C000127029

LOSS *of the* ASSUMPTIVE WORLD

The Series in Trauma and Loss
Consulting Editors
Charles R. Figley and Therese A. Rando

LOSS *of the*
ASSUMPTIVE WORLD

A Theory of Traumatic Loss

Jeffrey Kauffman,
Editor

Routledge
Taylor & Francis Group
New York London

Routledge is an imprint of the
Taylor & Francis Group, an informa business

Published in 2002 by
Routledge
29 West 35th Street
New York, NY 10001

Published in Great Britain by
Routledge
27 Church Road
Hove, East Sussex, BN3 2FA

Routledge is an imprint of the Taylor & Francis Group.

Copyright © 2002 by Jeffrey Kauffman.

All rights reserved. No part of this book may be reprinted or reproduced or utilized in any form or by any electronic, mechanical, or other means, now known or hereafter invented, including photocopying and recording or in any information storage or retrieval system, without permission in writing from the publisher.

10 9 8 7 6 5 4 3 2

Printed on acid-free, 250-year-life paper.
Manufactured in the United States of America.
Design and typography: Jack Donner

Library of Congress Cataloging-in-Publication Data

Loss of the assumptive world : a theory of traumatic loss / Jeffrey Kauffman, editor.
    p. cm.
  Includes bibliographical references and index.
  ISBN 1–58391–313–0
    1. Loss (Psychology) I. Kauffman, Jeffrey.
  RC455.4.L67 L67 2002
  616.89—dc21

                                                        2002018314

Contents

Note from the Editor

This book was written before September 11, 2001. Since that day, we are living in a new, dangerous world in which our basic sense of safety and security is threatened. Terror is now a destabilizing factor of the world order in which our psyches live, threatening the integrity of the experienced world as predictable and orderly. This is a loss of the assumptive world—the loss of protective beliefs, the loss of the constancy of internal constructs.

Trauma and grief therapy is faced with the responsibility of responding to new challenges in the treatment of traumatized persons. Understanding grief and trauma theory and treatment well, and taking care of one's own trauma, is now a responsibility of all psychotherapists, and I hope that the concept of the loss of the assumptive world will be of value to psychotherapists trying to help others struggling to understand the traumatic losses that are at hand.

Series Editor's Foreword

At this writing, workers continue to recover the bodies of those who died at the World Trade Center in New York on September 11, 2001. It has now been more than six months since America and the world in general began to seem more dangerous, and understanding trauma and loss has, as a result of the events of September 11, become that much more important. We are still at the beginning of a collective struggle to comprehend the implications of such an enormous trauma, one that has taken away many Americans' feelings of security and freedom. At this time there could not be a more fitting topic to explore than that examined in this book—the loss of assumptive world values. This book is about the destruction and rebuilding of life assumptions, and I can verify that my life assumptions, as well as those of many other people in this country, were destroyed on September 11, 2001.

My colleagues and I responded to the attack and the needs of traumatized New Yorkers under the banner of the Green Cross Projects. Green Cross volunteers facilitated 76 group defusing/educational sessions ranging from 1 to 1 and a half hours; 2 sessions even ran for 4 hours. Total attendance for group sessions was 635 people. Also, Green Cross volunteers facilitated individual defusing/crisis interventions spanning 20 minutes to 1 hour and, at times, even longer. There were 2,159 individual defusing/crisis interventions. In all, Green Cross volunteers came into contact with 2,794 survivors of the World Trade Center attacks.

Over and over, the theme that emerged from discussions with those who survived—particularly those who knew victims killed in the attack—was an extraordinary shift in worldviews. Never-before-experienced concerns about the welfare of a loved one became doubtful after September 11th. Never-before-experienced fears of working in tall buildings, as well as in New York City and in America in general, have now been replaced with new fears. This extraordinary sea of change in basic life assumptions is among the artifacts of this terrorist attack. Although Americans are now experiencing what most of the world has experienced for years, the threat of terrorism in our own hometowns, the shock of the 9/11 attacks may be greater for us. We have been lulled into a sense of complacency by our sense of invulnerability. Though we have fought many wars, none have been fought on United States soil for centuries.

The latest contribution to the Series in Trauma and Loss, *Loss of the Assumptive World: A Theory of Traumatic Loss*, edited by Jeffrey Kauffman, is about the extraordinary shift, the wake-up call, the "shattered assumptions" (Janoff-Bulman, 1985) caused by trauma and loss. Now more than ever, this book contributes to the emerging field of Traumatology and the theoretical practice of mental health applied to the grieving. Established in 1997, the Series's purpose is to attract significant contributions to the fields of both thanantology and traumatology. As Kauffman notes in the Introduction, the Series aims to foster dialogue between these two fields. Such a dialogue flourishes in this important book. Scholars and practitioners from both fields discuss the concept of loss of the assumptive world toward a new conceptualization. This new conceptualization expands upon what was established by Colin Murray Parkes (who wrote the Postscript to this volume), Ronnie Janoff-Bulman (author of the Foreword) and the individual chapter authors in terms of traumatic loss, relationship with self and others, psychological processes, and loss so great there are no words to describe it. Each of these extensions is organized in the four parts of this book.

Like other chapter authors, the Series co-editor, Dr. Therese Rando, discusses a critical aspect of shattered assumptions by focusing on the special challenges of people traumatized who, prior to experiencing a trauma, had led especially happy lives. All fourteen chapters in the book thoroughly examine the content of our assumptive world, with respect for the diversity of coping strategies. Each chapter approaches loss of the assumptive world toward a psychology of traumatic grief. What emerges is a perspective that is basic to the human experience, and an ordering principle that helps make sense out of changes in beliefs. In addition to the lessons for practitioners, which sensitize them to these basic responses to extraordinary change, there is recognition of how difficult this task is for the helper. Being with a client suffering from traumatic loss is "truly difficult (impossible but necessary) for clinical attention (and more so for theory) to be attuned to trauma and keep it present" (see p. 3 of this volume). It is very difficult but helping a client through a struggle with pre-trauma assumptions makes the work important and rewarding.

The Series in Trauma and Loss will continue to attract high-quality works that provide a conceptual bridge between the two fields of thanantology and traumatology. More books like this one will help to build a literature that will lead to an integration of theory, assessment, research, and practice with the traumatized, including those who have experienced loss. This library will be an indispensable resource for those who study and help people, families, and communities subjected to highly stressful events.

On behalf of the Editorial Board of the Series in Trauma and Loss I congratulate Dr. Kauffman for selecting useful and perfectly mixed chapters by some of the leading figures in this field and thank the contributors—Dr. Ronnie Janoff-Bulman for an insightful Foreword and Colin Murray Parkes for the Postscript. We look forward to publishing books these contributors write for the Series.

Charles R. Figley, Ph.D.
March 2002

Reference

Janoff-Bulman, R. (1985). The aftermath of victimization: Rebuilding shattered assumptions. In C. R. Figley (Ed.), Trauma and its wake (pp. 15–35). New York: Brunner/Mazel.

Foreword

I wrote *Shattered assumptions: Towards a new psychology of trauma* because it seemed time to pull together my previously disconnected thoughts and conjectures about trauma. For two decades I had written about the reactions of survivors, but my journal articles and chapters didn't provide a unified picture of traumatic loss and recovery. The book was also intended to provide me with a sense of closure after twenty years of research with survivors of many different types of victimization. I was feeling the need to move on to other questions and topics that had been put on the back burner for too long. Almost ten years have passed since the publication of *Shattered assumptions*, and work in the area of trauma and loss has continued to expand, evolve, and mature. This maturation is evident in this excellent edited volume, and both personally and professionally I feel I owe a debt of gratitude to the editor, Jeffrey Kauffman, and to the highly respected contributors of the individual chapters. The primary organizing concept in my book—the notion of lost or shattered assumptions—functions as the core metaphor for traumatic loss in the current volume. Thus it is particularly exciting for me to see that my own "closure" was far from an end, but rather another way station in the ongoing development of our understanding of trauma and loss. In this volume the notion of shattered assumptions functions as a starting point for the chapters' theoretical contributions; the authors dramatically strengthen and enrich this conceptualization and, in turn, our understanding of traumatic loss.

Although theory building may feel like a solitary process, in the course of normal science we typically add more bricks to a structure already partially constructed by others. In my case, the work of other psychologists provided me with the construct of the assumptive world, which proved indispensable in my efforts to make sense of trauma survivors' reactions. Coming from different theoretical backgrounds and using different vocabularies, these psychologists posited the equivalent of a fundamental set of assumptions that reside at the core of our psyches and enable us to navigate our course through life. Seymour Epstein's "theories of reality," John Bowlby's "working models," and in particular Colin Murray Parkes' "assumptive world" all speak to the unquestioned beliefs that constitute the bedrock of our cognitive-emotional worlds.

It was this conceptualization—the assumptive world—that provided me with clues to our utter lack of psychological preparedness in the face of traumatic life events. "I never thought it could happen to me" still echoes in my ears, having been voiced again and again in my years of work with survivors. What is the content of our assumptive world? Could these fundamental assumptions be a key to the terror and disintegration of traumatic loss? My preoccupation with these questions soon led me to posit a theory of trauma based on the core metaphor of "shattered assumptions."

We are psychologically unprepared for traumatic losses because our fundamental assumptions about the world and ourselves—assumptions embracing benevolence, meaning, and self-worth—generally afford us a sense of relative invulnerability. We may recognize that bad things happen "out there," but we believe that "our world" is good and safe; misfortune and tragedy won't strike us. When our fundamental assumptions shatter in the face of traumatic life events and losses, we are left confronting a seemingly malevolent, meaningless world; we are bereft of any adequate internal guides. Trauma entails a confrontation with mortality, real or symbolic, and with our own fragility. Survivors recognize their earlier assumptions for what they were—grand illusions—and experience the pain and disillusionment that accompany their collapse. Given the depth of the psychic wound, recovery is nothing short of remarkable. Survivors adopt supremely creative responses in interpreting their experiences; these coping efforts are in the service of helping survivors reconstruct new, viable assumptive worlds that are psychologically comforting yet can account for their traumatic losses. We now know that survivors fare far better than early studies of limited clinical samples had led us to believe. Their reconstructed assumptive worlds—no longer naive, but reflecting a new kind of wisdom born of experience—are a testament to survivors' incredible psychological strengths.

This respect for the experiences and coping abilities of trauma survivors is a subtext of this volume, for the contributors address the transformation of trauma from tragedy to integrated experience. The explicit common thread throughout the book is the breakdown and reconstruction of fundamental assumptions, which is approached from a variety of theoretical orientations. Together the fourteen chapters provide an impressive diversity of perspectives on the core metaphor and provide rich characterizations, vocabularies, and first-person accounts that further our understanding of traumatic loss. Reconceptualizations of shattered assumptions include the breakdown of psychological defenses, crisis of meaning, interpersonal betrayal, self-fragmentation, deprivation of self-object fantasies, and narrative disruption. These distinct interpretations are also the basis for fresh insights into the recovery process for survivors.

In the end, the chapters do not compete for theoretical dominance or acceptance, but rather complement, embellish, and strengthen each other and their fundamental similarities. The volume succeeds at extending earlier formulations of the loss of assumptions. In addition to the diversity of theoretical perspectives represented, important new distinctions are drawn, such as the difference between ordinary and extraordinary meanings and between local and global assumptions. New issues are raised and old ones creatively revisited, including the nature of traumatic loss in childhood, the role of story making and memory, and the special significance of meaning, safety, and spirituality in the process of traumatic breakdown and recovery.

This is a book for many audiences. Professionals, survivors, and friends and family of survivors will benefit from the depth and breadth of psychological analysis presented here. In fact, anyone interested in coping at the extremes of human experience will benefit from the wealth of insights and knowledge presented in the pages that follow.

Ronnie Janoff-Bulman

Acknowledgment

I wish to thank Therese Rando, who introduced me to the concept of loss of the assumptive world, who urged me to undertake this project, and whose friendship has been a gift to me.

Introduction

Jeffrey Kauffman

The assumptive world concept refers to the assumptions or beliefs that ground, secure, or orient people, that give a sense of reality, meaning, or purpose to life. The assumption may be that I am a good person, that I will grow old with my spouse, that God is just, that others may be trusted, that things are or will be a certain way, that there is a future. Or it may be that an assumption is such a familiar aspect of one's sense of reality that its disruption is hard to conceive, the loss of confidence in its truth putting one's very sense of identity at risk. All in all, the range of possibilities is extensive. Different perspectives and theories are presented here not only for the intrinsic interest that each point of view holds but also, and especially, for the way it elaborates and helps us better understand the concept of the assumptive world. With this intent the articles herein were solicited. Yet beyond this, the contributors of this book articulate a spirit of hope and resilience in the face of traumatic loss. Each bears witness to traumatic loss, makes revealing and useful assumptions about it, and points out the possibilities of healing and transformation. This book, as a theory of the traumatic loss of the assumptive world, is conceived in the spirit of advancing Parkes' crucial insight into the psychology of psychosocial change and Janoff-Bulman's new psychology of trauma. The theory of the assumptive world integrates a diverse range of basic clinical and theoretical concerns in the treatment of traumatic loss.

The collection of articles before you has been developed especially for the Brunner-Routledge series aimed at fostering dialogue between traumatology and thanatology. In this book there are chapters by thanatologists and by traumatologists representing diverse perspectives, including constructivist and narrative theory, Kohutian self-psychology, betrayal theory, Beckerian transference theory, psychoanalysis, phenomenology, coping theory, information-processing theory, ego psychology, and others that I can not fit so clearly under the heading of a specific theory name. Each chapter approaches loss of the assumptive world with concerns, perspectives, and assumptions that help to clarify and expand our understanding of the concept; it is to be hoped that the diverse voices and topics work together to illuminate the concept of loss of the assumptive world as especially useful for understanding and treating traumatic loss. With an interest in the interconnections between traumatology and thanatology—and, more so, in their common realities—this collection points toward a psychology of traumatic grief. There is a sense in which traumatic loss of the assumptive world is a paradigm for the psychology of change, in that there is a kernel of trauma at the psychological core of all change experience; when we understand the traumatic loss of the assumptive world, we understand a core wound in all bereavement. While trauma is a loss experience, the healing from it is a mourning process. The construct of loss of the assumptive world calls for the relationship between death and trauma to be rethought.

Before we take a bird's-eye view of the chapters in this book, I want to point out a root aspect of the concept of the assumptive world that we inherit from Parkes and from Janoff-Bulman, a consideration that is, I think, what makes this a most basic concept: that *the concept of the assumptive world is a psychological principle of the conservation of human reality or "culture."* The notion of the assumptive world was introduced into the thanatology literature by Parkes (1971, 1988). Parkes introduces the assumptive world as a concept for understanding changes in psychosocial reality. Most broadly, he defines the assumptive world this way: "The assumptive world is the only world we know and it includes everything we know or think we know. It includes our interpretation of the past and our expectations of the future, our plans and our prejudices. Any or all of these may need to change as a result of changes in the life space" (1971, p. 102). What is this assumptive world? It appears to be virtually all of specifically human reality. Talking this way about the world we know, and the world of remembering and expecting, Parkes is conceiving a basic organizing principle of human experience and of beliefs and temporality. The assumptive world is the ordering principle for the psychological or psychosocial construction of the human world.

Parkes is concerned with the psychology of change, specifically the psychology of healing from the wound of loss that is present in change. In other words the concept of loss of the assumptive world is a theory of grief. Assumptive worlds are constant internal constructs, and change is the disruption of the constancy of these constructs. Change also prompts the need to conserve, or maintain constancy, and for an assumptive world to reassert itself. The concept of the assumptive world is, in the broadest sense, a principle of the normative constancy of experience and belief, a constancy principle of the psychological organization of the human world and one's experience of oneself and the world. The assumptive world is the principle of the conservation of psychosocial reality.

Janoff-Bulman works up the theory of the loss of the assumptive world into a powerful argument for a "new psychology of trauma." An important part of her new psychology is the way she thinks about the normative constancy of beliefs and their disruption: "Our penchant for preserving rather than changing knowledge structure suggests the deeply embedded, deeply accepted nature of our beliefs about the benevolence and meaningfulness of the world and our own self worth" (1992, p. 51). Disruption of the normative constancy of beliefs, that is, loss of the assumptive world, is specifically loss of beliefs about goodness, meaningfulness, and self-worth. What is lost in traumatic loss is these value beliefs. In a theory of the assumptive world constituted by beliefs of goodness, meaningfulness, and self-worth, *belief is a value-intending act*; believing is an act of consciousness intending value. Traumatic loss of the normative authority of the assumptive world prompts rampant devaluations.

The assumptive world is constituted by the psychological act of *believing*. Assumptive worlds are believed worlds, worlds intended and constituted by believing or, as Janoff-Bulman also notes, illusions. The assumptive world is illusion believed to be reality. And in this way human culture is constituted. What is shattered in trauma are beliefs, in the sense of vitally valued illusions, or more especially the *ability* to believe or assume. "At the core of our internal world we hold basic truths of ourselves and our external world that represent our orientation towards the 'total push and pull of the cosmos'" (Janoff-Bulman, 1992, p. 4). This is not the cosmos of natural science, except metaphorically, but is the "total push and pull" of assumptions, the *power* of assumption in human beings. The being of human beings, the core of our internal world, the psychological truth of existence, is deeply valued illusion, *damaged in traumatization*. Janoff-Bulman indicates specifically the loss of goodness, meaning, and self-worth beliefs as the site of this damage. Psychological trauma is a shattering of the *conservancy* of assumptive world beliefs.

The construct of the assumptive world helps to frame or organize our understanding of the clinical presentation of traumatic loss, the object of clinical attention, the client. The concept may also be useful with regard to the therapist's own process in the presence of a traumatized client. (The *difference* between these two, therapist and client, is the containment function, or the secure boundary that makes treatment possible.) Assuming that being empathically attuned *is* this clinical boundary, *is* the basic tool for understanding or "holding" trauma, and *is* specifically therapeutic, then being present, or bearing witness in the face of the clients's bearing witness to trauma, is the basic clinical responsibility of the therapist. Yet it is *truly difficult* (impossible but necessary) for clinical attention (and more so for theory) to be attuned to trauma and keep it present. Trauma could be defined by this characteristic difficulty. When it is occurring, there is no presence at all; after its occurrence, it does not stop happening. It returns and returns, and continues to be absent (like God). The core of traumatic loss is mysterious, dangerous, contradictory, horrific, mortifying, uncanny. And neither client nor therapist can say what the implosive nucleus is. For the psychotherapist to be well attuned to trauma is *truly difficult*. How do you recognize and keep present what doesn't present itself? And at the core of the traumatic wound is recurring violence, a demolition of presence, unable to signify itself. The loss of the assumptive world of presence is described by Blanchot in *The instant of my death* this way: "As if the death outside of him could only henceforth collide with the death in him. 'I am alive. No, you are dead'" (Blanchot, 2000, p. 9). The assumption that I am is only clearly seen to be an *assumption* when it is lost.

"Outside the range of usual human experience," said the *DSM-III-R*, groping to express something that lies outside the realm and range of a diagnostic and statistical manual. The word *usual* here is ambiguous. Maybe it wants to say and not to say *normal*, and says instead *usual*. By saying *usual* rather than *normal*, the implication is, perhaps, that it is not commonly occurring. But this would be a hedge, for it surely does not refer to the frequency of events. If traumatic events occurred to many people often, the events, the experience, would be no less traumatic. Frequency of occurrence in a population, in the human race as a whole, or in an individual is not a factor in the definition or the differential diagnosis of psychological trauma. Perhaps the word *normal* better conveys the meaning here. "The range of normal experience," means "within the bounds established by a norm for human experience," and outside the range is a disruption of the sense of reality, order, meaning, familiarity, safety, and so on. The norms of human experience, like all cultural norms, are assumptive worlds.

The word *usual* also suggests something we are used to, a familiar experience. In the wake of traumatization the familiar has become unfamiliar. The unfamiliar familiar is, Otto Rank pointed out, the uncanny. Loss of the familiarity of the self and the world is the loss of a basic assumption that organizes identity. The uncanny shattering of identity in traumatic loss is a loss of the assumption that one exists, and a collapse of valuations that sustain the self, meaningfulness, and the world. Related to this is a sense in which shared familiarity and a feeling of being at home are subverted by the unfamiliarity, foreignness, strangeness, and undiscloseable nature of traumatic experience.

The assumptive world also is familiar in the sense of a normalcy that aims to exclude awareness of violence, even as violence repeatedly, predictably (one might think) violates norms and ruptures the boundaries of the assumptive world, and even as the exclusion of knowledge or awareness of violence is itself an act of violence. The norm of normal experience aims to conserve an assumptive world order. The power of assumptive world norms includes their power to exercise psychological and psychosocial violence. The conservation of experience, the conserving power of the assumptive world, fosters a disavowal of violence, itself an act of violence. The conserving power of assumptive world illusions tends to disavow violence.

There are many interesting and revealing angles for looking at the concept of the assumptive world. The concept "assumptive world" is itself an assumption, a theoretical construct, an illusion that organizes a considerable range of concerns in loss theory and trauma theory, and that brings clinically significant understanding to traumatic loss. The phrase "assumptive world" is said in many ways. The contributors to this book present an array of assumptions, each of which illuminates an aspect of the assumptive world concept. Many theories of the assumptive world are here cobbled together as chapters in order to tell a story about the unspeakable traumatic loss of the assumptive world.

Landsman understands the loss of the assumptive world to be "a crisis of meaning": "when we experience events that don't fit our schemas, or violate our assumptions, or shatter our illusions, we experience a crisis of meaning." Landsman develops her view by presenting a history of the concepts of "meaning" and "the assumptive world." This literature review synthesizes into a theory of the assumptive world as "systems of meaning." Her nuanced theory of the loss of meaning is perhaps best introduced by own words: "In the context of 'meaningless suffering' attention is drawn relentlessly to the problem of meaning; survivors attempt to determine, discover, or create a sense of meaning out of circumstances that seem most to lack it. As shattering experiences occasion these efforts, trauma constitutes a crucible of meaning—a crucible in which meaning is tested and transformed, and from which it may perhaps emerge renewed." An important distinction she makes is between "ordinary meanings . . . a profound need to restore basic assumptions of benevolence, justice, control, and self-worth to a pretrauma configuration" and "extraordinary meanings . . . existential meaninglessness . . . the spiritual crisis of trauma . . . confrontation with the existential givens of life." Landsman's theory of the crisis of extraordinary meaning underscores especially the possibility and meaningfulness of "posttraumatic resilience and growth."

Neimeyer, Botella, Herrero, Pacheco, Figueras, and Werner-Wildner take meaning to mean a narrative about oneself, a theory of the assumptive world as ethnobiography, an act of *constructing* narratives of the meaning of one's life. The act of construction is called "storytelling." The assumptive world is talked about in terms of life stories: "life stories can be disrupted by profound loss." The subject, and object, of ethnobiography is the narrative construction of *identity*. Neimeyer and colleagues say that "meaning-making processes, including the development of one's sense of personal identity, are hypothesized to assume a narrative as well as anticipatory structure." The anticipatory structure of narrative, its way of constructing the future, displays the assumptive nature of narration, particularly posttraumatic ethnobiographic autoconstructed narrations. Neimeyer and colleagues "describe and illustrate" a most "promising approach to understanding the breakdown in the assumptive world," "a constructivist perspective on meaning reconstruction, an organizing frame for human experience that both imparts order to the past and yields anticipations of an intelligible future." "Traumatic loss disrupts the continuity of our self-narratives, however, and undercuts our associated sense of identity." "From the standpoint of its author, a story stakes a claim, seeking a sustainable position for the self."

A revealing and clinically significant perspective on the loss of the assumptive world is that the assumptive world is spiritual, and the loss is a spiritual loss. Doka defines the spirituality lost in the loss of the assumptive world as loss of "the belief in, or nature of, a God or higher power that controls human destiny, a sense of fairness or justice in the operation of the world, or held beliefs about what makes life or death meaningful." The *grief* in the loss of the assumptive world comes about because the belief that God is just and good has been shattered. We may see here a congruence with, and an opening upon, the spiritual significance of Janoff-Bulman's understanding of the assumptive world as self-worth, meaningfulness, and world valuations. Doka is especially concerned about postloss reconstruction of the spiritual world, or, in a language of spiritual assumptions, *resilience and transcendence*. Doka discusses resilience in caregiver spirituality and in the spirituality of the bereaved. Considering Job, C. S. Lewis, and Harold Kushner, he says that "spiritual struggles led to a more resilient spirituality, one that allowed them to resolve issues about the unfairness of life, or the nature and existence of God. In fact, one might say that the key to a resilient spirituality is that it allows an individual to find meaning in the most difficult situations. Such systems must have a flexibility that allows individuals to confront the ambiguity and unfairness of life." "Finding meaning," a spiritual act, is *constructing an assumptive world*. Doka, further, says that transcending the crisis of faith in traumatic loss is an acceptance of mystery.

Attig presents a phenomenology of the *assumptions* of being in the world, of assuming one's place in the world, of living fully present and responsible in the social world. "We adopt ways of living and orient ourselves within . . . noncognitive, emotional, psychological, physical, behavioral, social, soulful, and spiritual forces and contexts." To understand how the lived practical world *is* a set of assumptions about how to live in the world, "we need to stretch our understanding of 'assumption' to encompass all that we have come to 'take for granted' as we have learned how to be and to act in the world in the presence of those we love." He says, "I call these ways of living 'assumptions' precisely because they come to be operative in our lives without our thinking self-consciously about them. . . . We carry such knowing how within us as practical abilities, dispositions, and habits. It is comprised of ways of doing and being that we hold in our bodies and characters." Attig presents a rich and poetic phenomenology of assuming one's place in the world and of resuming one's place after traumatic loss.

De Prince and Freyd examine the relationship of the loss of the assumptive world with Freyd's *betrayal theory*, noting that both go beyond the "fear paradigm" for understanding traumatization. "Freyd . . . initially proposed betrayal trauma theory to account for memory impairment for traumatic events. Betrayal trauma theory posited that there is a social utility in remaining unaware of abuse when the perpetrator is a caregiver." Betrayal trauma theory provides insight into the psychology of keeping secret, hidden, and dissociated. Coinciding with the traumatic loss of the assumptive world is the installation of a secret. We may note that betrayal, as a hidden narcissistic insult inherent in the loss of assumptive world, may be present in any traumatization, not just those in which there is a perpetrator betraying trust; that is, loss of assumptive world *is a betrayal*. DePrince and Freyd note an interesting sense in which the loss of the assumptive world concept is useful in understanding sociopolitical betrayals and silences: "McFarlane and van der Kolk . . . note that society becomes resentful of the ways in which victims of trauma shatter our illusions of safety. Society, therefore, is often resistant to recognizing the effects of trauma and inclined to engage in victim-blaming in order to maintain basic assumptions."

Liechty provides a Beckerian perspective on the loss of the assumptive world. From this perspective the assumptive world is our "cultural worldview drawing into one image the broad nexus of transference relationships." He says that "transference relationships are those that function as external sources of power by which one calms and represses innate human anxiety rooted in the mortal, human condition." Becker's concept of transference relationship helps us understand how assumptive worlds are constructed and maintained through the relationship with idealized objects. Liechty develops the concept of transference as a window onto the psychodynamics of the construction of the assumptive world. Transference objects in Becker are idealized, powerful containers of mortality anxiety. Transference is the process by which assumptive worlds are constructed. Liechty writes that "grief and mourning are understood in the context of this theory as the process of rebuilding the psychologically defensive character of one's assumptive world, a world constituted by transferential relationships involving place, possessions, self-esteem, and moral and religious commitments in addition to relationships with people."

Ulman and Miliora's model of trauma as shattered fantasy is a Kohutian self-psychological description of the traumatic loss of the assumptive world. Using this psychoanalytic perspective, they describe posttraumatic distortions in the self's valuations of itself. Ulman and Miliora present a depth psychology of traumatization, of the *subject* who loses the assumptive world, "the subject who assumes," that is, *the self*. They present three case studies corresponding to Kohut's three types of narcissistic transference, or, as Ulman and Miliora say, "the three major forms of archaic narcissism": (1) "the traumatic disillusionment of an archaic grandiose fantasy," (2) "the traumatic loss of a fantasy of merger with an idealized self-object," and (3) "the traumatic loss of a fantasized twinship."

Soloman presents a description of the treatment methodology called eye movement desensitization and reprocessing (EMDR), which "facilitate[s] the adaptive integration of traumatic information." EMDR is theoretically based upon the information-processing model called "accelerated information processing." Soloman clearly articulates the information-processing model of healing from traumatic loss. In traumatic loss there is an "inability to integrate the traumatic information into one's assumptive world." Unprocessed traumatic information "may result in intense feelings of vulnerability, helplessness, and low self-worth and efficacy." At the end of his chapter he introduces the concept of "expansion of basic world assumptions" as a normative outcome of "processing the traumatic situation." Expanded basic world assumptions involve "a deeper awareness of . . . vulnerability."

Corr examines "coping with challenges to assumptive worlds." "In the professional literature," he writes, "the term *coping* has been defined as 'constantly changing cognitive and behavioral efforts to manage specific external and/or internal demands that are appraised as taxing or exceeding the resources of the person.'" He presents careful conceptual analyses of "coping" and "the assumptive world," with thoughtful distinctions and refinements of the concept of the assumptive world. After an analysis of traumatic loss and other forms of death-related loss, he considers a loss of the assumptive world related to change that involves neither trauma nor death. "If trauma is, as we have seen, 'a psychologically distressing event that is outside the range of usual human experience,' it is not altogether fanciful to think that a stroke of good fortune or an experience of extraordinary gain may be distressing in ways that offer certain parallels to extraordinary loss. Surely gain can sometimes and in principle be as much a source of perceived stress as loss."

Bloom, examining "mourning and recovery from childhood maltreatment," provides many clinically astute descriptions of the consequences of damaged attachments, of "losses attendant upon child abuse and neglect," and of "little deaths." In articulating this she achieves a notable integration of traumatology and thanatology. Setting her bearings in this chapter, she says: "For some, the sources of grief constitute the loss of already established assumptions and beliefs about self, home, family and society. For others, the assaults to their integrity began when they were so young that they had no time to even develop a coherent assumptive world before their lives were shattered. Complicating the process of grieving for adult survivors is the fact that the losses that accompany child maltreatment are cloaked in silence, lost in the shrouds of history, and largely unrecognized. In general, their grief for these losses is unaccepted, rejected, denied, and stigmatized. . . . Child neglect represents particular challenges for adult survivors because they must grieve for things they never had, and thus never had the chance to lose." She examines the important connection between childhood attachments impacted by trauma and traumatic grief and clinical issues having to do with adult relationships and the *capacity* to grieve, noting that "the losses that adults must recapitulate and work through in order to recover are long delayed, sometimes tangible, but at other times metaphorical, spiritual, or moral losses."

Rando turns our attention toward specific vulnerablities of the capacity to *revise* a shattered assumptive world. She calls these assumptive world vulnerabilities "too good a childhood." There is irony in calling this assumptive world vulnerability "too good a childhood," or, as she says, there is irony in the very goodness of "too good a childhood." The irony is that when traumatic loss occurs, belief in the goodness or the assumption of goodness is also shattered by the betrayal that what was given as good turns out to be not good. Rando provides a careful, clinically well-tuned view of the disadvantages of an extremely good premorbid history for achieving assumptive world revision after trauma and major loss. Rando examines developmental precursors of complications in the ego's response to traumatic loss of the assumptive world. "The long-term impacts of ... negative life experiences [i.e., traumatic losses] are determined in large part by the preexisting assumptions maintained by the individual involved." "Too good a childhood" is one that is "so positive as to generate unrealistic assumptive world elements and/or [is] missing sufficient negative experiences to promote a requisite measure of capacity to contend with defense or revision of their assumptive world." She breaks it down into two types of assumptive world vulnerabilities. "The first group of persons (Group I) with assumptive world vulnerabilities have prior histories characterized by both overwhelmingly and unrealistically positive experiences *and* a lack of adversity. As a result, Group I individuals have life experiences that (1) generate overly positive, unrealistic, overgeneralized assumptive world elements and (2) result in an absence of adversity that could provide knowledge about and practice in defending and revising the assumptive world." In Group II are those individuals who "have had a relative lack of adversity in their premorbid life." She offers clinical guidelines for understanding and treating assumtive world vulnerabilities.

Goldman presents an account of the child's assumptive world and its loss. This chapter is not burdened by theoretical concerns and speaks in a simple, direct way (almost in the manner of telling a children's story) about the assumptive world of children and the child's vulnerabilities in loss of the assumptive world. What she has to say is of great value in understanding the loss of the assumptive world in children, yet in large part it applies as well to adults, in particular that part of the self injured in the loss of the assumptive world. "Children make basic assumptions about the world around them. They assume it will be kind, protective, safe, consistent, and meaningful. They assume their caretakers will be there to provide love, protection, and meaning. They need predictability, structure, and reassurance that their life and world have meaning and value." The grief issues of children in traumatic loss are lost assumptions of trust, worth, meaning, and faith. She concludes with recommendations for re-creating a safe assumptive world.

Kauffman emphasizes the importance of safety in the treatment of traumatic grief and focuses clinical attention on the psychodynamics associated with the loss of the assumptive world. He says that "traumatization is an exposure of the self in which the self fragments, loses its protective illusions and value, and hides in unnamable shame," and he examines each of these concepts—self, fragmentation, loss of illusions and value, and shame. He also analyzes the meaning of the concept "assumption." Kauffman sees the loss of safety and the narcissistic vulnerability associated with it to be the critical clinical element in the loss of the assumptive world. He says that the "the loss of the assumptive world is the inward elaboration of ... violence inwardly in terms of value and meaning and self-experience. In traumatic grief the sense of unsafety ... anticipates violence that has already happened but has not been sufficiently taken in and secured, violence that is *continuous* as the inner reality of self-experience and which keeps *repeating* in day-to-day experience of the self in the world."

"What cannot be remembered or forgotten," the topic of Krystal's chapter, is *traumatic memory*. Krystal says, "Traumatic memories are not repressed in the ordinary sense of the word. Something worse happens to them.... Some traumatic perceptions are not compatible with the survival of the self, and are never registered consciously or in a form that is recoverable by any normal means, and these are the memories that can never be forgotten or remembered." Krystal's chapter bears witness to the impossibility and the necessity of bearing witness. He says, "the need to go over some element of the past may become an all-consuming task. No amount of retelling relieves the inner compulsion. There seems to be not enough time, not enough listening to do justice to the compulsion." The relationship between memory and bearing witness is a central concern of this chapter. The storytelling or testimony is an act of recall and mourning, an act by which the trauma survivor attempts to rebuild an assumptive world. "Memory happens in the course of retelling. But memory is determined by a number of events.... Among the factors are the nature of the original perception, the degree and mode of registration, the nature of the retention, and, finally, the capacity for recall and the form in which the recall takes place." Krystal examines how each of these works in traumatic loss. His writing bears witness to the extreme that is signified by the word *trauma*, the force that shatters assumptive worlds and leads to "impacted mourning."

Caruth's chapter, the final one in this book, and a memorial to her mother, is a careful analysis of Freud's *Beyond the pleasure principle*, specifically his articulation of the repetition compulsion; then, in a striking leap, her text bears witness to a child who bears witness to death. The repetition compulsion is a key concept in the psychodynamics of trauma, yet the repetition compulsion is an important concept in assumptive world theory for a further reason: the assumptive world is, like the *da* in Freud's grandson's game, a compulsive repetition, and as Caruth points, a creative act. In the *fort* (gone) and *da* (there) of the child's game Caruth deciphers not a repetition of death but a symbolic reenactment of the creation of life, a repetition of a creation of life from death. "What is most surprising in the child's game ... is that this reenactment of reality in the game places repetition at the very heart of childhood, and links the repetition to a creative act of invention. In the introduction of the child's game Freud's original question—How does life bear witness to death?—is linked to another question: What kind of witness is a creative act?" And, finally, "the language of the theory, much like the child's stammering language, articulates the very notions of the trauma and of the death drive as a creative act of parting."

References

Blanchot, M. (2000). *The instant of my death* (E. Rottenberg, Trans.). In J. Derrida, *Demure*. Stanford, CA; Stanford Univerity Press.

Janoff-Bulman, R. (1992). *Shattered assumptions: Towards a new psychology of trauma*, New York: The Free Press.

Parkes, C. M. (1971). Psycho-social transition: A field of study. *Social Science and Medicine, 5*, 101–115.

Parkes, C. M. (1988). Bereavement as a psychosocial transition: Processes of adaptation to change. *Journal of Social Issues, 44(3)*, 53–65.

Rank, Otto. (1971). *The double* (H. Tucker, Trans.). Chapel Hill, NC: The University of North Carolina Press.

part 1.

Constructing Meaning in a World Broken by the Traumatic Loss of the Assumptive World

Meaning, Self, and Transcendence

1.

Crises of Meaning in Trauma and Loss

Irene Smith Landsman

Trauma and loss are experiences that push us to our limits. By definition, trauma overwhelms our usual abilities to cope and adjust, calling into question the most basic assumptions that organize our experience of ourselves, relationships, the world, and the human condition itself. The crisis of trauma is pervasive, altering emotional, cognitive, and behavioral experience, and the subjective experience of trauma not infrequently includes a crisis of meaning at a deep level of experience. As Victor Frankl wrote, humans possess a fundamental "will toward meaning" (1984); meaning is essential to human existence, despite the fact that the structures and essence of meaning are frequently outside of our awareness. The need for meaning is made clear in experiences that are at the same time overwhelming and without apparent meaning. In the context of "meaningless suffering" attention is drawn relentlessly to the problem of meaning; survivors attempt to determine, discover, or create a sense of meaning out of circumstances that seem most to lack it. As shattering experiences occasion these efforts, trauma constitutes a crucible of meaning—a crucible in which meaning is tested and transformed, and from which it may perhaps emerge renewed.

The evidence for a crisis of meaning in the wake of trauma is pervasive in the trauma literature. In a variety of studies across different populations, survivors are seen to ask "Why me?" or "Why this?" and to search for meaning in the aftermath of catastrophe.

The Search for Meaning

A "search for meaning" has been reported across a broad spectrum of traumatic experience. These phenomena have been observed among victims of serious physical injury, survivors of incest, rape victims, disaster survivors, bereaved persons, and others. Some writers have found more search for meaning to be associated with worse psychological outcomes, and "finding meaning" to be associated with better outcomes. Others have argued that it is the kind of meaning that is found that has implications for outcomes. In an early study, [Janoff-]Bulman and Wortman (1977) found that all spinal cord victims surveyed reported asking "Why me?" with regard to their injury, and most had generated some answers citing predetermination, chance, a divine plan, deservedness, and/or a selective focus on some positive consequences of their injury. Survivors of incest have also been seen to grapple with these issues (Silver, Boon, & Stones, 1983), asking "why me?" and searching for "some reason, meaning, or way to make sense out of their incest experience," with a continued (unproductive) search for meaning associated with worse outcomes. Bereaved persons ask "why me?" as well as searching for meaning in a broader sense (see, e.g., Downey, Silver, & Wortman, 1990; Schwartzberg & Janoff-Bulman, 1991; Landsman, 1993). Rape victims whose "themes" of meaning remained unresolved were more likely to have posttraumatic stress disorder (Newman, Riggs, & Roth, 1997).

While several studies have found subjects who search for meaning to be more symptomatic than those who do not, we cannot assume that the search itself contributes directly to worse outcomes. In a study of adjustment following bereavement or serious injury (Landsman, 1993), a majority of trauma survivors did search for meaning, but there was *not* a simple relationship between the extent of search for meaning and outcomes. Rather, more serious or debilitating traumas were associated with more search for meaning; after accounting for severity, the extent of search for meaning had no independent contribution to differences in adjustment.

What Does "Meaning" Mean?

While both the trauma and bereavement literatures contain many attempts to identify and understand phenomena such as the "problem of meaning," "search for meaning," or "crisis of meaning," there is discouragingly little consistency in how meaning is defined and operationalized. The relative neglect of questions of meaning in the empirical research on bereavement and trauma may well be related to the difficulties in defining and measuring these processes. As Lifton (1993) wrote, "Although psychiatrists and psychologists have sometimes declined to use the term *meaning* on the grounds that it cannot be defined scientifically, we must find a rigorous way of analyzing it because, without addressing this idea of meaning . . . we cannot understand post-traumatic stress disorder" (p. 13).

In the subset of trauma literature that deals with meaning, some authors' definitions of meaning are fairly specific and well-defined, while others are more inclusive and general; some authors use different terms to describe what appear to be similar constructs. In addition, there seems to be a qualitative difference between what might be termed "ordinary" meanings and what we might call "extraordinary" or existential meanings. A general assumption that life should be meaningful does not ordinarily require that we be specific about what meaningfulness entails. Ordinary meaningfulness probably includes a sense that life has a structure that is both comprehensible and satisfying; that we understand the world, our lives, and our roles; and that we feel sufficiently able to negotiate its demands and achieve our goals. This ordinary meaning rests on unexamined assumptions about such things as safety, control, and justice, and subsumes our basic needs for cognitive clarity, order, nonrandomness, and self-efficacy.

In the background, even further outside our usual awareness, lies "extraordinary" or existential meaning. The problem of existential meaning is made clear in rare encounters with the realization that meaning or purpose in life is not a concrete, measurable truth but must be discovered, if not invented, by ourselves. More abstract than beliefs about cause and effect, more inclusive than the specific systems of motivation and reward we each have, existential meaning is a sense of compelling emotional investment in existence itself, apart from the defining particulars of our individual life, roles, goals, and achievements.

Theoretical Overview

Theoretical and empirical descriptions of the impact of trauma focus on a variety of phenomena related to coming to terms with a shattering event. In order to establish an overall frame of reference for thinking about the many different tasks and challenges that are subsumed in the trauma response, the major theoretical approaches will be organized in terms of those dealing primarily with cognitive mastery (including attributions), those describing shattered assumptions or schemas, and those involving "extraordinary" challenges to meaning, or existential crisis.

Cognitive Mastery: Attributions in the Service of Control

In the immediate aftermath of a traumatic event, survivors face an essential and not always simple challenge of understanding the event itself. Before asking "Why?" or "Why me?" those who experience trauma must ask "What happened?" and, in a somewhat concrete sense, "How did it happen?"

Forming an Account

In the immediate aftermath of a traumatic event some confusion regarding exactly what occurred is typical. Survivors ordinarily need to review the sequence of events in some detail and may be frustrated and dismayed if information is inadequate to make possible the formation of a coherent account of the experience. Rumination about details, particularly cause and effect, is common. This perhaps most basic struggle with meaning is illustrated in Parkes and Weiss' (1983) study of the experience of widows. They asserted that "making sense of loss requires developing an 'account,' an explanation of how it happened" (p. 156). As a starting point in placing the experience of major loss in the context of one's life, it seems necessary to create a basic narrative that includes some plausible causal explanation, and provides an explanation that does not leave important questions unanswered. This level of meaning does not necessarily determine the emotional impact of a trauma, but represents the need for basic cognitive mastery, which may precede engagement with other tasks of adjustment. Parkes and Weiss maintained that an "adequate account" (p. 156) may be necessary but not sufficient for recovery, because in its absence it is not possible to restore a sense of safety and control.

Attributional Style

Forming attributions for a traumatic event involves both cognitive mastery, in the sense of generating a theory of the event(s) that culminated in a traumatic outcome, and efforts to reestablish a sense of safety and control for the future. The literature on attributions indicates that we generate attributions for events in ways that serve the function of enhancing our perception of control over our environment, and that this may be particularly true of traumatic events. Wortman (1976) wrote, "[P]eople minimize the role of chance in producing various outcomes, exaggerate the relationship between their behavior and 'uncontrollable' life events, and tend to be unaware of the extent to which their behavior is controlled by external forces" (p. 43). Specifically, we tend to attribute causality in ways that allows belief in personal control over future outcomes to be maintained.

As Rotter (1966) proposed, an internal locus of control—a belief that events that affect us are consequences of our own actions or attributes—is a generally adaptive attributional style. Some trauma researchers have suggested that becoming an "innocent victim" might destroy this healthy internal locus of control, while bearing some objective responsibility for even traumatic events might keep this healthy attributional style intact (Athelstan & Crewe, 1979). Other researchers suggest that causal attributions for traumatic events reflect not only attributional style but the magnitude of the trauma, such that the influence of locus of control or attributional style on attributions for extremely severe events may be overwhelmed by the objectively uncontrollable nature of disaster (Joseph, Yule, & Williams, 1993).

Blame and Self-blame

Attributions often involve blame. Here, too, much useful theory has been developed, resulting in some empirical research. Thirty years ago, Walster (1966) noted that, especially in the case of very negative events, people often find it necessary to assign some kind of blame or responsibility rather than to accept the randomness of such experiences. Thus, we understand blaming the victim of an accident or illness as an attribution that allows nonvictim observers to maintain a belief in their own invulnerability. In order to maintain a sense of personal control and safety, it is necessary to find ways to avoid recognizing noncontingency—that is, to reject randomness.

Similarly, Lerner's (1980) theory of "belief in a just world" suggests that most individuals have a need to believe that, in life, people "get what they deserve" (p. 11) and thus deserve what they get. Negative events, even those experienced by others, represent evidence that the world may *not* be just. In order to maintain an illusion of control, and therefore an illusion of one's own ability to avoid negative events, it may be tempting to believe that victims of trauma caused or brought on their own misfortune—thereby keeping intact the belief in a just world. Such beliefs may be maintained by attributing causal responsibility to the victimized individual, or if the objective circumstances make this impossible, by denigrating the individual's character in order to see the victim as "deserving" misfortune (Lerner & Matthews, 1967). Thus, observers overascribe culpability to victims of rape or assault, for example.

Not only do some onlookers tend to blame victims, but victims tend to blame themselves. In a study of spinal cord injury ([Janoff-]Bulman & Wortman, 1977), victims often blamed themselves regardless of the objective circumstances of their injury. Interestingly, those who had the most self-blame were actually coping *better* postinjury. Janoff-Bulman (1979) explored this issue further, trying to resolve the paradox of why self-blame (so often thought of as pathological and depressogenic) might be adaptive in some circumstances. She suggested that there are two different forms of self-blame—characterological and behavioral. The first is the kind of self-blame that relates to one's attributes as a person and is generally assumed to be pathogenic. The second is more specific in that one blames oneself for specific actions one took or failed to take that contributed to the trauma. (These concepts are similar to what other writers have distinguished as "shame" versus "guilt" [Joseph, Yule, & Williams, 1993].) Janoff-Bulman suggested that behavioral self-blame helps restore a sense of control and may be adaptive in this way. However, in numerous studies applying this construct, the evidence has been somewhat mixed—some researchers have found behavioral self-blame to be adaptive and some have not. For example, at least two studies of motor vehicle accidents found that victims who believed themselves responsible for an accident functioned better emotionally than did "innocent victims" (Delahanty et al., 1997; Hickling et al., 1999). A study of traumatic injury and bereavement (Landsman, 1993) found that while injured subjects exhibited distinguishable characterological and behavioral self-blame, neither type of self-blame was correlated with adjustment; among bereaved persons both types of blame were relatively rare, tended to coexist, and were associated with worse outcomes (p. 154).

In contrast to the mixed evidence on the adaptiveness of self-blame (which apparently can, in some circumstances, be helpful), there is little evidence that blaming other people in the wake of trauma serves a positive function. In a review of studies in which blame of others following trauma was assessed, Tennen and Affleck (1990) concluded that other-blame was almost always associated with worse outcomes. These reviewers asserted that the link between other-blame and poor outcomes is probably overdetermined. Objective circumstances of the trauma, for instance, may make other-blame inevitable while independently contributing to more difficult recovery. For example, homicide bereavement is a trauma that evokes, if not requires, the blame of another, but it is also an extremely difficult trauma to cope with in terms of suddenness, violence, human agency, loss, and other factors, so it may be expected to be associated with worse outcomes. Tennen and Affleck suggested that in some cases, blame of others may be a manifestation of a maladaptive preexisting personality and coping style—in other words, a symptom exhibited by someone who in a variety of ways may be expected to have a poor outcome following trauma. And finally, they emphasize that blame of others tends to alienate potential sources of support, which may additionally compromise recovery.

Since the Tennen and Affleck review there have been some other findings that "external attributions," including blame of perpetrator, may be associated with good adjustment in incest survivors, especially when contrasted with self-blame attributions. In a review, Dalenberg and Jacobs (1994) emphasized the complexity of blame and self-blame attributions in the case of sexual abuse. They pointed out that empirical studies frequently demonstrate that self-blame and other-blame may coexist and are often uncorrelated (p. 30). They cautioned against research paradigms that assume self- and other-blame to be mutually exclusive, concluding that "complex explanation[s]" (p. 47) combining some control-preserving self-blame and appropriate recognition of perpetrator culpability may be optimal.

The Assumptive World

The cognitive processes of "forming an account" of a traumatic event and of developing an understanding of the causes of such an event may be characterized

as asking "What happened?" and "How did it happen?" One of the most familiar operationalizations of a crisis of meaning in trauma is the degree to which
survivors ask "Why?" or "Why me?" in the wake of disaster. While these questions may be partly concerned with the concrete tasks of cognitive mastery of
determining causal factors, there seem to be deeper questions embedded here,
which may reveal a dawning perception that one's assumptive world cannot
encompass what has taken place.

Schemas and Illusions

There is an extensive literature in social psychology regarding the schemas,
assumptions, illusions, or meanings that operate in ordinary lives and that are called
into question or even shattered by extremely traumatic events. When we experience events that don't fit our schemas, violate our assumptions, or shatter our illusions, we experience a crisis of meaning. In Piaget's language, there is new
information to be assimilated or accommodated (1954). Either an event must be
interpreted and explained in such a way as to fit our schemas, which is a difficult
and painful task, or our schemas must be altered, an even more daunting task.

Parkes and Weiss (1983) described the threat of spousal bereavement and other
traumas to basic assumptions: "Each of us maintains an internal assumptive world,
a schema of the nature of our reality . . . events that are unwanted, and that invalidate a large part of our assumptive worlds, are likely to prove difficult for us to
assimilate" (p. 71). Several information-processing models focus on how new
information is incorporated into mental constructs.

Mardi Horowitz (1992) wrote of the "completion tendency," defined as a "need
to match new information with inner models based on older information, and
the revision of both until they agree" (1992, p. 92). This theory focuses on the
cognitive aspects of schemas and memory. In the ordinary course of events new
information and experience are incorporated into existing cognitive schemas—
change to schemas is slight, incremental, and/or relatively specific. Traumatic
events, however, require that schemas undergo *revision*. Horowitz points out that
this is a difficult and lengthy process because so much cognitive change is required.
Further, he pointed out that while the process of reworking these cognitive structures goes on, the repeated "recognition of the discrepancy between the new state
of affairs and the inner habitual model" (1992, p. 94) is so painful that it brings to
a halt, temporarily, the processing of traumatic material. This process of what
might be termed "interrupted information processing" is related to the alternating phases of intrusion and avoidance, also highlighted by Horowitz, which so
typify the symptoms of trauma response.

Seymour Epstein (1985, 1991) took a constructivist perspective, asserting that
"the essence of a person's personality is the implicit theory of self and the world
that the person constructs" (1985, p. 283). This statement highlights the centrality of meaning in human experience, asserting that schemas of meaning are the
essence of personality, without which we do not fully exist. In addition, Epstein
emphasized that meaning is only partially known—schemas of meaning are
implicit theories. Another important contribution of Epstein's theory is the inclusion, differentiation, and integration of both cognitive *and* emotional aspects of
meaning; schemas can operate at a preconscious, emotional level in addition to a
cognitive level. To the extent that important and fundamental schemas operate

out of usual awareness, they may exert an even greater influence on subjective experience and behavior. Trauma has the potential to disrupt schemas, both the more *general* and far-reaching schemas that ordinarily remain unchanged and the schemas that ordinarily operate outside of conscious awareness. Epstein asserted that this disruption destabilizes the personality and that regaining the self requires the development of modified schemas that can assimilate the reality of trauma. The most general, fundamental beliefs delineated by Epstein, and incorporated by Janoff-Bulman (1985, 1989), include schemas regarding the extent to which the world is benign and worthwhile as opposed to unrewarding, dangerous, or evil; a sense of "order and meaning" related to justice, predictability, controllability, and nonrandomness; schemas about others regarding trust; and schemas about the self with respect to basic self-worth, adequacy, wholeness, and invulnerability versus vulnerability.

Shattered Assumptions

Janoff-Bulman (1989, 1992) delineated a model of the shattered assumptive world that is vulnerable to traumatic experience. Schemas at risk in the wake of trauma include those involving personal invulnerability, a "meaningful world," and a positive self-image; coping strategies are generated in an attempt to rebuld these basic assumpsions. An instrument developed by Janoff-Bulman (1989) to operationalize this theory, the World Assumptions Scale (WAS), has been used in several studies of trauma survivors. That scale assesses the intactness of assumptions in three major areas: benevolence (of the world and of people), meaningfulness (justice, control, and nonrandomness), and self-worth (one's own goodness, control, and luck). As described later in this chapter, meaningfulness is operationalized in the WAS in a very specific fashion that differs in important ways from other concepts of meaning in the trauma literature.

Themes of Meaning

Susan Roth and colleagues explored both the content of trauma-relevant schemas and the processes by which trauma and recovery affect schemas. They incorporated Epstein's schemas in an expanded set of what they termed "themes," adding self-blame beliefs, a sense of reciprocity in human relationships, alienation versus connection to others, "legitimacy" with respect to one's response to trauma, and also feelings of rage, helplessness, fear, loss, shame, guilt, and distress (Roth & Newman, 1991; Newman, Riggs, & Roth, 1997). This model, following Epstein, incorporates both the emotional and cognitive disruptions of trauma. Specifically, these authors proposed that trauma may "challenge existing themes, foster the development of maladaptive themes, or prevent adaptive themes from emerging" (Newman, Riggs, & Roth, 1997, p. 198). In their empirical work, the extent to which themes have been "resolved" or not is evaluated. "Unresolved" themes, in this view, remain problematic and contribute to continued symptoms to the extent they remain "influenced by the trauma" and construct "an overly biased or confined way of relating to the world" (p. 198). An unresolved theme may be a maladaptively revised schema that incorporates the trauma but does not allow full engagement with life and one's future. (Thus it is somewhat different from Horowitz' description of incompletely revised schemas, which remain incongruent with traumatic experience). A "resolved" theme, by contrast, is one that "both incorporates the trauma and permits flexible emotional engagement with the world" (Newman, Riggs, & Roth, p. 198); this is consistent with Horowitz' model and can be seen as an adaptively revised assumption. Finally, Roth and her colleagues identified "nonrelevant" themes as those which are not disrupted by traumatic experience. The view of the process of recovery in Roth's work emphasizes that a developing awareness of the challenge to existing schemas or themes is necessary (highlighting the assumption that important schemas may not ordinarily be conscious), and that this conflict must be processed. Common to the information-processing perspective in general, this model incorporates the paradox that processes essential to integration and thus "recovery" themselves generate the painful symptoms of the trauma response.

Taylor's (1983) theory of cognitive adaptation to threatening events similarly delineates three "themes" in the adjustment process, focusing on three predominant concerns. The "search for meaning" in Taylor's model involves the need to assess "why a crisis occurred and what its impact has been" (p. 1162). A "sense of mastery," disrupted by trauma, must be restored via attributions and beliefs that maintain or enhance a perception of control. Finally, "self-esteem" is threatened by the perception of oneself as a victim, and self-enhancing social comparisons serve to preserve or restore self-regard. Draucker (1989) tested a model that incorporated Taylor's (1983) cognitive coping tasks as mediators of adjustment in the case of adult incest survivors. In that study, outcome was directly related to the cognitive tasks of meaning, mastery, and maintenance of self-esteem, and a successful search for meaning in the negative experience was associated with better outcomes.

Existential Crisis

The tasks of cognitive mastery, causal attribution, and confronting and restoring shattered assumptions may be considered to constitute crises of "ordinary meaning," as described earlier. In addition to—and perhaps because of—the crisis of ordinary meanings, there may be a crisis of finding or creating meaning that was not required before, of confronting the limits of ordinary meaning and of facing existential meaninglessness. Clinical experience, theory, and empirical research all contain reference to the existential problem inherent in bereavement and other traumas. A lack of meaning and purpose in life (the "existential vacuum"), while perhaps difficult to define, is clearly a major difficulty for many survivors.

Existential meaning has been more the realm of philosophers than of clinicians or researchers. In social psychology and even traumatology, much less is understood about this dimension of trauma than about attributions, control, blame, and self-blame. However, there is some useful groundwork for us to consider.

Viktor Frankl (1984) held that a fundamental will toward meaning is an essential motivational drive, not "a secondary rationalization of instinctual drives" (p. 105). Frankl held that personal meaning may be discovered and expressed in different ways, including individual accomplishments, one's experience of life, and one's stand toward suffering. He drew on his experiences in World War II concentration camps and said that the ability to find meaning was essential to survival in the overwhelmingly negative environment of the camps. By extension, he regarded meaning as essential in any circumstance of unavoidable suffering. While suffering may not be necessary in order to find meaning, a sense of meaning is possible despite—and even because of—extreme suffering. Frankl asserted that the ability to choose one's attitude toward suffering may be the "last of the human freedoms" (p. 74), and that such "attitudinal heroism" can make it possible to "transform a personal tragedy into a triumph . . . when we are no longer able to change a situation . . . we are challenged to change ourselves" (p. 116).

Irvin Yalom (1980) described an existential psychology in which the forces resulting in important intrapsychic conflict are in fact the "givens of existence" (p. 8)—inescapable, though painful, aspects of human experience. In Yalom's view, denial of the ultimate realities of death, freedom, isolation, and meaninglessness results in a pervasive anxiety characterizing the "normal but neurotic" functioning of everyday life. The confrontation and acknowledgment of the existential givens in each of these realms has implications for reactions to threatening life events. A confrontation with one's own mortality (as in the case of serious personal injury or the death of an important other person) may be terrifying or may be an impetus to live life more completely and fully, with increased "mindfulness of being." An acknowledgment of existential freedom may permit the survivor of a truly shattering event to be able to choose how to bear the ensuing suffering, and may relate to the fact that some survivors of traumatic events are able to focus on the positive aspects of the experience. Existential isolation (in contrast to interpersonal or intrapersonal isolation) is likely to be brought home to trauma survivors. Similar to the ultimate isolation of death, the experience of physical or psychic suffering is an isolating one. Despite the presence of family and social support, survivors realize that no other person can truly share their suffering. Finally, the problem of meaning, as Yalom has noted, arises from awareness of the existential givens of death, freedom, and isolation. Arguably, it is this existential confrontation that underlies the preeminence given by many victims to the search for meaning in the wake of devastating life events.

The Role of Denial

In trauma literature, as in the field of psychology generally, views and findings relating to the definitions and functions of denial vary. It may be useful here to consider three general kinds of denial—defensive denial, trauma-specific avoidance, and adaptive illusions.

Defensive Denial

First, we might use the term "defensive denial" to indicate a traditional psychodynamic view of denial as a defense against internal wishes, fears, and conflicts that are potentially threatening to one's sense of self. Defensive denial, which may take many forms, contributes to psychological neurosis. The more extensive and sustained the denial, the greater the attendant psychopathology, due to a loosening connection to reality (Hoffman, 1970).

In Yalom's existential psychological model, the dynamic forces in conflict within individuals are not the instinctive drives of Freudian theory, but those posed by the "givens of existence"—of which the most central is mortality (1980, p. 8). Denial of the reality of death is ubiquitous, and personality styles, in Yalom's view, emerge as a function of particular death-denying defensive styles. Overall, Yalom considered denial of death to be normal but neurotic, arguing that "death anxiety is inversely proportional to life satisfaction" (p. 207). On one hand, *restor-*

ing denial defenses in the wake of personally threatening events such as personal injury, serious illness, or the death of a close other person may permit recovery and return to baseline functioning. In contrast, facing the existential reality of death—a confrontation that may be forced by such experiences—can provide a new perspective for life concerns. The abandonment of denial creates a strong sense that "existence cannot be postponed" (p. 161), perhaps prompting individuals to live more fully in their present lives. An existential confrontation, abandoning denial—and not completely restoring it—has the potential for personal growth over and above a return to baseline.

Similarly, Antonovsky (1984) maintained that a healthy sense of coherence (as described below, a sense that the world and one's life is comprehensible, manageable, and meaningful) should in general result in less need for illusion and denial.

Trauma-Specific Avoidance

In cognitive-processing models such as Horowitz's (1992), trauma-specific denial or avoidance states alternate in a dynamic fashion with periods of intrusion of traumatic memories, thoughts, and feelings. During such periods individuals may be dazed, have complete or partial amnesia for the event, feel emotionally numb, engage in fantasies to avoid thinking about the event and its implications, experience somatic symptoms, and engage in either frantic activity or in withdrawal (Horowitz, 1982). While these phenomena may be at odds with "normal" (that is, pretrauma) functioning, and are by definition part of the psychopathology of posttraumatic stress disorder, it is likely that such avoidance is a necessary part of coming to terms with a traumatic experience. The function of such states is best understood as permitting a gradual assimilation of a potentially overwhelming, unwelcome, negative reality. Repeated cycles of intrusion and avoidance allow the survivor of trauma to alternate periods of active work on the problem of incorporating novel, inconsistent information into existing views of oneself and the world with periods of withdrawal, avoidance, or denial that allow the individual to gather strength and maintain adaptive functioning.

Adaptive Illusions

Another kind of trauma-specific denial may be qualitatively different from cognitive avoidance. Even when the reality of trauma has been assimilated and accepted, survivors may selectively focus on specific aspects of an experience in ways that lessen its negative implications. Taylor, Wood, and Lichtman (1983) made a distinction between denial of the reality of a threatening event and "minimization of victimization." In their research on cancer patients they only occasionally observed those who denied "that they had ever had it, despite clear evidence ... that it had existed" (p. 36). In contrast, many survivors minimized the victimizing aspects of the diagnosis by making positive comparisons with others or with hypothetical worse outcomes. In another report, Taylor (1983) stated that illusions, "that is, beliefs that have no factual basis or that require looking at known facts in a particular way" (p. 1171), ought not to be regarded as synonymous with defensiveness. Defensive denial, according to Taylor, is often held to connote pathological behavior, which may be maladaptive if it prevents people from seeing and taking necessary actions. She argued that illusions can be adaptive to the extent they enable people to maintain a sense of hope and perceived control over their lives. The literature on "depressive realism," for example, demonstrates that appraisal of situations and performance tend to be more objectively accurate in depressed individuals than in nondepressed persons; the latter exhibit an adaptive (if inaccurate) optimism (see, for example, Alloy and Abramson, 1979).

Whether denial is adaptive or maladaptive appears to depend on when it is used, how extensive it is, and especially the *function* it serves. Janoff-Bulman and Frieze (1983) speculated that an "illusion of invulnerability" might have negative consequences if it leads people to take unnecessary chances. On the other hand, they argued, such illusions help maintain an assumptive world that protects people from feeling overwhelming anxiety and stress. In more recent work, Janoff-Bulman (1989, 1992) suggested that the illusion of invulnerability and a resulting "sense of safety and security" is a fundamental prerequisite to emotional stability and well-being, citing personality and object relations theory.

Taylor (1983, 1989) emphasized that illusions are normal, and cited the adaptive function of illusions in protecting victims from overwhelming emotions, thus enabling them to engage in constructive behavior. In a more recent report, Taylor and Brown (1988) asserted that illusion is valuable, despite a theoretical tradition to the contrary, and perhaps especially so under conditions of threat.

A Delicate Balance

The adaptive functions of denial in the recovery process, *and* the benefits of giving up denial eventually, are integrated in Janoff-Bulman and Timko's (1987) article on the role of denial in recovery from trauma. Because traumatic negative events severely challenge and often shatter fundamental assumptions, there is an important adaptive role for denial in recovery from trauma, especially in the early stages. The process of change in such fundamental assumptions needs to be gradual and slow, and denial may serve the function of regulating the pace of this revision. Thus, denial may be most necessary in the early stages of the aftermath of trauma, as it ameliorates what would otherwise constitute a "dramatic, unmodulated attack on the primary postulates of the assumptive world" (p. 145). This type of denial is the trauma-specific "avoidance" detailed in cognitive-processing models such as Horowitz's, described above.

In their review of empirical research on the "natural course of denial," Janoff-Bulman and Timko found that denial is sufficiently common in the wake of negative life events as to be considered normal. Further, denial appeared in the studies reviewed to be adaptive in the short run, to decrease with time in most cases, and to be associated with worse psychosocial functioning when it does not decrease over time. Much less is known, they point out, about the long-term effects of denial.

Individual survivors of trauma may vary a great deal with respect to their utilization of denial in coping with the task of restructuring shattered assumptions. Janoff-Bulman and Timko speculated that some individuals—for instance, those whose assumptive worlds are less threatened by the event or who have a higher tolerance for anxiety—may have less of a need to use denial. It also seems likely that certain kinds of trauma will be less threatening to these assumptions than others. Over time, people's assumptive worlds are altered sufficiently to accommodate the traumatic experience, and survivors emerge "sadder but wiser" (Janoff-Bulman & Timko, 1987, p. 154), their assumptive worlds both less rigid and less unreservedly positive than before.

Like Yalom, Janoff-Bulman and Timko (1987) also pointed out the possibility of benefits ensuing from the process of confronting directly, without denial, "the reality of one's situation" (p. 154). Such benefits may include a sense of mastery, resulting from the successful effort to integrate the experience in one's world-view. Further, they argued, the ability of survivors to experience hope and optimism may be enhanced. Hope, they asserted, involves the ability to identify and focus on the positive aspects of even negative experience, and is activated when denial is no longer needed for coping. Survivors often express having a greater "appreciation of life," a sharpened perception of "what is really important," and a positive regard for oneself and one's attributes. The decline of denial and the emergence of hope may mark the completion of the process of recovery from trauma. Denial is one of the mechanisms "that serve to shield us from experiencing utter misery and despair; when its work is completed, hope can take its place" (p. 155).

A useful distinction may be made between denial that is specific to the particulars of a given traumatic experience and more general, overarching denial. The first, event-specific denial (or avoidance), may be essential to early phases of coping with trauma. Denial as a defensive style, like Yalom's denial of death or Janoff-Bulman's invulnerability assumption, is part of one's usual psychological makeup. The coping denial (avoidance) may be more common to early stages of adjustment and be specific to the event and its implications. The global denial that can be part of one's assumptive world may be altered by the experience of extremely negative events.

Sorting out the Meaning Muddle

As reviewed, definitions of "meaning" in the literature vary, conflict, and/or overlap. Single phenomena of meaning may exist, such as forming an account, asking "Why this?" and "Why me?" assessing impact and consequences, finding meaning, and making meaning. Definitions of meaning are also embedded in more elaborated models. In Taylor's model of cognitive adaptation, for example, "meaningfulness" concerns cognitive issues similar to forming an account, attributing causality, and assessing impact. Janoff-Bulman's World Assumptions Scale operationalizes "meaningfulness" assumptions as concerning beliefs in a just world, controllability of outcomes, and nonrandomness. These definitions exemplify what was described above as "ordinary" meanings.

Antonovsky's "sense of coherence" (1984) includes both kinds of meanings—ordinary and extraordinary—and provides a welcome degree of definitional clarity. He describes a sense of coherence as consisting of three related yet separate components, reflecting cognitions, beliefs, and feelings that are adaptive and healthy. First, "comprehensibility" is the experience of things in the world and our lives making sense—an assurance based on cognitive understanding of how things work and why things happen. Second, "manageability" is the sense that in this (comprehensible) world, we have the abilities required to make our way, to deal with the forces and facts of life. Finally, "meaningfulness" is the "emotional counterpart to comprehensibility" (p. 119). Not only do things make sense cognitively, but these things matter to us. Not only is the world understandable and manageable, but it is worth caring about and investing energy in. It is important to note that Antonovsky's concept of meaning is quite different from that embedded in measures such as Janoff-Bulman's World Assumptions Scale (1989).

Positive Change: The Paradox of Good Outcomes

Conventional concepts of trauma and even of bereavement are often shaped, explicitly or implicitly, by a medical model. In that paradigm, an event of trauma or loss is essentially defined as a pathogen, the phenomenology of grief or trauma response regarded as a disease process, and recovery defined as a return to baseline. A major limitation of such an approach lies in its inability to account for positive changes in the wake of loss and pain.

The subject of good outcomes has only fairly recently, and somewhat tentatively, been addressed in the trauma and loss literatures. Judith Lyons (1991) identified the imbalance between our ability to quantify and explain posttrauma pathology and our limited and mostly anecdotal knowledge about posttrauma resilience and growth. Some types of events may be more or less conducive to positive adjustment, as may different preexisting personality styles. Differences in the ways in which survivors process the trauma, including their search for meaning, may, she suggested, explain how positive as well as negative outcomes are reached. She also reminded us of evidence that sometimes those who ultimately adjust well, even transcend the trauma, pass through an initial period of distress and even despair.

Where measures assessing positive change have been applied, evidence of subjective perception of benefit, growth, and positive change has been found. In studies of disaster, incest, and bereavement a variety of positive changes related to a traumatic experience have been identified, many consistent with greater existential awareness. Typically, survivors cite positive *and* negative changes, apparently coexisting without necessarily being offsetting. Survivors of a cruise ship disaster endorsed both positive (e.g., "I don't take life for granted anymore") and negative (e.g., "I don't look forward to the future anymore") items on a "change in outlook" questionnaire developed by Joseph, Williams, and Yule (1993). Positive-response items were endorsed more frequently than were negative items. Negative item endorsement was correlated with higher levels of distress and traumatic stress, while endorsement of positive items was not correlated with symptomatology.

Tedeschi and Calhoun (1996) developed a Posttraumatic Growth Inventory comprising items reflecting subjective positive changes in areas of relationships, future hopes, personal strength, and appreciation of life (p. 460). Traumatized college students' endorsement of these items was not associated with a desire to appear socially acceptable, nor was identification of positive change correlated with psychological symptoms. Those with more severe trauma identified even more positive change than those with lesser trauma.

In a study of serious physical injury and bereavement (Landsman, 1993), a significant minority rated themselves as better off overall about a year and a half postevent. These individuals cited existential factors, such as a heightened appreciation of life's fragility, and identified positive implications of this change in perspective. Many valued their personal relationships more highly, felt they had a clearer sense of priorities, and found life more meaningful. Compared to those who considered their posttrauma lives to be about the same, the survivors who felt better off had *not* experienced less severe trauma, nor did they have fewer PTSD or other psychiatric symptoms. Injured subjects who considered themselves worse off following the trauma *and* those who felt better off reported the most concern with seeking meaning; those who had more or less returned to baseline had the *least* concern with meaning. Some kind of crisis of meaning, in other words, characterized the extremes of outcome.

Yalom and Lieberman (1991) observed that "existential awareness"—consciousness of mortality, concern with purpose and meaning, and acknowledgment of "regrets"—was associated with postbereavement growth in a study of widows and widowers. Interestingly, existential awareness was associated with more initial grief but also with more "personal effectance" (p. 343). They concluded that symptoms of trauma and grief were orthogonal to personal growth (p. 345). In other words, the experience of suffering did not make an experience of growth less likely.

In fact, a growing number of studies seem to illustrate that existential confrontation (as evidenced by a search for meaning), while not related in straightforward ways to conventional measures of adjustment, is frequently associated with perceptions of benefit or positive change.

Despair and Transcendence—A Model of Existential Confrontation

The crisis of meaning in bereavement and other traumas is a crisis on two major levels, with different implications. The crisis of "ordinary meanings" is perhaps inevitable; there is a profound need to restore basic assumptions of benevolence, justice, control, and self-worth to a pretrauma configuration, and the difficulty in doing so is a fair reflection of the extent to which an event has been traumatic. When ordinary meanings cannot be restored to their original configuration, major assumptive worlds or systems of meaning are *changed*, with sometimes powerful results, both good and bad.

The model shown in Figure 1-1 outlines three possible paths of adjustment following trauma. What this model suggests is that *revision* of the assumptive world (in contrast to rebuilding or restoration) is common to both the best and the worst outcomes in the wake of bereavement and other trauma; such revision and existential confrontation may explain important aspects of both despair and transcendence.

First, in any trauma that meets the definition of the word, the shattering of assumptions of control, justice, and nonrandomness creates a primary set of recovery tasks. The survivor must work through the trauma in ways that will allow the traumatic experience to be integrated into existing schemas or assumptions, and also make adjustments to these assumptions to accommodate experience that cannot be fully assimilated. The tasks of forming an account and developing attributions of causality may be considered common to all trauma reactions.

A variety of factors may influence the extent to which restoring shattered assumptions is possible. For some people, and for some kinds of trauma, it may be that basic assumptions can be restored to their pretrauma configuration. It may be that in these cases attributions such as behavioral self-blame help to restore assumptions of control over future events and that a continued search for meaning will *not* be necessary. These particular survivors may, in fact, return to baseline.

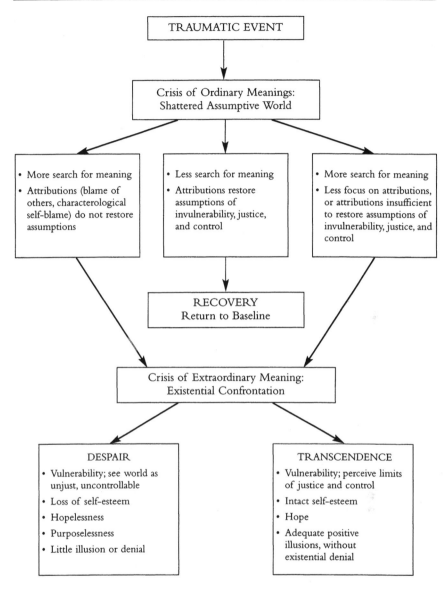

Figure 1-1. Crises of meaning and paths of adjustment.

In some situations, however, basic assumptions cannot be restored. Experiences such as the murder of a loved one, for example, make it difficult to hold an unaltered belief in the benevolence of the world. In fully confronting the fact of murder, we must recognize that there is evil in the world, that there are evil people. While some survivors may be able to identify factors specific to a trauma that they can avoid in the future, others will be forced to accept, more than before, the fact of randomness and attendant vulnerability.

When ordinary meanings cannot be fully restored the confrontation with extra-ordinary meanings—the problem of existential meaninglessness—becomes more likely. Herein lies the spiritual *crisis* of trauma—a crisis, true to the meaning of the word, that entails both danger and opportunity. Confrontation with the existential givens of life may lead either to despair or, perhaps, to transcendence.

On one hand, some victims confront the realities of existence and find them bleak. They see the world as without justice and feel unable to control their destiny. Their schemas of meaning, or world assumptions, have been changed, but in a way that is ultimately negative. Without hope, they lack even what Shelley Taylor (1989) has termed "positive illusions," and are not able to escape the pain, disappointment, and loss they have experienced—they are in despair. On the other hand, because of this existential confrontation, others are able to accept the limits of justice and control. They perceive life's fragility and their own vulnerability but find it a motivating force that makes life more meaningful. Without existential denial, they are still able to maintain hope, self-esteem, and a sense of purpose in life. Schemas or assumptions have been altered by trauma, have not been rebuilt to a pretrauma configuration, but leave room for an engagement with life and with the future. Despite a trauma and sometimes radical change to some schemas, some survivors retain a sense of meaningfulness in the sense of Antonovsky's model—assumptions of nonrandomness, justice, and control may have been altered, but life continues to be found worthy of emotional investment.

And sometimes these are the same people. While despair and transcendence are vastly different states, it may be that transcendence cannot be truly experienced without a close encounter with despair.

Conclusion

In considering the crisis of meaning in bereavement and trauma, we must consider both despair and transcendence, recognizing the elements that these extremes of outcome may have in common. In particular, they may share the phenomenon of existential confrontation that sometimes, although not always, ensues from trauma.

Transcendence is still very much a mystery in the wake of trauma. We know it exists, we believe we recognize it when we see it, we may even experience it. But we are at a loss to quantify it and even more at a loss to foster it. In the words of one of the existentialist philosophers, Karl Jaspers, "one cannot prove Transcendence, one bears witness to it" (Blackham, 1952, p. 54).

It is important to struggle with the difficult issues of definition and measurement so that the phenomenon of transcendence not remain mysterious, so that it can be assessed, understood, and thus witnessed in the research literature as well as in the consultation room. While we may not prove transcendence, we must continue to bear witness to the struggle with meaning and meaninglessness, to bear witness to despair, and—sometimes—to bear witness to transcendence.

Notes

This chapter is based in part on the author's doctoral dissertation and related material presented at the Fifth International Conference on Grief and Bereavement in Contemporary Society (June 26, 1997, Washington, DC); the Second Annual Conference on Trauma,

Loss and Dissociation (March 3, 1996, Alexandria, Virginia); and the Fourth European Conference on Traumatic Stress Studies (May 10, 1995, Paris).

The author acknowledges with gratitude the encouragement and assistance of Diane A. Arnkoff, Catherine L. Anderson, and Bonnie L. Green.

References

Alloy, L. B. & Abramson, L. Y. (1979). Judgment of contingency in depressed and nondepressed students: Sadder but wiser? *Journal of Experimental Psychology, 108(4)*, 441–485.

Antonovsky, A. (1984). The sense of coherence as a determinant of health. In J. D. Matarazzo et al. (Eds.), *Behavioral health: A handbook of health enhancement and disease prevention* (pp. 114–129). New York: Wiley.

Athelstan, G. T., & Crewe, N. M. (1979). Psychological adjustment to spinal cord injury as related to manner of onset of disability. *Rehabilitation Counseling Bulletin, 22*, 311–319.

Blackham, H. J. (1952). *Six existentialist thinkers.* London: Routledge & Kegan Paul, Ltd.

Dalenberg, C. J., & Jacobs, D. A. (1994). Attributional analyses of child sexual abuse episodes: Empirical and clinical issues. *Journal of Child Sexual Abuse, 3(3)*, 37–50.

Delahanty, D. L., Herberman, K. J. C., Hayward, M. C., Fullerton, C. S., Ursano, R. J., & Baum, A. (1997). Acute and chronic distress and Posttraumatic Stress Disorder as a function of responsibility for serious motor vehicle accidents. *Journal of Consulting and Clinical Psychology, 65*, 560–567.

Downey, G., Silver, R. C., & Wortman, C. B. (1990). Reconsidering the attribution-adjustment relation following a major negative event: Coping with the loss of a child. *Journal of Personality and Social Psychology, 59*, 925–940.

Draucker, C. B. (1989). Cognitive adaptation of female incest survivors. *Journal of Consulting and Clinical Psychology, 57*, 668–670.

Epstein, S. (1991). The self-concept, the traumatic neurosis, and the structure of personality. In D. Z. Ozer, J. M. Healy, Jr., & A. J. Stewart (Eds.), *Perspectives on personality* (Vol. 3, pp. 63–98). London: Jessica Kingsley Publishers.

Epstein, S. (1985). The implications of cognitive-experiential self-theory for research in social psychology and personality. *Journal for the Theory of Social Behaviour, 15*, 283–310.

Frankl, V. E. (1984). *Man's search for meaning: An introduction to logotherapy* (3rd ed.). New York: Simon & Schuster. (Original work published 1959, 1962 as *From death-camp to existentialism*).

Hickling, E. J., Blanchard, E. B., Buckley, T. C., & Taylor, A. E. (1999). Effects of attribution of responsibility for motor vehicle accidents on severity of PTSD symptoms, ways of coping, and recovery over six months. *Journal of Traumatic Stress, 12*, 345–353.

Hoffman, P. S. (1970). *Psychoanalysis and psychopathology.* New York: McGraw-Hill.

Horowitz, M. J. (1982). Psychological processes induced by illness, injury, and loss. In T. Millon, C. Green, & N. Meagher (Eds.), *Handbook of clinical health psychology* (pp. 53–67). New York: Plenum Press.

Horowitz, M. (1992). *Stress response syndromes.* Northvale, NJ: Jason Aronson Inc.

Janoff-Bulman, R. (1979). Characterological versus behavioral self-blame: Inquiries into depression and rape. *Journal of Personality and Social Psychology, 37*, 1798–1809.

Janoff-Bulman, R. (1985). The aftermath of victimization: Rebuilding shattered assumptions. In C. R. Figley (Ed.), *Trauma and its wake* (pp. 15–35). New York: Brunner/Mazel.

Janoff-Bulman, R. (1989). Assumptive worlds and the stress of traumatic events: Applications of the schema construct. *Social Cognition, 7*, 113–136.

Janoff-Bulman, R. (1992). *Shattered assumptions: Towards a new psychology of trauma.* New York: The Free Press.

Janoff-Bulman, R., & Frieze, I. H. (1983). A theoretical perspective for understanding reactions to victimization. *Journal of Social Issues, 39(2)*, 1–17.

Janoff-Bulman, R., & Timko, C. (1987). Coping with traumatic life events: The role of denial in light of people's assumptive worlds. In C. R. Snyder & C. E. Ford (Eds.), *Coping with negative life events: Clinical and social psychological perspectives* (pp. 135–159). New York: Plenum.

[Janoff-]Bulman, R. J., & Wortman, C. B. (1977). Attributions of blame and coping in the "real world": Severe accident victims react to their lot. *Journal of Personality and Social Psychology, 35,* 351–363.

Joseph, S., Williams, R., & Yule, W. (1993). Changes in outlook following disaster: The preliminary development of a measure to assess positive and negative responses. *Journal of Traumatic Stress, 6,* 271–279.

Joseph, S., Yule, W., & Williams, R. (1993). Post-traumatic stress: Attributional aspects. *Journal of Traumatic Stress, 6,* 501–514.

Landsman, I. S. (1993). Variability of outcome following traumatic life events: Adjustment to injury and bereavement. (Doctoral dissertation, Catholic University of America, 1993).

Lerner, M. J. (1980). *The belief in a just world.* New York: Plenum.

Lerner, M. J., & Matthews, G. (1967). Reactions to suffering of others under conditions of indirect responsibility. *Journal of Personal and Social Psychology, 5,* 319–325.

Lifton, R. J. (1993). From Hiroshima to the Nazi doctors: The evolution of psychoformative approaches to understanding traumatic stress syndromes. In J. P. Wilson & B. Raphael (Eds.), *International handbook of traumatic stress syndromes* (pp. 11–23). New York: Plenum Press.

Lyons, J. A. (1991). Strategies for assessing the potential for positive adjustment following trauma. *Journal of Traumatic Stress, 4,* 93–111.

Newman, E., Riggs, D. S., & Roth, S. H. (1997). Thematic resolution, PTSD, and Complex PTSD: The relationship between meaning and trauma-related diagnoses. *Journal of Traumatic Stress, 10,* 197–213.

Parkes, C. M., & Weiss, R. S. (1983). *Recovery from bereavement.* New York: Basic Books.

Piaget, J. (1954). *The construction of reality in the child.* New York: Basic Books.

Roth, S. H., & Newman, E. (1991). The process of coping with sexual trauma. *Journal of Traumatic Stress, 4,* 279–297.

Rotter, J. (1966). Generalized expectancies for internal vs. external control of reinforcement. *Psychological Monographs, 80, 1 (whole number 609).*

Schwartzberg, S. S., & Janoff-Bulman, R. (1991). Grief and the search for meaning: Exploring the assumptive worlds of bereaved college students. *Journal of Social and Clinical Psychology, 10.* 270–288.

Silver, R. L., Boon, C., & Stones, M. H. (1983). Searching for meaning in misfortune: Making sense of incest. *Journal of Social Issues, 39,* 81–102.

Taylor, S. E. (1983). Adjustment to threatening events: A theory of cognitive adaptation. *American Psychologist, 38,* 1161–1173.

Taylor, S. E. (1989). *Positive illusions: Creative self-deception and the healthy mind.* New York: Basic Books.

Taylor, S. E. & Brown, J. D. (1988). Illusion and well-being: A social psychology perspective on mental health. *Psychological Bulletin, 103* (2), 193–210.

Taylor, S. E., Wood, J. V., & Lichtman, R. R. (1983). It could be worse: Selective evaluation as a response to victimization. *Journal of Social Issues, 39*(2), 19–40.

Tedeschi, R. G., & Calhoun, L. G. (1996). The Posttraumatic Growth Inventory: Measuring the positive legacy of trauma. *Journal of Traumatic Stress, 9(3),* 455–471.

Tennen, H., & Affleck, G. (1990). Blaming others for threatening events. *Psychological Bulletin, 108,* 209–232.

Wortman, C. B. (1976). Causal attributions and personal control. In J. H. Harvey, W. J. Ickes, & R. F. Kidd (Eds.), *New directions in attributions research* (Vol. 1) (pp. 23–51). Hillsdale, NJ: Erlbaum.

Yalom, I. D. (1980). *Existential psychotherapy.* New York: Basic Books.

Yalom, I. D., & Lieberman, M. A. (1991). Bereavement and heightened existential awareness. *Psychiatry, 54,* 334–345.

2.

The Meaning of Your Absence

Traumatic Loss and Narrative Reconstruction

Robert A. Neimeyer, Luis Botella,
Olga Herrero, Meritxell Pacheco, Sara Figueras,
and Luis Alberto Werner-Wildner

As the publication of this book testifies, bereavement theory has evolved considerably in recent years. Gone is its unquestioning reliance on presumably universal stage models of recovery, its preemptive focus on emotional responses to loss in isolation from both cognition and action, and its penchant for quantifying grief in terms of psychopathological symptomatology (Neimeyer, 1998). In their place is a newfound sensitivity to different patterns of adaptation as a function of age, gender, and ethnicity (Martin & Doka, 2000), concern with the disruption of life assumptions (Janoff-Bulman, 1989), and the quantitative and qualitative study of the transformations of self and world occasioned by loss (Neimeyer & Hogan, 2001; Tedeschi, Park, & Calhoun, 1998). Our goal in the present chapter is to extend this latter effort by applying the concepts and methods of one recent contribution to grief theory—namely, a constructivist and narrative approach—to the idiographic account of a man contending with traumatic loss of his son through suicide. We hope that this intensive case study will suggest the conceptual, methodological, and clinical relevance of a meaning reconstruction model (Neimeyer, 2001b) to grief studies, and point to some directions for its further refinement.

A Forward Glance

Like most projects, this chapter represents the convergence of both planned and accidental factors. At one level, it represents a systematic application of a conceptual model of human beings as meaning-makers that we have found to provide a fertile framework for psychotherapy (Botella & Feixas, 1998; Neimeyer & Raskin, 2000) and grief counseling (Neimeyer, 1998; Neimeyer, 2001b; Neimeyer, Fortner, & Melby, 1999). On another level, it represents a shared response to an unpredictable event—the enrollment of one of this chapter's authors (Luis Alberto Wener-Wildner) in a graduate psychology course offered by another (Luis Botella) at a critical moment during his attempt to reconstruct the meaning of his life following his son's tragic act of self-destruction. The evocative personal journal and poetic reflections that trace his journey from emotional decimation to existential regeneration form the heart of this chapter, with interpretive commentary provided by the other authors. Our unanimous decision to coauthor the chapter rather than treat this archival material as anonymous "clinical data" reflects our shared conviction that autoethnographic personal accounts are professional contributions in their own right (Ellis, 1998), as well as our constructivist respect for many voices, regardless of their academic pedigree.

We will begin by providing a brief background for a narrative model of the construction of meaning, and consider how life stories can be disrupted by profound loss. We will then draw on material from Luis Alberto's diary to illustrate key features of this approach as it applies to suicidal bereavement. Finally, we will close with some thoughts on current directions we are pursuing as we strive to configure a more delicate understanding of the ways in which human beings struggle, often successfully, to accommodate their life stories to the brute realities of loss in a progressive rather than regressive fashion.

The Narrative Construction of Identity

When considered from a constructivist standpoint, human psychological processes can be considered "efforts after meaning" (Bartlett, 1932). Being human entails active efforts to interpret experience, seeking purpose and significance in the events that surround us. In this sense, constructivists view people as incipient scientists developing personally and consensually validated theories of life experiences that enable them to organize the past, direct their choices in the present, and anticipate an intelligible future (Kelly, 1991). In recent years, this personal–scientist metaphor has been expanded to encompass the conception of humans as inveterate storytellers (Hermans, 2001; Mair, 1988). In this extended sense, meaning-making processes, including the development of one's sense of personal identity, are hypothesized to assume a narrative as well as anticipatory structure.

Anticipation as a fundamental human tendency to interpret experience is at the heart of personal construct psychology (PCP) (Kelly, 1991), the prototypical constructivist theory. Narrative conceptualizations coherent with a Kellian approach echo the anticipatory quality of storytelling, as in Mair's (1989) postulate that "persons' processes are psychologically channelized by the stories that they live and the stories that they tell" (p. 5). In a similar vein, Sarbin (1986) proposed a "narratory principle" intrinsic to human sense making: "Human beings think, perceive, imagine, and make moral choices according to narrative structures" (p. 8).

To approach human processes in general (and self-identity in particular) from a narrative standpoint requires a definition of narrative. Although such a definition could be formulated on literary grounds, we prefer an approach that emphasizes the psychological functions served by "storying" experience, such as that offered by Sarbin (1986):

> The narrative is a way of organizing episodes, actions, and accounts of actions; it is an achievement that brings together mundane facts and fantastic creations; time and place are incorporated. The narrative allows for the inclusion of actors' reasons for their acts, as well as the causes of [their] happening. (p. 9)

Ultimately, because all knowledge depends on the structure of the knower (Maturana & Varela, 1987), and the ordering of our world is inseparable from our experiencing of it (Guidano, 1995), all knowledge is self-referential and all narratives can be broadly considered self-narratives. In order to clarify the narrative construction of identity, however, a more restrictive definition of self-narrative is needed, along the lines of the social constructionist account offered by Gergen (1994):

> Our present identity is not a sudden and mysterious event but a sensible result of a life story.... Such creations of narrative order may be essential in giving life a sense of meaning and direction.... The term "self-narrative" will refer to an individual's account of the relationship among self-relevant events across time. In developing a self-narrative we establish coherent connections among life events. Rather than see our life as simply "one damned thing after another," we formulate a story in which life events are systematically related, rendered intelligible by their place in a sequence or unfolding process. (p. 187)

If self-identity is organized as a narrative construction, then the self can be viewed as a storyteller or as "someone who has a story to tell about his or her own life. In telling this story the person gives special significance to particular events (or groups of events), which function as units of meaning" (Hermans, 1995, p.1).

From a traditional psychological approach the development of personal identity is seen as an individual achievement. The grand metanarrative implicit in such a romantic vision is one of the mythical hero who faces a series of tasks and who returns from an odyssey as a complete and finished being, with a consolidated identity. The individualistic emphasis is inherent in apparently different developmental theories such as psychoanalysis or humanistic psychology (Gergen & Gergen, 1986). It is also implicit in the daily discursive practices of laypeople— at least in Western cultures, in which adolescence is positioned as a stage of "crisis" and "discovery" of one's own "real" identity in all its dimensions; relational, vocational, sexual, and so on.

Nevertheless, as Geertz (1983) reminds us from an anthropological point of view:

> The western conception of the person as a limited, unique, and more or less motivationally and cognitively integrated universe, with a dynamic center of consciousness, emotion, judgment and action organized in a characteristic set, and opposed by contrast to other similar sets and to his social and cultural background is, convincing as it may seem to us, a quite unique idea in the context of the cultures of the world. (p. 77)

In a more discursive approach, individual identity emerges in the process of interaction, not as a final product, but as constituted and reconstituted in relation to others (Davies & Harre, 1990). That is, any sense of ourselves as protagonists in our self-narrative relies critically on our construction of other important characters, and their loss therefore undermines our own identity-in-relation. As a social as well as personal action, storying one's experience also entails (1) learning to attribute meaning in terms intelligible to one's community, and (2) positioning oneself (or, sometimes, being positioned) in the context of such accounts. Tragic loss in particular challenges the intelligibility of previously adequate self-narratives, and calls for the development of new narrative forms in which images of both self and other can find a new "fictional" plausibility (Neimeyer, 2000). Restated, profound disruptions of our self-narratives occasioned by loss call for "narrative repair," whose goal is not so much to represent the final "truth" of our experience as to construct an account in which both people and events can be rendered once again meaningful.

A further dimension along which our self-narratives are ordered is that of time. As implicit in the very definitions of narrative cited above, narration serves to link otherwise isolated events and self-images in a coherent fashion, giving rise to an explicit sense of self that strives to capture the subtle implicit transitions of lived experience. When loss experiences intrude into a previously coherent self-narrative, one's sense of continuity in time is disrupted, and with it the apparent authority of one's previous self-understanding (Neimeyer & Levitt, 2000b). The resulting tension challenges the *I* (or self-as-knower/author) to accommodate new perspectives on the *me* (or self-as-known/actor) (Guidano, 1991). When such accommodation is successful, a new self-theory results, one that bridges the preexisting self and the one that has survived the unbidden transition. A similar process of accommodation may be called for in connection with one's construction of other key figures in the self-narrative, resulting in a reconstruction of their motives and intentions along with one's own (Hermans & Kempen, 1993).

In elaborating one's narrative of identity across time, the dialectical tension between continuity and discontinuity plays a crucial role. Rarely do the events of our lives conform to a simple plot structure, as most self-narratives are critically fragmented by life events that introduce an unexpected discontinuity—with major loss experiences being quintessential examples. Our first impulse when faced with invalidation of our scripts of identity often focuses on becoming our "old self" again. Unfortunately, such a "narrative rewind" is impossible by definition, as we cannot turn back time and must instead struggle with ways of bridging what once was and what now is, in a way that yields different intimations of what might yet be. Thus, as M. C. Bateson (1993, p. 45) notes, "Much of coping with discontinuity has to do with discovering threads of continuity. You cannot adjust to changes unless you can recognize some analogy between your old situation and your new situation." Such recognition, as Sarbin (1986, p. 6) aptly noted, "provides the basis for analogy, and if linguistic translation is necessary, the partial similarity is expressed as a metaphor." Elaborating metaphors that grasp the contours of identity transformations—perhaps by describing grief as a "journey" or bereavement as a "test"—assist in this process of reconstruction by identifying elastic "superordinate constructs" (Kelly, 1991) that help assign meaning to whole "chapters" in one's autobiography, including the disruptive events themselves.

A final consideration in the construction and reconstruction of self-narratives concerns their dialogic function, the way in which any account is located in the context of a polyphony of competing discourses, and always represents an implicit answer to the real or imagined speech acts of others (Bakhtin, 1986). In the case of apparently personal accounts of loss, for example, such self-narratives represent not only resources for self-reflection on a difficult experience but also responses to other potential discourses on the experience. For this reason, all self-narratives incorporate rhetorical devices to undermine alternative versions and to avoid being undermined by them (Potter, 1996). From the standpoint of its author, a story stakes a claim, seeking a sustainable "position" for the self in a social field of competing accounts (Neimeyer, 2000).

These remarks regarding the personal and interpersonal functions of narrative, and the temporal challenges to self-continuity occasioned by profound transition, provide a schematic framework for understanding the disruptive influence of catastrophic loss. After a brief consideration of the convergence of this account with recent trends in grief theory, we will return to these themes in the context of the self-narrative of a father contending with suicidal bereavement.

Toward a New Theory of Grieving

The past decade has witnessed a great deal of development in grief theory and research, development that is both evolutionary and revolutionary. In this section we will highlight a few of these trends that have special relevance for our current work, and leave to other comprehensive sourcebooks the task of presenting more fully the "new look" in bereavement studies (Neimeyer, 2001b; Stroebe, Stroebe, Hansson, & Schut, 2001). Here we will briefly summarize six trends that converge with the constructivist conceptualization of identity development outlined above, and which provide interpretive resources for analyzing the personal journal to follow. These include (1) the shift toward idiographic approaches and away from stage models of grieving, (2) the growth of qualitative research, (3) notions of sense making, benefit finding, and identity reconstruction, (4) the adoption of nonpathologizing models of transformation, (5) a focus on the continuing bond with the deceased, and (6) explicitly narrative models of grieving.

Idiographic Approaches

Despite the near hegemony of stage models of grief since the 1969 publication of Kubler-Ross's (1969) *On Death and Dying* (Downe-Wambolt & Tamlyn, 1997), the shortcomings of such models have been increasingly recognized. Corr (1993), for example, notes the virtual absence of empirical support for a conception of bereavement as involving identifiable universal stages of adaptation, and Worden (1991) has offered a more active, task-based model of what the bereaved person needs to accomplish in order to reinvest in living. This critical effort has been supplemented by growing recognition of subtle ethnic and gender variations in grieving (Braun & Nichols, 1997; Martin & Doka, 2000), further undermining the presumed authority of a one-size-fits-all approach to postloss adaptation.

With the critique of traditional models has come a call for more personal, idiographic approaches to loss, which seek not so much to offer alternative models of human experience as to afford new windows on human complexity. Thus, Attig (1996) depicts the many ways in which bereaved persons "relearn" the world following loss, and Gilbert (1996) underscores the quite different fashion in which different family members, by dint of their different positions, accommodate the "same" loss. Constructivist theorists in particular have developed a range of methods for studying and facilitating individual processes of bereavement adaptation (Neimeyer, Keesee, & Fortner, 2000; Vickio, 1999), contributing to many of the remaining trends discussed below.

Qualitative Research

Coinciding with the upsurge of interest in idiographic approaches has been a proliferation of qualitative approaches to grief, supplementing the traditional emphasis on quantitative assessment of grief symptomatology (Neimeyer &

Hogan, 2001). Much of this work concerns the unique experiences of bereaved parents, whose belief in a benign and predictable universe can be cruelly undercut by the experience of such "off time" deaths (Walsh & McGoldrick, 1991). Braun and Berg (1994) and Milo (1997), for example, have performed grounded theory analyses on accounts of bereaved parents, identifying the core meanings that parents attach to their loss, and discussing how such meanings relate to their broader adaptation. Both Nadeau (1997) and Rosenblatt (2000) have studied meaning making regarding loss as an interactive process within families, tracing the delicate discursive "dance" performed by survivors as they renegotiate their intimate relationships and "mind-read" the probable reactions of the deceased to his or her own death. Some investigators have also begun to promote a cross-fertilization of qualitative and quantitative methods, for example, by using grounded theory analyses of the discourse of bereaved persons to provide the raw material for constructing conventionally validated items for grief inventories (Hogan, Greenfield, & Schmidt, 2001). Our present hermeneutic interpretation of a grief diary represents one further example of this qualitative research tradition.

The Various Faces of Meaning

Perhaps the most common and least satisfactory approach to the problem of meaning in the wake of loss is one that views it as a narrowly cognitive achievement, a kind of "positive reframing" of a "stressful life event." In our view such a conception trivializes meaning making by turning it into a "cognitive coping strategy" rather than revealing it in all its complexity as a quest for a new orientation in the world in both practical and existential terms (Neimeyer, 2001c). This anguished process of searching for new significance draws on symbolic resources in the self, family, community, and broader culture, and often requires a metaphorical "stretching" of the expressive power of language to be adequate to the nuances of loss (Neimeyer, 2001a).

Viewed over time, meaning reconstruction includes several processes, which vary in their impact and relevance at different points in the experience. For example, longitudinal research by Davis, Nolen-Hoeksma, and Larson (1998) has established that the ability to "make sense" of the loss itself predicts early adjustment to bereavement, whereas only the capacity to find indirect benefits in the loss (e.g., learning important life lessons) predicts longer term outcome. Additionally, the large-scale interview study performed by Frantz, Farrell, and Trolley (2001) documents the important shifts in personal identity noted by bereaved persons over the first two years following loss, capturing their sense of greater strength, diminished fear of death, and heightened sensitivity to the suffering of others. Clearly, the reconstruction of meaning at these levels is more than simply a way of putting a positive face on unpleasant events, representing instead a profound reorganization of one's constructions of self and world.

Transformative Processes in Grieving

These considerations lead naturally to an acknowledgment that grief is—or can be—a transformative process, one that can trigger not only posttraumatic stress but also posttraumatic growth (Tedeschi et al., 1998). Although some theorists have attempted to accommodate these observations by extending conventional stage models to include a final stage of transformation (Prend, 1997), others have viewed grief as inherently transformative, requiring qualitative changes in one's sense of self, world, and spirituality (Klass, 1999). In our view, however, the transformation of any system can be regressive as well as progressive, in the sense of reducing or augmenting its richness or complexity, or moving a self-narrative farther from or closer to its own fictional goals (Neimeyer, 2000). At least in favorable social and personal circumstances, however, this system transformation can go deep, establishing whole new core sets of values and organizing principles for living. A qualitative shift of this kind has been documented in the longitudinal research of Richards and her colleagues (Richards, Acree, & Folkman, 1999; Richards & Folkman, 1997) on gay partners of men who have died of AIDS, as well as in case studies of grief diaries of the kind analyzed here (Balk & Vesta, 1998).

Continuing Bonds

One of the most fundamental recent changes in grief theory has been the growing recognition of the importance of continuing bonds with the deceased, in place of the immensely influential psychodynamic concept of withdrawing "emotional energy" from the lost loved one in order to "invest" it elsewhere (Klass, Silverman, & Nickman, 1996). The traditional emphasis on "seeking closure" or "letting go" is being reevaluated even within the dynamic camp, leading to the belated recognition that maintaining symbolic connection with the deceased can assist rather than hinder the process of adaptation (Hagman, 2001). Indeed, current data suggest that even vivid sensory forms of "contact" with a deceased spouse (e.g., sensing his or her presence, hearing his or her voice) not only are commonplace but also are typically welcomed by the bereaved as a source of comforting connection (Datson & Marwit, 1997). Developing a continuing bond with the "inner representation" of the one who has died seems especially useful in the case of bereaved parents, particularly when such reconnection is validated by the community of others who have suffered similar losses (Klass, 1999).

In keeping with these findings, a number of authors have been exploring concepts and strategies for understanding and facilitating a helpful ongoing connection between the bereaved and those they have lost. For example, Attig (2000) has described grieving as a process of moving from "loving others in their presence" to "loving them in their absence," figuratively creating a "place in the heart" in which ongoing contact with memories of the deceased is possible and such memories are freely accessed and shared. Both Vickio (1999) and Neimeyer (1998) have provided various guidelines and exercises for facilitating constructive connections of this kind, along with clinical examples of their application. From the standpoint of the present chapter, such techniques could be seen as means of restoring a measure of relational continuity to the construction of self, by again finding some anchoring in a relationship that can be carried on in symbolic rather than literal ways.

The Narrative Trend

Finally, a number of theorists and investigators have begun to adopt an explicit narrative model for conceptualizing trauma and loss, in a way that is highly compatible with our own analysis. For example, Walter (1996) construes grieving as a social process of constructing a biography of the deceased through discussion with others who also knew him or her:

> Bereavement is part of the never-ending and reflexive conversation with self and others through which the late-modern person makes sense of their existence. In other words, bereavement is part of the process of (auto)biography, and the biographical imperative—the need to make sense of self and others in a continuing narrative—is the motor that drives bereavement behaviour. (p. 20)

In a more strictly psychological vein, Sewell (1997) has developed a "life event grid" methodology for examining the extent of personal meaning attribution to traumatic and nontraumatic life experiences, and Neimeyer and Stewart (1996) have used similar methods to assess the way in which trauma survivors "emplot" their loss. Thus, our efforts to conceptualize loss in terms of narrative disruption (Neimeyer & Levitt, 2000a) and to develop comprehensive methods for the qualitative analysis of loss narratives (Pacheco & Botella, 1999) are part of a broader trend toward understanding loss in the context of the breakdown and reorganization of life stories. The analysis that follows represents a modest extension of this effort.

Luis Alberto's Quest for Meaning

The foregoing themes provide conceptual resources for the analysis of a unique document consisting of one father's personal diary following the tragic suicidal death of his son. This father, Luis Alberto Werner-Wildner, was a successful South American businessman who sought overseas training in psychology for the first time in the wake of this tragic event. It was in the course of this study that he encountered constructivist ideas through contact with another of the authors (Luis Botella), finding in them a helpful reformulation of the perturbing questions generated by his son's fateful decision. In particular, Kelly's (1955) discussion of suicide as an "elaborative choice," whose goal was to preserve a person's system of meaning by warding off further invalidation, struck him deeply, and instigated the written reflections that became his diary.

Although the presentation of a complex document such as the diary could take several forms, we have chosen to follow the structure imposed by the author himself, allowing him to segment or punctuate the story of his bereavement through the titles of his literal and poetic reflections. This approach is congruent with a personal-construct view that people carve up the unending flow of experience in terms of personally significant themes. As Kelly (1991, p. 52) notes, experience

> presents itself from the beginning as an unending and undifferentiated process. Only when man attunes his ear to recurrent themes in the monotonous flow does his universe begin to make sense to him. Like a musician, he must phrase his experience in order to make sense out of it. The phrases are distinguished events. The separation of events is what man produces for himself when he decides to chop up time into manageable lengths. Within these segments, which are based on recurrent themes, man begins to discover the bases for likenesses and differences.

In the case of an explicit self-narrative such as the present one, the decision to let the author express his own organization of a multifaceted experience seems particularly apt. We were impressed, however, by the way in which his own intuitive punctuation of his bereavement journey corresponded closely to Kelly's (1991) description of the "experience cycle," whereby a person (1) frames certain anticipations for life experiences, (2) invests in these foreseen outcomes, (3) encounters the outcomes, (4) experiences emotionally significant validation or invalidation, and (5) reformulates or reaffirms the anticipatory system of constructs on the basis of these consequences (Neimeyer, 1987). We will therefore draw occasionally on this cycle, which was spontaneously cited by Luis Alberto as well, in the discussion that follows.

Haciendo un Poco De Historia: *Going Back in Time*

Luis Alberto begins his diary by providing a backward glance at his life prior to the tragedy, antedating the suicide by approximately a decade. Interestingly, he writes in the third person, in keeping with Kelly's (1991) suggestion that doing so permits one to take greater perspective on a deeply personal "self-characterization" such as the present one. Luis Alberto's description of his own "academic and professional success, built with his daily efforts," is attributed chiefly to "his desire to improve in life," signaling a culturally supported individualistic theme of self-determination that is reflected in much of his subsequent prose.

The author's initial description of his domestic life is similarly idyllic, consisting of "a beautiful family made up of three children: a girl of fifteen, a young boy of thirteen, and a child of four, plus an intelligent and cultivated wife, an excellent companion. Nothing disturbed this peaceful family whose father used to keep problems from work separated from the ones at home." Luis Alberto positions himself in the narrative as someone who is the virtual embodiment of a cultural discourse of balanced investment in work and family, underscoring the children's "peaceful childhood and adolescence" and the extent to which the "family built itself and grew up apart from the common problems of other mortals." However, he also hints in his opening passage that cracks were beginning to appear in this façade, noting his "slight arrogance in seeing how his children were beginning to walk a triumphant path in life." He thereby skillfully leads the reader to expect a reversal in the narrative of self-assured success in his life and in that of the children who "were their father's pride," a reversal ushered in by the gathering storm of his elder son's adolescence.

Una Nube Negra: *A Black Cloud*

Up to this point, the themes of Luis Alberto's self-narrative seem to preclude loss or tragedy as personal realities, as he notes at one point that such things "are only witnessed in the lives of others." In terms of the experience cycle, it seems clear that this father was highly invested in the anticipation of his children's academic and career success and was ill prepared for the encounter with his son's devastating melancholy, which quickly came to dominate family life. Luis Alberto signals this dramatic turn thus:

> Suddenly a sort of black cloud imposed itself on that previously peaceful home, as the adolescent son began to change. He looked strange, he would lock himself in his room to cry, he gave up his studies and entered into a profound depression.
>
> He was treated in the country's best centers, improving and starting to become his old self, only to fall into his depression again.

One day he left home and never returned. He was found dead, his car having plunged from a cliff [in the Chilean Andes] under circumstances never explained. He was twenty-one.

In his diary, Luis Alberto shares his responses to this traumatic narrative invalidation in two distinct voices, each of which strikingly parallels his external and internal reactions. On the surface, he notes that

the family faced the fact calmly, keeping their pain to themselves, but questioning absolutely every paradigm that they until then had respected. All their constructs, products of years of social and professional successes, were absolutely shattered. What happened? Who was to blame? Was it an accident? All these questions passed again and again through the family members' minds, and especially the father's. Eventually the suicide hypothesis became inescapable, and as a consequence their personal constructs were absolutely shattered and psychological destruction began to threaten the family group, especially its head.

Luis Alberto's surface composure in the face of catastrophic loss is mirrored in his controlled, intellectual prose, even when acknowledging the devastating disruption of family paradigms and narrative themes that resulted. On the other hand, he clearly invites the reader to imagine the more tumultuous inner world of the family, "and especially the father," as they struggled to make sense of the death and grappled with the associated questions of causality, responsibility, and guilt. Luis Alberto underscores this sensed division:

Time passed by and the period of grief was carried out internally. Outwardly it was strength, personality, and endurance; inwardly it was destruction, questioning, and conflicting emotions. After two years, the grieving still continues.

In the journal, this more hidden, emotionally plaintive voice finds expression mainly in poetic form. The first of these poems explores the profound disruption and anguish associated with the ending of his son's life. In a manner reminiscent of Gergen's (1999) concept of "relational being," Luis Alberto contemplates the discontinuity in his own sense of self that was triggered by his son's death:

Tu Ausencia: Your Absence
Your laughter was my laughter.
Your tears were my tears.
Your dream was my dream.
You left, and your laughter and your tears left.
Your dreams were cut short, my dreams ended one day in spring.
Today I recall your face and my soul aches and cries.
There is no warmth in my heart or hope in my life
That consoles me for your absence,
And that takes away the anguish of living without your life.

En Busca de Luz: In Search of Light

Dislodged from a relationship that once anchored his sense of identity as a father, Luis Alberto begins the anguished process of searching for meaning in his son's elective death. As noted in his journal, this search occurs not only in the inner world of his questioning, but also in the physical world, as he relocates to study psychology abroad. The tumult of this psychological and literal journey is captured in a second poetic entry, entitled "My Rebelliousness."

Mi Rebeldía: My Rebelliousness
And it was my rebelliousness that one night drove me
To travel through the uncertain world of my mind,
Plotting my stories.
My time is coming to an end, my mind is restless,
Looking for the answer to the disquieting emptiness that life leaves you.
But the more I search, the fewer answers I find,
And time imprisons you with bolts of time.
The fog of years obscures your memories,
And today, more rebellious than before,
I deny the gods and lose myself in myself, without knowing my destiny.

In this poem, Luis Alberto implicitly emplots his personal story in a broader cultural metanarrative of an odyssey, a "restless" quest for answers to a troubling riddle too insistent to be ignored. Prompted by a "disquieting emptiness," he searches unsuccessfully for a framework of meaning that would grant intelligibility to his son's suicide, while the very memories that would link him to his son are locked away in the dark prison of time. Significantly, the once forward-looking narrative of Luis Alberto's life now lacks an anticipatory dimension, as he acknowledges his denial of "the gods" and the loss of his "destiny."

Commenting on this "first step in the process of reconstruction" in his retrospective diary, Luis Alberto notes that it was a period of profound "personal and social questioning," one filled with "denial, unhappiness, and long silences." But he also draws attention to his writing of numerous "hard poems" during this period, "which served as an escape valve for the intense pressure that day by day accumulated" in his soul. This writing was not the only visible expression of this private anguish, however, as he "in parallel developed a self-destructive anxiety that translated itself into such things as risking his life in unnecessary ways, searching for something he could not know, or even explain."

Eventually, three months after the suicide, Luis Alberto's desperation led him to consult a psychologist specializing in such cases. The resulting "flow of sympathy" between the two men "served to strengthen the spirit of the father and little by little he began to look at the world, first accepting the fact [of the suicide] and second beginning to rebuild a better plan for the future." This plan included his decision to undertake graduate study in psychology as an extension of his quest for meaning. As Luis Alberto noted, "this step was one of the longest, in which his entire system of constructs was completely reworked, so that he could start anew."

This lengthy process of narrative reconstruction is suggested in the following poem, whose very title and final line hint at the unfinished nature of the process of meaning attribution that has begun:

Y: And ...
And ... that beautiful evening you kissed death
Without noticing that you were leaving a thousand pains in your wake.
You embarked on your journey,

Embracing that bride who subjugated your soul and shadowed your spirit.
What journey did you face that has no return?
Is there meaning in the journey that crossed your destiny?
I shall never find answers to my eternal question.
I shall never know if the road ends with life.
And . . .

Significantly, Luis Alberto's process of narrative repair involves a dramatic metaphoric connotative shift or "transvaluation" (Shawver, 1998) in the meaning of his son's death: rather than being viewed only as an expression of his mental illness, the son's suicide is reconstructed as a romantic liaison, albeit one with painful implications. Likewise, death is metaphorically transvaluated as a "bride" whom one can "kiss" and "embrace." Luis Alberto's ambivalence about this alternative narrative, however, is signaled in his description of the metaphorical bride who "subjugated" his son's soul and "shadowed his spirit." Interestingly, suicide is also reconstructed as a "journey," a metaphor that recurs in several of the poems. The negative face of this transvaluation is again that it has "no return" and that it "leaves a thousand pains in its wake." The poem concludes by elaborating the journey metaphor, wondering if the road that literally and figuratively led to his son's suicide carried him to a meaningful destination or simply came to an end with his life.

Reconstruction

In his diary, Luis Alberto notes that he "began his own reconstruction in the light of constructivist psychology, which helped him to leave the deep pit in which he had been immersed for almost two years of his life." It is interesting to conjecture that his phrasing of the intellectual context of his reconstruction—"in *light* of constructivist psychology"—implicitly positions this most recent phase of his grieving as the fulfillment of the earlier one he phrased as "in search of light." Stated differently, a constructivist emphasis on agency even in the midst of suffering and despair illuminated a different potential theme underpinning his son's tragic decision, one that suggested that his suicide, phenomenologically, represented an elaborative choice rather than meaningless symptom. Luis Alberto ponders this meaning in the last of his poems, entitled "Your Search."

Tu Busqueda: Your Search
You were looking for a rainbow hidden in the mountain
And, to your encounter,1 you flew in endless freedom.
Your wings covered you with a blanket of silence
And from the highest summit we get intoxicated with your light.
Your peace makes us stronger, your freedom unites us.
Your flight without return is our pain and our punishment.
But more, that eternal flight that released your soul comforts us;
It is our guide and our hope.
Your never-ending search took you to the mountain
And from there you flew to encounter your destiny.
Today we weep for your absence, we yearn for your hours.
But the same memory comforts us for your departure.
Will we again someday, in remote places,
Exchange memories, joys, and pains?

In the last of Luis Alberto's poems, his son's death is transvaluated as a "search" in its very title. The poem emphasizes the freedom and release entailed in his son's launching his car from the cliff by making recourse to metaphors such as "looking for a rainbow hidden in the mountain" and "flying in endless freedom." Although Luis Alberto construes such "flight without return" as "our pain and punishment," he also transvaluates it as "our comfort, our guide, and our hope," viewing it as a quest for peace and freedom. In this case, the juxtaposition of the unfamiliar (suicide) and the familiar (flight) that allows the metaphor to speak to the reader derives partly from the way in which Luis Alberto's son's throwing himself from a cliff in his car literally involved flying. This implicit connection adds emotional relevance and impact to the metaphor.

At the end of the poem, Luis Alberto seems to hint at the prospect of reconnection not only with others ("your freedom unites us") but also with his son, conjuring the possibility of a remote future beyond the present yearning in which joys and sorrows can again be exchanged. This theme of a continuing bond with his son is also reinforced more subtly in the narrative phrasing of their respective agonizing quests in different poems as deeply personal "searches," each of which finds at least a provisional conclusion that comforts the protagonist. As in Kelly's experience cycle, Luis Alberto ends his poetic reconstruction with an anticipatory conjecture rather than with a spurious sense of certainty. This epistemological humility seems more appropriate a stance than the "slight arrogance" that characterized his life prior to the tragedy, and hints at the broader reconstruction of identity that coincided with the authoring of a new self-narrative.

What Learning Can I Take from This Experience?

Luis Alberto concludes his reflections by considering the life lessons he has carried away from his son's traumatic death, including the critical roles of a renewed spirituality and emotionality in "permitting him to view life anew" and "provoking a rebirth of intellectuality." This triad of core themes—spiritual, affective, and cognitive—allowed him to devote himself to finding his "lost physical strength and a proactive vision of the future and of life in general." In keeping with transformative models of loss, Luis Alberto's painful process of meaning reconstruction led to a renewed vision of his life and himself, one that helped him reposition himself in a world that, albeit shattered, could be rebuilt again.

The narrative repair exemplified in this reconstructive process consists precisely in finding a new guiding theme for Luis Alberto's life and his identity, one that does not marginalize his loss but includes it and even uses it as a cornerstone. Thus, the emerging narrative is no longer focused exclusively on professional and social success, but on a newly found sense of "spirituality, love, intellectuality, creative strength, and sociability." Luis Alberto equates this process to the creation of "a new system of constructs" that "give a different meaning to a life that undoubtedly has a *before* and an *after*." By bridging the chapters of his life that had been fragmented by his loss, such constructs allowed him to "live again, probably more intensely than before, enjoying life in all that that means: at home, in the workplace, with one's friends and acquaintances," to "laugh again, simply put, to live."

This emerging narrative and sense of renewed identity allows Luis Alberto to benefit from the richness of the here and now; it increases his mindfulness and his reflexive awareness that there is more to life than social and professional success, even if such experiences are also important. In short, Luis Alberto seems to have found his own "rainbow" hidden behind the "dark cloud" of his son's tragic death, and with it a sustainable self-narrative that holds the pain of his loss without being eclipsed by it. In a sense, Luis Alberto's reconstructive process can be seen as a shift from "the absence of meaning" to "the meaning of absence," as reflected in the new metaphors he was able to find for death and loss, and the implications these carried for a new life.

Concluding Comments

Our goal in this chapter has been to describe and illustrate one promising approach to understanding the breakdown in the assumptive world occasioned by loss, in the form of a constructivist perspective on meaning reconstruction. We began by considering the many functions of narrative, which provides an organizing frame for human experience that both imparts order to the past and yields anticipations of an intelligible future. Traumatic loss disrupts the continuity of our self-narratives, however, and undercuts our associated sense of identity. Faced with such profound invalidation, we struggle to attribute sense to the tragedy, find something of value in the loss, and reconstruct a new and viable sense of ourselves as protagonists. Contemporary trends in grief theory dovetail with this narrative conception and provide a rich interpretive repertoire for understanding grieving as a process of meaning reconstruction.

Applying these concepts to the qualitative analysis of one father's grief journal, we were gratified by the extent to which a narrative approach fit the unique contours of his bereavement. Interestingly, the father himself drew upon not only constructivist ideas in interpreting his son's suicide and his own response to it, but also upon narrative methods—reflective journaling and poetic exploration—to pursue his own healing journey. As constructivists, psychotherapists, and human beings, we cannot help but experience a profound sense of respect and awe in the face of such spontaneous meaning-making processes, which helped the author regain a sense of coherence and direction even in the wake of cataclysmic loss. Stories such as this one are a reminder of what led us to become psychotherapists: our faith and celebration of the human capacity to find significance in the experience of suffering, and transformation in the midst of tragedy. We hope that our efforts in this chapter to highlight the possible contributions of narrative to the understanding and facilitation of meaning reconstruction will encourage other readers to consider its relevance for their own lives and work.

Note

1. The Spanish *encuentro* that Luis Alberto uses here is much richer in connotation than its English equivalent. *Encuentro* can mean literally "encounter," but also "finding" and "collision." Thus, in a single artfully chosen word, the author evokes the themes of searching, finding, and romantic liaison captured in his other poems, as well as the literal means by which his son took his life.

References

Attig, T. (1996). *How we grieve: Relearning the world*. New York: Oxford University Press.

Attig, T. (2000). *The heart of grief*. New York: Oxford University Press.

Bakhtin, M. (1986). The problem of speech genres. In M. Bakhtin (Ed.), *Speech genres and other late essays* (pp. 60–102). Austin: University of Texas Press.

Balk, D. E., & Vesta, L. C. (1998). Psychological development during four years of bereavement: A longitudinal case study. *Death Studies, 22,* 23–41.

Bartlett, F. C. (1932). *Remembering*. Cambridge: Cambridge University Press.

Bateson, M. (1993). Composing a life. In C. Simpkinson & A. Simpkinson (Eds.), *Sacred stories*. San Francisco: Harper Collins.

Botella, L., & Feixas, G. (1998). *Teoría de los constructos personales: Aplicaciones a la práctica psicologica* [Personal construct theory: Applications to psychological practice]. Barcelona: Laertes.

Braun, K. L., & Nichols, R. (1997). Death and dying in four Asian American cultures. *Death Studies, 21,* 327–359.

Braun, M. L., & Berg, D. H. (1994). Meaning reconstruction in the experience of bereavement. *Death Studies, 18,* 105–129.

Corr, C. A. (1993). Coping with dying: Lessons we should and should not learn from the work of Elisabeth Kübler-Ross. *Death Studies, 17,* 69–83.

Datson, S. L., & Marwit, S. J. (1997). Personality constructs and perceived presence of deceased loved ones. *Death Studies, 21,* 131–146.

Davies, B., & Harre, R. (1990). Positioning: The discursive production of selves. *Journal for the Theory of Social Behavior, 20,* 43–63.

Davis, C. G., Nolen-Hoeksema, S., & Larson, J. (1998). Making sense of loss and benefiting from the experience: Two construals of meaning. *Journal of Personality and Social Psychology, 75,* 561–574.

Downe-Wambolt, B., & Tamlyn, D. (1997). An international survey of death education trends in faculties of nursing and medicine. *Death Studies, 21,* 177–188.

Ellis, C. (1998). Exploring loss through autoethnographic inquiry. In J. Harvey (Ed.), *Perspectives on loss: A sourcebook* (pp. 49–68). Philadelphia: Brunner/Mazel.

Frantz, T. T., Farrell, M. M., & Trolley, B. C. (2001). Positive outcomes of losing a loved one. In R. A. Neimeyer (Ed.), *Meaning reconstruction and the experience of loss*. Washington, DC: American Psychological Association.

Geertz, C. (1983). *Local knowledge*. New York: Basic Books.

Gergen, K. J. (1994). *Realities and relationships*. Cambridge: Harvard University Press.

Gergen, K. J. (1999). *An invitation to social construction*. Cambridge, MA: Harvard University Press.

Gergen, K. J., & Gergen, M. M. (1986). Narrative form and the construction of psychological science. In T. R. Sarbin (Ed.), *Narrative psychology*. New York: Praeger.

Gilbert, K. R. (1996). "We've had the same loss, why don't we have the same grief?" Loss and differential grief in families. *Death Studies, 20,* 269–284.

Guidano, V. F. (1991). *The self in process*. New York: Guilford.

Guidano, V. F. (1995). Constructivist psychotherapy: A theoretical framework. In R. A. Neimeyer & M. J. Mahoney (Eds.), *Constructivism in psychotherapy* (pp. 93–108). Washington, DC: American Psychological Association.

Hagman, G. (2001). Beyond decathexis: Towards a new psychoanalytic understanding of mourning. In R. A. Neimeyer (Ed.), *Meaning reconstruction and the experience of loss*. Washington, DC: American Psychological Association.

Hermans, H. (1995). *Self-narratives: The construction of meaning in psychotherapy*. New York: Guilford.

Hermans, H. J. M. (2001). The person as a motivated storyteller. In R. A. Neimeyer & G. J. Neimeyer (Eds.), *Advances in personal construct psychology* (Vol. 5, pp. in press). New York: Praeger.

Hermans, H. J. M., & Kempen, H. J. G. (1993). *The dialogical self*. New York: Guilford.

Hogan, N. S., Greenfield, D. B., & Schmidt, L. A. (2001). Development and Validation of the Hogan Grief Reactions Checklist. *Death Studies, 25*, in press.

Janoff-Bulman, R. (1989). Assumptive worlds and the stress of traumatic events. *Social Cognition, 7*, 113–116.

Kelly, G. A. (1991). *The psychology of personal constructs.* New York: Routledge. (Originally published 1955.)

Klass, D. (1999). *The spiritual lives of bereaved parents.* Philadelphia: Brunner Mazel.

Klass, D., Silverman, P. R., & Nickman, S. (1996). *Continuing bonds: New understandings of grief.* Washington, DC: Taylor & Francis.

Kübler-Ross, E. (1969). *On death and dying.* New York: Macmillan.

Mair, M. (1988). Psychology as story telling. *International Journal of Personal Construct Psychology, 1*, 125–137.

Mair, M. (1989). Kelly, Bannister, and a Story-Telling Psychology. *International Journal of Personal Construct Psychology, 2*, 1–15.

Martin, T., & Doka, K. (2000). *Men don't cry, women do.* Philadelphia: Brunner/Mazel.

Maturana, H., & Varela, F. (1987). *The tree of knowledge.* Boston: New Science Library.

Milo, E. M. (1997). Maternal responses to the life and death of a child with developmental disability. *Death Studies, 21*, 443–476.

Nadeau, J. W. (1997). *Families making sense of death.* Newbury Park, CA: Sage.

Neimeyer, R. A. (1987). An orientation to personal construct therapy. In R. A. Neimeyer & G. J. Neimeyer (Eds.), *Personal construct therapy casebook* (pp. 3–19). New York: Springer.

Neimeyer, R. A. (1998). *Lessons of loss: A guide to coping.* New York: McGraw-Hill.

Neimeyer, R. A. (2000). Narrative disruptions in the construction of self. In R. A. Neimeyer & J. Raskin (Eds.), *Constructions of disorder: Meaning-making frameworks for psychotherapy* (pp. 207–241). Washington, DC: American Psychological Association.

Neimeyer, R. A. (2001a). The language of loss. In R. A. Neimeyer (Ed.), *Meaning reconstruction and the experience of loss.* Washington, DC: American Psychological Association.

Neimeyer, R. A. (Ed.). (2001b). *Meaning reconstruction and the experience of loss.* Washington, DC: American Psychological Association.

Neimeyer, R. A. (2001c). Searching for the meaning of meaning: Grief therapy and the process of reconstruction. *Death Studies, 25*, in press.

Neimeyer, R. A., Fortner, B., & Melby, D. (1999). Intervening in suicide: Do personal or professional factors make a difference? *Australian Journal of Grief and Bereavement, 2*, 43–46.

Neimeyer, R. A., & Hogan, N. (2001). Quantitative or qualitative? Measurement issues in the study of grief. In M. Stroebe, H. Schut, & R. Hansson (Eds.), *Handbook of bereavement.* Washington, DC: American Psychological Association.

Neimeyer, R. A., Keesee, N. J., & Fortner, B.V. (2000). Loss and meaning reconstruction: Propositions and procedures. In R. Malkinson, S. Rubin, & E. Wiztum, (Ed.), *Traumatic and non-traumatic loss and bereavement* . Madison, CT: Psychosocial Press.

Neimeyer, R. A., & Levitt, H. (2000a). Coping and coherence: A narrative perspective. In C. R. Snyder (Ed.), *Perspectives on coping* . New York: Wiley.

Neimeyer, R. A., & Levitt, H. (2000b). What's narrative got to do with it? Construction and coherence in accounts of loss. In J. H. Harvey & E. D. Miller (Eds.), *Loss and trauma.* Philadelphia: Brunner/Mazel.

Neimeyer, R. A., & Raskin, J. (Eds.). (2000). *Constructions of disorder: Meaning-making frameworks for psychotherapy.* Washington, D.C.: American Psychological Association.

Neimeyer, R. A., & Stewart, A. E. (1996). Trauma, healing, and the narrative emplotment of loss. *Families in Society, 77*, 360–375.

Pacheco, M., & Botella, L. (1999). La transformación narrativa-dialógica durante el proceso psicoterapéutico [Narrative-dialogical transformation during the psychotherapeutic process]. *Revista de Psicología i Ciencias de la Educación* [Journal of Psychology and Educational Sciences], 5, 195–208.

Potter, J. (1996). *Representing reality.* London: Sage.

Prend, A. D. (1997). *Transcending loss*. New York: Berkley.

Richards, T. A., Acree, M., & Folkman, S. (1999). Spiritual aspects of loss among partners of men with AIDS: Postbereavement follow-up. *Death Studies, 23*, 105–127.

Richards, T. A., & Folkman, S. (1997). Spiritual aspects of loss at the time of a partner's death from AIDS. *Death Studies, 21*, 515–540.

Rosenblatt, P. (2000). *Parent grief: Narratives of loss and relationship*. Philadelphia: Brunner/Mazel.

Sarbin, T. R. (1986). The narrative as a root metaphor for psychology, *Narrative psychology: The storied nature of human conduct*. New York: Praeger.

Sewell, K. W. (1997). Posttraumatic stress: Towards a constructivist model of psychotherapy. In G. J. Neimeyer & R. A. Neimeyer (Eds.), *Advances in personal construct psychology* (Vol. 4, pp. 207–235). Greenwich, CT: JAI Press.

Shawver, L. (1998). *Notes on the concept of transvaluation*. Available: http://www.california.com/~rathbone/transval.htm.

Stroebe, M., Stroebe, W., Hansson, R., & Schut, H. (2001). *New handbook of bereavement: Consequences, coping, and care*. Washington, DC: American Psychological Association.

Tedeschi, R., Park, C., & Calhoun, L. (Eds.). (1998). *Posttraumatic growth: Positive changes in the aftermath of crisis*. Mahwah, NJ: Lawrence Erlbaum.

Vickio, C. (1999). Together in spirit: Keeping our relationships alive when loved ones die. *Death Studies, 23*, 161–175.

Walsh, F., & McGoldrick, M. (1991). *Living beyond loss*. New York: Norton.

Walter, T. (1996). A new model of grief: Bereavement and biography. *Mortality, 1*, 7–25.

Worden, J. W. (1991). *Grief counseling and grief therapy: A handbook for mental health practitioners*. New York: Springer.

3.

How Could God?

Loss and the Spiritual Assumptive World

Kenneth Doka

Ryan was only twenty-three years old. Already in his life he had achieved much. He had been an honor student, Eagle Scout, the recipient of many athletic trophies and scholastic awards. He had just become engaged and held a new, exciting job. But that year he developed cancer and died. His fiancée still questions, "Why him?"

John and Mary are grieving the death of their son, who died two years ago at the age of eleven, when his bicycle was struck by a hit-and-run driver. John has stopped attending church: "I refuse to believe in a God that could allow this." Mary still regularly attends but avoids events and holidays that remind her of her son, such as the Christmas pageant. She has also stopped teaching Sunday school. Mary feels that John's prior erratic attendance may have been a factor in their son's death. "Maybe," she says, "this was God's wake-up call."

In both of these cases, persons are struggling to redefine their faith, to find meaning in the loss of a person they loved. In both cases, the nature or circumstances of the loss have challenged their assumptions or beliefs about God or the fairness of the world. They are seeking to redefine their spirituality, now challenged by loss.

Throughout this book, there is a concern with the assumptive world, or the personal constructs that individuals use to make sense of their world (see Rando, 1993; Kelly, 1955). Loss often challenges those assumptions, causing the bereaved to attempt to reconstruct their assumptive world. As Rando (1993) and Parkes (1988) note, after a traumatic loss nothing can be taken for granted anymore. Rando (1993) also makes a useful distinction between *global* and *specific* assumptions. Specific assumptions are related to the loss, such as expectations that one would grow old together. But global assumptions also exist. These are more general beliefs about the world. Loss sometimes challenges these assumptions as well, causing bereaved persons to question earlier beliefs, challenging faith and philosophy, and complicating the search to find meaning in the loss. In fact, I had earlier suggested building on Worden's (1991) model, that one of the most significant tasks in grief is to reconstruct faith or philosophical systems, now challenged by the loss (Doka, 1993).

The goal of the chapter is to focus specifically on the ways that loss challenges the spiritual assumptive world. To accomplish this, it is first necessary to define and discuss spirituality and to describe the ways that loss can cause individuals to question prior beliefs. A second issue then needs to be explored—how individuals can reconstruct their spirituality in the face of loss.

The Challenge to Spirituality

Spirituality is a difficult concept to define. First, it needs to be distinguished from *religion*. The latter refers to an organized set of beliefs or dogma shared by a defined group. Spirituality, though, is broader than that. Morgan (1988) defines it as a "specialness." To Morgan an individual's spirit refers to that person's uniqueness— the individual as thinking, willing, and deciding. This means that humans—driven by an ability to think, feel, and decide—seek to attribute meaning to their world and life. Out of that quest for meaning emerges philosophy, knowledge, ethics, and religion. The way any given individual combines these to find and determine meaning is the essence of that individual's spirituality. Religion may be part, even a large part, of any given individual's spirituality, but it is not identical to it.

Not every loss challenges meaning. Some losses may reaffirm one's meaning. For example, Robert's father died at age ninety-two after a short and comparatively painless illness. Robert misses and mourns his dad, a close companion throughout life. His father's death does violate some specific assumptions—including that his father would continue to be a companion. But while Robert will grieve, the issue of rebuilding faith does not loom large. To Robert, his father had a model life and death, reinforcing the comforting concept that one ages and then drifts off to a gentle death. Ann's son died at a relatively young age, in his early thirties, from a drug overdose. While Ann struggles with her grief, especially a sense of guilt and ambivalence, the loss does not challenge her sense of the world. To Ann, "you reap what you sow." Ann always warned her son, who struggled with drugs since adolescence, that his abuse of drugs would lead to his early death.

But other losses do challenge an individual's spiritual assumptions or beliefs about the nature of the world. The introductory cases illustrate this. In Ryan's case, his fiancée has begun to question the fairness or justice of the world. John's loss has made it difficult to believe in a loving God. His wife, Mary, is struggling to find meaning as well in her faith. Underlying her spirituality is a sense that every act, however hurtful, has a reason. She now seeks to find God's rationale in the death of her son. Both John and Mary may struggle with the issue of justice, as the hit-and-run driver responsible for their son's death has yet to be apprehended. Moreover, they question the fairness of their son's life being ended so prematurely, before he could experience much of what life offered.

These are just some of the challenges that can occur. A loss such as a death can cause individuals to challenge many of their global assumptions that relate to spirituality. These can entail such issues as the belief in or nature of a God or higher power that controls human destiny, a sense of fairness or justice in the operation of the world, or beliefs about what makes life or death meaningful.

Reconstructing the Spiritual World

Job

Job was an upright man. For many years God lovingly blessed him. But Satan challenged God. "Why should he not be good? It's in his interest." So God allowed Satan to torment Job. And this he did. Job experienced multiple losses as well as financial reversals. Impoverished, alone, and now with a loathsome and painful illness, Job asks plaintively, "Why?" His friends suggest answers— "God is testing you, or perhaps you have sinned—secretly or even unawares." Their answers reflect their assumptions, and Job's former assumptions, about the world—it is a fair place, with order and justice. But these assumptions have now been shattered for Job. The world cannot be fair. There is no justice in what has happened, in what Job sees happen all the time. Goodness is not always rewarded, nor evil punished. He demands God answer him. God does. In a powerful speech he reminds Job that Job is unable to comprehend the mind of his creator. "Where were you when I laid the foundation of the earth?" (RSV Job 38, v.4). Job finds peace in God's presence and is able to accept the mystery of God's way.

C. S. Lewis

C. S. Lewis' life story is known to many through the movie Shadowlands. *A scholar and Christian apologist, he authored many books on the nature of faith. His own early life was relatively uncomplicated. A confirmed bachelor, he quietly enjoyed the pleasures of academic life. Late in his life he fell deeply in love with a woman. But she soon developed cancer. He was with her as she painfully and slowly succumbed to her illness.*

Like Job, C. S. Lewis' spiritual assumptive world was challenged. In A grief observed *(1961) he wrote: "Not that I am (I think) in much danger of ceasing to believe in God. The real danger is of coming to believe such dreadful things about Him" (pp. 9–10). Later, like Job, C. S. Lewis is able to accept, after a spiritual struggle, a sense of mystery. He no longer seeks to answer the question "Why?"*

Rabbi Harold Kushner

Rabbi Harold Kushner wrote a very personal book entitled When bad things happen to good people *(1981). It documents his own spiritual struggle over how a benevolent God could allow his young, bright, and happy son Aaron to die from progeria, a genetic illness that brings accelerated aging.*

"Why do the righteous suffer?" he asked. Caught in the paradox between God's merciful benevolence and omnipotence, Kushner's struggle leads him to believe that God has allowed the world to run on its own natural laws. God, to Kushner, will support humans with His presence, but He will not change the laws of the universe to accommodate a single individual.

Loss and the Assumptive World

All of these three cases deal with individuals who have struggled with their spiritual assumptive world. These struggles can have four outcomes.

In some cases the bereaved individual may go through a period of intense introspection and simply reaffirm his or her earlier beliefs. Here, the earlier beliefs do sustain and create meaning. For example, the death of Ann's son from a drug overdose was expected, but it was still painful. Yet while it raised many issues, it supported a belief, a global assumption that bad actions and choices will inevitably entail devastating consequences.

In other cases the bereaved may simply find that their own belief system is not adequate but fail to find a suitable replacement. Here they have lost a belief that gave life meaning. The loss of that belief can be one of the most enduring and painful aspects of the bereavement experience. Richard offers an illustration of this. A self-proclaimed "secular humanist," Richard believed that all persons harbor a spark of the divine. On both a macro and micro level, he tried to encourage that spark. On a macro level his legal career focused on peace and justice issues, eschewing the lucrative legal opportunities his expertise might have offered. On a micro level he worked at a homeless shelter, often befriending the persons he met there. Believing work was a road to self-respect and dignity, Richard would often employ the homeless men and women once he got to know them. He would pay a decent wage and treat workers with great dignity. But one day, one of the men he befriended brutally raped and killed his daughter. Years later, when he sought counseling, he expressed this issue as a loss of belief: "I have come to terms with the loss of Laura: I have not yet come to terms with the loss of everything I believed." For Richard, the major issue was restoring or rebuilding a philosophical system changed by loss.

Other individuals may extensively redefine spirituality. For example, when Tom's family died in a fire, he found little comfort in his own spiritual tradition. For years he explored a variety of alternative spiritual traditions before embracing Buddhism.

Another alternative, illustrated by the earlier three cases, is that the struggle to find meaning may allow one to modify or deepen one's belief structure. Job could not reconcile his experience with the belief in a just God. C. S. Lewis and Rabbi Kushner found that their experiences no longer allowed them to affirm that God was both good and omnipotent. Yet their experiences did not turn them away from their beliefs, but rather forced them to examine and modify their belief systems and their spiritual assumptive worlds. For Job and C. S. Lewis, their faith now included a deeper sense of the mystery, the unknowableness of God. For Kushner, it meant revising his notion of God's omnipotence.

In each of these cases, their spiritual struggles led to a more resilient spirituality, one that allowed them to resolve issues about the unfairness of life, or the nature and existence of God. In fact, one might say that the key to a resilient spirituality is that it allows an individual to find meaning in the most difficult situations. Such systems must have a flexibility that allows individuals to confront the ambiguity and unfairness of life.

How can a counselor help an individual struggling with spiritual beliefs? Perhaps two things can assist. The first is simply to allow and witness their struggle. In many cases their struggle can be invalidated by others, perhaps family or clergy who fear the questioning of their own spiritual assumptions. Clients, then, sometimes need only the opportunity and invitation to examine the way their beliefs address their current crisis. Allowing that, offering a ministry or presence that validates and addresses that struggle is in itself a great gift.

Second, individuals may need assistance in finding resources that can assist them in exploring the ways that their belief systems speak to them in this crisis. Those resources can come in many forms—rituals, individuals within the faith community, lessons, and books. All of these can contribute to that quest to find meaning as one struggles with the implications of the loss. As an example, stories or principles from a given spiritual or religious tradition can be solicited, offered, and reviewed. For instance, a woman felt guilty that she was angry with God for the death of her child. Yet when she reviewed the story of Job, she was reminded that God commended Job for his honest anger. Rituals, too, can offer meaning. For example, funeral rituals offer opportunities to address the ways that a religious tradition or philosophical stance both understands a death and offers solace to survivors. There may be other ways to assist as well in accessing and understanding struggles with spirituality. Counselors, for example, can invite clients to understand their own spiritual journeys by having them review the ways that their spiritual understanding developed and changed throughout their lives. Asking clients to recount their favorite spiritual stories and lessons also can assist clients in exploring spiritual beliefs. Reminiscence and life review activities can be powerful tools to release memories, thereby assisting in the reconstruction of meaning.

It may be useful as well to assist clients in identifying individuals within their own faith traditions that can assist them, in print or in person, with their own spiritual struggle. For example, C.S. Lewis' *A grief observed* can validate spiritual anger and the quest for spiritual inquiry. Counselors would do well to network with local clergy to identify potential resources within a variety of faith traditions.

Clients can be encouraged to utilize their spiritual practices. Meditation and prayer, for example, can offer opportunities for reflection and expression of spiritual conflicts and questions.

Counselors should directly ask clients about the ways in which their beliefs speak to current crisis. In this way the client can acknowledge the beliefs that both facilitate and complicate the struggle for meaning.

However, caregivers need to be cautious about challenging beliefs. First, caregivers ought to be wary of imposing their own belief system on that of a client. Second, challenging beliefs that the caregiver finds troubling may deprive clients of an effective belief system when they may have neither the internal nor external resources to reconstruct their belief system. The caregiver's goal is to accompany the client on that spiritual journey and to assist the client in identifying resources, not to compel a direction that the client is not yet willing or ready to take.

Conclusion

Perhaps there is one more cautionary note—crises can be the most difficult times to reassess beliefs, as one's energy is sapped and strengths taxed. If one attends to one's own spirituality, constantly reviewing the ways that it addresses the vicissitudes of life, one is less likely to be challenged at a time of loss. The cautionary note extends beyond the individual to clergy and religious leaders. There is a challenge, then, for clergy and religious leaders to encourage existential examination in their preaching and teaching.

And there is a challenge to caregivers as well. Vachon (1987) noted that resilient caregivers possessed a spirituality, however defined, that allowed them to address the unfairness of life, an unfairness they inevitably encountered in their work among the ill, dying, and bereaved. Caregivers need to continually address and replenish their own spirituality not only as a model to those they help but also so they they themselves have something to offer.

References

Doka, K. J. (1993). The spiritual crisis of bereavement. In K. J. Doka and J. Morgan (Eds), *Death and spirituality.* Amityville, NY: Baywood.

Kelly, G. (1955). *The psychology of personal constructs.* New York: Norton.

Kushner, H. (1981). *When bad things happen to good people.* New York: Avon Books.

Lewis, C. S. (1961). *A grief observed*. New York: Bantam Books.

Morgan, J. (1988). Death and bereavement: Spiritual, ethical and pastoral issues. *Death Studies, 12,* 85–90.

Parkes, C. M. (1988). Bereavement as psychosocial transition: Processes of adaptation to change. *Journal of Social Issues, 44(3),* 53–55.

Rando, T. (1993). *Treatment of complicated mourning*. Champaign, IL: Research Press.

Vachon, M. (1987). *Occupational stress in the care of the critically ill, the dying and the bereaved*. New York: Hemisphere.

Worden, J. W. (1991). Grief counseling and grief thereapy (2nd Ed.). New York: Springer.

4.

Questionable Assumptions About Assumptive Worlds

Tom Attig

We assume too much when we assume that the loss of the assumptive world following the death of someone we love is predominantly a cognitive matter requiring adjustment in explicitly held beliefs about or interpretations of reality. We need to stretch our understanding of "assumption" to encompass all that we have come to take for granted as we have learned how to be and to act in the world in the presence of those we love. Bereavement undermines not only our cognitive and intellectual understandings but also our taken-for-granted emotional, psychological, behavioral, social, soulful, and spiritual ways of being in the world. Once we have overcome the cognitive bias in our thinking about loss of assumptive worlds, we must rethink ways of helping mourners to modify this broader range of assumptions.

Cognitive Bias in the Discussion

Colin Murray Parkes (1971) begins the discussion of loss of the assumptive world in an essay on psychosocial transitions. He focuses on major changes in life that require us to restructure our "ways of looking at the world" and "plans for living in it." He defines assumptive world as the "total set of assumptions which we build up on the basis of past experience in carrying out our purposes." He says:

> The assumptive world is the only world we know and it includes everything we know or think we know. It includes our interpretation of the past and our expectations of the future, our plans and our prejudices. Any or all of these may need to change as a result of changes in the life space.

This life space includes those (typically local) parts of the environment with which individuals interact and in relation to which they organize their behavior. Parkes goes on to define "psycho-social transitions" (including coming to terms with the death of someone we love) as "those major changes in life space which are *lasting in their effects*, which *take place over a relatively short period of time* and which *affect large areas of the assumptive world.*" The assumptive world comprises not only "a model of the world as it is" but also "models of the world as it might be, "including representations of "probable situations, ideal situations or dreaded situations."

Parkes continues with extensive discussion of such things as *recognition* of the familiar, *cognitive* orientation within and mastery of the environment, active components in *perception, predictions* about external objects, the process of *realization* that ordinarily follows bereavement, resistance to *questioning* assumptions, and the aim of psychotherapy as the *insight* that "occurs when a person *recognizes* a discrepancy between his assumptive world and his life space."

In a later article on bereavement (1988), Parkes writes about the capacity of the central nervous system to "organize the most complex impressions into internal models of the world, which enable us to recognize and understand the world that we experience and to predict the outcome of our own and others' behavior." He argues that grief is an emotion that arises from "awareness of a discrepancy between the world that is and the world that 'should be.'" He describes this latter world as an "internal construct" unique to each individual. This internal world that must change following the death of a loved one consists of "all those expectations and assumptions invalidated by the change in our life space." He goes on to describe this assumptive world as an "organized schema" that contains "everything that we assume to be true on the basis of our previous experience." He urges that we are constantly matching this *schema* against *sensory input* in order to orient ourselves, *recognize* what is happening, and *plan* our actions. He says that Freud (1917) called the process of *reviewing the internal world* after bereavement "the work of mourning" and cautions that the mind that is doing the reviewing is also the mind under review. Because this is so, the reviewing mind is likely to be disorganized and compromised by anxiety and fear deriving from "lost confidence" in its "world model." He says that those making the psychosocial transition following bereavement need three things: emotional support, protection through a period of helplessness, and "assistance in discovering new models of the world appropriate to the emergent situation."

Parkes wonders about the accessibility of our fundamental assumptions to *introspection*. He says that we resist bringing them to the surface due to anxiety and fear about possibly acknowledging their unreliability and losing the orientation and stability they provide. His references to Freud and to the insight that is said to result from successful psychotherapy reflect his recognition that we hold the assumptions in question deep within us in places (the unconscious perhaps) that elude our reflective glance and challenge our capacity to explicitly articulate them. Parkes seems confident, however, that the assumptions in question are one and all perceptual, propositional, and therefore cognitive in character: they are matters of what we know (or think we know) or what we believe about the way the world is.

Therese Rando (1993) is representative of many other authors who have subsequently touched on the subject of loss of the assumptive world. In passages where she writes of the need to relinquish attachments to the old assumptive world, she expresses concern about mourners who continue "to operate with an out-of-date and invalid construct system." She writes of such things as "the human being's need for meaning and cognitive control—understanding, sense, security, and predictability," the need to "relinquish ideas" about the world in general and about the deceased and the relationship in particular, "cognitive dissonance" between aspects of the assumptive world and the new reality brought about by death, the need to discard (or at least reexamine) fundamental beliefs, and how "our ways of perceiving things, our expectations, and our beliefs" are deeply ingrained. She goes on to recommend therapeutic interventions that support "cognitive readjustment," including approaches that address psychosocial transition (following Parkes), personal construct dislocation and adaptation, cognitive processing aspects of the stress response syndrome, the search for meaning, rehabilitating belief in personal invulnerability, and promoting positive self-perception.

The emphasis in these writings on loss of the assumptive world and much of the discussion in the literature falls upon cognitive processes and beliefs and their role in orienting us in the world. The discussion stresses what we have been thinking or believing about the world in general and about the particular corners of it that we inhabit. And it treats the rethinking and adjustment of beliefs that may be required when someone we love dies.

But this persistent emphasis on cognition misses something central about the nature of assumption. Commonly when we assume, we take something for granted without really thinking about it at all. That is, there is something fundamentally deeper—beneath the level of our thoughtful awareness, prior to thought, and often quite noncognitive—that we can easily miss if we are not careful in trying to understand just what is involved in loss of the assumptive world. To be sure, we have sometimes consciously entertained, critically examined, and deliberately assumed (adopted or made our own) beliefs that we come to question when someone we love dies—ideas about such things as the trustworthiness of the world, the fairness of the deity, or the meaning of life. And we have sometimes entered upon courses of action as a result of conscious weighing of alternatives and deliberate planning based in self-consciously held and articulated beliefs about what will work and what is desirable, only to find that we must change course when someone we love dies.

But more often, what we assume has never become the object of reflection or been explicitly articulated. Yes, the loss of the assumptive world is very much a matter of the disruption of our taken-for-granted orientation in the world. But it is doubtful that such orientation comes primarily or even very much at all from beliefs explicitly held or plans deliberately executed. Let us turn now to closer examination of the nature of this taken-for-granted orientation in the world and of the variety of assumptions upon which it is grounded.

How We Assume Places in the World

We come into the world as strangers when we are newborns. Others must welcome us in some minimal sense, or we will perish. We depend utterly upon parental figures to meet our most elementary needs for food, water, clothing, shelter, comfort, warmth, touch, attention, affection, and love. We know *how* to cry for these things. But we do not know self-consciously *that* we need them: we have no capacity for beliefs, for we lack language within which to have and articulate them. We have no self-awareness to ground self-understanding, for we lack the ability to distinguish between ourselves and the world around us. And we do not self-consciously *plan* how to meet our own needs: we lack the capacity to identify what our needs are and to deliberate about alternative means of meeting them. Most of us develop reflective abilities to do these things later in life, though—sadly—some of us never do.

But before we ever develop even these minimally sophisticated cognitive capacities, we begin to engage practically, directly, straightforwardly, and unselfconsciously with the world around us. As we do, we learn *how* to live in that world. Such knowing *how* precedes any knowing *that* or knowing *about* that we ever achieve.

We extend our know-how in the world in incremental steps through infancy and early childhood. Gradually, we establish a foothold of our own in that world. At first, we are confined to the arms that hold and nurture us and the places where our caregivers take us for sleep, feeding, bathing, and visits with others. Within the attention to our basic needs, we begin to feel safe, secure, and at home in the world. In these places we engage only with the things that are placed with us or that others bring into view. Our caregivers and these few things and places are our first introduction to the rich variety the world holds. They attract our attention and fascinate us. We cling to and grow attached to them.

As we develop abilities to move on our own, to reach and grasp, to hold our heads up, to sit, to crawl, and to walk, we bring more and more things, places, and eventually people, into the range of our experience. We begin to venture forth into the world on our own, very tentatively at first. We learn how far we can safely go, returning often to the security we have come to sense close to those who love us. Gradually, we extend the range and duration of our forays and learn our way around rooms, homes, and their immediate vicinities. When our caregivers take us to new places, we explore them cautiously at first and then with greater confidence as we learn our ways around in them. Some things and places hold our attention more than others. We are often taken with and become entirely immersed in them. We become attached to familiar things and take some as our own, caring about many and treasuring some. We become accustomed to and come to feel at home in familiar places.

As we learn how to use our bodies, we expand the range of and enrich our experiences. As we learn how to use our senses and to manipulate things with our hands, the world reveals its sensory aspects to us. We learn how to take delight in some of them and to avoid others, to satisfy our curiosity about and probe things, and to explore new places. We become accustomed to and at home with familiar sights, sounds, textures, odors, and flavors. As we grow in hand-eye coordination and dexterity and gain control of other parts of our bodies, we extend the repertoire of what we know how to do. We learn to hold a bottle or cup and to drink, to bring food to our mouths, to play with simple toys, to open and close doors, to climb, to participate in elementary games, to dress ourselves, to run, to jump, to catch and throw, to mimic the movements of others, and to master simple tasks.

As we mature, we expand our repertoire of activities and experiences within the limits of our capacities and aversions to danger and risk. We take in more of what our experiences have to offer and find a fuller range of satisfactions in them. We become more adept and effective in more refined, complex, and varied activities. Often we learn from and imitate others; sometimes we adopt our own distinctive styles. We begin to sense and learn how to exercise our freedom. We choose our own paths and venture down them in our own ways. We try and fail and try again, learning how to go on as we do. We come to care about and enjoy doing and experiencing some things more than others. We blend activities and experiences into routines and make distinctive daily life patterns our own. We continually weave and reweave those patterns as our interests and abilities change, creating life histories uniquely our own.

As we extend our spheres of experience and activity, our social contacts expand as well. We meet and interact with others in our immediate and extended families, members of their social circles, and eventually peers, friends, teachers, mentors, colleagues, and acquaintances. We assume roles in relationships with them. We learn how to act within those roles. We accept the responsibilities that come with the roles and develop the skills to meet them. We attune ourselves to and rely on the abilities and sensibilities of others and benefit from what they have to offer us. We develop abilities and sensibilities of our own that enable us to offer others something in turn. We learn how to sense and respond to the emotions, motivations, and dispositions that underlie and shape others' actions and characters. We learn how to sense and express our own emotions. And we assume motivations, dispositions, and characters of our own. We learn how to share interests, tolerate differences, play and work together, cooperate, and respect one another. In all of these ways we learn how to be with others, to maintain connections with them while we are apart, to walk the earth with them, to feel at home and at ease with some, to accommodate many others, to be wary of and cautious around some, and to defend ourselves against still others. We enter into distinctive patterns of give and take, patterns that we constantly weave and reweave as different individuals come and go in our lives. As we do, we live unique individual and collective life histories and establish our identities within them.

Our learning how to live in the world takes root in our capacities to both retain what we have learned from past experience and to anticipate the future. We carry our fundamental needs with us always. We develop wants and desires as means to meeting those needs and satisfying our curiosities. We learn what works and what does not, which experiences, actions, and interactions meet our needs and wants and which do not. As we do, we grow accustomed to doing things and interacting with others in certain ways. We hold what we have learned in the dispositions and habits that carry us forward virtually automatically.

We also learn how to rely on the stability of the world and the regularity of others' behaviors and responses. We learn how to anticipate what will happen next and what will result from our actions. At first, the time horizon of our anticipations is very limited, barely stretching beyond the present moment. But as we gradually find our bearings, our anticipations become expectations and hopes that extend further and further into the future. Our expectations rest in our sense of what is probable or likely given what we have experienced of the stability and regularity in the world around us and the confidence we have acquired in what has worked reliably for us up to now. We come to rely upon our expectations as the basis for our sense of daily purpose and the ground for our capacity to shape and hold to many of our long-term goals and objectives. Our hopes rest in our sense of what is possible or worth a try given what we have experienced of the openness of the world and what we have learned from extending our efforts beyond previous limits. We come to rely upon our hopes as the basis for our striving to overcome adversity, to better our lot in life and that of those we love, and to grow and become more than we have been.

And so it is that we assume, or take for ourselves, places in the world. We orient ourselves within our physical surroundings, our social surroundings, individual and collective life histories, and the limits of our own capacities fundamentally and primarily through practical engagement in the world. We orient ourselves in and through the needs, wants, emotions, motivations, abilities, habits, dispositions, interaction patterns, expectations, and hopes that arise within and shape that practical engagement.

We seek regularity, stability, order, and constancy in our surroundings. We struggle to feel comfortable, safe, and secure within them. We learn how to respond to what we find in them in emotionally appropriate ways. We become accustomed to ways of meeting our needs and fulfilling our desires. We assume positions and postures and situate ourselves in physical and social space and time. We immerse ourselves in and extend the ranges of our experiences and activities. We steady ourselves as we assume habits and routines and become accustomed to life patterns. We establish and sustain patterns of connections to things, places, and other people. We learn to trust and rely upon the abilities and effectiveness of our bodies, the dispositions of our characters, and the viability of our expectations and hopes for the future. We become who we are (assume identities and characters) as we embody the orienting forces within us and live the histories they generate. We come to feel at home, that we belong within these familiar experiences, activities, patterns of connection, histories, and identities.

To be sure, as we mature, most of us develop abilities to reflect upon and articulate beliefs about the nature of the world around us and about the life we live within it. We adopt beliefs and theories, sometimes without even realizing that we have, often without question from others, and more rarely after careful critical examination. Beliefs and theories orient us in frameworks for understanding and interpreting the world and our places in it. Most of us also develop abilities to anticipate the consequences of our actions and to deliberate about goals and means to achieving them. We adopt plans and strategies for action, often following others without question and sometimes making or altering plans through critical deliberation. Plans orient us in time and within the courses of our life histories.

But it is important to notice that the orientation that comes with the exercise of these higher cognitive powers is by no means the most fundamental or the primary orientation that supports and sustains us. Fundamentally, we adopt ways of living and orient ourselves within the noncognitive, emotional, psychological, physical, behavioral, social, soulful, and spiritual forces and contexts I have been describing. I call these ways of living "assumptions" precisely because they come to be operative in our lives without our thinking self-consciously about them. They function habitually and automatically to shape and direct our lives in ways that we take for granted. We would not get very far in life if this were not so. Knowing *how* to live grounded in practical assumptions provides a stabilizing momentum that makes it possible most of the time to meet our needs, satisfy our wants, express ourselves, sustain connections, and move into the future without stopping to think about every step along the way. If we had to examine explicitly every implicit belief or deliberate self-consciously about every alternative, our lives would grind to a halt.

Motivations for reflection, examination of beliefs and theories, and deliberation about plans arise within contexts of practical engagement in the world already well under way. At most, the orientation that derives from the exercise of these higher cognitive powers complements, enhances, or enables us to modify the more fundamental orientation that we have found and achieved and continue to benefit from in prereflective experience and activity. We spend most of our time actively engaged in the world. We spend but a small fraction of our time in reflection, theorizing, and deliberation. We tend to use these powers when our practical assumptions (knowledge of *how* to live in the world that we carry in our bodies and characters) let us down in some way, we feel confused or frustrated, our lives lose the rhythm or momentum we've grown accustomed to, we sense a need to change direction, or we long to understand the broader contexts or the greater scheme of things within which we live, suffer, and die.

Sometimes coming to know more *about* (or reviewing our beliefs *about*) the way the world is or should be (locally or globally) or deliberating self-consciously *about* possible courses of action enables us to live more effective, satisfying, and fulfilling lives, and sometimes it does not. When we turn our reflective glance toward and attempt to understand our own know-how and practical success in the world, we manage to reflect on and consciously articulate but a small fraction of what we have accomplished prereflectively and what we continue to accomplish.

Even when we have reflected and critically examined beliefs or consciously deliberated about courses of action based upon beliefs about what will work and what is desirable, such beliefs and plans usually recede from conscious awareness into the background we bring to subsequent experience of and action in the world. They become operative in our encounters with the world at the level of disposition, not consciously held belief or plan.

What We Lose When Someone We Love Dies

When we come to love someone—a parent, sibling, family member, friend, spouse or companion, teacher, mentor, or colleague—we assume particular places in their worlds, and they assume particular places in ours in all of the ways I have described. As we learn how to live with them, each comes to have a presence in our daily living, in our unfolding life stories, and in the shaping of our characters. Each person and each relationship is unique and irreplaceable, complex and multidimensional, and subtly nuanced in ways beyond our abilities to fathom and articulate. As the song says, we grow accustomed to their faces—and oh so much more! With each, we weave an intricate pattern of give and take with aspects of dependence and independence, satisfaction and disappointment, ease and tension, joy and sorrow, and love and hate to which we grow accustomed. Many of our emotions, needs, desires, motivations, dispositions, habits, expectations, and hopes find their targets in beloved individuals. These forces become operative within us as we come to be at home with and take for granted the continued presence of our loved ones and all that it means to us

We often consciously adopt beliefs *about* our loved ones and our relationships and deliberately develop plans that influence aspects of our lives with and within them. And we sometimes consciously reflect upon and adopt beliefs about the broader contexts of our lives and the scheme of things within which we, those we love, and our relationships find places. We explicitly articulate and adopt global, ultimate assumptions about the way the world works and how and where we fit in it. But first there is practical, embodied involvement with those we love that is shaped by the kinds of local, here-and-now, particular, lived assumptions, or practical knowing *how*, that I have described. And often within that practical engagement in life with others we come to feel safe, secure, at home within the world we experience, and confident in the viability of the life we are living without ever consciously reflecting or examining possible reasons for feeling as we do or explicitly adopting beliefs about the matter. Ongoing life already under way with those we love precedes and provides the context within which we are only sometimes motivated to reflect and deliberate in ways that give rise to explicitly held beliefs, plans, and global assumptions.

When those we love die, we lose their continuing presence. But even in their absence, the myriad particular, multidimensional assumptions that have shaped our lives in their presence do not cease to operate within us. We are profoundly confused and disoriented in bereavement precisely because the orienting forces within us no longer find their target. That is, much that is within us and that in part makes us who we are no longer fits in a world irrevocably changed by death. We had no idea how much we had become accustomed to and taken for granted in life with our loved ones. Life cannot now hold its familiar shape. Our daily life patterns are shattered, many of the regular rhythms interrupted and routines no longer practicable. Life cannot now sustain its familiar momentum. Our life histories are disrupted, veering from anticipated to unknown courses. We cannot hold to our ways of acting and being in the world that depended upon their continued living. The lived assumptions that enabled us to live in these ways are no longer viable. We lose the orientation in the world that these assumptions supported until death changed everything. And whatever feelings of safety, security, being at home, and confidence in living that took root in life with them are undermined.

Such is the true character and depth of the loss of the assumptive world that we experience when someone we love dies. Yes, we lose whatever cognitive anchoring or orientation in reality that explicitly held beliefs or deliberately adopted plans provided. But we also lose the more fundamental and far more pervasive anchoring and orientation that the full range of particular lived, practical assumptions grounded in sharing life with them provided. This because we have taken so much more for granted (assumed so much more) than simply the validity of our beliefs or the viability of our plans. We have also taken for granted the fit, effectiveness, and sustainability of the noncognitive orienting forces that became second nature to us as we learn how to live with our loved ones. And we have also take for granted the feelings of safety, security, sense of belonging, and confidence in living we experienced in life with them.

Perhaps my point about the loss of assumptive world being fundamentally a matter of loss of practical, lived assumptions can be more readily grasped if we consider young children. They do not orient themselves in the world through consciously entertaining beliefs, theories, or faiths or deliberating about and developing plans. They find their ways in the world, learn how to live in it, prereflectively and practically through the orienting life forces within them, the practical abilities they embody, and the characters they develop in interaction with their physical and social surroundings. And when someone they love dies, their lives are disrupted in the fundamental ways I have described. The daily life patterns they have grown accustomed to are shattered, and the established momentum of their lives is disrupted every bit as much as they are in our adult lives. The same is true for others whose capacities for reflection and deliberation either have not fully developed or have been compromised. We miss the heart of the experiences of bereavement of children and these other populations when we overlook the pervasive loss of assumption their bereavement entails. Indeed, overlooking this loss may be a central reason why we have long tended to disenfranchise their grief.

Relearning What We Have Assumed

We knew how to live while our loved ones were with us. And we knew how to love them. With so many of our life assumptions no longer viable after bereavement, we are challenged to relearn our ways in the world (Attig, 1996). We must establish and grow accustomed to new constellations of life assumptions. We must learn how to live in the absence of our loved ones and to love them still, how to give them places in our hearts, how to hold them in our memories, practical lives, souls, and spirits (Attig, 2000).

We must relearn how to live in all dimensions of our lives. Emotionally, we are challenged to learn how to address and carry the pain of missing those we love, to work toward a new emotional equilibrium in physical and social surroundings pervaded with their absence, and to love them in new ways. Psychologically, we must learn ways to renew our self-confidence, self-esteem, and self-identity. Behaviorally, we struggle to learn new ways of doing things and to modify our motivations, dispositions, and habits. And we are challenged to once again find satisfaction in the variety and patterns of our activities and experiences. Physically or biologically, we must learn to blend old and new ways of meeting our needs for food, shelter, and especially closeness. And we must expend the great energy that meeting the challenges of relearning requires. Socially, we are challenged to find our way in changed patterns of give and take with others, including our fellow survivors and others we may yet meet on life's paths. Intellectually, we seek answers to the questions that trouble us, and pursue satisfactory understandings and interpretations of the meanings of what has happened. Soulfully, we struggle to learn how to be at home again with the things and within the places our loved ones have left behind, with our families and communities, and within ourselves. We have to learn to trust again the remnants in life that can still sustain us. And spiritually, we muster the courage to learn new life patterns and redirect our life stories. We must learn ways of overcoming our suffering, finding peace and consolation, and modifying our hopes.

Such relearning and coming to terms with the loss of our assumptive worlds is no more a matter of taking in information or mastering ideas and theories than was our learning how to live in the world in the first place. It is not fundamentally a matter of rethinking beliefs, faiths, and theories *about* the world or our place in it. To be sure, intellectual coping is a part of coming to terms with loss of our assumptive worlds. Intellectual coping includes realizing that another has died in the sense of coming to accept the truth of the proposition *that* he or she no longer lives. Parkes and his followers are correct when they say that we incline toward denial of this central proposition about our new reality: we resist taking it in. Intellectual coping also often includes rethinking some of our most cherished beliefs about ourselves, our relationships, the way the world works, and our place in that world. And it can be very difficult to acknowledge that such beliefs may be questionable and, even more difficult, to actually reexamine and modify them. Parkes and others are also correct when they say that such intellectual assumptions are difficult to access through introspection because of fears and anxieties about where such rethinking may lead us.

Similarly, although relearning the world and coming to terms with the loss of our assumptive worlds is primarily a practical matter, this is no more a matter of deliberately revising life plans than was learning how to live in the world in the first place. It is not fundamentally a matter of consciously rethinking goals and alternative means of meeting them. To be sure, this can be a part of the practical coping that is required of us. When those who have died have figured centrally in plans we have deliberately adopted, we must acknowledge that the plans are no longer viable. Parkes and others are again correct when they note that we may resist accepting the necessity here because we cherish such plans and prefer known to unknown courses in life. But as I have said above, very little of our practical engagement in the world is guided by deliberate planning. Our involvement in living has a momentum all its own beneath the surface of reflection, self-consciousness, explicitly held belief, and deliberation.

Relearning the world or coming to terms with the loss of our assumptive worlds is primarily about learning new ways of acting and being in the world. In great part, and fundamentally, this relearning is a matter of rechanneling the practical momentum of the stream of prereflective, unselfconscious, predeliberative life within which we are immersed and at home. It is a matter of coming to know *how* to go on in the world where so much of what we have taken for granted in the emotional, psychological, behavioral, social, soulful, and spiritual dimensions of our lives is no longer supportable or practicable.

Realizing, or making real, the deaths of those we love is so much more than simply assenting to the truth of the proposition that they no longer live. It is a matter of taking in that truth in the depths of our being, allowing ourselves to feel the impact of the absence in all dimensions of our lives, experiencing the differences that absence makes in the world around us and in our daily lives and life histories, practically reorienting ourselves to those differences, and making the truth our own in our bodies and characters.

Rechanneling the practical momentum of our lives in the aftermath of bereavement is so much more than simply revising plans we have adopted. It is a matter of modifying all of the lived assumptions that were grounded in the continued presence of those we love, changing in all of the dimensions of our being, becoming accustomed to new life patterns, reorienting and immersing ourselves in the flow of life in new directions, and coming to be at home once again in our life histories and the identities we find within them.

Unlike beliefs or plans that we have come to take for granted, most practical assumptions are not propositional in character at all. That is, they are not matters of knowing or believing *that* the world is or should be one way as opposed to another. They are instead matters of knowing *how* to act and be in the world. We know *how* to do so many things—walk, run, tie a knot, strike a golf ball, bake a cake, play an instrument, tell a joke, paint a picture, comfort a friend, love one another, get along with a difficult person, or make a marriage work, to name but a few. Yet these matters of practical repertoire are most often very difficult, even impossible, to put into words. If someone asks us to explain how we do what we know perfectly well how to do, most of us quickly concede that we cannot articulate it easily, if at all. Our knowing how is simply not that kind of thing. But, just as we take beliefs and plans for granted, we come to take such knowing how for granted. Our bodies become able, and our characters become disposed. We take such knowing how upon ourselves. It comes to operate within us without thinking.

This knowing how eludes introspection for reasons different from those Parkes discusses. We do not carry it within us as conscious constructs, internal models or schemata checked against reality, or beliefs explicit or implicit. It does not consist of ways of understanding, conjecturing, or theorizing about the world that we hold in our minds. We carry such knowing how within us as practical abilities, dispositions, and habits. It comprises ways of doing and being that we hold in our bodies and characters. It is because these orienting practical assumptions are noncognitive in character to begin with that they elude our introspective grasp: We are looking in the wrong place if we are looking for beliefs. And we are asking a great deal if we expect that most, or any, of us will be very adept at articulating the practical assumptions that we seek to bring to awareness.

Helping with the Relearning

If the loss and relearning of our assumptive worlds have the character I have described, then there are clear implications for the nature of helping with the relearning. Such helping must be like teaching. The range of cognitive therapies Rando describes can only be part of the story. When they are used effectively, they help us to relearn our beliefs *about* the way the world is or should be. They are useful in helping us (teaching us) to acknowledge and understand whatever orientation in the world we have lost that was grounded in our beliefs or in plans we have developed. And they can help and support us as we rethink and modify those beliefs and plans in ways that help us to find new orientation in the world based in them.

We can learn all that there is to know in books, lectures, or workshops or from counselors *about* the full range of practical challenges we confront when our loved ones have died and about means of addressing them, just as we can read late-nineteenth-century manuals (often extending to hundreds of pages) about what is practically required to ride a bicycle. But such theoretical knowledge is simply different from the practical knowledge we require to actually come to terms with loss of our assumptive worlds. Our knowledge about practical assumptions and means to changing them provides no guarantee that we will know *how* to do and be what the world now challenges us to do and become (just as readers of those manuals acquired no guarantee that they would know how to ride their bicycles). Knowledge about such practical matters provides at most a useful framework for understanding what we must yet do. There is still the matter of learning how to do it, acquiring and effectively using the sensibilities, abilities, and dispositions that will reorient and enable us to feel once again at home in the world.

Cognitive therapies do not, and on principle cannot, reach the far broader range of practical assumptions that operate within us beneath the surface of our self-conscious awareness. Such cognitive therapies are designed to help us (teach us) to rethink our places in the world. But more pervasively and fundamentally, we must learn how to live in those places. What we have taken for granted about such living has been undermined. Relearning the practical assumptions that have shaped our lives can only be aided and supported by teaching that helps us to redirect and refine many of the practical orienting forces within our bodies and characters and transform ourselves in all dimensions of our being, reposture and reposition ourselves in our physical and social surroundings, rehabituate ourselves in our daily life patterns, rechannel the practical momentum that carries us into the next chapters of our life histories, and reconnect with those who have died and love them in their absence. By such practical means we will, if we are successful, recover our sense of belonging and being at home in a world transformed by death.

We can benefit from teaching (counseling) that enables and supports our trying and testing familiar ways in the world, to learn if they are still trustworthy and satisfying. Teaching that encourages and prepares us to try what we have not tried before (through such things as imagining alternative approaches and strategies, anticipating possible consequences, envisioning successful outcomes, even rehearsing). Teaching that supports our learning from our mistakes and trying again (through such things as listening and debriefing, helping us to express and come to terms with our emotions, and helping us to maintain our confidence and motivation). Teaching that nurtures our developing and refining the abilities, habits, sensibilities, and dispositions that enable us to be effective in everyday activities and in our physical surroundings and social surroundings and to find satisfactions in experience and thrive again. Teaching that encourages, prepares, and supports us as we change life courses and redirect our life histories. Teaching that helps us make the transition from loving in presence to loving in absence, that encourages and supports our remembering our loved ones, appreciating their legacies, and drawing upon their practical, soulful, and spiritual influences.

Thus far, I have focused primarily on the kind of teaching we need to relearn the local, everyday assumptions that orient us within our immediate physical and social surroundings, in our particular life circumstances. We also need teaching that helps us to relearn the more global assumptions that orient us within the greater scheme of things. We are already practically engaged in existence within that scheme before we are ever motivated to reflect about our places in it. Typically, as we come to feel safe, secure, and at home in our everyday lives and within our personal life histories in all of the noncognitive ways I have described, we also come to feel safe, secure, and at home within this broader world context. We learn how to live in the world at large with at least minimal confidence that there is a point to going on day to day, caring, pursuing purposes, hoping, and aspiring. We experience living itself as meaningful and worthwhile without really thinking about it very much at all. Thought about such global matters typically arises only when we feel that this baseline confidence is shaken, that the fabric of our lives is unraveling, that our prereflective ways of acting and being in the world are coming undone, as we do, for example, when someone we love dies.

When we do, we need teaching that supports our recovering the confidence in our footing in the world that has been undermined. Here, too, cognitive approaches to helping us have their limitations because the understandings that beliefs and faiths on such matters provide go only so far in grounding such confidence and orienting us within this broader scheme. No doubt many of us have found great steadiness and strength in beliefs and faiths that we have self-consciously adopted. Some teaching (counseling) can help us to reexamine such beliefs and faiths when our confidence in them has been shaken. It can enable us to find deeper significance and unsuspected support in beliefs we already hold or to find alternative beliefs that steady us and restore our confidence on new foundations. Others of us have come to hold similar beliefs on such global matters without realizing that we have. The same kind of cognitively oriented teaching can help us to acknowledge and articulate such implicit beliefs and reexamine them in similar ways.

Within many traditions there are spiritual practices that complement adherence to faith and belief. They enable us to experience connection with and feel at home within the broader scheme of things directly, to orient ourselves within it through practice, not theory. They include such things as meditation, prayer, walking in silence, retreats for respite and renewal, communing with nature, chanting and singing, listening to music, participation in ritual, joining others in fellowship and communion, and giving to others from compassion. Teaching that introduces us to and supports us as we engage in such practices can also contribute to our recovering confidence of our place in the greater scheme of things.

But we should not underestimate the great contribution of teaching that enables us to reorient ourselves practically in our particular life circumstances. Typically it was learning how to live in our everyday life patterns and our unfolding life histories in the presence of our loved ones that first led us to experience the more global confidence that has now been shaken. Teaching that restores our practical effectiveness in living in the absence of those we love goes a very long way in restoring that global confidence. It is difficult to conceive a better, more direct, and effective way to restore confidence that life is meaningful and worthwhile than to return to living effectively, purposefully, and satisfyingly in our particular life circumstances. We rarely seriously question the place of our lives in the greater scheme of things when life is going well. And our most fervently held beliefs and cherished faiths are often shaken and sorely tested when it is not. Teaching that supports our reexamining and modifying such beliefs at most complements or reinforces teaching that enables us to recover the more fundamental, practical orientation in our particular life circumstances that commonly grounds our confidence that life is meaningful and worthwhile.

We also need practical teaching that will support us in the ongoing struggle to find our bearings and to assume viable postures within a greater scheme of things pervaded with the mysteries of impermanence, change, uncertainty, fallibility, life, love, suffering, and death. We need wise counsel that enables us to learn to live with these mysteries rather than attempt to fully understand or master them. We need teaching that supports our changing in response to them rather than trying futilely to change them. We need wise counsel that helps us to learn how to live with the realization that our grasp on reality through beliefs and faiths is tenuous and that our postures before mysteries are temporary at best. Ultimately, we need teaching that supports our learning to hold ourselves steady and to recover and sustain momentum in living once again in the ever-present shadows of these mysteries.

References

Attig, T. (1996). *How we grieve: Relearning the world*. New York: Oxford University Press.

Attig, T. (2000). *The Heart of grief: The desire for lasting love*. New York: Oxford University Press.

Freud, S. (1917)). Mourning and melancholia. In *The complete psychological works of Sigmund Freud* (Vol. 14). New York: Norton.

Parkes, C. M. (1971). Psycho-social transition: A field of study. *Social Science and Medicine*, 5, 101–115.

Parkes, C. M. (1988). Bereavement as a psychosocial transition: Processes of adaptation to change. *Journal of Social Issues, 44(3)*, 53–65.

Rando, T. (1993). *Treatment of complicated mourning*. Champaign, IL: Research Press.

part 2.

Relationships with Self and Others

5.

The Harm of Trauma

Pathological Fear, Shattered Assumptions, or Betrayal?

Anne P. DePrince and Jennifer J. Freyd

Recent research using a random sampling of individuals across the United States found that 72 percent of respondents reported having experienced at least one serious traumatic event, ranging from childhood abuse to car accidents to murder of a loved one (Elliott, 1997). This study is in line with other research indicating that a significant portion of the population has experienced serious trauma. Research also indicates that a substantial number of those individuals exposed to trauma go on to experience psychological distress related to the trauma (for reviews, see van der Kolk & McFarlane, 1996; McFarlane & DeGirolamo, 1996). According to accepted wisdom in the traumatic stress field, fear is the central reaction associated with traumatic events, and pathological fear is at the core of post-traumatic distress. We refer to this almost exclusive focus on the emotion of fear as the "fear paradigm."

This chapter examines the limitations of this "fear paradigm" and proposes that fundamental changes in the types of research questions asked occur when reactions beyond fear are considered. To illustrate this, we will consider the influence on theory development stemming from Janoff-Bulman's (1992) "shattered assumptions" framework with its emphasis on cognitive appraisal. In addition, we will outline changes that occur in the range of research questions posed when the current fear paradigm is broadened to include a focus on Freyd's "betrayal trauma" theory. Based on distinctions drawn between affect and cognition, between fear and betrayal, and between explicit and implicit appraisals, we propose that a broad range of reactions should be considered in trauma research and clinical work. We suggest that fear, shattered assumptions, and betrayal are all important core insults stemming from the most damaging traumas.

The reactions and emotions that psychologists assume individuals experience in response to traumatic events necessarily affect research design, data collection, and interpretation. The paradigm within which research occurs affects both the content of and value placed on research questions (Kuhn, 1970). We consider cognitive and affective reactions other than fear to examine how research and treatment questions are altered depending on the primary emotion or reaction response assumed by the researcher. In particular, we consider the research questions that arise when theoretically driven studies move from a paradigm that assumes fear to be the core reaction associated with the trauma response to a framework that also considers as central shattered assumptions and betrayal (including both implicit and explicitly experienced betrayal) associated with trauma.

Historical Focus on the Reaction of Fear

Since the mid-1980s, conceptualizations of trauma have increasingly centered on the fear invoked by trauma and resulting anxiety related to that fear. Most psychological research on trauma during the late twentieth century focused on the specific diagnosis of posttraumatic stress disorder (PTSD). The PTSD diagnosis requires that the individual has experienced intense fear, helplessness, or horror in response to a traumatic event. This criteria has likely influenced research inasmuch as fear tends to be the reaction most frequently examined and considered in theories about PTSD onset, maintenance, and recovery. The focus on fear can be seen in the current classification of posttraumatic stress disorder as an anxiety disorder and the requirement that the traumatic stressor invoke fear or helplessness in the individual (*DSM-IV*).

The current conceptualization of PTSD has its origins in work with Vietnam combat veterans (for a review, see Herman, 1992). Evidence used to support the placement of PTSD in the anxiety disorders includes arguments by Barlow that PTSD developed in the same way as other anxiety disorders (for a review, see Brett, 1996). From this view, when individuals with biological and psychological vulnerabilities experience stressful life events, they begin to organize their lives around beliefs that stressful events are largely unpredictable, thereby leading to increased fear and chronic hyperarousal (Brett, 1996).

The assumption that fear is at the core of the PTSD response has influenced research, theory, and treatment development. Information-processing approaches to PTSD have stressed the role of emotional networks in the onset and maintenance of PTSD. Lang's model for emotional processing, which suggests that emotion is defined as an information structure in memory that includes stimuli, responses, and the meaning assigned to the stimulus-and-response data, has been extended to fear in PTSD (e.g., Foa & Kozak, 1986). Within this framework the underlying assumption in research and treatment has been that the individual with PTSD has pathological elements in the fear structure that require modification (Rothbaum & Foa, 1996). Treatment, therefore, is based on activating fear structures and introducing corrective emotional information, which is thought to lead to decreased symptomatology (e.g., see Meadows & Foa, 1998). The focus on fear has likely also contributed to a focus on the anxiety symptoms of PTSD (e.g., arousal and intrusive symptoms), with relatively less attention paid to dissociative symptoms. Dissociation and alexithymia have recently gained increasing attention in research and intervention work (e.g., Wagner & Linehan, 1998; Cloitre, 1998; Putnam, 1997). In addition, the relationship between avoidance and maintenance of PTSD anxiety symptoms has also gained increased attention (e.g., Meadows & Foa, 1998).

Recent Theoretical Development Beyond Fear:
Shattered Assumptions

In recent years, new theories have increased the breadth of reactions considered with respect to responses to trauma. We will focus on influential theories of reactions to the most damaging traumas—those that are human-caused and involve interpersonal violence and violation. Janoff-Bulman (1992) suggested that such traumas shatter three basic assumptions held about the world: the world is benevolent, the world is meaningful, and the self is worthy. Janoff-Bulman's (1992) theory shifted the emphasis from the emotion and biology of fear to a cognitive appraisal of the world and the self following trauma. Janoff-Bulman employed information-processing approaches to explore the ways in which schemas and other cognitive factors influence humans' cognitive conservatism and resistance to changing these basic assumptions. Given that humans are resistant to any change in these assumptions, traumatic experiences shatter the assumptions. Within this shattered assumption framework, coping with and healing from trauma require that individuals reconcile their old set of assumptions with new, modified assumptions. Empirical investigations have resulted in good support for this theory and provided additional information about how the type of trauma experienced influences which assumption(s) are affected.

In addition to contributing to both research and clinical domains, the shattered assumptions framework is a useful way to consider some of the sociopolitical influences on the field. McFarlane and van der Kolk (1996) note that society becomes resentful of the ways in which victims of trauma shatter our illusions of safety. Society, therefore, is often resistant to recognizing the effects of trauma and inclined to engage in victim blaming in order to maintain basic assumptions.

The shattered assumptions theory provides a framework through which to understand effects of trauma that might not be related to fear or terror associated with the event. Instead, some posttraumatic distress may be primarily related to violations of important assumptions. This framework opens up a new set of research questions that might otherwise not be asked when researchers focus primarily on fear. For example, one might ask about the impact of violation of assumptions in distress and recovery.

Recent Theoretical Development Beyond Fear: Betrayal

Freyd's (1996, 1999) betrayal trauma theory has challenged the field to move beyond conceptualizations of fear as the sole motivating reaction in traumatic responses. Freyd (1994, 1996) initially proposed betrayal trauma theory to account for memory impairment in regard to traumatic events. Betrayal trauma theory posited that there is a social utility in remaining unaware of abuse when the perpetrator is a caregiver (Freyd, 1996). The theory accounts for memory failure in a way that can be empirically tested, and it stresses a reaction that previously had not been focused on to any large extent in research.

In delineating the theory, Freyd (1996) lays out the evolutionary basis for why and how humans are usually excellent at detecting betrayals while exploring the critical proposal that under some circumstances detecting betrayals may be coun-terproductive to survival. Specifically, in cases where a victim is dependent on a caregiver, survival may require that she or he remain unaware of the betrayal. In the case of childhood sexual abuse, a child who is aware that her or his parent is being abusive may withdraw from the relationship (e.g., withdraw in terms of proximity or emotionally). For a child who depends on a caregiver for basic survival, withdrawing may actually be at odds with ultimate survival goals. In such cases, the child's survival would be better ensured by being blind to the betrayal and isolating the knowledge of the event. Betrayal trauma theory invokes disso-ciation as a likely mechanism in isolating awareness of abuse and betrayal. The betrayal trauma framework has been primarily applied to child abuse to date but likely informs processing in other types of trauma, such as domestic violence and combat (see Shay, 1994, for discussion of betrayal in combat).

In more recent work Freyd (1998, 1999, in press) noted that traumatic events likely involve differing degrees of fear and betrayal, depending on the context and characteristics of the event. Looking at a two-dimensional model with fear on one axis and social betrayal on the other, the possibility that traumas may involve mainly betrayal or fear, or a combination of both, extends the traditional assump-tions in PTSD research that fear is the emotion at the core of responses to trauma.

Shay (1994) also invokes the role that betrayal plays in response to trauma, particularly in the case of combat. Shay draws on the ways in which betrayal influ-enced the experience of many Vietnam veterans. Combat, much like a family, creates the world in which the soldiers live by controlling such things as bodily function (when they can sleep, eat) and creating barriers to escape. Shay discusses the utter dependence of the soldier on the military, and the ways in which soldiers were betrayed both in Vietnam and upon returning to the United States. Shay highlights the centrality of betrayal when he suggests that a soldier's trust in his own perceptions and cognitions probably recovers upon leaving combat, unless the soldier has experienced some betrayal that has altered his reality (e.g., being told, "This didn't happen to you").

Betrayal as an Implicit Factor or an Explicit Appraisal in Reaction to Trauma?

The role of betrayal in betrayal trauma theory was initially considered an implicit but central aspect of some situations. If a child is being mistreated by a caregiver he or she is dependent upon, this is by definition betrayal, whether the child recog-nizes the betrayal explicitly or not. Indeed, the memory impairment and gaps in awareness that betrayal trauma theory predicted were assumed to serve in part to ward off conscious awareness of mistreatment in order to promote the dependent child's survival goals. In contrast, the traditional focus on fear has generally seemed to assume that individuals are consciously aware of fear. Similarly, Janoff-Bulman's theory of shattered assumptions placed the cognitive appraisals within the conscious domain. Shattered assumptions theory leads us to ponder the possibil-ity that in some cases betrayal is a conscious appraisal in response to trauma—an appraisal that combines both elements of cognitive information processing and powerful emotional responses. While conscious appraisals of betrayal may be inhibited at the time of trauma and for as long as the trauma victim is dependent upon the perpetrator, eventually the trauma survivor may become conscious of strong feelings of betrayal. This framework raises the important question as to what role the emotional perception of betrayal has in distress and recovery.

Combining Betrayal Trauma and Shattered Assumptions: Affect Versus Cognition

Both betrayal trauma theory and the shattered assumptions framework primarily focus on the impact of trauma on cognitive systems. These theories do not focus on the explicit experience of emotions, in comparison to the fear paradigm, which focuses primarily on the emotion of fear. Taken together, the conceptual perspectives from betrayal trauma theory, shattered assumptions theory, and the fear paradigm can be combined such that affective and cognitive components are jointly considered in a way that deepens our understanding of the effects of trauma. Betrayal trauma theory alone suggests that the experience of betrayal is implicit in the situation and is not experienced as an emotion per se; in fact, betrayal trauma theory predicts that victims will use various cognitive mechanisms to stay unaware of the betrayal. The shattered assumption framework adds to this conceptual picture by illustrating that betrayal may move to an explicit phenomenon in terms of an awareness that core assumptions, such as that the world is benevolent, have been violated. Theoretical traditions from the fear paradigm that focus on experiences of emotion lead us to then consider betrayal as an explicit emotion.

The trauma literature includes research and clinical approaches that seek to integrate dimensions, such as explicit versus implicit influences and affect versus cognition. For example, Roth and colleagues have incorporated the role of assumptions in their work with survivors of sexual assault as well as identified and examined additional responses associated with sexual assault (e.g., Roth & Lebowitz, 1988; Roth & Newman, 1993; Newman, Riggs, & Roth, 1997; Roth & Newman, 1991; Lifton, 1996). Within this conceptualization, Roth and Newman (1993) have defined themes affected by sexual trauma; these themes include both affect (e.g., rage) and schemas (e.g., meaningful world). Roth and Newman (1991) note that the survivor must grapple with the emotional impact of the trauma in order to end preoccupation with negative feelings and recover. Research involving a coding system to assess these themes has examined their relationship to posttraumatic distress (e.g., Roth & Newman, 1993; Roth, Lebowitz, & DeRosa, 1997). During the *DSM-IV* field trials, Roth and colleagues used the coding system to successfully predict whether individuals would meet criteria for PTSD alone or no PTSD, compared to concurrent PTSD and complex PTSD (Newman, Riggs, & Roth, 1997).

Roth and Newman (1991) specify four major schemas that are affected by trauma; these include the three assumptions outlined by Janoff-Bulman as well as a fourth notion that people are trustworthy and worth relating to. This fourth assumption can be viewed as a way that betrayal trauma theory and shattered assumptions theory intersect. One of the core assumptions that people may operate under is that others are trustworthy; when traumatic events are perpetrated by trusted individuals, this core assumption is shattered.

Fear and Betrayal:
Why Does It Matter Which We Examine?

To date, fear has been the most widely discussed reaction associated with traumatic experiences. The research questions asked within this fear paradigm typically differ from the questions asked when betrayal is also considered. The current fear paradigm will be examined in contrast to a framework that incorporates implicit and explicit appraisals of betrayal as central to posttraumatic responses.

Research on posttraumatic reactions has largely centered on how fear associated with traumatic events relates to symptoms of anxiety (e.g., increased arousal, hypervigilance). Many important findings that inform intervention and prevention work have come from the fear paradigm. For example, the focus on fear has led to important research concerning cognitive-behavioral therapies that are related to significant decreases in self-reported anxiety symptoms (see Follette, Ruzek, & Abueg, 1998).

There are limitations to research that has occurred under the fear paradigm. With a focus on fear, mainstream psychology has tended to pathologize trauma survivors' reactions by assuming that the pathology resides within the traumatized individual. Either implicitly or explicitly, responsibility for the experience of fear is placed on the individual survivor. In assuming that posttraumatic pathology is contained within the individual, research has often failed to examine the social context within which the trauma occurred and with which the survivor interacts after the trauma.

Shifts in Perspective with Betrayal: New Research Questions

Incorporating betrayal into theories of posttraumatic responses affects the research questions posed on at least three levels. Considering betrayal changes the extent to which research focuses on the context of the traumatic event, the range of outcomes, and the influence of sociopolitical factors. Examples of research questions at each of these levels will be considered.

Context of the Traumatic Event

When betrayal associated with the traumatic event is considered, the research questions asked necessarily shift to focus on relational issues and social context. The very inclusion of betrayal as an important reaction requires that the researcher ask by whom or what the survivor was betrayed. By asking this question, the individual is placed in a relational and social context. When questions are asked from a relational perspective, the pathology is not placed solely within the mind of the individual. Instead, both the individual and the context inform conceptualization of the survivor's response to trauma. The context may include the traumatic events itself, the relationship to the perpetrator, the societal response to the event, and cultural influences on the individual, among many other critical variables.

With betrayal, research must necessarily ask more detailed questions about the traumatic event itself. In particular, closer attention is paid to the relationship between the perpetrator and victim in interpersonal violence. The perpetrator-victim relationship offers insight into the extent of the betrayal. Specific predictions can be made as to how information related to the betrayal will be processed (see Freyd, 1996). For example, current research examines the extent to which memory impairment is related to perpetrator-victim relationship (Freyd, 1996; Freyd, DePrince, & Zurbriggen, in preparation). Individuals report greater memory impairment for sexual trauma perpetrated by family members than nonfamily members (Freyd, 1996; DePrince & Zurbriggen, in preparation).

Types of Distress Examined

Considering betrayal also changes the types of distress research will address. Predictions about the relationship of betrayal to distress can be extended from other work in the field. For example, Roth and colleagues have looked at whether overall disruption in emotion themes is related to posttraumatic symptoms. Roth and colleagues have illustrated that alterations in important themes are related to overall symptomatology. However, using the presence of specific emotions to predict symptom configurations has not been examined to date. Within a betrayal trauma framework, predictions about symptoms other than PTSD are tested. For example, Freyd's (1996) betrayal trauma theory implicates dissociation as an important mechanism in keeping threatening information from awareness. Indeed, DePrince and Freyd (1999; in submission) have found empirical support for the relationship between dissociation and knowledge isolation in laboratory tasks. Under the betrayal trauma theory framework, betrayal may be related to dissociative responses that will help the individual keep threatening information from awareness (DePrince & Freyd, 1999; in submission). DePrince and Freyd (in preparation) predict that betrayal will be correlated with dissociative and numbing symptoms, but not arousal; fear will be correlated with arousal symptoms and not dissociative or numbing symptoms.

Influence of Sociopolitical Context

A betrayal framework highlights the need to examine the historical and cultural contexts within which traumas occur in order to understand betrayal at a societal level. Recent work addressing the importance of historical context in understanding the needs of the Native American community speak to the central role that cultural considerations of reactions, such as betrayal, can and must play in research and theory. Duran, Duran, Brave Heart, and Horse-Davis (1998) discuss the soul wound created by generations of oppression set in the context of historical trauma; even when trauma occurs in the present, these events cannot be addressed without considering the historical context within which the individual lives. Treatment models and research geared toward Native American communities must take into account the effects of generations of oppressive policies, such as boarding schools, as well as stressors such as racism and disease, in order to address the individual. Without considering the individual in this historical context, psychologists may fail to recognize the ways in which current trauma is exacerbated by the effects of the intergenerational transmission of trauma. Psychologists also risk pathologizing the individual instead of critically examining the sociocultural forces at play.

Betrayal also forces researchers to consider the influence of the response that the survivor receives from others following the event. Betrayal may come in the form of disbelief, minimizing, or otherwise devaluing the individual's experience. For example, assault survivors might be betrayed by disbelief and accusations of fabricating the events. Vietnam veterans experienced betrayal when they returned to a country that blamed them rather than celebrated their return, as had happened following previous wars (e.g., Shay, 1994). Betrayal may occur in terms of the justice system's treatment of the trauma (see Herman, 1992, for a discussion of revictimization through the courts) or the media's portrayal. The cultural response may include betrayal for events that did not necessarily involve interpersonal violence. For example, failure of the government to respond following a natural disaster, or perhaps responding differentially such that aid is not administered equally, may represent a betrayal that affects the level and type of distress reported by survivors.

Shay (1994) discusses betrayal of what is right in terms of Vietnam veterans. From a perspective examining betrayal of what is right, researchers may begin to ask what the appropriate response to trauma is at both individual and cultural levels. When only the fear experienced by survivors is examined, researchers are not forced to think about the community's role in addressing the transgression. In contrast, asking what is right addresses the sense of fairness that has been violated when traumas include betrayal and invokes consideration of the community and cultural response.

Why Haven't We Gone Far Enough?

Considering interpersonal betrayal in trauma requires that we confront the reality of the harm humans can cause one another. As individuals, as well as a society, we remain defended against awareness of the betrayals that so often occur in traumatic events. The field of psychology has witnessed ebbs and flows of interest and commitment to understanding the complexities of human trauma (for a review, see Herman, 1992). Stopping with a focus on fear allows researchers and clinicians to view the pathology as occurring within the individual, thereby maintaining distance from the more challenging awareness of the ways in which humans have historically betrayed other humans. Interesting parallels can be drawn with research on women and death in order to understand why the field may not include reactions, such as betrayal, that inherently challenge basic assumptions about the world as benevolent and people as trustworthy.

Anderson, Armitage, Jack, and Wittner (1990) reflect on why and how researchers frequently fail to listen to the experiences of women. In a discussion of oral history and feminist methods, they note that oral history methods "incorporate the previously overlooked lives, activities and feelings of women ... When women speak for themselves, they reveal hidden realities: new experiences and new perspectives emerge that challenge the 'truths' of official accounts and cast doubt upon established theories" (p. 95). Similarly, when we listen to those who have experienced trauma, in many cases we are listening to groups who traditionally have been voiceless in this culture and whose stories have been at times suppressed (e.g., Roth, Lebowitz, & DeRosa, 1997).

Anderson et al. (1990) note that researchers can miss critical information about the meaning individuals assign to their lives in a number of ways. First, we can fail to ask the questions that access information about the meaning each individual ascribes to a traumatic event. As researchers working within empirical paradigms, we may often take emotion-laden information from participants and respond with neutral questions. Our neutrality as researchers suggests to the participant that the emotion they share is not valued and sought in our explorations.

Researchers may listen to survivors through the lens of our own theories in a way that limits our ability to hear information that is inconsistent with our paradigm. When theories dictate that fear is the central response to trauma, researchers may fail to consider other emotions and reactions, such as betrayal, related to traumatic events. This problem is confounded by psychology's tendency to distrust the reliability of self-reported states (Anderson et al., 1990). Most of our research paradigms either implicitly or explicitly state that researchers are the experts. Working within such a paradigm, we may listen until we hear our expectation of the centrality of fear met by the survivor. In addition, empirical methods may at times limit the ability to examine the meaning people make of trauma because meaning is created by the individual, while research has tended to examine the component parts of the individual (Yalom, 1980).

Yet another impediment to the examination of reactions other than fear may be biases that defend against an acute awareness of interpersonal betrayal. In a related discussion, Yalom (1980) identifies an adult bias in examining how children understand death. Yalom argues that adults' fear and denial of death affect how they interpret research on children's knowledge of death. Adults may in fact fail to ask the questions that would elucidate children's knowledge of death, or even misperceive children's statements, in the service of defending against an awareness that even children can comprehend and fear death.

Similarly, researchers must grapple with the biases that lead to defending against knowing the ways in which interpersonal and societal betrayals have occurred in the context of trauma. When a trauma is experienced and researchers assume the person responds with fear, the focus can easily move away from the traumatic event to the "pathological fear" of the individual. This keeps societal denial of trauma and betrayal in place. When betrayal is introduced as a response to trauma, a revolutionary shift in focus occurs; the focus moves from the individual to the relationship and the social context of the event. A betrayal perspective raises questions about the relationship with the perpetrator, the context of the event, the response of others, of society. Asking about betrayal demands that the trauma be acknowledged and the event be examined, not just the individual's response. Betrayal places the pathology in the traumatic event, not in the individual. This perspective requires researchers and clinicians to recognize, with a frequently painful awareness, that trauma happens. Asking about betrayal requires that we break through our own denial, as well as challenge societal denial, of the existence and high rates of trauma that humans perpetrate on other humans. If we look only at fear, we risk asking only what is wrong with this fearful individual. We risk remaining complacent in both our own and society's denial of trauma, particularly betrayal trauma.

Summary and Conclusions

In the recent history of the traumatic stress studies field, fear has been the focus of study. Work derived from research on fear and anxiety has provided critical information to aid researchers' and clinicians' understanding of the impact of trauma. The literature arising from the fear paradigm has informed clinical and research endeavors, including the development of many treatment protocols used today with victims of various types of trauma.

Over the last ten years, we have seen an increase in study of reactions other than fear (e.g., Janoff-Bulman, 1992; Shay, 1994; Freyd, 1996; Roth & Newman, 1991). In particular, shattered assumptions and betrayal have been introduced as important factors in understanding how the victim responds to the world changes that follow trauma. When researchers ask questions from the perspective of reactions such as betrayal, interpersonal relationships and the social context of the trauma are more likely to be examined than when we focus mainly on fear and the pathology of the individual. As we look to relationships to understand the impact of betrayal, we are forced to consider the individual who experienced the trauma, the event itself, the sociopolitical context, and the community response. From this perspective, researchers ask new and exciting questions that examine the ways in which relationships and society beyond the circumscribed event potentially affect survivors' reactions and recovery.

Incorporating reactions beyond fear into research and theory will likely assist researchers and clinicians in capturing more of the complexity and heterogeneity of trauma and posttraumatic responses. Increasingly, researchers are noting that the current conceptualization of PTSD may not capture the heterogeneity of human responses (Putnam, 1997; Finkelhor & Kendall-Tackett, 1997). Likely, the focus on fear does not capture the full breadth of reactions that influence coping and recovery following trauma.

References

Anderson, K., Armitage, S., Jack, D., & Wittner, J. (1990). Beginning where we are: Feminist methodology in oral history. In J. M. Nelson (Ed.), *Feminist Research Methods* (pp. 94–114). San Francisco: Westview Press.

Brett, E. A. (1996). The classification of posttraumatic stress disorder. In B. A. van der Kolk, A. C. McFarlane, & L. Weisaeth (Eds.), *Traumatic stress: The effects of overwhelming experience on mind, body and society* (pp. 117–128). New York: Guilford Press.

Brett, E. A. (1993). Classifications of posttraumatic stress disorder in DSM-IV: Anxiety disorder, dissociative disorder, or stress disorder? In J. R. T Davidson & E. B. Foa (Eds.), *Posttraumatic stress disorder: DSM-IV and beyond* (pp. 191–206). Washington, DC: American Psychiatric Press.

Cloitre, M. (1998). Sexual revictimization: Risk factors and prevention. In V. M. Follette, J. I. Ruzek, & F. R. Abueg (Eds.), *Cognitive-behavioral therapies for trauma* (pp. 278–304). New York: Guilford Press.

DePrince, A. P. & Freyd, J. J. (1999). Dissociative tendencies, attention and memory. *Psychological Science, 10*, 449–452.

DePrince, A. P. & Freyd, J. J. (2001). Memory and dissociative tendencies: The role of attentional context and word meaning in a directed forgetting task. *Journal of Trauma and Dissociation, 2,* 67–82.

DePrince, A. P. & Freyd, J. J. (in preparation). Fear, betrayal and posttraumatic symptoms.

Duran, E., Duran, B., Brave Heart, M. Y. H., and Horse-Davis, S. Y. (1998). Healing the American Indian soul wound. In Y. Danieli (Ed.), *International handbook of multigenerational legacies of trauma* (pp. 341–354). New York: Plenum Press.

Elliott, D. M. (1997). Traumatic events: Prevalence and delayed recall in the general population. *Journal of Consulting and Clinical Practice, 65,* 811–820.

Finkelhor, D., & Kendall-Tackett, K. (1997). A developmental perspective in the childhood impact of crime, abuse and violent victimization. In D. Cicchetti & S. L. Toth (Eds.), *Developmental perspectives on trauma: Theory, research and intervention* (pp. 1–32). Rochester, NY: University of Rochester Press.

Foa, E. B., & Kozak, M. J. (1986). Emotional processing of fear: Exposure to corrective information. *Psychological Bulletin, 99*, 20–35.

Follette,V. M. Ruzek, J. I., & Abueg, F. R. (1998). *Cogitive behavioral therapies for trauma.* New York: Guilford Press.

Freyd, J. J. (1994) Betrayal-trauma: Traumatic amnesia as an adaptive response to childhood abuse. *Ethics & Behavior, 4*, 307–329.

Freyd, J. J. (1996). *Betrayal trauma: The logic of forgetting childhood abuse.* Cambridge: Harvard University Press.

Freyd, J. J. (1998). Science in the memory debate. *Ethics & Behavior, 8*, 101–113.

Freyd, J. J. (1999). Blind to betrayal: New perspectives on memory for trauma. *The Harvard Mental Health Letter, 15(12)*, 4–6.

Freyd, J. J. (in press). Memory and dimensions of trauma: Terror may be "all-too-well remembered" and betrayal buried. In J. R. Conte (Ed.), *Child sexual abuse: Knowns and unknowns—A Volume in honor of Roland Summit.* Oakland, CA: Sage Publications

Herman, J. L. (1992). *Trauma and recovery.* New York: Basic Books.

Janoff-Bulman, R. (1992). *Shattered assumptions: Towards a new psychology of trauma.* New York: The Free Press.

Kuhn, T. S. (1970). *The structure of scientific revolutions.* Chicago: University of Chicago Press.

Lifton, N. (1996). *The thematic assessment measurement system: A measurement for systematically tracking the recovery from sexual abuse.* (Doctoral dissertation, Duke University, 1996). Dissertation Abstracts International, 57, 2937.

Meadows, E. A. & Foa, E. B. (1998). Intrusion, arousal, and avoidance: Sexual trauma survivors. InV. M. Follette, J. I. Ruzek, & F. R. Abueg (Eds.), *Cognitive-behavioral therapies for trauma* (pp. 100–123). New York: Guilford Press.

McFarlane, A. C. & de Girolamo, G. (1996). The nature of traumatic stressors and the epidemiology of posttraumatic reactions. In B. A. van der Kolk, A. C. McFarland & L. Weisaeth (Eds.) *Traumatic stress: The effect of overwhelming experience on mind, body and society (129–154). New York: Guilford Press.*

McFarlane, A. C. & van der Kolk, B. A. (1996). Trauma and its challenge to society. In B. A. van der Kolk, A. C. McFarland, & Weisaeth (Eds.), *Traumatic stress: The effects of overwhelming experience on mind, body, and society* (24–46). New York: Guilford Press.

Newman, E., Riggs, D. S., & Roth, S. (1997). Thematic resolution, PTSD, and complex PTSD: The relationship between meaning and trauma-related diagnoses. *Journal of Traumatic Stress, 10*, 197–213.

Putnam, F. W. (1997). *Dissociation in children and adolescents.* New York: Guilford Press.

Roth, S. & Lebowitz, L. (1988). The experience of sexual trauma. *Journal of Traumatic Stress, 1*, 79–107.

Roth, S., & Newman, E. (1991). The process of coping with sexual trauma. *Journal of Traumatic Stress, 4*, 279–296.

Roth, S., Lebowitz, L., & DeRosa, R. R. (1997). Thematic assessment of posttraumatic stress reactions. In J. P. Wilson & T. M. Keane (Eds.), *Assessing psychological trauma and PTSD* (pp. 512–528). New York: Guilford Press.

Rothbaum, B. O., & Foa, E. B. (1996). Cognitive-behavioral therapy for posttraumatic stress disorder. In B. A. van der Kolk, A. C. McFarlane, & L. Weisaeth (Eds.), *Traumatic stress: The effects of overwhelming experience on mind, body and society* (pp. 491–509). New York: Guilford Press.

Shay, J. (1994). *Achilles in Vietnam: Combat trauma and the undoing of character.* New York: Touchstone Books.

van der Kolk, B. A. (1996). The complexity of adaptation to trauma: Self-regulation, stimulus discrimination, and characterological development. In B. A. van der Kolk, A. C.

McFarlane, & L. Weisaeth (Eds.), *Traumatic stress: The effects of overwhelming experience on mind, body and society* (pp. 182–213). New York: Guilford Press.

van der Kolk, B. A., & McFarlane, A. C. (1996). The black hole of trauma. In B. A. van der Kolk, A. C. McFarlane, & L. Weisaeth (Eds.), *Traumatic Stress: The effects of overwhelming experience on mind, body, and society* (pp. 3–23). New York: Guilford Press.

Wagner, A. W., & Linehan, M. M. (1998). Dissociative behavior. In V. M. Follette, J. I. Ruzek, & F. R. Abueg (Eds.), *Cognitive-behavioral therapies for trauma* (pp. 191–225). New York: Guilford Press.

Yalom, I. (1980). *Existential psychotherapy*. New York: Basic Books.

6.

The Assumptive World in the Context of Transference Relationships

A Contribution to Grief Theory

Daniel Liechty

Life is an act of faith. Most of what we do most of the time, and some of what we do all of the time, is done on faith. Acts of faith are so intrinsic to the common sense of daily living that it strikes us as comical when such acts of faith are pointed out to us by skeptics—for example, by philosopher David Hume, who in the eighteenth century pointed out that just because the sun has risen every morning so far, this is not absolute proof it will rise again tomorrow (Hume, 1935). When we act on faith that the sun will rise tomorrow, this is a well-justified act of faith. Nonetheless, it is an act of faith. Even in science and mathematics, all "proofs" are built on other assumptions and axioms for which there are no proofs.

Once the basic point is made that we skate in our daily living on a thin sheet of certainty above a lake of faith, it becomes clear just how integral acts of faith are to normal human existence. At the same time, it must also be recognized that there are multiple levels of faith based on multiple levels of evidence yielding multiple levels of justification for given acts of faith.

Some acts of faith are very well justified. For example, my action based on the faith that when I walk out my front door the ground will not open up and swallow me is justified not only by my repeated experience of walking out my door without event, but also by a wide body of learning concerning geological formations and gravity theory. I know intellectually that there is a minute, statistical possibility that the earth could part just in that time and place where next I set my foot. The probability of that event actually occurring, however, is so small that I am not just being reckless with my life when I ignore it entirely in my daily routine. Toward the other end of the probability scale, the odds are relatively high, given indicators such as my family history, that I could have a myocardial infarction at any time. This possibility comes to mind much more often than the ground swallowing me up, even causing a certain amount of behavioral change in me, though not enough to satisfy either my physician or my wife. Yet even this eventuality is not in my conscious thought at least 99 percent of the time.

We build up a psychological approach in our everyday living that emphasizes safety, routine, and predictability and at the same time deemphasizes danger, chaos, and randomness. I know intellectually that this worldview is an optimistic construct and not an empirical description of reality. Yet it is also true that my optimistically constructed worldview, almost all of the time, allows me to navigate the real world better than I would be able to were I constantly filled with thoughts, however arguably realistic, of what could happen to me at any given moment. This was well understood by philosopher Hans Vaihinger, who in 1923 published a systematic philosophical construction based on the concept of living "as if ..." (Vaihinger, 1952). It is understood no less well by the modern cheerleaders for "positive thinking." It also shows up in the medical field, where it is well accepted that positive expectations on the part of the patient (and maybe also the healer) facilitate positive treatment outcomes. Most recently, the "placebo effect" is being subjected to empirical research and is proving to be at least as therapeutically significant in many areas as pharmaceutical interventions (Blakeslee, 1998). It will be interesting to see how attitudes shift in the ethical proscription against administering placebos after double-blind studies have demonstrated their effectiveness and brain research studies outline a clear, biochemical explanation for the positive outcomes.

Optimism yields positive functional survival benefits (Taylor, 1989). It is therefore understandable that most of the time we are paradigmatic optimists in our assumptive worlds. R. Janoff-Bulman summarized this optimism as consisting of three general assumptions, the maintenance of which to at least some degree is more or less a definition of mental health. The first of these is that the world is a benevolent place: the immediate environment in which we live is friendly toward us as a species and as individuals. Secondly, the world is a meaningful place: the world we live in "makes sense," is just, and reflects orderliness. And finally, the self is worthy: each of us as individuals is able to perceive himself or herself as good, valuable to others, and able to act with significance in the environment (Janoff-Bulman, 1992, pp. 3–25).

Janoff-Bulman demonstrates how devastating it is when force of circumstance undermines this optimistic assumptive worldview. She characterizes the situation of the traumatized individual as that of living in a world of "shattered assumptions." This was aptly drawn upon by T. A. Rando and applied to people experiencing complicated grief and mourning (Rando, 1993). Taken together, we see in the work of these two writers just how desperately people will try to hang on to this assumptive world. Most important for clinical symptom formation, people are often willing to let go of and alter aspects of the third assumption, the worthiness of the self, in order to rescue the first two assumptions, keeping them plausible and intact in the face of adverse circumstances. That is to say, in situations of tragedy or adversity, very large numbers of people would rather view themselves personally as morally evil or in some other way deserving of punishment (thus preserving the notion of just rewards) than entertain the notion that we live in a random universe in which there is neither rhyme nor reason as to why they have suffered from adversity.

This willingness to judge oneself as evil or unworthy, and therefore deserving of what fate has delivered, is noted as often as any phenomenon in the clinical literature. It may be the closest thing we have to a human psychological constant and illustrates the depths of the human need to maintain and protect structures of collective and cultural meaning in human life. Although this move against the self might seem like choosing a Pyrrhic victory, its puzzling nature invites us to pursue an existential analysis of what occurs when the contours of one's assumptive world are threatened by life's events.

As I have tried to understand this maneuver of the human psyche, I have been most impressed by the contribution of Ernest Becker (Becker, 1971, 1973, 1975; Liechty, 1995). Becker examined the logic of transference in the therapeutic relationship within the context of a broad range of social scientific literature. Although he was primarily intending to describe the interaction between a group and its leader, Becker soon saw that the logic of transference applied to many of the relationships in which people engage in society, not only relationships between people but also symbolic relationships, as for example in the relationship between a person and material objects that the person endows with protective, symbolic significance. Thus Becker demonstrated a close connection between the logic of therapeutic transference and wider social phenomena such as religious fetishism and superstitions.

Drawing especially on cultural anthropological literature, Becker outlined five basic questions to which a viable cultural worldview must give answer: What are the innate dispositions of human beings? What is the relationship between human beings and nature? What is the direction in time of the action process? What type of personality is most valued? What is the dominant modality of human relationships (Becker, 1962)? Here Becker was pointing toward a pattern of components very similar to those Janoff-Bulman outlined as necessary for good mental health. What Janoff-Bulman refers to as the assumptive world is in essence the same as what Becker referred to as a cultural worldview.

Becker suggested that our cultural worldview, our constructed assumptive world, itself functions in the manner of a transference relationship. In its very character of normalcy and taken-for-grantedness, it acts as an integral anesthetizing buffer against unconscious and repressed death anxiety, which is inherent in human existence. If this suggestion can be maintained, then what we find in Becker's work is nothing less than a biopsychosocial approach to depth psychology, unveiling the anxious nature of human thought and emotions, which is profoundly unitive of individual and social psychological theory. In this context, viewing object relations as that which in large part constitutes the assumptive world, we see that the function of such relationships is not only to orient us in the world but also to assist us in the psychological denial of the mortal human condition. A closer look at Becker's basic theory may help us better understand some of the contradictions and paradoxes intrinsic to grief and mourning. What observations led Becker to the theory he propounded?

Prompted especially by the work of Otto Rank and Norman O. Brown, Becker made two simple but very important observations about human existence. The first of these was that human beings, like all other animal species, have at least one basic drive, that primary narcissism all living organism share: the basic drive to continue existing. We can call it the survival instinct if that language better suits. Becker noticed that all successful species have, through the evolutionary process, developed a myriad of survival strategies. For most living things low down on the food chain, the central strategy for survival is the ability to procreate in massive numbers. Though in terms of percentage, very large numbers of the individual members of such species end up as food and nourishment for other species, nevertheless they reproduce in such massive numbers that in each generation enough are left over to procreate again and thus ensure the survival of the species.

Moving up the food chain, other kinds of survival strategies are employed. Speed, sharp claws and teeth, impenetrable hides, thick fur, camouflage coloring, and keen eyesight and hearing are just a few of the most obvious of these survival strategies. These are survival mechanisms the human species sorely lacks. Even our best human specimens are relatively slow and thin-skinned; have pitifully weak powers of sensory perception, no claws, no fur, and no camouflage, and produce extremely small litters (at least before the days of fertility drugs). Yet even though our history is still being written, our species arguably has been the most adaptive and successful species on the face of the earth. In an evolutionary eye blink, our species covered the earth, surviving and thriving in climates and conditions as diverse as the planet has to offer. How could this be?

Becker noticed that while in many ways the human species is poorly constructed compared to other species, humans do have one survival mechanism that other species lack: our powerful brain capacity. Brain capacity allowed our species to thrive and eventually dominate other species, which on the physical level are much better adapted to the environment than we humans. Our species is the only species that has the brain capacity for the kind of abstract thinking necessary to create environments that conform to our own specifications and not simply to adapt ourselves to existing environments. That a cave offers shelter from storms and that fire makes things warm is experiential knowledge that might be shared by any number of species. This basic information is only the beginning for humans, however. The human being is able to abstract, to put these two unrelated tidbits of learning together: to imagine a fire within a cave, objectify the self and project the self into that imaginary environment, see that it is good, and then set out to create that environment where it did not before exist. It is this ability to think abstractly, and, collapsing past, present, and future together, to objectify and project the self into not-yet-existing environments that is the source of our success as a species. It is a survival mechanism more powerful than claws, muscles, speed, teeth, or massive procreation could ever be.

Recognition of the central importance of our intellect as our specific species survival mechanism leads to Becker's second simple but very important observation about the human condition. Like all species, we exist. Like very few species, we know that we do exist. But as far as we know, we are the only animal species that exists, knows that it exists, and knows that it knows it exists. In short, we are the only species (as far as we know) that has developed self-consciousness, consciousness of ourselves as objects. And here, said Becker, is the rub. For once we develop self-consciousness and can think of ourselves as objects projected into past, present, and future environments, we very soon run smack into one very sobering fact: we are mortal. We will all die. We will die, we know we will die, and we know we know we will die. What has happened, Becker observed, is that the evolutionary process created in the human species an animal whose very mechanism for survival runs absolutely counter, psychologically speaking, to the primary narcissism that evolution planted in all living things, that first and most deep urge of all living things to continue existing. We are saddled like all species with the overriding urge to live, to continue breathing. But unlike other species, we are well aware from a relatively young age that this is doomed to failure.

★ ★ ★

Becker suggested that *this basic contradiction in our nature is the root source of human anxiety.* The sublimated psychological energy created by this contradiction is in turn the most basic source of human motivation and of human creativity. This mortality anxiety and the concurrent desire for immortality (that is, the denial of death) are the very energy cooking in the unconscious. A significant and growing body of empirical research in social psychology strongly supports the hypothesis that the content of the unconscious is not antisocial sexual or aggressive drives; it is not the will to power and domination; it is not the archetypal structures of the collective unconscious; neither is it simple pleasure or conformity drives. Each of these is there in the human psyche, to be sure. But each in turn can best be understood as manifesting specific applied strategies for expression of that even deeper psychological drive, the denial of death (cf. Greenberg, Solomon, & Pyszczynski, 1997; Solomon, Greenberg, Pyszczynski, 1991, 1998). Since all human beings must face the reality of death as both a physical and a symbolic entity, this formulation accounts for the similarities in human psychology across cultural boundaries while avoiding Jung's mysticism on one hand and becoming mired in Freud's biologism on the other. Grounded in the biological reality of death, both individual psychological response and collective behavior are integral elements of the theory, making it a truly comprehensive biopsychosocial interpretation of human behavior.

The next point to be made is obvious to those who initially encounter Becker's theory, for it is usually the first objection to the theory that springs to mind. Most of us have no ongoing consciousness of fear of death. Most of us never really think much about it. Most of us would not see it as a healthy trait were someone to be preoccupied with constant thoughts and fears of death. These objections are exactly on track to guide us into the depth psychological aspect of Becker's thought. Becker suggested that were we constantly conscious of just how fragile our existence really is (not just that we will die someday, but that it really could happen to any one of us by a thousand different means before even finishing the reading of this essay), we would be psychotically stunned and unable to act. Therefore, the simple forward movement of everyday living presupposes an ability to repress the fact of death from consciousness. Death comes to consciousness at best in small and manageable doses now and then, usually in disguised and symbolic form. Becker's theory brings into play the entire spectrum of ego defenses, showing how the manifest goal of the defense (e.g., maintaining self-esteem) is on a deeper level a defense against mortality awareness (if I can be deflated, defeated, dispensed with, I can also die). Becker interpreted the psychological character types in the same light, that is, as stereotypical strategies for managing mortality anxiety, shielding the symbolic self from confrontation with its own emptiness, its no-thing-ness, its transience, its ultimate limitation, its impermanence—all signifiers of its basic mortality.

The very normalcy of everyday living assumes that most people most of the time are able to employ successfully the array of defense mechanisms against the overwhelmingness of death anxiety. We learn psychological defenses as part of the socialization process itself, finally giving ourselves over to culturally prescribed roles in the assurance that by obedient participation in the transcendently heroic projects of culture itself, we will be worthy of the symbolic immortality that transcending culture bestows (and since we soon recognize that eternal life in the body is not possible, absorption into the objectively larger whole of transcending cultural projects is the best shot we have at immortality). Full explication of the defense mechanisms in Becker's theory cannot be undertaken here. But here we do begin to better comprehend the importance of Becker's enlargement of the mechanism of transference.

In psychoanalytic theory, transference usually refers to the extraordinarily exaggerated sense of power and importance that the patient projects upon the analyst. Transference analysis is fruitful in psychotherapy exactly because it is a door directly into the patient's unconscious conceptions of power and power relationships. Becker's treatment of transference began with this psychoanalytic concept. He then expanded on it by use of key concepts of power, magic, and fetishism current in anthropological literature. Becker painted a picture of transference as a phenomenon occurring not simply within the confines of the analyst's office. Transference occurs whenever an exaggerated sense of power is projected onto any object and then that object is used to cope with and calm an otherwise overwhelming sense of anxiety. Prototypical transference objects are parents and close caregivers, although because they are literally its whole world the infant has no way of knowing that the power it perceives in these people is exaggerated. We see the transference dynamic emerge even more clearly in what Winnicott referred to as *transitional objects*. Such transitional objects may be external material objects, such as a favorite toy or blanket, or even objectified parts of the body itself, such as the thumb. When a man fumbles through his pocket for a rabbit's foot or saint's medallion in times of stress or when an adoring throng of worshipful admirers scream "*Heil!*" to their Führer, transference dynamics (of varying levels to be sure) are at work. That is, people project onto transference objects the power and ability to save and protect them from evil, fear, and anxiety (of loss, separation, annihilation—all psychological symbols of mortality) and then proceed to act toward these objects as if it really did have that power.

What we see in Becker's conception of transference is not limited to a dynamic that happens in therapy (though it encompasses that dynamic also) but rather is a way of life in which we all participate. Human beings spend most of their psychic energy creating and attaching to cultural symbols of immortality that promote an immediate suppression from consciousness the terror that arises from awareness of mortality and through which people vicariously participate in immortality. A viable cultural worldview, that is, the individual and collective assumptive world, provides what Becker called an "immortality ideology" in which people find security and protection from the extreme anxiety-provoking awareness of human mortality. Like the experience of trauma in war or natural disasters, in which the taken-for-grantedness of the assumptive world collapses, the sudden loss of a person who is an especially key figure in the symbolic life of the individual or group may well provoke an emotional reaction that is far more heavily layered than the reaction to the loss of that person alone. It may well provoke an emotional reaction responding to an eruption of one's most basic and vitally repressed material suddenly and brutally exposed to consciousness.

Let us listen to one person's description of a shattered assumptive world.

> I opened the door to my car, swinging my feet out onto the dark asphalt of the driveway. Suddenly I found myself out of balance for a moment, found myself swaying

into the gravel path edged by the shadow yew bushes as if I were going to spill, chin first, onto the ground. I righted myself abruptly, jerked up marionette-style, strings taut again, and heard at that moment—with a sort of auditory hindsight—that I had been screaming, moaning really, but low and powerful, like a train coming through. The sound shocked me more than the dizziness. I had never felt a sound like that in myself before. My husband had just left me, suddenly, mysteriously, and the sound in my body came from the strange rift his leaving had made. Of all the parts of my life that I had just lost—the two of us nested in bed at night, our working hip-to-hip in the narrow kitchen, the family's joking after dinner, elbows sprawled around the plates and glasses—the most startling loss was this, the crack in the spirit, the gyroscope tumbling over, the compass points scattered.

In this recently published recollection, Molly Layton (1998) bravely, graphically, and revealingly recounts her experience at that moment when realization of the loss of her husband brutally forced its way into her consciousness. This passage demonstrates an unusual depth of self-awareness and candor in expressing that awareness. Here Molly acknowledges clearly that she was reacting to more than just the loss of her husband; she was reacting to the loss of that normalcy, the taken-for-granted security that he represented symbolically in her life—the picture of middle-class American family life symbolized in communion at the table, family closeness, communicative intimacy. As the lid is torn off, she swoons in an experience of the earth itself moving, jumping up to swallow her. Like all the horror displayed in the most eerie dream-world episodes of *The Twilight Zone*, she experiences disorientation, dislocation, disembodiment, even dismemberment. Her usual sense of unity between body and spirit, her at-homeness in her body, is fractured into the alien strangeness of depersonalization. She hears her own voice as if it were the voice of another. Her movements are felt not as those of her own volition, but rather as involuntary responses to the will of a puppeteer. She experiences a "crack in the spirit," a fracturing, that is, of the part of the self most often associated symbolically with immortality, with that part of the human being that (it is often insisted) does not die and decay.

Our reaction in reading this passage may be like the reaction I often have reading firsthand accounts of tragic suffering in war or other disasters: I find myself subtly distancing myself as subject from the account as object. That is, I defend myself against the shock and pain expressed in the passage by subconsciously pretending that this does not have to do with me. Yet I do think that moment when Molly's defenses against anxiety were shattered is a moment with which all of us feel connected, for we too have experienced that disorienting terror. It has been experienced, by many of us as a consequence of our own losses, our own shattered compass points, and by all of us in those terrifying dreams when, through the symbols of nightmare, subconscious voices communicate to consciousness the repressed awareness of the fragility of our being.

In my own practice with hospice patients and their families, I found this perspective of immediate and practical value in understanding the interaction between worldview collapse and issues of grief and loss (Liechty 2000). In many American families, parents retain a transference function for the children long after the children are grown and are parents themselves. We would expect that parents would be loved as family members and respected for their sage advice and experience. However, in working with families particularly around the impending death of parents, one sees clearly how often an exaggerated sense of power is projected onto the parental objects and the function that parent has fulfilled within the family system to allow family members to cope with what would otherwise be a potentially overwhelming sense of existential anxiety. In some ethnic groups it tends to be the father who is placed in this role, while in others it may be the mother. Conceivably a family system could be contoured around any family member in this role. The point is, within a given family system, the very stability of the family structure and the normalcy of the family's existence are based on this primitive sense that protection, security, and safety are channeled to the family through a venerated patriarch or matriarch. Although family members would be consciously unaware of the magical reliance on the revered family member, the crushing collapse felt by the family when circumstances force into consciousness the fact of that person's mere mortality will often be as dramatic as any they could experience.

In one particular family I worked with in 1996, it often seemed as though in their remarks they were reading from my script. In the throes of this collapse, the adult male children expressed such feelings as: "I just can't accept this—I always thought Dad would be there somehow. How could this be happening to *Dad?* If this can happen to Dad, what can we really hold on to in life? What is solid? It feels like nothing is really real, and that I am just a shell."

Repeatedly the sentiments expressed by family members, in particular the adult male children of the dying patient, pointed not simply toward grief and pain of loss, but toward a world falling apart. Grief and the pain of loss was for a number of days and weeks actually secondary to a kind of stunned questioning of reality itself, of God and the human place in the universe. During this time, as family members found themselves living in this collapsed assumptive world, normally repressed anxiety would often flare in very primitive emotional outbursts, particularly in the form of feuding and fighting among the adult male children of the family (with wives entering in on the side of each). The need to find someplace to lay blame for everyday mistakes or problems was far out of proportion to the trivial nature of most of these incidents. It appeared clear to me that this need to place blame had little to do with actual circumstances of the everyday events and much to do with a deeply emotional need to reestablish some sense of order and predictability, at least to those areas of life over which these people still imagined a semblance of control.

This understanding of the transferential nature of the assumptive world, gained by a conjunctive reading of R. Bulman-Janoff, T. Rando, and E. Becker, is a significant addition to grief theory and the practice of grief therapy. It starkly underlines the extent to which the assumptive world is a mechanism of defense against the onslaught not so much of grief as an isolated emotion but of the existential anxiety of the human situation itself. Recognition of this transferential aspect in relationships with those significant others who constitute the assumptive world is an important key to deeper understanding of the range of emotional responses therapists find in their patients, especially responses that may seem extremely out of proportion to the situation. This in turn yields some useful suggestions for assessment and intervention for grief counselors and therapists. While these suggestions are not necessarily new, and are already followed intuitively by many practice professionals, this approach serves to ground such practice wisdom in firm, empirically investigated theoretical sources, yielding a solid foundation for understanding why such interventions are important to the therapeutic process. I will limit myself here to just three such suggestions.

First, this perspective suggests that in assessing patients for possible complications in the mourning process, whether that assessment takes place before or after the death or loss has occurred, the counselor or therapist would do well to pay close attention to the magnitude of the role the dying or deceased person has played in the assumptive world of the patient. The loss of one on whom a patient primarily has relied for financial, emotional, familial, and social support signals a higher likelihood of complication than loss in a situation where more diffuse support systems are present. In short, this perspective yields another helpful angle of understanding for assessment of the supporting networks within which a patient functions.

Approaching such assessment in this light more easily allows attention to focus beyond immediate family and friends as integral to the networks of support in which a patient functions. In this context, it is apparent that the depth of love between the patient and the dying or deceased person is not itself an infallible indicator of complications of mourning, nor, conversely, are complications in the mourning process necessarily indicative of the depth of love between the patient and the lost loved one. More likely is that a relationship of concentrated dependence will more adequately signal possible complications. Especially in such cases of concentrated dependence, therapeutic intervention must focus on assisting the patient in diversifying his or her sources of support (Langs, 1997). In initiating this expansion, a key source may be the patient-therapist relationship itself. The overall assumption, however, is that stability in the mental and emotional reconstruction of a newly functioning assumptive world is directly related to the diversity of the sources from which it is constituted. This suggests that therapeutic group work will almost always be the preferred mode of grief therapy. Individual psychotherapy, in conjunction with a good medication consultation, will be most helpful when the mourning process has veered into deep depression or is entangled with an unrelated mental or emotional problem. In general, given this need to expand connective resources in rebuilding and repairing the assumptive world of the patient, therapeutic group work much more clearly models the desired outcome than individual work alone.

Second, viewing the patient's experience of loss within a context of the transferential nature of the assumptive world suggests that the oftentimes extreme verbalization of despair counselors and therapists hear from patients in the initial phases of loss (including thoughts of death and suicide) are not merely emotional exaggerations. The sudden loss of a key figure in one's assumptive world does indeed place one in front of the condition of human mortality with greatly weakened defenses against the terror and anxiety this condition provokes. Lucid and despairing thoughts of death, hopelessness, meaninglessness, and suicide are one intelligible response to this condition. In this light, counselors or therapists will understand that when a patient exhibits such response in the initial phases of loss, it is neither a time for dismissing such expressions as emotional exaggerations nor the moment for overreaction on the part of the counselor or therapist. Active listening, with assurances that such thoughts are themselves normal, will help the patient in the slow process of rebuilding his or her assumptive world.

The assumptive world and the transferential relationships by which it is constituted primarily perform a psychologically defensive function. In its very normalcy, predictability, and taken-for-granted character, it creates a bulwark against the intrusion of existential anxiety. Seen in this context, the complications of grief and mourning may be rooted in misplaced psychological defenses, to be sure. But even more apparent is the grounding of such complications in the breakdown of previously functioning psychological defenses. This is an important point for grief counselors and therapists to grasp, for it implies that for the most part, grief work is aimed toward assisting the client in creating and enhancing functional psychological defenses to replace those shattered by the loss (Firestone, 1994). Viewed in this perspective, the grief therapist will gain a healthy and positive respect for psychological defenses such as denial and displacement, in contrast to the view in much of the psychotherapy literature, which implies that such defenses are barriers to positive therapeutic outcomes. Once it is firmly understood that psychological defenses are absolutely essential to well-functioning mental health (Taylor, 1989; Goleman, 1996) the grief therapist will be better able to tolerate and accept the presence of denial, displacement, and other psychological defense mechanisms, better respect the patient's right to his or her defenses, and be able to better assess such defenses as therapeutic assets in relation to their actual functioning in the life of a particular patient.

Finally, approaching the grief and mourning process in light of the transferential nature of the assumptive world makes it much more apparent that grief and mourning are not issues unrelated or tangential to overall human mental health, to be confined to a very specialized subfield focusing on death and dying. We see here, rather, that the basic issues of grief and the mourning process are *paradigmatic for the human condition itself*. As mentioned above, a growing body of empirical research work strongly suggests that E. Becker was right on target in his suggestion that the energy cooking away in the subconscious is mortality anxiety and that repression of this anxiety is one of the most basic human psychological functions.

When grief and mourning are understood in the context of this theory as the process of rebuilding the transferential, psychologically defensive function of one's assumptive world, involving place, possessions, self-esteem, and moral and religious commitments, in addition to direct human relationships, then we see that for human beings, emotional and spiritual growth is itself a mourning process (Kauffman, 1993; Pletcher, 1995). This brings grief work and grief therapy from the periphery of psychotherapeutic theory and practice directly into its most creative center.

References

Becker, E. (1962). *The birth and death of meaning: A perspective in psychiatry and anthropology.* New York: The Free Press.

Becker, E. (1971). *The birth and death of meaning: An interdisciplinary perspective on the problem of man.* New York: The Free Press.

Becker, E. (1973). *The denial of death.* New York: The Free Press.

Becker, E. (1975). *Escape from evil.* New York: The Free Press.

Blakeslee, S. (October 13, 1998). Placebos prove so powerful even experts are surprised. *The New York Times.*

Firestone, R. W. (1994). Psychological defenses against death anxiety. In R.A. Neimeyer (Ed.), *Death anxiety handbook: Research, instrumentation and application* (pp. 217–241). Washington, DC: Taylor and Francis.

Goleman, D. (1996). *Vital lies, simple truths: The psychology of self-deception.* New York: Touchstone Books.

Greenberg, J., Solomon, S., & Pyszczynski, T. (1997). Terror management theory of self-esteem and cultural worldviews: Empirical assessments and conceptual refinements. In M. Zanna (Ed.), *Advances in experimental social psychology* (Vol. 29) (pp. 61–139). San Diego: Academic Press.

Hume, D. (1935). *Dialogues concerning natural religion.* Oxford: Clarendon Press.

Janoff-Bulman, R. (1992). *Shattered assumptions: Towards a new psychology of trauma.* New York: Free Press.

Kauffman, J. (1993). Spiritual perspectives on suffering the pain of death. In K. J. Doka and J. D. Morgan (Eds.), *Death and spirituality* (pp. 165–170). Amityville, NY: Baywood Publishing Company.

Langs, R. (1997). *Death anxiety and clinical practice.* London: Karnac Books.

Layton, M. (1998). Ripped apart. *Family Therapy Networker, 22(6),* 24–31.

Liechty, D. (1995). *Transference and transcendence: Ernest Becker's contribution to psychotherapy.* Northvale, NJ: Jason Aronson, Inc.

Liechty, D. (2000). Touching mortality, touching strength: Working with dying patients. *Journal of Religion and Health, 39,* 247–260.

Pletcher, G. (1995). Meaning and the awareness of death. In J. Kauffman (Ed.), *Awareness of mortality* (pp. 63–73). Amityville, NY: Baywood Publishing Company.

Rando, T. A. (1993). *The treatment of complicated mourning.* Chicago: Research Press.

Solomon, S., Greenberg, J., & Pyszczynski, T. (1991). A terror management theory of social behavior: The psychological function of self-esteem and cultural worldviews. In M. Zanna (Ed.), *Advances in experimental social psychology* (Vol. 22., pp. 91–159). San Diego: Academic Press.

Solomon, S., Greenberg, J. and Pyszczynski, T. (1998). Tales from the crypt: On the role of death in life. *Zygon: Journal of Religion and Science,* 33 (1), 9–44.

Taylor, S. E. (1989). *Positive illusions: Creative self-deception and the healthy mind.* New York: Basic Books.

Vaihinger, H. (1952). *The philosophy of "as if": A system of the theoretical, practical and religious fictions of mankind.* London: Routledge and Kegan Paul.

7.

A Self-Psychological Study of Experiences of Near Loss of One's Own Life or the Dying or Death of a Close Relative

The Shattered-Fantasy Model of Traumatic Loss

Richard B. Ulman and Maria T. Miliora

This chapter presents psychoanalytic case material illustrating the interconnection that exists between the work of Janoff-Bulman (1985, 1992) on the loss of the assumptive world and that of Ulman and Brothers (1987, 1988) on the shattered-fantasy model of trauma. An examination of traumatic loss reveals a key connection between the fields of traumatology and thanatology. Traumatic loss is defined in terms of a close encounter with death, either a near loss of one's own life or the loss of a close relative.

The self-psychological vantage point we employ aims at an empathic understanding of the unconscious meaning of the near loss of one's own life or the death or dying of another as determined by the psychic disruption of archaic narcissistic fantasies, or self-object fantasies. This chapter provides clinicians and therapists with an illuminating way of understanding and treating the patient suffering a traumatic loss.

The work of Janoff-Bulman is especially valuable because she has focused, to a significant degree, on the phenomenon of grief, mourning, and bereavement following the traumatic loss of a loved one; this dovetails with the viewpoint of Ulman and Brothers. These latter authors have focused on the traumatic and faulty restoration of archaic narcissistic fantasies as evidenced in the form of posttraumatic stress disorder (PTSD) in Vietnam combat veterans as well as survivors of incest and rape. The convergence of the foci of Janoff-Bulman and of Ulman and Brothers serves as a bridge linking our application of the shattered-fantasy model of trauma to experiences of nearly losing one's own life and the death or dying of a close relative.

Three case studies of patients, representative of the interrelationship of traumatology and thanatology, are detailed. These case studies support the hypotheses that (1) experiences of nearly losing one's own life may break down, or psychologically destroy, magical illusions of the self as, for instance, all-powerful, all-knowing, and/or in total control; and (2) experiences of dying, in the form of the death or terminal illness of a close relative or loved one, may undermine illusory views of the external (outside) world as an imaginary domain governed by rationality, orderliness, meaningfulness, intentionality, responsiveness, accountability, fairness, and justice.

Our methodology is based on the representative case study as developed by Spotts and Shontz (1976). We have used this same methodology in our studies of trauma survivors (see Ulman and Brothers, 1987, 1988), addicts (see Ulman and Paul, 1989, 1990, 1992, 2002), patients with panic disorder (Miliora and Ulman, 1996a) and the obsessive-compulsive character (Ulman and Miliora, in submission). The representative case study method is designed as an in-depth exploration of the inner psychological lives of a relatively small number of research subjects. These people have personal life histories that depict, in a graphic manner, the salient features of a much larger group of individuals with similar life histories.

The three case studies, inasmuch as they are representative of a group of patients, allow us to make valid and reliable generalizations about our larger pool of patients, a sample that currently numbers approximately twenty-five. Our representative case study method, with its focus on the intensive rather than the extensive, is particularly well suited to the psychoanalytic study of the unconscious fantasy lives of our research subjects. Moreover, the therapeutic analysis and working through of the PTSD symptoms of our three patients enabled us to first deconstruct and then reconstruct the unconscious meaning of traumatic loss as determined psychologically by the disillusionment of specific fantasies, illusions, and assumptions. (See Miliora and Ulman, 1996b, for a discussion of a psychoanalytic method of first deconstructing the symptoms of certain psychiatric disorders, such as panic and obsessive-compulsive disorder, and then reconstructing the unconscious meaning, as determined psychically by fantasy, of these disorders.)

Review of Literature

There is an enormous and ever-growing body of work on the topics of grief, mourning, and bereavement. The theoretical perspective adopted by Janoff-Bulman is that of academic and empirical psychology, whereas that employed by Ulman and Brothers is psychoanalytic and, more specifically, self-psychological. Janoff-Bulman (1985) argues that "post-traumatic stress disorder is largely attributable to the *shattering* of victims' basic assumptions about themselves and the world" (p. 18, emphasis added). She indicates that three basic assumptions are shattered by traumatic experiences, especially trauma based on experiences of death and dying: "(1) the belief in personal invulnerability; (2) the perception of the world as meaningful and comprehensible; and (3) the view of ourselves in a positive light" (p. 18). These three basic fantasies make up what Janoff-Bulman (1992) labels the "assumptive world" (p. 69).

The assumptive world is, Janoff-Bulman contends, based on "generalizations" that are derived from childhood experiences and then applied to experiences occurring during adulthood. She believes, therefore, that everyone has a tendency to overgeneralize from experiences as children to experiences as adults. In the process, she asserts, people make certain assumptions, or presumptions, about their own nature and that of the world. We would describe this tendency as the fantasy of the "good old days." These are the illusions, we believe, that are shattered by trauma, in particular by traumatic loss.

The traumatic loss of the assumptive world is, in the context of experiences of death and dying, the basis for reactions of grief, mourning, and bereavement. Janoff-Bulman maintains that a person who is unable to reconstruct or reinvent a new assumptive world is vulnerable to a pathological form of grief, mourning, and bereavement. Such a reaction is manifested, she argues, in the dissociative symptoms of PTSD.

Janoff-Bulman (1992, p. 186 n.13) cites the 1988 work of Ulman and Brothers as "related" and similar to her own. Ulman and Brothers presented psychoanalytic case material in support of their central thesis that PTSD is a dissociative (rather than anxiety) disorder. They claim that PTSD is constituted by the shattering and faulty restoration of archaic narcissistic fantasies. Evidence of such psychic devastation exists, they posit, in the form of PTSD patients reexperiencing and numbing symptoms.

These authors define archaic narcissistic fantasies as involving prototypical and imaginary scenarios about the self in relation to the world of self-objects. These phantasmagorical scenes may be about three types of unconscious visions, including (1) the self as exhibited grandly before an admiring, worshipful, and awestruck audience (that is, the mirroring self-object); (2) the self as merged with another imagined as idealized and as being omnipotent and/or omniscient (that is, the idealized self-object); and (3) the self as joined at the psychic hip, so to speak, to an imaginary and identical twin (that is, the twinship or alter ego self-object).

From a self-psychological perspective, these illusory scenes may be thought of as being representative of the three major forms of archaic narcissism, namely the mirroring of grandiosity, the idealization of another as an omnipotent and/or omniscient presence, and the twinning with another as an alter ego.

In their psychoanalytic treatment of combat, incest, and rape survivors, Ulman and Brothers found that such archaic narcissistic fantasies were utterly deprived of their illusory meaning. Thus, the victims of trauma were deprived, either temporarily or permanently, of the prior status of these self-object fantasies as psychic organizers of subjective experience. In line with Janoff-Bulman, Ulman and Brothers contend that such fantasies, like the assumptive world, must be restored in some shape or form in order for a trauma victim to recover successfully from PTSD.

The pioneering work of Lifton (1967, 1968, 1973, 1982) offered numerous studies constituting the foundational basis for any theoretical synthesis of the fields of traumatology and thanatology. Lifton, in documenting the traumatic impact of death ("the death imprint") on the lives of survivors of various catastrophic disasters, has paved the way for all of us who have followed in his footsteps. In particular, we are building on and providing a self-psychological version of Lifton's (1988) concept of the "traumatized self" (p. 9). Lifton (1988, p. 11) is quite emphatic about distinguishing his notion of the self, which is traumatized by the imprinting of death, from the Kohutian and self-psychological version of the self (in relation to self-object). However, Lifton's distinction notwithstanding, we believe that the two notions of the self are actually quite compatible. Consequently, in contradistinction to Lifton, we argue that they need not be so sharply contrasted.

Important to theoretical and empirical support of our position is research focusing on the meaning of traumatic loss in the context of its impact on narcissism and the self, or self-experience. Horowitz, Wilner, Marmar, and Krupnick

(1980), in their study of patients who were survivors of traumatic loss, "found that troublesome preexistent self-images and role relationship models were common precursors to pathological grief" (p. 1159). These authors employ a theoretical perspective that anticipates our own self-psychological viewpoint. They hypothesize: "To submerge [a] traumatic view of the needy self abandoned by a caretaker, the patient developed a role relationship model in which the other served not as supplier but as stabilizer of the strength of the self." They continue: "With recognition of the death, the patient was forced to once again contemplate his vulnerability" (p. 1160).

Several psychoanalytic studies on death and mourning have been conducted by self-psychologists. Shane and Shane (1990), for example, report on a self-psychological analysis of an adult patient who lost a parent early in life. They stress the narcissistic damage that occurred to this patient, as a child, as a result of the loss of the self-object functions of the deceased parent. These authors contend that the loss of the mirroring self-object functions of a parent affects a "child's sense of power and omnipotence" (p. 118), whereas the loss of the idealizing self-object function of a parent may weaken a child's "sense of comfort and security" (p. 118).

The works of Hagman (1995a, 1995b, 1996a, 1996b), another self-psychologist, are important to our argument for two reasons. First, he places great importance on the role of (unconscious) fantasy in his self-psychological understanding of the mourning of the death of a loved one. And second, in the course of his psychoanalytic therapy with patients in such self-states of mourning, he works clinically with fantasy.

Clinical

In this section of the chapter we present three representative case studies illustrative of our self-psychological understanding of and approach to analytic therapy with patients suffering from traumatic loss or the loss of the "assumptive world." The cases illustrate the ways in which the unconscious meaning of such traumatic loss—either in the form of an experience of nearly losing one's own life and/or an experience of the dying or death of a close relative—may be determined by the shattering and faulty restoration of archaic narcissistic fantasies. The presentation of these cases provides analytic data in support of our two hypotheses concerning the loss of narcissistic illusions, which in turn may trigger the disillusionment of heretofore undetected imaginings about the nature of the self and the world.

Case 1: Grant's Near Loss of His Own Life

The case of Grant illustrates the ways in which the traumatic disillusionment of an archaic grandiose fantasy determined the unconscious, narcissistic meaning of the near loss of his own life occurring as a result of a plane crash. (We believe that grandiosity is archaic to the degree to which it has failed to undergo sufficient developmental transformation and is, therefore, in a state of developmental arrest.)

Late one night, the therapist received an alarming phone message: Grant had crash-landed his plane, almost killing not only himself but his adopted son as well as the latter's girlfriend, both of whom had been passengers on the plane. A close friend of Grant's had left a message on the therapist's answering machine about the crash. According to the friend, Grant had run out of fuel; consequently, he was forced to make an emergency landing in which the plane crashed into a field. Apparently Grant had lost control of the plane and had driven it nose first into an embankment. Not only was Grant badly injured and nearly killed, but his son and the latter's girlfriend also suffered serious injuries. In fact, all three of them required emergency surgery and weeks of hospitalization, followed by months and months of physical rehabilitation.

This case presents an example of the psychoanalysis of PTSD symptoms, and more specifically numbing symptoms, as a means of empathically grasping how a life-threatening accident shattered an archaic narcissistic fantasy. This narcissistic illusion had been central to organizing the unconscious meaning of Grant's self-experience. In the course of analytic therapy with Grant, we discovered how this core fantasy organized Grant's unconscious experience of himself. It defined his sense of his own personal greatness, uniqueness, specialness, and grandeur. We demonstrate that, unconsciously, Grant was unable to restore this grandiose fantasy, which was central to his assumptive world, and that this faulty restoration contributed to the narcissistic meaning of the trauma.

Finally, we illustrate the therapeutic ways in which Grant was helped to work through the symbolically encoded meaning of his PTSD symptoms. In the process, he modified his grandiose vision of himself. At the same time, he revised the unconscious meaning of the trauma as it had been determined psychically by the loss of a phantasmagorical vision of himself.

Early Phase of Therapy

Grant, a divorced white male now in his mid-sixties, is a college professor in an academic field related to medicine. (When he entered therapy, he was a nonprac-ticing physician.) Approximately thirteen years ago, he entered analytic therapy because of severe depression stemming from a chronically bad marriage. He has remained in therapy during this entire period on a twice-a-week basis.

As the early phase of the therapy unfolded, the following picture emerged of Grant's personal history. The only son of hardworking, stern, and very unemo-tional parents, Grant had lost a young sister from spinal meningitis when he was only four years old. After the death of his sister, Grant said that he and his parents never uttered her name again and that they never talked about nor even mentioned her death.

Grant graduated from college, then medical school. Subsequently, he pursued a career as a medical researcher rather than practicing clinical medicine. In pursu-ing his research career, Grant suffered from what has been referred to as the "Nobel prize complex" (Tartakoff, 1966). According to Grant, he did not feel that it was grand and glorious enough to work as a senior medical researcher at a prestigious institution of higher learning. In this regard, he spoke exultingly of his prized daydreams of actually winning the Nobel prize in medicine.

Given the extremely grandiose nature of Grant's expectation of becoming a Nobel prize winner, it was not at all surprising that he was very upset with himself as a result of having not succeeded in garnering this coveted prize. Interestingly, at about this same time, he conceded that he began what became a pattern of extramarital affairs. Unconsciously, Grant had decided that if he could not win the Nobel prize, then at least he could win the hearts (and bodies) of a series of attractive, beautiful, and intelligent women. Apparently, Grant imagined that, as if by magic, a bevy of beauties would compensate for the absence of the desired Nobel prize.

As part of Grant's unconscious fantasy life, he imagined that becoming a Don Juan would serve as an alternative means of living out his grandiose fantasy of professional fame and acclaim. Grant fancied that his amorous conquests would allow him to puff up himself, thus reinflating his deflated sense of archaic grandiosity. This narcissistic deflation resulted from his subjectively perceived professional shortcomings and failures. In Grant's fantasy world, he imagined that he could substitute adoring woman as mirroring self-objects, thus successfully replacing professional colleagues as an awestruck and worshipful audience.

Eventually, Grant left medical research and pursued a career at a first-rate university as a tenured professor in a field related to his background in medicine. As a professor, Grant took foolhardy risks, which presaged his tragic error in judgment as the pilot of the doomed plane. In a way most cavalier, he took several female graduate students as lovers. It seemed that he was oblivious to the possible negative effects that his amorous adventures might have on his reputation and job. Instead, he reveled in these sexual encounters with these young women, literally fornicating with them on the floor of his office.

Grant was flying high, so to speak, fueled psychically by his grandiose fantasies of himself as an irresistible Don Juan. He imagined himself as the seducer par excellence of the most beautiful and sexy female graduate students. At the lofty psychic heights to which Grant's archaic grandiosity carried him, he envisioned himself as having achieved such a grand stature that nothing and nobody could hold him down. He had become a captive of his own phantasmagorical vision of himself. As such a captive, he imagined himself in the context of a flying act as a sexual conquistador of unparalleled potency. He also fancied that he had launched himself into a narcissistic orbit in which he circled high above the world of mere mortals.

Middle Phase of Therapy

During this middle phase of the therapy, the analyst attempted to empathize with Grant's narcissistic desire for an archaic mirroring self-object. On the basis of this empathic stance, the therapist hoped that unconsciously Grant would form a transference fantasy of the therapist as a mirroring self-object. Such a self-object fantasy might transferentially alleviate the symptoms of Grant's empty/depleted depression, including suicidality. However, the antidepressant effect of the transference fantasy was limited. (See Ulman and Paul, 2002 for a discussion of the various "psychopharmacotherapeutic" effects of different self-object transference fantasies.)

Grant needed more than the therapy alone could offer in the way of providing for archaic mirroring of his grandiose fantasy. So he turned to an extra-analytic source of narcissistic nourishment and sustenance. Many years in the past, Grant, as a physician in the military, had done some flying in the air force. Grant spoke glowingly in sessions of having been bitten again by the flying bug. He returned to flying with a frenzy expressive of a narcissistic bliss that in recent years had been sorely missing from his life. He took up flying lessons and was soon taking long trips, excursions that, in hindsight, were well beyond his flying abilities as a pilot.

In a fashion typical of narcissistic denial, Grant paid little attention to the dangers incumbent upon exceeding his flying abilities. Impulsively, he literally flew ahead. Grant imagined that he could make up for lost time, thus becoming in no time a flying ace. Having just received a beginner's flying license, Grant, in an act of being a true daredevil, flew off into the wide blue yonder.

In sessions, Grant recounted, in great detail and with great gusto, his various flying adventures. Failing to heed the therapist's warnings about the dangers of exceeding his limits, Grant soared, literally and figuratively, unrestrained and unburdened through the skies. In the process, he reinflated his previously flagging and sagging sense of archaic grandiosity. Unconsciously, Grant was operating on the basis of a narcissistic illusion of personal greatness that provided him with a blissful feeling of well-being. This archaic narcissistic fantasy was similar in nature and function to the earlier one Grant had entertained of being a Don Juan and sexual conquistador.

The therapist, despite his capacity as a mirroring self-object, could not provide Grant with a frame within which to adequately and safely contain his rapidly and ever-expanding sense of greatness and grandeur. In his own mind, Grant had reduced the therapist to a mere spectator. As such, the therapist was forced to sit by idly as Grant grandly exhibited himself without any restraint.

Recent Phase of Therapy

Following the plane crash, Grant returned to therapy almost immediately after he completed his physical rehabilitation. At first, he spoke reluctantly, and only with considerable prodding from the therapist, about his near loss of life. With a sense of resignation, he gave the following account of the events leading up to the accident.

Grant had concocted a grand scheme: he would fly his son as well as the son's girlfriend from a local airport in New England, where the plane was hangared, to a distant southern college to which his son had applied. With great exasperation Grant related that his son was late as usual, thus delaying the takeoff. Blinded by narcissistic rage, Grant took off with only one of the two fuel tanks filled. He said that he had reasoned to himself as follows: at some point in the flight he could take on additional fuel by landing at an airport well within the flying range afforded him with just one tank of gas.

Unfortunately, Grant did not take into consideration the possibility of bad weather and the resulting necessity of making changes in his flight plan. And, as fate would have it, he did run into a storm. He was forced to go around the bad weather, thus necessitating a totally unfamiliar route. Flying with only one tank of fuel, Grant eventually ran out of gas in midair, and made a crash landing.

On Grant's part, there was considerable narcissistic resistance to talking about the accident, resistance that was motivated unconsciously by the desire to avoid a sense of shame. In addition, Grant was quite amnesic about the events immediately preceding the plane crash. Physically, the amnesia was caused by a serious concussion, which Grant had suffered when the plane hit the embankment. Psychologically, the amnesia was also a symptom of a full-blown case of PTSD.

From a clinical perspective, numbing symptoms were the most prominent aspects of Grant's PTSD. Slowly, Grant recovered memories of the events immediately leading up to the accident. However, he spoke about the traumatic event with little or no affect, evidencing almost no emotion. In fact, he described the terrifying moments just prior to crashing, and shortly thereafter, when he regained consciousness, as if he were talking about the accident as having happened to someone other than himself.

In a state of dissociation, which was characterized by both depersonalization and derealization, Grant entertained an unconscious fantasy of the accident as having never happened to him; instead, he imagined that it had befallen someone else. (See Arlow, 1966, for a discussion of the nature of unconscious fantasy in determining a state of dissociation marked by depersonalization and derealization. See also Arlow, 1969a, 1969b.) Perhaps even more shockingly, Grant showed almost no remorse, regret, or guilt about the fact that he had been directly responsible for serious and permanent injury to both of his two young passengers.

The unconscious fantasy that supported Grant's dissociation and denial was in the service of attempting to restore his shattered sense of archaic grandiosity. Unconsciously, Grant was responding to his near loss of life as he had learned to do in the earlier, developmental context of his sister's death. Thus he sought to put the accident out of his mind by simply not talking about it. It appeared that Grant imagined that if he succeeded in putting the accident out of his conscious awareness, then he could disavow the meaning and reality of the event. (See Basch, 1981, on the distinction between the unconscious defense mechanisms of denial and disavowal.)

Gradually, the therapeutic analysis and working through of the PTSD symptoms revealed the unconscious and narcissistic meaning of the trauma. Grant's grandiose fantasy of himself had been smashed up, just as had the plane and all its passengers. Narcissistically, he was mortified by an undeniable and irrefutable fact: that he had once again used extremely poor judgment and had been negligent. However, in this instance, his error in judgment nearly cost him his life as well as the lives of others near and dear to him. He was consumed narcissistically by a mortifying sense of shame, which stemmed from the humiliation and embarrassment of feeling exposed as one who was a danger to both himself and others.

Grant had failed in his unconscious attempt to restore, by a "denial in fantasy" (see Freud, 1966), his traumatically shattered sense of personal greatness. This was the narcissistic meaning of the accident and an experience of nearly losing his life. In a state of narcissistic denial, Grant refused unconsciously to accept the actuality of the plane crash. He cut off or numbed out (that is, canceled out) all feelings associated with this traumatic event. Having broken through this numbed-out and dissociated state with the help of therapy, Grant became more introspective and thus began to grasp the narcissistic meaning of the trauma. The unconscious meaning of Grant's near loss of his own life centered not on that trauma nor, for that matter, on the near death of his son and the latter's girlfriend; instead, it involved the loss of Grant's grandiose fantasy of himself, a fantasy that was at the heart of his assumptive world.

Without this core fantasy, Grant was a total and complete stranger to himself; that is, he was in a state of dissociation characterized by depersonalization. As part of working through the numbing symptoms of his PTSD, Grant began a long overdue process of psychological growth. He reorganized himself psychically on the basis of a vision of himself that was now, as a result of therapy, less phantasmagorical and more reality-based. In developing a more realistic and adaptive view of himself, Grant unconsciously replaced the loss of his grandiose fantasy with a more developmentally mature sense of himself.

Three factors attested to this therapeutic process of self-transformation. First, Grant extricated himself from unhealthy relationships with both his wife and a mistress. Subsequently, he established a healthy relationship with a new and mature girlfriend. Second, he gave up flying, and instead he took up horseback riding. The latter represented a far more suitable, and certainly safer, means of giving expression to a healthy form of grandiosity. And third, Grant took a major and bold leap in his professional life: he managed to get the training and experience necessary for him to take up for the first time the clinical practice of medicine.

Case 2: Huck's Experience of Nearly Losing His Own Life and His Experience of the Death of His Mother

Huck is a transition case positioned midway between the cases of Grant (just discussed) and Marianne (to be discussed next): the former is an example of an experience of nearly losing one's own life, whereas the latter is an instance of the dying of a loved one. In contrast to both of these cases, Huck was involved in a tragic automobile accident, one that almost took his life and did, in fact, take the life of his mother. In comparison to Grant, for whom as a youngster the death of his baby sister appears not to have been traumatic, for Huck losing his mother at a relatively young age (he was ten years old when she was killed) did, indeed, constitute a "massive trauma" (Krystal, 1971; Krystal and Niederlands, 1968). And in comparison to Marianne, who currently is experiencing the dying process of her twin sister, Huck was still a youngster at the time when his mother was killed in a car in which he was also a passenger.

Huck is a transitional case in another way, too. The narcissistic meaning of Grant's loss was organized unconsciously in terms of the traumatic loss of a grandiose fantasy. Marianne's is organized unconsciously in terms of the traumatic loss of a fantasized twinship.

Huck, in contrast to both Grant and Marianne, is representative of a case in which there is the traumatic loss of a fantasy of merger with an idealized self-object (his mother). This traumatic loss resulted in the pathological alteration (or transmogrification) of both Huck's self-experience and his experience of the world, (that is, his assumptive world), which he had imagined as the symbolic equivalent of an empathic self-object milieu.

Early Phase of Therapy

Huck, a recently divorced white male in his mid-forties, has been in analytic therapy on a twice-a-week basis for approximately six years. Huck entered therapy ostensibly to deal with serious emotional difficulties resulting from long-term marriage problems. During the early phase of the therapy Huck separated from and then divorced his wife.

Following Huck's divorce, he adopted the lifestyle of a lone wolf; he lived alone and kept to himself. He maintained an emotional stance that ensured he would not form any new relationship with a female companion.

Huck works extremely hard running a trade-oriented business of his own. In the context of his work life, he takes great pride in his self-sufficiency and independence. He likes to imagine that he needs nobody and requires nothing from anyone. He related daydreams about taking care of all of his needs on his own without the assistance of anyone else. Huck has an illusion that he owes nothing to anyone, and nobody owes him anything.

During the early phase of the therapy, Huck related in vague, fuzzy, and hazy terms the barest details of the trauma surrounding the car accident. With little affect or emotion in his voice he recounted that on a cold, snowy night, Huck and his parents were all on their way to see a movie. Huck's father, who had been drinking moderately that evening, was driving the family car. Huck was sitting in the front seat, safely tucked between his father and mother. Suddenly, and without any warning, the car hit a patch of black ice. His father lost control of the car, and it slid off the road, slamming front end first into a huge oak tree.

Huck was knocked unconscious; several minutes later, after regaining consciousness, he discovered himself in a pool of blood on the floor of the car with his mother's body slumped over him. His father was not seriously injured; he had hit the steering wheel, which stopped him from being thrown violently into the dashboard or windshield.

Huck's father managed to pull Huck and his mother out of the tangled mess. He then waved down a passing car and summoned emergency aid. Huck and his mother were rushed by ambulance to a nearby hospital, where they both received emergency medical treatment.

Slowly and over time, the therapist managed to help Huck to remember more of the emotionally laden details surrounding the accident. For instance, Huck recalled that both he and his mother were placed on hospital gurneys, where they lay side by side for what seemed to Huck like an eternity. In addition to a severe concussion, Huck had sustained serious injuries to his face and mouth. One of his eyes had been knocked completely out of its socket, his nose had been smashed to the side of his face, and his entire mouth had been ripped open from the inside of his gum line right down to his lower jaw.

Huck referred to himself as a "bloody mess." However, as Huck described these details, he said, with a hint of black humor, that, compared to his mother, he had been the relatively lucky one! The emergency medical team worked frantically to save his life by stopping his profuse bleeding; unfortunately, however, they lost the battle to save his mother's life.

Later, Huck learned that his mother had sustained massive head injuries as a result of being thrown against the windshield. Again with a note of gallows humor, Huck indicated that upon arrival at the ER his mother was DOA. Thus, in reality, she had been lying for quite a while next to him on the hospital gurney as a dead and lifeless corpse.

Trying to hold back his tears, Huck stressed his conviction that instinctively and intentionally his mother had placed herself between him and the dashboard and the windshield. In true idealized fashion, Huck believed firmly that she sacrificed her own life in order to protect her little boy.

Following the accident, Huck went to a physical rehabilitation center, where he spent several months recovering from his life-threatening injuries. He said that he was actually fortunate to have survived. Surgeons saved his eye and repaired the massive physical damage to his mouth, teeth, gums, and jaw.

There was no doubt, based on Huck's more complete accounting of the accident, that he had been through a traumatic event, one that involved both nearly losing his own life and the loss of a parent. Yet the unconscious (and narcissistic) meaning of the trauma remained, for some time, more of a mystery. Nonetheless, early in the therapy it was possible to make a definitive diagnosis of chronic (rather than acute) PTSD. The passage of so much time notwithstanding, Huck still suffered from the dissociative symptoms of PTSD. His reexperiencing symptoms consisted of both intrusive, daytime thoughts as well as flashbacks. He did not remember, however, having had any recurrent nightmares, nor, for that matter, did he recall having had any dreams that involved his mother.

In addition to the reexperiencing symptoms, Huck also suffered from PTSD numbing. As was true in the case of Grant, Huck spoke initially of the traumatic accident as if he were talking about an event that had happened to someone else. The PTSD numbing and reexperiencing symptoms were part of a chronic state of dissociation involving both depersonalization as well as derealization. Unconsciously, Huck had constructed a fantasy system, or an assumptive world, the meaning of which can be translated as follows: "This event did not happen to me, and, in fact, it did not happen at all! Rather, it's all just a bad dream; I will awake soon and everything will be okay!"

Middle Phase of Therapy

As the therapy progressed, the therapist confirmed the original diagnosis of PTSD, without, however, any further success at understanding the narcissistic meaning of the traumatic loss. As a result, the therapist could not help Huck come to terms with the traumatic meaning of his loss as it affected both his experience of himself and his immediate social (self-object) milieu.

From an analytic point of view, it became clear that unconsciously Huck was resisting the formation of an idealizing self-object transference. Clinical evidence of this resistance to the transference was present in a very negative attitude on Huck's part toward the therapist, whom Huck felt he could not trust, rely on, or depend upon.

In analyzing this resistance, the therapist communicated to Huck his empathic understanding of Huck's unconscious dread of ever again putting his trust in a person whom he depended upon as he had his mother (see Ornstein, 1974, 1991 on the dread to repeat and the hope for a new beginning). The therapist's empathic communication enabled Huck to start the difficult process of rediscovering and remembering the deeply buried emotions he had felt for his mother before she was killed.

Prior to his mother's death, Huck recalled that he had been a painfully shy and introverted little boy. Huck described himself as a child who was always afraid and frightened of people; in fact, he emphasized that he felt intimidated by just about everyone with whom he came into contact. In stark and dramatic contrast to himself as a little boy, Huck remembered his mother as being extremely outgoing, extroverted, and gregarious.

A picture emerged of Huck's mother as an idealized maternal presence with whom he felt merged in fantasy. As his imaginary go-between, she functioned as an idealized self-object. Her fantasized existence as such an omnipotent presence made it possible for Huck to interact somewhat more successfully with other people.

With Huck's mother as his personal emissary to the world, he felt less self-conscious and more secure as well as confident. Imagining his mother as literally by his side, Huck managed to venture forth more boldly into the world. This was the intersubjective context (or self/self-object matrix) in which Huck developed some initial ability to conduct himself as a semiautonomous agent in relation to the outside world.

The Recent Phase of Therapy

The analysis of Huck's resistance to the idealizing self-object transference opened the way to the therapeutic process of reconstructing the narcissistic meaning of the trauma surrounding the car crash. Eventually, Huck trusted the therapist in a way that could be said to approximate the pattern of trust that likely existed between Huck and his mother. From an empathic perspective, the parallel pattern of trust was based on the fact that, notwithstanding Huck's initial and grave misgivings about the trustworthiness of the therapist, the latter had proved to be very instrumental to Huck in helping him to extricate himself from a marriage that he felt had been a travesty for almost seventeen years. In this intersubjective context, Huck began to talk about the therapist in a different way than he had in the past. His present references to the therapist indicated the presence in Huck's unconscious of a transference fantasy of the latter as an imaginary functionary who served in a self-object capacity similar to that of his idealized mother. In other words, this was analogous to the self-object functioning of Huck's mother.

Huck imagined the therapist as an idealized self-object in whose presence he had been able to resolve a previously unsolvable problem. Thus, Huck seemed to fantasize about the therapist as a self-object replacement for his mother. Imagining the therapist/mother as once again by his side, Huck felt empowered and strong enough to navigate more successfully through the inevitable crises of separating from and then divorcing his wife.

In the emergence of a series of dreams about his mother, there was striking clinical evidence of Huck's transference fantasy of the therapist as a self-object reincarnation of his dead mother. (Interestingly, these were the first dreams involving his mother that Huck could recall.) In one of these dreams, Huck indicated that he was back at his high school, where he was attending his senior prom. He was dancing with his mother, who had returned, as if by magic, from the dead.

In associating to this dream, Huck connected his mother with the therapist in that he experienced both of them as a guiding and reassuring presence in his life. Huck also associated dancing with his mother at the prom with his renewed confidence and security in appearing in public before other people. In the dream, Huck noted that he did not feel any of his usual tinges of self-consciousness in such a situation.

Apparently Huck had set up the therapist, in his unconscious mind, as a self-object who functioned narcissistically as an imaginary substitute for his dead mother. However, in making such a self-object substitution, Huck unwittingly set off a paradoxical reaction within himself: unconsciously, he dreaded the repetition of the traumatic loss of this idealized self-object presence, and thus he resisted any conscious awareness of the similarity between the self-object functioning of the therapist and his mother.

The transference resistance (in contrast to the resistance to the transference) was also fueled for Huck by the unconscious meaning of the disastrous outcome of his marriage. Huck and the therapist realized together that unconsciously Huck had set up his wife as a fantasized replacement for his dead mother. There were several factors that helped account for this joint realization. First, his wife was already the mother of a young daughter (Huck's stepdaughter); then she quickly became the mother of his own biological daughter. Both of these factors were important in the unconscious process in which Huck imagined his wife as a maternal presence of great power and significance. Unconsciously, he fantasized that his wife would serve in the same self-object capacity as had his mother prior to her death.

Understandably, Huck's wife did not empathically grasp the narcissistic meaning of the role to which he had assigned her in the psychic world of his unconscious fantasy life. Thus, at the beginning of therapy, Huck had already been disappointed by one imaginary replacement for his mother, that is, his wife. Yet despite his initial dread-based resistance to the transference, Huck eventually did create an unconscious fantasy of the therapist as another maternal substitute.

At this point in the still ongoing therapy, the following picture has emerged of the narcissistic meaning for Huck of his experience of nearly losing his own life as well as that of the traumatic loss of his beloved mother. Prior to the accident, Huck had been organized unconsciously on the basis of a powerful self-object fantasy of merger with an idealized maternal presence. This archaic narcissistic fantasy was central to how Huck experienced both himself and his immediate surroundings, the latter functioning, to some degree, as an empathic self-object milieu.

Without his mother, Huck lost this "central organizing fantasy" (Nurnberg & Shapiro, 1983). In the absence of this fantasy, his whole inner world was devastated. He retreated from the outer world, populated by other people, and existed for a long time (that is, until his marriage) in his own private fantasy world. On an unconscious level, the loss for Huck of the self-object fantasy of being merged with an idealized maternal presence constituted the narcissistic meaning of both his experience of nearly losing his own life and the experience of the death of his mother.

Only now, in the intersubjective context of his current therapy, has Huck begun the long-overdue process of once again organizing himself psychically on the basis of an idealized self-object fantasy. In other words, he is establishing a new basis and a new set of premises for his assumptive world. However, in the present situation, the fantasy has arisen in an analytic setting in which it can undergo therapeutic modulation and tempering.

Case 3: Marianne's Experience of Her Twin's Dying

Marianne, a forty-four-year-old married woman and the mother of two latency-aged boys, owns and manages a successful sales business that employs about ten people. She entered analytic therapy on a weekly basis about four years ago. During the third year of treatment, Marianne's twin sister, Meg, was diagnosed with inoperable lymphatic cancer. Meg is herself a mother of three children and the only family member with whom Marianne enjoyed a close relationship. It was discovered that Meg's cancer had metastasized. The physicians who were treating Meg estimated that she had only a few months to live. Marianne reacted to the news of her twin's imminent death by manifesting symptoms associated with PTSD—more specifically, numbing.

Early Phase of Therapy

Marianne described her family in a manner that underscored the propensity of her parents and siblings to suffer from a number of serious forms of emotional illness. Marianne emphasized that among her five siblings she was the only one who had not been diagnosed as suffering from a psychiatric disorder.

Marianne admitted that she did not like or respect her parents; she acknowledged an equal degree of disrespect toward most of her siblings. She insisted that she was different from her family not only in being mentally sound but also in regard to setting and achieving goals, having a sense of personal responsibility for her life, and enjoying material success. In relating her feelings and dreads about her family, Marianne seemed to be stressing that she did not want to be like them. She experienced some degree of narcissistic mortification in regard to any sense of twinship or kinship with her family, including her fraternal twin sister, Meg.

Marianne explained that she experienced extreme ambivalence even in the case of Meg. On one hand, Marianne loved Meg more than any other family member, speaking to her by phone every day and giving her money and gifts. Marianne characterized her relationship with Meg as providing her with some sense of belonging to her family (that is, some sense of twinship). On the other hand, Marianne was angry with Meg for allowing herself and her children to live in abject poverty and without adequate health care.

In addition to her concern about the possibility of being stricken, like all other members of her family, with mental illness, Marianne feared becoming poverty-stricken as were her parents and her twin sister. Her successful business notwithstanding, Marianne was consumed with narcissistic mortification emanating from a dreaded fantasy of losing everything and living in squalor. This mortifying fantasy scenario derived from her early experiences of growing up in a lower-middle-class family that provided little in the way of material comforts. In fact, Marianne related that she had not been given adequate toys and clothing even when she was a child; later, as an adolescent, she was not provided with the opportunity to go to college. Marianne described the level of familial poverty as exemplified by paint peeling off the walls of her family home, which she described derisively as dilapidated.

To some extent, Marianne was organized unconsciously by a blissful version of a grandiose fantasy of being a big shot and a high roller. This narcissistic fantasy was the flip side of the dreaded fantasy of being poor and living in squalor. Paradoxically, although dreading poverty, Marianne spends most of her earnings, setting aside almost no money to safeguard her financial future.

In addition to her early life, an existence that gave her little in the way of material comfort, Marianne reported that her parents had provided almost no emotional support. She described her mother as frequently "losing it," that is, screaming at and terrorizing the children, while her father remained silent and sat passively on the sidelines. Marianne recollected that she was the "good child," the high achiever, the strong one. Because her parents were seemingly preoccupied with her siblings, all of whom already were evidencing signs of emotional distress, Marianne claimed she never received much attention from them. In other words, she felt her parents were completely unempathic to her unconscious need for them to function narcissistically as mirroring self-objects.

As a child, Marianne unconsciously learned to cut herself off (that is, dissociate) from feelings and, hence, become numb to the emotional pain she experienced as a member of her family. She recounted that one of the ways in which she accomplished what amounted to a form of dissociation was to immerse herself in the Sears-Roebuck catalog. She imagined herself as being one of the models pictured in the catalog. She fantasized wearing the clothes that the models wore and living their glamorous life, an existence that she imagined as being much more exciting and fulfilling than her own.

Marianne explained that she "lost herself" in the catalog and created an imaginary existence for herself. In her make-believe world, that is, her assumptive world, she could entertain the illusion of being safely removed from the pain associated with her family.

Moreover, Marianne described how her parents had contributed to creating a sense that she and Meg were unequal twins (or halves). According to Marianne, her twin was considered the better half with regard to physical appearance and activities, whereas Marianne was thought to be the better half concerning intellectual pursuits.

In her activities as an adult, Marianne noted that she sought to be different from her family in terms of both material success and mental health. In the familial context of her ambivalent kinship relationship with her parents and siblings (including her twin sister, Meg), Marianne's business success apparently enabled her to envision herself as the better half. In stark contrast, she imagined her family members as lesser halves. However, in the area of physical appearance, Marianne continued to experience herself, relative to her twin, as the lesser half.

During the early course of therapy, it became clear that Marianne did not experience her feelings as emotions, but rather somatized them. These somatized emotions manifested as gastrointestinal symptoms. The therapist worked with Marianne to help her feel her emotions more directly and immediately, and, as a result, to integrate the emotional meaning of her experience as a mental content of her mind.

Middle Phase of Therapy

When Marianne first learned that Meg was terminally ill, she was frightened and sad. "What will I do without the one person in my family with whom I have a sense of connection?" she lamented. Her lament points to Marianne's feeling that her sense of connection to her family had been mediated by her twin and that she felt she was in danger of losing this mediating function if she lost Meg. Furthermore, Marianne gave expression to her fear that a diagnosis of cancer could befall her as well. This fear suggests that Marianne's fantasy of personal invulnerability, which was at the core of her assumptive world, was seriously disturbed as a result of her twin's illness.

Marianne did not experience her feelings for long, however. Rather, she dissociated herself from her feelings and unconsciously attempted to deal with her twin sister's impending death in a matter-of-fact manner. It would be business as usual.

In narcissistic denial and refusing to accept the prognosis, Marianne had her sister transferred to a world-class cancer treatment center. Meg was treated for four months with aggressive chemotherapy; she underwent a number of ups and downs, some of the latter pointing to the inevitability that death was close at hand.

In effect, Marianne operated as if she were the point man for all discussions and decisions regarding her sister's care. She met with the oncology team, learned about the various chemotherapy drugs, and discussed the pros and cons of different drug regimens with her sister and brother-in-law.

In one therapy session, when the situation regarding Meg looked particularly bleak, Marianne broke down in tears, crying about the impending loss of her sister. She asked poignantly: "Why her, a good person, a kind person, only forty-four years of age and with three children?" With this question, Marianne seemed to be giving expression to the disturbance of her narcissistic illusions, or her assumptive world, about life as rational, sensible, ordered, and fair.

The therapist assured Marianne that she was not going through this ordeal alone. The therapist explained that she would join Marianne in her time of need, thus sharing the emotional burden of her pain. In the intersubjective context of the treatment, the therapist was offering to function narcissistically for Marianne as a self-object "twin."

In this way, the therapist hoped to compensate transferentially for the imminent loss of Marianne's twin sister. Marianne responded to this offer by saying that she was afraid to rely on the therapist for support because the therapist, like her sister, might get sick and die.

Marianne's doubts and reservations about relying on the self-object functioning of the therapist as an imaginary twin is indicative of her unconscious resistance to forming a transference based on a fantasized twinship. Nonetheless, the therapist remained available during this difficult period to Marianne for emergency phone calls, and Marianne took advantage of this availability on a number of occasions. In so doing, she signaled that the unconscious resistance to a twinship with the therapist had diminished to a considerable degree.

In subsequent therapy sessions, it was clear that unconsciously Marianne was defending herself against feeling any further pain. She focused entirely on the practical aspects of managing a cancer patient's care. She described to the therapist the various drugs that were being considered and the kind of prognosis each held out.

Marianne no longer seemed to have any feelings about her twin sister's illness. When the therapist asked explicitly about such feelings, Marianne responded almost in a rote manner that she felt sad. However, she quickly returned to the practical. In an intellectual fashion that was devoid of emotion, Marianne described, for example, the basis of the various decisions which she had made concerning her sister's care.

After her sister's chemotherapy regimen ended and Meg had gone back home, Marianne talked to the therapist about a number of other concerns. These included her worries about her husband's unsuccessful business ventures, her fears that her former best friend was spreading rumors about her within their shared social circle, and her anxieties about her mother's hip operation. Marianne seemed to have substituted these worries, all of which involved a sense of personal loss, for any dread about her sister and the latter's extremely limited life expectancy. Unconsciously, she had distanced (that is, dissociated) herself from her sister as a twin, whom she had unconsciously fantasized as functioning narcissistically as an alter ego self-object. However, it was apparent that, despite her attempt to dissociate herself emotionally from Meg's life-and-death struggle with cancer, Marianne was being traumatized by the impending loss of her twin. In other words, a major premise of her assumptive world was being seriously challenged and threatened.

Marianne acknowledged the possibility that she was indeed attempting to distance herself emotionally from her twin, stating that she had been feeling terribly exhausted and that she had felt pain in her legs all that week. She explained that she had never felt tired during her sister's hospitalization and that during the early days of her sister's illness she had once felt the same pain in her legs; however, it had quickly disappeared. The therapist interpreted that unconsciously Marianne had dissociated from her painful feelings about the imminent loss of her twin during the traumatic period of the latter's hospitalization. The therapist's empathic inference was confirmed by Marianne's own subjective experience.

Moreover, the therapist began an analytic dialogue with Marianne regarding the unconscious meaning of her PTSD symptoms. They discussed her twin sister's imminent death in terms of the disturbance of Marianne's narcissistic illusions about possessing megalomaniacal control over her life and of the functioning of the world, which she imagined as her private domain.

In cutting herself off from emotions concerning the possible death of her twin, Marianne attempted unconsciously to defend herself from the sense of disconnection engendered by the loss of twinship with Meg. She defended herself by arming herself with knowledge about all aspects of Meg's care. This knowledge provided Marianne with an illusory sense of omniscience and megalomaniacal control. These narcissistic illusions represented Marianne's unconscious attempts at the restoration, albeit faulty, of her fantasized twinship with her sister, a fantasy that had been vital to her assumptive world.

During this period of therapy, Marianne reported a recurrent type of nightmarish dream in which she lost all of her possessions. In a more explicit version of this dream, Marianne reported approaching the street where she lived and discovering much to her dismay that the road was gone. It had been utterly destroyed by a bomb.

In the dream, she remembered that one of her children was at home; thus she assumed that he had been killed. However, when she reached the area where her house once stood, she was told by her neighbor that her husband and her other child had died as well. Marianne felt totally devastated and bereft, and, believing that she could not tolerate this massive loss, entertained the possibility of killing herself.

In associating to the dream, which was indicative of PTSD reexperiencing symptoms, the primary feeling that Marianne could relate to was that of a sense of aloneness. Marianne and the therapist talked about Marianne's ambivalence and her earlier fantasy of being like her twin, and, in the process, of losing everything and becoming destitute. Yet, now with her sister literally on death's doorstep, Marianne unconsciously believed that if she lost the fantasized twinship, not only would she be alone, but she too would be destroyed.

Another dream was interpreted as being symbolic of the twinship merger that Marianne (unconsciously) fantasized with Meg. In the dream, Marianne was in her doctor's office and discovered that she had become anorexic, weighing only eighty-seven pounds. In associating to the dream, Marianne remembered that Meg had weighed eighty-seven pounds when she first left the hospital and returned home.

Recent Phase of Therapy

Marianne acknowledged that she feared she might lose herself and that, at times, she felt invisible and had no clear impression of her physical appearance. The dream was about Marianne's mortifying fantasy of herself as the lesser half in relation to her twin as regards physical appearance.

This fantasy of narcissistic mortification seemed to be at the heart of Marianne's body image distortions. In other words, Marianne "disappears," that is, merges with Meg and thus becomes physically embodied by Meg. In Marianne's unconscious mind, if she loses her twin, she loses all ability to experience herself as a physical being. Apparently, Marianne can only see her body (that is, experience her physical self) through her sister, who functions narcissistically as a self-object twin. In the absence of Meg, Marianne imagines a dreaded scenario in which she disappears as a physical being.

Marianne related that although she continues to speak to Meg every day, their conversations are brief and perfunctory. She explained that she does not want to be too close emotionally to Meg at this point because she does not know how much longer Meg will be alive.

The therapist referred back to Marianne's dread of losing the therapist as analogous to her worry of being alone or losing herself if she loses her twin sister. Marianne confirmed her narcissistic dread of losing the therapist. In this context, she admitted that she had missed two previous therapy sessions because she was afraid of closeness with the therapist, who she worried might become sick and die. As with her actual twin, Marianne dreaded that she might lose her therapist in the latter's self-object functioning as a twin and, thereby, lose herself.

As the therapy continued, a self-object transference emerged that was more stable. It was organized unconsciously in terms of the therapist's self-object functioning as a twin. The therapist and Marianne spoke openly about Marianne's former perception of her husband as well as of her sister as being her lesser half or, in the case of her sister as regards physicality, being her better half.

Slowly, Marianne began to experience herself as involved transferentially with the therapist in the intersubjective context of a fantasized twinship. In a number of therapy sessions, Marianne used expressions such as "We work well together" and "We are a good match." Marianne's constant use of *we* is reflective of her increasing sense of twinship with the therapist.

The ultimate goal of therapy is for Marianne to experience the therapist as her equal half. The therapist hopes that this twinship transference will, through transmuting internalization, allow Marianne to experience herself as a whole self, that is, neither a lesser half nor a better half. Ideally the twinship transference will result in a therapeutic restoration on Marianne's part of more tempered and modulated fantasies about herself and of her existence, that is, her "assumptive world." The more archaic version of these narcissistic fantasies had been seriously threatened as a result of the illness and impending death of her twin.

Conclusion

Our psychoanalytic case material makes clear that traumatic loss, either in the form of an experience of nearly losing one's own life or an experience of the dying or death of a close relative, may be understood and treated self-psychologically not only in terms of object loss but also as regards the loss of self-object fantasies. From our self-psychological point of view, it is important to remember the following fact: as human beings we exist in a psychological world that is populated symbolically not only by internal objects (that is, introjected images of other people) but by self-objects (that is, imaginary functionaries) as well. A psychoanalytic focus on this dimension of unconscious mental life is essential for the analytic therapist working psychotherapeutically with survivors of traumatic loss of the "assumptive world" in the form of archaic narcissistic fantasies or self-object fantasies of the self and the surround. In the course of conducting such important psychotherapeutic work, the analytic therapist has entered the psychic domain constituted by the fields of traumatology and thanatology.

References

Arlow, J. A. (1966). Depersonalization and derealization. In R. M. Lowenstein, L. M. Newman, M. Schur, and A. J. Solnit (Eds.), *Psychoanalysis—A general psychology* (pp. 456–478). New York: International Universities Press.

Arlow, J. A. (1969a). Unconscious fantasy and disturbances of conscious experience. *Psychoanalytic Quarterly, 38*: 1–27.

Arlow, J. A. (1969b). Fantasy, memory, and reality testing. *Psychoanalytic Quarterly, 38*: 28–51.

Basch, M. F. (1981). Psychoanalytic interpretation and cognitive transformation. *International Journal of Psycho-Analysis, 62*: 151–175.

Freud, A. (1966). Denial in fantasy. In *The ego and the mechanisms of defense* (pp. 69–82). New York: International Universities Press.

Hagman, G. (1995a). Death of a self-object: Toward a self psychology of the mourning process. In A. Goldberg (Ed.), *Progress in self psychology: The impact of new ideas* (pp. 189–205). Hillsdale, NJ: The Analytic Press.

Hagman, G. (1995b). Mourning: A review and reconsideration. *International Journal of Psycho-Analysis, 76*: 909–925.

Hagman, G. (1996a). The role of the other in mourning. *Psychoanalytic Quarterly, 65*: 327–352.

Hagman, G. (1996b). Flight from the subjectivity of the other: Pathological adaptation to childhood parent loss. In A. Goldberg, (Ed.), *Progress in self psychology: Basic ideas reconsidered* (pp. 207–219). Hillsdale, NJ: The Analytic Press.

Horowitz, M. J., Wilner, N., Marmar, C. & Krupnick, J. (1980). Pathological grief and the activation of latent self-images. *The American Journal of Psychiatry, 137*: 1157–1162.

Janoff-Bulman, R. (1985). The aftermath of victimization: Rebuilding shattered assumptions. In C. R. Figley (Ed.), *Trauma and Its Wake* (pp. 15–35). New York: Brunner/Mazel.

Janoff-Bulman, R. (1992). *Shattered assumptions: Towards a new psychology of trauma.* New York: The Free Press.

Krystal, H. (1971). Psychotherapy after massive traumatization. In H. Krystal and W. G. Niederland (Ed.), *Psychic traumatization* (pp. 223–229). Boston: Little, Brown & Co.

Krystal, H., & Niederland, W. G. (1968). Clinical observations on the survivor syndrome. In H. Krystal (Ed.), *Massive Psychic Trauma* (pp. 327–348). New York: International Universities Press.

Kohut, H. (1971). *The analysis of the self: A systematic approach to the psychoanalytic treatment of narcissistic personality disorders.* New York: International Universities Press.

Kohut, H. (1977). *The restoration of the self.* New York: International Universities Press.

Kohut, H. (1984). *How does analysis cure?* Chicago: University of Chicago Press.

Leon, I. G. (1999). Bereavement and repair of the self: Poetic confrontations with death. *Psychoanalytic Review, 86*: 385.

Lifton, R. J. (1967). *Death in life.* New York: Random House.

Lifton, R. J. (1968). Observations on Hiroshima survivors. In H. Krystal (Ed.), *Massive Psychic Trauma* (pp. 168–189). New York: International Universities Press.

Lifton, R. J. (1973). *Home from the war: Vietnam veterans*. New York: Simon & Schuster.

Lifton, R. J. (1982). Psychology of the survivor and the death imprint. *Psychiatric Annals, 12:* 1011–1020.

Lifton, R. J. (1988). Understanding the traumatized self: Imagery, symbolization, and transformation. In J. P. Wilson, Z. Harel, and B. Kahana (Eds.), *Human adaptation to extreme stress: From the Holocaust to Vietnam* (pp. 7–31). New York: Plenum Press.

Lifton, R. J., & Olson, E. (1976). The human meaning of total disaster. *Psychiatry, 39,* 1–18.

Miliora, M. T., & Ulman, R. B. (1996a). Panic disorder: A bioself-psychological perspective. *Journal of the American Academy of Psychoanalysis, 24,* 217–256.

Miliora, M. T., & Ulman, R. B. (1996b). Deconstruction and reconstruction: A self-psychological perspective on the construction of meaning in psychoanalysis. In J. R. Brandell (Ed.), *Narration and therapeutic action: The construction of meaning in psychoanalytic social work* (pp. 61–81). New York: The Haworth Press.

Nurnberg, G. H., & Shapiro, L. M. (1983). The central organizing fantasy. *Psychoanalytic Review, 70:* 493–503.

Ornstein, A. (1974). The dread to repeat and the new beginning: A contribution to the psychoanalysis of the narcissistic personality. *The Annual of Psychoanalysis, 2:* 231–248.

Ornstein, A. (1991). The dread to repeat: Comments on the working-through process in psychoanalysis. *Journal of the American Psychoanalytic Association, 39:* 377–398.

Spotts, J. V., & Shontz, F. C. (1976). *The life styles of nine american cocaine users.* Research Issue No. 16. National Institute on Drug Abuse. Washington, DC: United States Government Printing Office.

Stolorow, R. D., & Lachmann, F. M. (1980). *Psychoanalysis of developmental arrests: Theory and treatment.* New York: International Universities Press.

Tartakoff, H. H. (1966). The normal personality in our culture and the Nobel prize complex. In R. M. Lowenstein, L. M. Newman, M. Schur, & A. J. Solnit (Eds.), *Psychoanalysis—A general psychology* (pp. 222–252). New York: International Universities Press.

Tolpin, M. (1974). The Daedalus experience: A developmental vicissitude of the grandiose fantasy. *The Annual of Psychoanalysis, 2,* 213–228.

Ulman, R. B., and Brothers, D. (1987). A self-psychological reevaluation of posttraumatic stress disorder (PTSD) and its treatment: Shattered fantasies. *Journal of the American Academy of Psychoanalysis 15:* 175–203.

Ulman, R. B., and Brothers, D. (1988). *The shattered self: A psychoanalytic study of trauma.* Hillsdale, NJ: The Analytic Press.

Ulman, R. B., & Miliora, M. T. (In submission). A bioself-psychological approach to understanding and treating the obsessive-compulsive character.

Ulman, R. B., & Paul, H. (1989). A self-psychological theory and approach to treating substance abuse disorders: The "intersubjective absorption" hypothesis. In A. Goldberg (Ed.), *Progress in self psychology: Dimensions of self experience* (pp. 121–141). Hillsdale, NJ: The Analytic Press.

Ulman, R. B., & Paul, H. (1990). The addictive personality disorder and "addictive trigger mechanisms" (ATMs): The self psychology of addiction and its treatment. In A. Goldberg (Eds.), *Progress in self psychology: The realities of transference.* Hillsdale, NJ: The Analytic Press.

Ulman, R. B., & Paul, H. (1992). Dissociative anesthesia and the transitional selfobject transference in the intersubjective treatment of the addictive personality. In A. Goldberg (Ed.,), *Progress in self psychology: New therapeutic visions* (pp. 109–139). Hillsdale, NJ: The Analytic Press.

Ulman, R. B., & Paul, H. (2002). *The self psychology of addiction and its treatment: Narcissus in wonderland.* New York: Brunner-Routledge.

Weinstein, N. D. (1982). Egocentrism as a source of unrealistic optimism. *Personality and Social Psychology Bulletin, 8,* 195–200.

part 3.

Psychological Processes

8.

Treatment of Violated Assumptive Worlds with EMDR

Roger M. Solomon

People need a sense of meaning, understanding, and safety regarding the world, the people within it, and their role in the world (Everly, 1995). In trying to understand the world, people create an assumptive world—organized schemas—that contain everything a person assumes to be true about the world and the self on the basis of previous experience (Rando, 1993). These assumptions about the world and self provide a basis to organize one's experience and a stable conceptual system that enables psychological equilibrium in an ever-changing world (Janoff-Bulman, 1992).

Three fundamental assumptions about the self and world that traumatic events may violate are: (1) the world is benevolent, (2) events in the world are meaningful, and (3) the self is positive and worthy (Janoff-Bulman, 1992). The benevolent world is where good things happen and people are good. Bad things are not supposed to happen. In a meaningful world, events are just, fair, predictable, and controllable. There is a self-outcome contingency—a relationship between a person and what happens to him or her. A positive view of the self involves seeing oneself as a worthy, decent person, deserving of good outcomes. Bad things do not happen to good people. An event that violates or contradicts these assumptions can be traumatic: "The tragedy is not supposed to happen—not to me. I am supposed to be control, so it has to be my fault. I am a worthless person or this would not have happened."

A traumatic event can violate or contradict a person's basic assumptions about the world and one's self, shattering the foundation that makes the world safe and predictable, and disrupting one's sense of control and efficacy (Bulman, 1995; Everly, 1995; Solomon, 1995; Rando, 1993). The inability to integrate the traumatic information into one's assumptive world may result in intense feelings of vulnerability, helplessness, and low self-worth and efficacy.

Eye movement desensitization and reprocessing (EMDR) is a treatment methodology that can facilitate the adaptive integration of traumatic information. Controlled studies of the effectiveness of EMDR on single-trauma PTSD have demonstrated that after the equivalent of two or three 90-minute sessions,

84–100 percent of the single-trauma subjects no longer met criteria for PTSD posttest (Marcus, Marquis, & Sakai, 1997; Rothbaum, 1997; Scheck, Schaeffer, and Gillette, 1998; Wilson, Becker, & Tinker, 1995, 1997).

The method's claim of treatment success and its rapid spread throughout the world have instigated a wealth of critical research and debate (DeBell & Jones, 1997; Rosen, Lohr, McNally, & Herbert, 1998; Shapiro, 1996a, 1996b). Although the critical elements of the procedure still need dismantling and the theoretical rationale for EMDR needs more documentation and probably revisions, the amount of research documentation is now formidable. Interest seems to be moving from "Does it work?" to "How does it work?" Spector and Read's review article (1999) concludes that EMDR is an effective psychotherapy, but EMDR's relative efficacy in comparison to behavioral exposure therapies has yet to be established; the role of eye movements or other bilateral stimulation is controversial, and there is not sufficient research to know whether the theoretical model of EMDR is valid. More thorough reviews of the EMDR research and critiques can be found in Muris and Merckelbach (1999), Devilly and Spence (1999), and Shapiro (1999).

The Theoretical Model

The model underlying EMDR is the accelerated information-processing model (Shapiro, 1991, 1993a, 1993b, 1993c, 1994a, 1994b, 1995). This model posits an innate information-processing system that is physiologically configured to facilitate mental health in much the same way the rest of the body is designed to heal itself when injured (Shapiro, 1995). When operating appropriately, this system takes the perceptual information from a traumatic event to an adaptive resolution—useful information is stored with appropriate affect and is available for future use. The physiological and emotional arousal stemming from a traumatic event may disrupt the information-processing mechanism. This can result in the information taken in during the time of the trauma (disturbing images, thoughts, sensations, beliefs, and the like) becoming stored in disturbing, excitatory, state-specific form. The blocked processing prevents the traumatic information from progressing through the normal steps of adaptive integration. Nightmares, flashbacks, intrusive thoughts and sensory imagery, and other symptoms of PTSD may result from continual activation of this dysfunctionally stored information by internal or external stimuli, or perhaps because of repeated unsuccessful attempts of the information-processing mechanism to complete its own processing. Since the nonadaptively stored trauma is functionally compartmentalized apart from the appropriate information, the perceived event cannot be integrated into one's assumptive world.

EMDR organizes the memory selected for processing, catalyzes the information-processing system, maintains it in a dynamic state, and facilitates the processing of the information surrounding the event. Processing is defined as the forging of the associations and connections required for learning to take place so that the traumatic information can be "adaptively resolved" (Shapiro, 1999). Adaptive resolution refers to the client (1) being able to glean useful information from the event (e.g., take appropriate cautions under certain circumstances or around certain people) and discard what is not useful (e.g., negative sensations, irrational cognitions, etc.), (2) experiencing and manifesting appropriate affect in relation to the event, and (3) acquiring the capacity to effectively guide his/her future actions (Shapiro,

1999). Reprocessing the dysfunctional information enables the client to progress through the appropriate stages of affect and insight regarding such issues as appropriate levels of responsibility, present safety, and the availability of future choices.

EMDR is not a shortcut to resolution. After a traumatic incident, including significant loss, people have been found to face obstacles in the recovery process—for example, traumatic images from a death may prevent a person from proceeding in his or her grief work (Dyregrov, 1993b; Pynoos, 1992). Such intrusive symptoms result from dysfunctionally stored information that is unable to be processed, (van der Kolk & Fisler, 1995; Herman, 1992). By processing the dysfunctionally stored information, EMDR allows the information to move toward adaptive resolution. Hence, rather than skipping tasks in the recovery process, EMDR enables a natural progression.

EMDR is not a stand-alone method but an approach that needs to be integrated within an overall treatment framework. A person may not have sufficient information to resolve the trauma. In other words, schemas, or assumptive worlds, may be narrow or rigid and not contain the information needed to resolve the trauma. The person must have the necessary information in his or her schemas in order for the dysfunctional information to be assimilated and accommodated into existing schemas. If a person does not have sufficient information to conceptualize the event in a realistic way, therapy must first take the course of assisting the client in gaining relevant information. The victim does not have to totally believe the information, only have it available. For example, victims often blame themselves for the crime. A person may believe he or she should have been in control, seen it coming, been able to influence the situation into another outcome, and so on. Even though a person can conceive of the notion that the control was in the hands of the perpetrator, he or she may emotionally not believe this. People say, "I know it was not my fault, but it feels like it is." EMDR can assist the connection between the adaptive information and dysfunctionally stored information to facilitate integration.

A person may not have sufficient ego strength to process the dysfunctionally stored information. During EMDR, there can be an intense reliving of the event. The client has to have sufficient inner resources to deal with the emotional impact. Therefore, assessment of functioning, history taking, teaching of relaxation and safe-place exercises, and building of internal and external resources may be necessary before EMDR is initiated. Such steps are built into the EMDR protocol.

The generic therapeutic protocol underlying comprehensive EMDR treatment includes a three-pronged approach subsequent to appropriate therapeutic stabilization and client preparation (Shapiro, 1995). The client engages in (1) processing the past experiences contributing to present dysfunction, (2) processing present triggers that elicit present disturbance, and (3) incorporating positive patterns of behavior for future adaptive actions. Hence the clinician needs to assess whether the client has the skills and behaviors necessary for adaptive functioning, and provide appropriate information and learning experiences.

Eight-Phase Method

EMDR is currently an eight-phase treatment approach where the eye movement itself is only a small part of the method. EMDR undoubtedly includes a number of elements that could be viewed as nonspecific factors, such as therapeutic alliance and expectancy (Shapiro, 1999). The first phase is history taking. It must first be determined whether the client is suitable for EMDR treatment because the reprocessing of traumatic material may precipitate intense emotions. The client's ability to deal with high levels of disturbance, personal stability, and life constraints are evaluated. If the client is determined to be appropriate for EMDR treatment, the clinician obtains the information needed to design a treatment plan. The clinician evaluates the entire clinical picture, including the dysfunctional behaviors, symptoms, and characteristics that need to be addressed. The clinician then determines the specific memories that need to be reprocessed, including events that initially set the pathology in motion, present triggers that stimulate the dysfunctional material, and the kinds of positive behaviors and attitudes important for adaptive future functioning.

The second phase is client preparation. This involves establishing a therapeutic alliance, explaining the EMDR process and its effects, dealing with the client's concerns, and teaching the client relaxation techniques for coping with high levels of emotion. Informed consent about the possibility of intense emotions being evoked is obtained. The preparation phase also includes briefing the client on the theory of EMDR and the procedures involved and explaining what can realistically be expected.

The third phase is assessment. In this phase the clinician identifies the components of the target to be treated and takes baseline measures before reprocessing begins. The client is asked to select the image that best represents the memory. Then the therapist assists the client in identifying the negative cognition that expresses the dysfunctional, negative self-attribution related to participation in the event. Then a positive cognition or a more rational, realistic, and empowering self-assessment is identified. While utilized later to replace the negative cognition in the installation phase (phase five), the initial purpose of the positive cognition is to provide a therapeutic direction. To provide a baseline measurement, the client is asked to report how valid the positive cognition feels on a seven-point Validity of Cognition (VOC) Scale, with 1 being that it feels totally false and 7 being that it feels totally true.

The client and therapist also explore the emotions and physical sensations associated with the traumatic experience. The client is asked to rate the intensity of the emotion on a ten-point Subjective Units of Disturbance (SUD) Scale, with 0 being neutral and 10 being the worst it could be, to provide a baseline from which to assess changes during the procedure.

The next three phases have to do with the accelerated processing of information. During these phases there is simultaneous remediation of negative affect, cognitive restructuring, and generation of insights that can guide the client in the future. The individual phases are designated according to the elements that are used to determine treatment effects. For instance, desensitization uses the Subjective Units of Disturbance (SUD) Scale, installation uses the Validity of Cognition (VOC) Scale, and the body scan (where the client is asked to scan his or her body for sensations) uses the evaluation of bodily sensations. However, all treatment effects are viewed as by-products of accelerated information processing. Bilateral stimulation, such as sets of eye movement (where the client tracks the clinician's fingers back and forth across the visual field), alternating taps on the client's palms, or the therapist snapping his or her fingers alternately on each side of the client's head, are utilized to stimulate information processing according to appropriate protocols.

The fourth phase is desensitization. This phase focuses on the client's negative affect with clinical effects measured by the SUD Scale. While the client holds in mind the visual image, the negative cognition, and the sensations associated with the image, processing is activated during a focused clinician/client interaction involving sets of eye movement (or other stimulation) until the SUD level is reduced to 0 or 1, or higher if that is appropriate to client circumstance.

Phase five is installation, where the positive cognition is paired with the memory. After the distress level has dropped to a 0 or 1 on the SUD Scale, the focus becomes enhancing and strengthening the positive cognition identified earlier (or a more appropriate cognition that may have arisen spontaneously) as the replacement for the original negative cognition. Clinical effects are evaluated on the basis of the seven-point VOC Scale. This phase is complete when the positive cognition feels valid in relation to the incident, that is, the cognition reaches a VOC rating of 6 or 7 (completely true).

Phase six is the body scan. The client is asked to hold in mind both the target event and the positive cognition and scan his or her body for residual tension in the form of body sensation. Congruent with the work of van der Kolk and Fisler (1995), body sensations may indicate that additional information is dysfunctionally stored. Upon adequate processing, usually the tension will simply resolve, but not uncommonly additional targets may be revealed.

Phase seven is closure. The client must be returned to a state of emotional equilibrium at the end of the session, whether or not the reprocessing is complete. Relaxation and other coping skills learned during the preparation phase can be utilized when the client is experiencing discomfort. The client is briefed as to the possibility of other memories, feelings, or images emerging as the material continues to process between sessions. The client is asked to keep a journal or a log so that what comes up may be discussed in the next session.

Phase eight is reevaluation. In the next session, treatment results are reviewed to ensure complete treatment effects. The log is examined and the client is asked to reaccess the material previously worked on to see if there are any reverberations of the already reprocessed information that need to be addressed.

Applicability of EMDR

Given that EMDR is utilized to process dysfunctionally stored information, it is applicable to a wide range of disorders. Unless the symptons are chemically or physically based, it is assumed that they result from past learning situations (Shapiro, 1995). The clinician utilizes his or her clinical framework to identify the past memories and experiences underlying present symptoms. EMDR can then be utilized to reprocesses these memories, process present triggers, and incorporate adaptive patterns of behavior for the future. For example, one component of a client's depression or anxiety disorder may be the learned belief that he or she is inadequate and an unworthy person. During history taking, past learning experiences underlying the dysfunctional self-beliefs are identified. This may include pivotal parent-child interactions, school experiences, interactions with friends, and so on. After appropriate stabilization and preparation, these memories, and present triggers, can then be processed with EMDR. EMDR is not a substitute for the clinical procedures utilized to treat a disorder but an addition to the therapeutic framework and treatment methodology.

Although accelerated information processing is hypothesized as an important underlying mechanism of EMDR, several hypotheses have been proposed to explain how EMDR works to mobilize the rapid processing of cognitive and emotional material. For example, reciprocal inhibition where emotional distress is paired with a compelled relaxation response has been offered by Wilson, Silver, Covi, and Foster (1996). There may be a reduction in neurological abnormalities in traumatized persons following EMDR as shown on SPECT scans of the brains for these subjects (Levin, Lazrove, & van der Kolk, 1999). Another mechanism could be the suppression of avoidance by an optimal range of distraction stimuli, allowing traumatic memories to be processed (Shapiro, 1999). Other mechanisms that may contribute to the clinical effects of EMDR include exposure, synchronization of memory components, guided imagery, and cognitive restructuring (Shapiro, 1999).

EMDR is not a rigid protocol but a highly interactive procedure individualized for each client. Competent clinical skills and knowledge are needed for the successful utilization of EMDR. Identifying appropriate negative and positive cognitions is an exercise in case formulation. Knowledge of personality dynamics and psychopathology are necessary for the therapist to identify the beliefs and self-attributions underlying symptoms. Establishing rapport, eliciting a complete history, assisting the client in accessing traumatic memories, and steering the EMDR process take a strong clinical background.

Case Example

EMDR can facilitate the assimilation of the trauma into the assumptive world and the accommodation of the assumptive world to the traumatic event, as illustrated in the following case example.

A seventeen-year-old male was home alone with his father, who had a history of heart attacks, when the father had a massive heart attack and collapsed. The son called 911 and then administered CPR until paramedics arrived. The father died within a few minutes. The son felt guilty and responsible, believing he had done CPR wrong or had done something inappropriate to cause his father's death. Despite many assurances from different medical personnel that he did nothing wrong or inappropriate and there was nothing that could have been done, the son still felt guilty. In the next six months, the son became increasingly depressed and irritable. He still experienced flashbacks and intrusive imagery from the day his father died. Usually a responsible student, he began cutting classes and not doing his homework, and stole money from his mother's purse several times. This acting out had not been present prior to the father's death. He was receiving grief counseling, and was referred for EMDR as an adjunctive therapy to help deal with his loss and the trauma of his father's death. After five sessions with the EMDR therapist to take a history, develop rapport, discuss the father's death and the meaning to him, provide additional education about grief and trauma, and introduce EMDR, EMDR was utilized.

The worst moment of the tragedy, when he was attempting CPR and realized it was not working, was targeted with EMDR. His negative cognition was "It's my fault," and the positive cognition was "I did the best I could." He had feelings of guilt and powerlessness. During EMDR, he relived the feelings of horror experienced when his father fell to the ground, clutching his chest, and passed out. With more processing he started getting in touch with the thought processes and actions that next took place, including aspects that he had forgotten about or previously minimized. He recalled calling 911, remaining calm, and attempting CPR. He remembered shifting CPR rhythms and his position several times when he saw what he was doing was not working, and continuing CPR until the paramedics came. He remembered asking God for help and encouraging his father to hang on. At the completion of the processing session, the son realized he had done all he knew how to do and had done the best he could, and the death was not his fault (nor the fault of the paramedics or doctors who attended his father).

This example illustrates how people involved in a traumatic event can take too much responsibility and blame themselves for situations beyond their control. The son assumed he had control over the situation and took responsibility for the death despite having rational knowledge that it was not his fault. In terms of the EMDR model, the trauma was dysfunctionally stored in state-specific form and was unable to be integrated into existing schemas. The most traumatic moment was targeted. Typical of EMDR processing, the client relived moments of the event, getting in touch with intense emotions, aspects of the event that may have been dissociated, and relevant details that may have been minimized or overlooked because of the strong focus on his guilt. He was able to recall the many things he had done for his father in attempting to revive him. After processing, he could view the situation more objectively and realize he had done the best he could.

EMDR results in the client taking an appropriate level of responsibility; it does not absolve a person from responsibility. After reprocessing, the son who had previously blamed himself was now able to differentiate what was under his control and what was beyond his control.

The next session took place a week later. The treatment gains of believing the father's death was not his fault were stable. However, with the worst moments of the situation and irrational self-blame processed, deeper layers of dysfunctionally stored information and contradictions in his assumptive world emerged. During the week he had experienced a strong sense of helplessness and felt there should have been something that could have been done to prevent his father's death, even though he knew there was no more he could do. At a deeper level, he could not accept that there was no more he or anybody else could do. This was something that was not supposed to have happened, and he felt guilt and shame that it had. Hence, though issues of personal responsibility had been resolved, the client was experiencing distress emanating from the violation of his worldview.

EMDR was utilized on the image of his father lying on the floor, the negative cognition being "I'm helpless and ineffective" and the positive cognition being "I can be capable." He had feelings of powerlessness, vulnerability, and guilt. During the processing, he again relived the events of the day his father died. Feelings of helplessness, and anger over being helpless, were experienced at an intense level. With further processing he realized that he had not given up, but had kept trying and continuing to respond until the paramedics came. With continued processing another layer of emotion emerged. He experienced a strong sense of loss and pain over his father's death. He verbalized that his father was gone, he had not been able to prevent it, and neither he nor anyone else could do anything about it. Something that was not supposed to have happened did happen. With more processing the intense emotions subsided, and he described that the death now felt more real; it did happen. With more processing, he said he now felt a deeper realization that the death was beyond his control and that he had done the best he could. Further, he felt a sense of efficacy as he realized that he had not backed away, panicicked, or given up. Though not in control of what had happened to his father, he felt good about his response to the situation. He also felt more secure and safe in the world. Though bad things can happen, he was not helpless.

In this session, the distress emanating from violated assumptions was targeted. The client believed that the death of his father was something that should not have happened and he should have been able to do something to prevent it. As the distress was being processed, intense feelings of deep pain and anger related to the loss and his sense of helplessness were experienced. With completion of processing, the death now felt more "real." This indicates a deeper level of acceptance and integration of the loss. The deeper awareness that the death "happened" also indicates further trauma resolution with the situation starting to be placed in the past, instead of being continually relived in the present.

Processing also led to a broadening of his assumptive world. He could now accept that something that was not supposed to have happened did happen. Continuing with what evolved from the first session, he felt more of an affirmation that the death was beyond his control but that he have been able to respond and had done the best he could. No longer feeling guilty, he now experienced a sense of personal efficacy for not giving up or backing away from trying to help his father. He also felt more secure in the world. What seemed to have integrated into his worldview was that things can happen beyond one's control, but one has control over one's response to the situation. Hence, processing enabled progression through the issues (1) appropriate responsibility, (2) personal safety, and (3) control and the availability of choices.

EMDR does not take away or neutralize appropriate emotions or truncate phases of trauma resolution or working though a loss. The son still mourned his father and felt pain at his loss. What processed were the obstacles to integration and movement through the grief process.

A follow-up session showed treatment gains to be stable, with no more flashbacks or intrusive imagery. EMDR was used to reinforce treatment gains by focusing on his feelings that the death was beyond his control and he did the best he could, his sense of efficacy emanating from not giving up, and his sense that he may not have control over what can happen but can control his response. He continued counseling with his regular therapist to do further grief work. His acting out stopped and he resumed regular school attendance and responsible study habits.

This example illustrates the importance of focusing beyond the specifics of a traumatic event to the core beliefs and assumptions that may have been violated. Accessing, addressing, and processing the contradiction in assumptive world beliefs enabled a broadening of the worldview and integration of the trauma.

Conclusion

EMDR is a therapeutic approach that supplements a clinician's ability to help clients integrate traumatic material into world assumptions. EMDR is not a stand-alone method and needs to be embedded within a therapeutic framework. Although the working therapeutic elements and theory behind the procedure are debated and need further research, the method offers a promising avenue for the adaptive processing of trauma, distressing memories, present anxieties, dysfunctional elements of grief, and other psychological problems.

References

DeBell, C., & Jones, R. D. (1997). As good as it seems? A review of EMDR experimental research. *Professional Psychology: Research and Practice, 28*, 153–163.

Devilly, G., & Spence, S. (1999). The relative efficacy and treatment distress of EMDR and a cognitive-behavior trauma treatment protocol in the amelioration of posttraumatic stress disorder. *Journal of Anxiety Disorders, 13*, 131–157.

Dyregrov, A. (1993b). The interplay of trauma and grief. *Association for Child Psychology and Psychiatry Occasional Papers, 8*, 2–10.

Everly, G. S. (1995). An integrative two-factor model of post-traumatic stress. In G. S. Everly (Ed.) *Psychotraumatology* (pp. 27–48). New York: Plenum Press.

Herman, J. L. (1992) *Trauma and Recovery*. New York: Basic Books.

Janoff-Bulman, R. (1992). *Shattered assumptions*. New York: Free Press.

Levin, P., Lazrove, S., & van der Kolk, B. (1999). What psychological testing and neuroimaging tell us about the treatment of posttraumatic stress disorder by eye movement desensitization and reprocessing. *Journal of Anxiety Disorders, 13*, 159–172.

Marcus, S., Marquis, P., & Sakai, C. (1997) Controlled study of treatment of PTSD using EMDR in an HMO setting. *Psychotherapy, 34*, 307–315.

Muris, P., & and Merckelbach, H. (1999). Traumatic memories, eye movements, phobia, and panic: A critical note on the proliferation of EMDR. *Journal of Anxiety Disorders, 13*, 209–223.

Pynoos, R. S. (1992). Grief and trauma in children and adolescents. *Bereavement Care, 11*, 2–10.

Rando, T. A. (1993). *Treatment of complicated mourning*. Champlain, IL: Research Press.

Rosen, G. M., Lohr, J. M., McNally, R., & Herbert, J. D. (1998). Power therapies, miraculous claims, and the cures that fail. *Behavioural and Cognitive Psychotherapy, 26*, 99–101.

Rothbaum, B. O. (1997). A controlled study of eye movement desensitization and reprocessing in the treatment of posttraumatic stress disordered sexual assault victims. *Bulletin of the Menninger Clinic, 61*, 317–334.

Scheck, M. M., Schaeffer, J. A., & Gillette, C. (1998). Brief psychological intervention with traumatized young women: The efficacy of eye movement desensitization and reprocessing, *Journal of Traumatic Stress, 11*, 25–44.

Shapiro, F. (1991). Eye movement desensitization and reprocessing procedure: From EMD to EMDR—a new treatment model for anxiety and related traumata. *Behavior Therapist, 14*, 133–135.

Shapiro, F. (1993a). Eye movement desensitization and reprocessing (EMDR) in 1992. *Journal of Traumatic Stress, 6*, 417–421.

Shapiro, F. (1993b). The status of EMDR in 1992. *Journal of Traumatic Stress, 6*, 413–421.

Shapiro, F. (1993c). Eye movement desensitization and reprocessing: A cautionary note. *Behavior Therapist, 14*, 188.

Shapiro, F. (1994a). Eye movement desensitization and reprocessing: A new treatment for anxiety and related trauma. In L. Hyer (Ed.), *Trauma victim: Theoretical issues and practical suggestions*. Muncie, IN: Accelerated Development.

Shapiro, F. (1994b). Eye movement desensitization and reprocessing: A new treatment for trauma and the whole person. *Treating Abuse Today, 4,* 5–13.

Shapiro, F. (1995). Eye movement desensitization and reprocessing: Basic principles, protocols, and procedure. New York: The Guilford Press.

Shapiro, F. (1996a). Eye movement desensitization and reprocessing (EMDR): Evaluation of controlled PTSD research. *Journal of Behavior Therapy and Experimental Psychiatry, 27,* 209–218.

Shapiro, F. (1996b). Errors of context and review of eye movement desensitization and reprocessing research. *Journal of Behavior Therapy and Experimental Psychiatry, 27,* 313–317.

Shapiro, F. (1999). Eye movement desensitization and reprocessing (EMDR) and the anxiety disorders: Clinical and research implications of an integrated psychotherapy treatment. *Journal of Anxiety Disorders, 13,* 35–67.

Solomon, R. M. (1995) Critical incident stress management in law enforcement. In G. S. Everly (Ed.), *Innovations in disaster and trauma psychology* (pp.123–157). Ellicott City, MD: Chevron Publishing.

Spector, J., & Read, J. (1999) The current status of eye movement desensitization and reprocessing. *Clinical Psychology and Psychotherapy, 6,* 165–174

van der Kolk, B., & Fisler, R. (1995). Dissociation and the fragmentary nature of traumatic memories. *Journal of Traumatic Stress, 8,* 505–525.

Wilson, S. A., Becker, L. A., & Tinker, R. H. (1995). Eye movement desensitization and reprocessing (EMDR) treatment for psychologically traumatized individuals. *Journal of Consulting and Clinical Psychology, 63,* 928–937.

Wilson. S.A., Becker, L. A., & Tinker, R. H. (1997). Fifteen-month follow-up of eye movement desensitization and reprocessing (EMDR) treatment for posttraumatic stress disorder and psychological trauma. *Journal of Consulting and Clinical Psychology, 65,* 1047–1056.

Wilson, D., Silver, S. M., Covi, W., & Foster, S. (1996) Eye movement desensitization and reprocessing: Effectiveness and autonomic correlates. *Journal of Behavior Therapy and Experimental Psychiatry, 27,* 219–222.

9.

Coping with Challenges to Assumptive Worlds

Charles A. Corr

This chapter examines issues related to coping with challenges to assumptive worlds. To do this, we begin with a discussion of the concept of coping and a review of the most prominent accounts of what is involved in the notion of an assumptive world. We then turn to a survey of several of the principal types of challenges that might arise to assumptive worlds. Finally, these discrete elements are brought together in a description of what might be involved in coping with challenges to assumptive worlds and some suggestions for helping individuals who are coping with challenges to their assumptive worlds.

Coping

The American humorist Josh Billings (1818–1885) is reported to have observed that "life consists not in holding good cards but in playing those you do hold well" (Corr, Nabe, & Corr, 2000, p. 135). How one plays the cards that one holds is a matter of how one copes. In the professional literature, the term *coping* has been defined as "constantly changing cognitive and behavioral efforts to manage specific external and/or internal demands that are appraised as taxing or exceeding the resources of the person" (Lazarus & Folkman, 1984, p. 141; compare Monat & Lazarus, 1991). Three elements are central in this definition: "constantly changing," "efforts to manage," and perceived stressors. We can most easily understand these three elements by considering them here in reverse order.

If individuals were not confronted by perceived stressors—"specific external and/or internal demands that are appraised as taxing or exceeding the resources of the person"—routine or habitualized behavior would suffice and there would be no need to try to cope. This suggests that what a person perceives to be a stressor in his or her life is essentially individual in nature. I might perceive as stressful situations or specific stimuli that you would not at all view in the same light. Alternatively, I might perceive some situations or specific stimuli to be stressful in some circumstances, such as when I first encounter them, or at certain times, such as when I am burdened by many additional demands on my psychic energies.

There may, of course, be many demands or challenges that all healthy persons at all times would perceive to be stressful. In any event, the perception of a demand as taxing or exceeding one's resources is a key point to which we will return later in this chapter.

The second central point in the definition of coping has to do with the responses that an individual makes to a perceived stressor. Whatever the source or origin of the perceived stressor, however it is thought to tax or exceed the individual's resources, and whether that appraisal is or is not accurate, coping involves efforts to manage the challenge(s) that is/are represented by the perceived stressor.

A third feature of coping is that it is typical that any efforts to manage perceived stressors will be constantly changing in character. Most often, coping efforts are dynamic, varying with an individual's personality, energy and moods, developmental status, social circumstances, and historical situation. These are familiar variables in all aspects of living; it is hardly likely that they would not be important variables in coping with perceived stressors. A key feature of the dynamic aspect of coping is that efforts at coping are likely to undergo change as they are found or perceived to be more or less effective in responding to the stressors from which they originated. This is not always the case. One might simply continue to try to cope in ways that are familiar but ineffective in the face of a particular stressful demand. However, the lesson for those who critically review coping efforts is that we should not assume a priori or without good evidence that an individual's coping efforts will be static, inflexible, or otherwise limited.

This understanding of coping has many desirable features. First, it accentuates *processes* of coping and the dynamic character of human responses to stress. Second, it emphasizes *efforts to manage* stressful demands. This focuses attention on the activity of coping, on whatever an individual is thinking or doing in response to stress, not merely on psychological traits that are either simply thought to or that actually do characterize internal feeling states. It also depicts coping as acting with a positive orientation that is not restricted to negativity, defending against, or pushing away problems (Weisman, 1984).

Third, this definition identifies coping as efforts to address demands that are *perceived as stressful*. As noted above, demands that are not perceived as stressful do not call for a coping response. Similarly, unperceived demands are not sources of stress. Also, because perceptions may change, coping processes may adjust to fit ways in which new perceptions present new situational challenges.

Fourth, this definition distinguishes coping from routine, automatized, rote behaviors that do not involve an effortful response. Such routine or habitual behaviors make up a large portion of everyday activity, serving our needs well until something goes wrong or until they are recognized to be inadequate and our stress level rises. Once again, coping refers specifically to efforts undertaken in response to demands that are appraised as *taxing or exceeding the resources* of the individual.

Fifth, this definition *does not confuse coping with outcome*. All too often, this point is misunderstood and people say that an individual "is just not coping" with his or her situation, when in fact they mean that the individual is not coping with the stressor in ways that are thought to be productive or successful or to which they attach approval. For example, submerging oneself in an extended alcohol-induced stupor is usually not considered to be a desirable way of coping with stress. It may do harm to the individual involved as well as to others with whom he or she might come into contact. But its real failing as a coping strategy lies in the fact that when one eventually sobers up, the stressor usually still remains to be addressed. Nevertheless, setting aside the question of its effectiveness as a way of dealing with stress, excessive consumption of alcoholic beverages may in fact be one way in which some people try to cope with stress-induced pain. In other words, even though it is unsuccessful, this behavior does represent *an effort* to cope.

In truth, there is good coping, bad coping, and a broad range of coping in between those extremes. Individuals and groups can debate the merits of various ways of coping both in themselves and in particular situations. But the concept of coping itself includes *all efforts* to manage stressful demands, however successful or unsuccessful such efforts might be.

A sixth feature of the way in which coping is defined here is that it spotlights efforts to *manage* stressful demands, not necessarily to *master* them. A person who is making efforts to cope may try—more or less successfully—to master a particular situation, but individuals are often willing to settle for less than mastery. They may, for example, simply accept, endure, minimize, or avoid stressful demands. When we confuse efforts to manage stress with efforts to master stress, we limit our understanding of coping to its most extreme forms and our focus tends to shift from processes to outcomes of coping.

There is a rich literature on coping. For example, Moos and Schaefer (1986) distinguished five coping tasks, nine coping skills, and three focal domains. We need not enter into that discussion, but we can suggest something of its richness and its utility for our present purposes by sketching the three focal domains identified by Moos and Schaefer. *Appraisal-focused coping* has to do with efforts to understand, assess, and perhaps redefine, minimize, or deny the stressful situation. *Problem-focused coping* has to do with efforts to identify and obtain information about alternative courses of action and their probable outcomes, to take action to deal directly with the crisis or its aftermath, or to attempt to replace losses involved in certain transitions by changing one's activities and creating new sources of satisfaction. *Emotion-focused coping* has to do with efforts to maintain hope and control one's emotions, vent one's feelings, or come to terms with and accept a situation as it is.

In view of an ambiguity in many uses of the term *emotion*, whereby it may mean either the overall reaction pattern of the whole organism (including somatic, feeling, behavioral, and other aspects), or only the feeling components of that reaction pattern (Elias, 1991), I would prefer to speak of this last coping focus as *reaction-focused coping* rather than *emotion-focused coping*. However, that point is not substantive for this tripartite distinction between coping efforts directed toward appraising the situation, trying to do something about the situation itself, or trying to do something about one's reactions to the situation. In each of these three focal domains, Moss and Schaefer (1986) argued, there is potential work or tasks to be undertaken and there are skills that can be developed and applied in various ways as part of one's coping.

The relevance of the concept of coping to issues related to the loss of or challenges to assumptive worlds, and the value of that concept in illuminating such issues, will become evident after we review what the literature has to say about assumptive worlds and after we survey some of the principal types of challenges to assumptive worlds.

Assumptive Worlds

The concept of an "assumptive world" was apparently first employed by Parkes (1971, 1975) in the sense in which it is used here, although the phrase itself has been credited to an earlier source, where it was used in a different context (Cantril, 1966). Parkes (1975, p. 132) defined an "assumptive world" as "a strongly held set of assumptions about the world and the self which is confidently maintained and used as a means of recognizing, planning and acting ... Assumptions such as these are learned and confirmed by the experience of many years."

Janoff-Bulman (1992), who developed this concept in a stimulating book entitled *Shattered assumptions: Towards a new psychology of trauma*, noted that although other writers have used different terms, "there is clearly congruence in these descriptions of a single underlying phenomenon." That common reference is to an assumptive world as "a conceptual system, developed over time, that provides us with expectations about the world and ourselves" (p. 5). Because some of our assumptions or internal representations are more central and basic than others, Janoff-Bulman referred to a network of diverse theories and representations organized hierarchically in which "our most fundamental assumptions" are those "that are most abstract and general, as well as most pervasive in their applicability" (p. 5). Because they form the nucleus of our internal world and are so basic, Janoff-Bulman thought of our fundamental assumptions as "the bedrock of our conceptual system," those "that we are least aware of and least likely to challenge" (p. 5).

Janoff-Bulman (1992, p. 6) proposed the following basic beliefs about ourselves, the external world, and the relationship between the two as our three fundamental assumptions: "The world is benevolent," "the world is meaningful," "the self is worthy." The *benevolence of the world* is thought to relate both to people and to events, and especially to one's own limited world and future expectations, if not to the world at large. The *meaningfulness of the world* seems to be founded on a conviction that there is a relationship between a particular person and what happens to him or her, and that this relationship is characterized by justice and control. In this context, "justice" refers to the view that good, decent, moral persons deserve positive outcomes, while misfortune is most appropriate for those who are morally corrupt; "control" implies a conviction that we can personally control or influence what happens to us or that there is some other principle of control (e.g., God) that ultimately influences outcomes in an appropriate way. If there is justice and control in the world, then there is order and comprehensibility rather than randomness and absurdity. The belief in *one's own self-worth* rests on the overall conviction that one is essentially good, decent, and moral in character, as well as wise and effective in one's actions.

Janoff-Bulman concedes that everyone may not hold these three beliefs. But she suggests that these convictions may lie at the foundation of individual world outlooks even when the individuals in question do not think this is what they believe. She cites a variety of data from object relations theorists, attachment theorists, and others who have studied early infant development to argue that the formation of a global model of self and world involving security, trust, and invulnerability is prototypical of her description of fundamental beliefs in one's assumptive world. Finally, Janoff-Bulman contends that our fundamental assumptions are not simply the result of foolhardy wish fulfillment, arguing that while they may be overgeneralizations, they are not maladaptive. The key is the position of fundamental assumptions as most basic in our conceptual system:

> It is at this basic level, I believe, that illusions are most adaptive, for their adaptiveness derives not only from the positive emotions directly tied to these assumptions but also from their implications for motivation.
>
> Our positive illusions at this level afford us the trust and confidence that are necessary to engage in new behaviors, to test our limits. (Janoff-Bulman, 1992, p. 23)

Rando (1993) has added a useful distinction that is perhaps implicit in Janoff-Bulman's account of assumptive worlds but not brought to the fore there, possibly as a result of Janoff-Bulman's concentration on fundamental assumptions and trauma. The distinction advanced by Rando is one between *global assumptions,* which "pertain to the self, others, life, or the world in general," and *specific assumptions,* which are "about the loved one's continued interactive presence" and about the countless expectations the mourner held for that person's forming a significant part of the world" (p. 51).

Challenges to Assumptive Worlds

Trauma

The focus of Janoff-Bulman's work in relation to assumptive worlds is on fundamental assumptions and trauma. As she notes, the revised edition of the *Diagnostic and Statistical Manual (DSM-III-R)* of the American Psychiatric Association (1987, p. 247) describes trauma in relation to its classification of posttraumatic stress disorder (PTSD) as "a psychologically distressing event that is outside the range of usual human experience." Trauma refers to events that can strike psychologically healthy individuals in such a way as to induce an intense psychological crisis, one that seriously challenges an individual's guiding paradigms or fundamental assumptions.

According to Janoff-Bulman, traumatic events have three characteristics: they are out of the ordinary, directly experienced, and perceived as threats to survival and self-preservation. This means that traumatic events always involve an appraisal process, since it is how the event is understood—its interpretation and meaning—that determines whether it will be experienced as traumatic or not. Whatever is perceived as trauma consists of overwhelming life events that pose intense threats to both biological and symbolic survival and generate terror. In trauma, individuals confront their own mortality and recognize their fragility as physical creatures. They recognize that what has happened does not readily fit their long-standing, fundamental, comfortable, and comforting assumptions about themselves and about the world. In short, trauma challenges both the physical survival of the survivor and the most basic assumptions in his or her conceptual system.

Janoff-Bulman suggests that trauma may be distinguished in terms of discrete and chronic events, individual and group victimizations, or child versus adult victimizations. Each of these has its own distinctive qualities, and each may affect an individual's fundamental assumptions in different ways. But the distinction in trauma that she emphasizes and which is perhaps most relevant here is the distinction between events that involve a perpetrator with malicious intent versus natural disasters or so-called acts of God (which might include technological disasters involving human error or negligence but generally do not include specific intent to harm).

In the case of *human-induced victimizations,* as in cases of rape, battering, incest, other criminal assaults, robbery, torture, terrorism, and war-related atrocities, Janoff-Bulman (1992, p. 78) observes that survivors must "confront the existence of evil and question the trustworthiness of people," whether the victimizer is a stranger or someone they know and have trusted. In this type of trauma, survivors are also likely to question themselves and to be questioned by others, asking why this happened to them and why they were selected as the target of this injury. In these ways, assumptions about the benevolence of the world and one's own self-worth are likely to be challenged.

In the case of *natural disasters,* as in instances of life-threatening disease, serious accidents, earthquakes, hurricanes, tornadoes, and floods, issues of randomness and powerlessness are often central for survivors. A sense of interpersonal betrayal is usually absent in these traumatic events, social support is often forthcoming, and one's own sense of self-worth may not be negatively impacted. But the world frequently seems more capricious and frightening after one experiences a natural disaster. Thus the meaningfulness of the world is likely to be at the heart of assumptions that are challenged.

Once again, it is the meaning of the traumatic event for the survivor that determines which assumptions are most affected. How the event is perceived and which assumptions are challenged will depend upon how the event is understood and interpreted. Fundamental convictions in the assumptive world are likely to be shattered or at least challenged. Disillusionment in some degree or other is likely. Alternatives of despair or hope depend on how the survivor copes, as does the new set of basic beliefs that emerges from that coping.

What we learn from this discussion is that trauma takes different forms, that it may or may not involve death, that it may involve both shared and highly individual reactions, and that different types of trauma may challenge different aspects of an individual's assumptive world. In general, trauma reaches deeply into the fundamental convictions of an individual's assumptive world. Often, the extraordinary and overwhelming nature of the traumatic events acts to shatter fundamental assumptions, although Janoff-Bulman notes that an individual's fundamental assumptions may have been tempered or inoculated when they have previously been questioned or challenged. That is, prior stressors of moderate magnitude may contribute to resiliency in responses to subsequent challenges to fundamental assumptions. In any event, "the coping task for survivors of traumatic life events is that of reconstructing fundamental schemas in the face of psychological breakdown and cognitive-emotional disintegration" (Janoff-Bulman, 1992, p. 90).

Death Without Trauma

Confronting death as a survivor or a survivor-to-be, particularly the death of a significant other, is often quite understandably perceived as stressful. The finality and absoluteness of death can have a powerful effect on grief and mourning both before and after its actual occurrence (Rando, 2000). Against this, in some circumstances death may be perceived as the completion of a natural cycle or as providing relief from suffering for the person who has died. This may, but need not always, soften its perceived impact on a survivor.

We have already described some of the implications of situations in which death is the result of trauma. But even nontraumatic forms of death can be associated with particular stressors. For example, deaths that are perceived as "off time"—sudden and unexpected deaths not involving trauma, or deaths that follow upon a protracted and perhaps difficult dying trajectory—as well as deaths that are perceived as violating what is assumed to be the "natural order" of things (such as the death of a child or situations in which an adult child predeceases his or her parent) and deaths that the survivor perceives as having been preventable (such as those involving carelessness or negligence) can all pose special challenges that may interfere with coping and complicate mourning (Rando, 1993).

The lesson for us to note is that even when trauma is not a factor, any death may challenge some aspects of an individual survivor's assumptive world, and some deaths may have special potency to bring into question even the fundamental convictions of that assumptive world. For example, how can my fundamental assumption about the benevolence of the world be maintained when the harshness of death rudely intrudes into a world that I had previously perceived as essentially positive and good? How can my fundamental assumption about the meaningfulness of the world be sustained "When bad things happen to good people" (Kushner, 1981) or when death seems to be random, unpredictable, and uncontrollable—that is, when justice, fairness, order, and comprehensibility are challenged? And how can I continue to uphold my fundamental assumption about my own self-worth when I perceive myself as having failed to fulfill my parental obligation to protect my child from harm?

Even when a survivor's fundamental or global assumptions about the world and the self are not perceived to be directly or overwhelmingly challenged by the death of a loved one, his or her specific assumptions will almost always be violated. Questions about the survivor's identity are often prominent, even when his or her self-worth is not central. This can occur in many ways. Some surviving parents ask themselves, "Am I still a mother or father?" Many bereaved parents find it difficult to respond when they are asked by others, "Do you have any children?" or "How many children do you have?" And after the death of a brother or sister some siblings ask, "Am I still a big/little sister/brother?" Other challenges revolve around whether or how the deceased person can be understood to constitute an ongoing presence in the survivor's assumptive world: Should I just forget her and acknowledge that my life with her is over? Can I construct a new relationship with him in which he can still somehow remain in my life in a new way? How can I "learn to be without the particular interaction, validation, reinforcement, and role-fulfilling behaviors previously existing in the relationship" (Rando, 1993, p. 51)?

Loss Without Death or Trauma

If nontraumatic forms of death can challenge an individual's global or specific assumptions, much the same can be true for other types of losses that involve neither death nor trauma. As in other forms of challenges to one's assumptive world, however, the interpretation and meaning of the loss are again central.

Some losses are of little consequence to an individual, while others are perceived to be of great importance. Some losses are or would be matters of large magnitude in some circumstances or at some points in the life of an individual, but are not so perceived under other conditions. Some losses are quite significant to an individual but are not appreciated by society. These latter include disenfranchised losses (Doka, 1989), which do not receive social recognition, validation, and support.

Losses that challenge one or more aspects of an individual's assumptive world may involve a significant person (such as a child put up for adoption, a lover who ends a relationship, or a spouse who seeks a divorce) or animal (such as a pet who is lost), a valued physical object (such as a family farm or home that must be sold to meet financial obligations, a prized collection lost to fire, or an expensive piece of art that has been stolen), or a symbolic object (such as a social role or status).

It is not possible to inventory here all of the losses an individual might suffer. Nor can we survey all of the ways in which such losses might challenge one or more aspects of an individual's assumptive world. But it is obvious that all relationships and attachments imply the possibility of endings, separations, and loss. And at least some of those losses have the capacity to challenge some of the global and/or specific assumptions that are part of the constellation of beliefs held by some of the individuals who have experienced such losses. Trauma and death are undoubtedly of great importance in human life, but the intensity of the difficulties they present should not be allowed to obscure the very real challenges to an individual's assumptive world that may result from other forms of loss, from primary or secondary losses, or from other challenges in life.

Stress Without Loss, Death, or Trauma

Discussions of assumptive worlds have been dominated by a focus on traumatic loss and, to a lesser degree, by an emphasis on other forms of death-related loss. Losses that are related neither to trauma nor to death have generally received less attention in this context, although they are manifold in both number and type, and despite the fact that they too can lead to challenges to individuals' assumptive worlds. I want to suggest, however, that there is an additional possibility to consider, one involving stressful challenges to assumptive worlds that do not directly incorporate, trauma, death, or loss.

In 1964, the French existentialist writer and philosopher Jean-Paul Sartre declined the Nobel prize for literature because he did not wish to permit his identity to be defined by others. Sartre seemed to believe that even the positive implications of becoming a Nobel laureate—being designated or set apart from his contemporaries and so recognized by others in this way—would unavoidably limit his self-definition through his own free choices. As a result, Sartre turned down a boon that most of the rest of us in similar circumstances would have eagerly embraced.

Sartre's situation can serve here as an example of a challenge to an individual's assumptive world arising not from loss but from actual or potential gain. If trauma is, as we have seen, "a psychologically distressing event that is outside the range of usual human experience," it is not altogether fanciful to think that a stroke of good fortune or an experience of extraordinary gain may be distressing in ways that offer certain parallels to extraordinary loss. Surely gain can sometimes and in principle be as much a source of perceived stress as loss.

Consider the following two examples. Joe Smith has a serious health problem. One of his major bodily organs is failing, and he is told that if the ability of that organ to function declines much further or ceases altogether, he will die very shortly thereafter. Clearly, he faces an immediate crisis and a difficult set of challenges.

The possibility of an organ transplant is raised; Joe is evaluated for transplantation, approved, and placed on the national waiting list. Joe's health continues to decline; he copes as well as he can, waits in suspense and agony, and tries to prepare himself as much as possible for the likelihood that he will die before a suitable organ becomes available.

One day, Joe's doctor suddenly informs him that it appears that a suitable organ has become available. The operation is successful, and we might think Joe lives happily ever after. But everything is not necessarily that simple.

Prior to transplantation, Joe faced major challenges to his assumptive world, along with significant coping tasks. After transplantation, he faces a different but no less compelling set of challenges to his assumptive world and a substantial but no less important set of coping tasks (compare Doka, 1993). In his new life after transplantation, Joe is likely to ask himself questions such as the following: What is now the meaning of my life? Was it fair that someone had to die so I could go on living? Why did that particular person die and why am I the one who is now alive? Is the organ that I received now mine or does it still belong to someone else? How can I ever hope to repay or even properly thank the family members of the donor, those amazing people who made the difficult decision to donate his or her organ? Can I maintain for the remainder of my life the health regimen and self-care obligations which are necessary to sustain my life as a transplant recipient?

This is not an exhaustive list of perceived challenges that might be faced by a transplant recipient. Rather, it is meant only to illustrate some of the stressful challenges confronting individuals who have received the gift of life through a major organ transplant.

A second example of challenges to assumptive worlds that arise from stressors that do not directly involve trauma, death, or loss might be found in winning the lottery or some similar prize. Janoff-Bulman (1992, p. 56) wrote that "winning a lottery . . . may present difficulties in adjusting to one's new economic status, but it is not a stressor that would induce a traumatic response." That may be so, but traumatic events are not the only potential challengers to assumptive worlds and traumatic responses are not the only ones that deserve our attention. Further, winning an incredible prize such as a lottery jackpot does not merely alter one's economic status. It can affect one's personal identity (Who am I—someone who has never before won anything—as a winner and as an individual of sudden and hitherto unparalleled financial resources?), social relations (How do I best act to preserve and maximize my new resources? How do I best respond to new demands placed upon me by relatives, friends, and strangers for financial assistance, for investment, or even for mere access to the glow of the spotlight thrown upon me?), and spiritual convictions (How can I find meaning in these events? How should I best use my gains to serve others and advance the values that I uphold?).

Janoff-Bulman believes traumatic events are more than out of the ordinary, directly experienced occasions that tax our resources. Trauma, as she views it, embodies powerful assaults on our most fundamental assumptions, threatening both bodily and symbolic survival. All of this generates fear and anxiety, hyperarousal and hyperreactivity, and a sense of terror.

We need not quarrel with this, even as we continue to argue (as earlier in this chapter) that challenges to assumptive worlds are not confined to trauma, that some nontraumatic events may challenge both fundamental (global) and/or specific assumptions, that challenges to symbolic assumptions are not necessarily inferior to challenges to physical survival, and that traumatic responses are not the only coping activities that deserve recognition, respect, and support.

Coping with Challenges to Assumptive Worlds

With respect to trauma and fundamental assumptions, Janoff-Bulman (1992, p. 69) has written that "in the end, it is a rebuilding of this trust—the reconstruction of a viable, nonthreatening assumptive world—that constitutes the core coping task of victims." In a sense, this is true, but stated in this way it seems to imply an overoptimistic appreciation of assumptive worlds that is not justified elsewhere by Janoff-Bulman's comments. For example, it is not the case that every individual is in possession of a viable, nonthreatening assumptive world or that every individual's assumptive world contains the three fundamental assumptions that she describes. Janoff-Bulman herself acknowledges that, "of course, not everyone holds these basic assumptions" (p. 6), and not everyone is in possession of a firm sense of basic trust. Some individuals do not perceive the world to be benevolent and meaningful; others do not have a strong sense of their own self-worth. Moreover, challenges to assumptive worlds do not occur merely via trauma or solely at the level of fundamental assumptions.

However, a key goal in life may well involve the establishment, maintenance, and (if need be) reconstruction of an assumptive world in which one can live as well as one is able. To this end, individuals are tasked with a responsibility to cope with challenges to their assumptive worlds. Such coping responds to challenges as they are perceived to arise. Such coping is dynamic, multifaceted, holistic, and highly individualistic in character.

Janoff-Bulman proposed (essentially following Piaget) that coping with challenges to assumptive worlds is likely to involve both assimilation and accommodation. *Assimilation* includes making changes in new, incoming information or challenges in order to achieve a good fit with preexisting schemas or assumptions; by contrast, *accommodation* embodies making changes in preexisting schemas or assumptions in order to maximize their fit with the new input. This means that there are essentially three possibilities for coping: maintaining existing assumptions unchanged in the face of and in spite of events, whose meaning might then be reinterpreted; abandoning existing assumptions completely and adopting new ones shaped by the events; or developing some kind of integrative middle ground in the ongoing negotiation between challenges and assumptions.

Since the stance of most individuals toward their assumptive worlds is essentially conservative, change in those frameworks is typically gradual or incremental, and often more likely at the subordinate level of more limited convictions than at the basic level of our most fundamental assumptions. As Janoff-Bulman argues, sudden and powerful challenges associated with trauma are most likely to break through this essentially conservative posture and reach down to fundamental assumptions, although she does not claim that change at that level is impossible in other ways or in association with other challenges.

Some Implications for Helping Individuals Who Are Coping with Challenges to Their Assumptive Worlds

Helping individuals who are coping with challenges to assumptive worlds may range from simple befriending—which offers the presence of a caring person who accepts and values the bereaved person, practical assistance, useful information, and/or human companionship—through various forms of professional intervention from mental health workers, counselors, and/or therapists. Perhaps the central point in any of these ways of helping is a recognition of the challenges the bereaved person has encountered and is likely still to be struggling with, and an appreciation of the nature of the efforts being made by that individual in response to those challenges to his or her assumptive world.

One key point in all efforts to be helpful is sensitivity (either implicitly or explicitly) to the central role of how the individual is coping. This sensitivity challenges helpers to:

- Appreciate the efforts that individuals make as part of an active process of coping with challenges to their assumptive worlds
- Be respectful of the global and specific convictions that make up an individual's assumptive world
- Be aware of differences and similarities in coping efforts undertaken over time and across persons and social groups
- Remain sensitive to individual perceptions of stressors that call for coping responses
- Recognize the diverse and changing efforts that are involved in coping responses
- Situate coping responses as elements in a holistic and ongoing process of responding to perceived stress, one that may involve physical, psychological, social, and spiritual dimensions
- Evaluate coping responses in terms of their effectiveness in managing (not necessarily mastering) stressful situations
- Try to avoid speaking too facilely of "recovery" or using any other similar term which implies a return to a previous condition ("healing," "getting back to normal") or a simple end point ("getting over," "closure," "completion"), rather than an ongoing process of reinterpreting and integrating past, present, and future challenges in a resilient way that promotes healthy living
- Appreciate coping not primarily in terms of external evaluations but—more importantly from the standpoint of the individual coper—in terms of how he or she is playing the cards that are available (often poor and difficult ones) in response to major challenges in living

From this point of view, we have much to learn from Janoff-Bulman's (1992, pp. 174–175) concluding comments about survivors who have coped effectively with challenges arising from traumatic events that affect their assumptions and fundamental convictions:

> [T]hese survivors recognize the possibility of tragedy, but do not allow it to pervade their self- and worldviews. . . .

[For such survivors] the world is benevolent, but not absolutely; events that happen make sense, but not always; the self can be counted on to be decent and competent, but helplessness is at times a reality....

There is disillusionment, yet it is generally not the disillusionment of despair. Rather, it is disillusionment tempered by hope....

[In the end, this view] involves an acknowledgement of real possibilities, both bad and good—of disaster in spite of human efforts, of triumph in spite of human limitations.

These comments describe the great capacities of the human spirit in individuals who, in the face of sharp and deep challenges to their fundamental convictions, have successfully involved themselves in a creative process of coping that embodies a reconstruction of encounters, events, relationships, and attitudes in their lives and in their assumptive worlds.

References

American Psychiatric Association. (1987). *Diagnostic and statistical manual of mental disorders* (3rd ed., rev.). Washington, DC: American Psychiatric Association.

Cantril, H. (1966). *The pattern of human concerns.* New Brunswick, NJ: Rutgers University Press.

Corr, C. A., Nabe, C. M., & Corr, D. M. (2000). *Death and dying, life and living* (3rd ed.). Belmont, CA: Wadsworth.

Doka, K. J. (Ed.). (1989). *Disenfranchised grief: Recognizing hidden sorrow.* Lexington, MA: Lexington Books.

Doka, K. J. (1993). *Living with life-threatening illness: A guide for patients, their families, and caregivers.* Lexington, MA: Lexington Books.

Elias, N. (1991). On human beings and their emotions: A process–sociological essay. In M. Featherstone, J. Hepworth, & B. S. Turner (Eds.), *The body: Social process and cultural theory* (pp. 103–125). London: Sage.

Janoff-Bulman, R. (1992). *Shattered assumptions: Towards a new psychology of trauma.* New York: The Free Press.

Kushner, H. S. (1981). *When bad things happen to good people.* New York: Avon.

Lazarus, R. S., & Folkman, S. (1984). *Stress, appraisal, and coping.* New York: Springer.

Monat, A., & Lazarus, R. S. (Eds.). (1991). *Stress and coping: An anthology* (3rd ed.). New York: Columbia University Press.

Moos, R. H., & Schaefer, J. A. (1986). Life transitions and crises: A conceptual overview. In R. H. Moos & J. A. Schaefer (Eds.), *Coping with life crises: An integrated approach* (pp. 3–28). New York: Plenum.

Parkes, C. M. (1971). Psycho-social transitions: A field of study. *Social Science and Medicine, 5,* 101–115.

Parkes, C. M. (1975). What becomes of redundant world models? A contribution to the study of adaptation to change. *British Journal of Medical Psychology, 48,* 131–137.

Rando, T. A. (1993). *Treatment of complicated mourning.* Champaign, IL: Research Press.

Rando, T. A. (Ed.). (2000). *Clinical dimensions of anticipatory mourning: Theory and practice in working with the dying, their loved ones, and their caregivers.* Champaign, IL: Research Press.

Weisman, A. D. (1984). *The coping capacity: On the nature of being mortal.* New York: Human Sciences Press.

10.

Beyond the Beveled Mirror

Mourning and Recovery
from Childhood Maltreatment

Sandra L. Bloom

When someone close to us dies, society generally accepts and even expects us to undergo a process of mourning. Death presents a tangible and comprehensible loss. Throughout history, cultures have built traditions and customs to provide a passage for the bereaved that enables us to let go of those who have died, in order to prepare us to create new attachments.

But society has yet to recognize the necessity and value of grieving for other kinds of losses besides those associated with death. A common denominator among our now more than seven thousand Sanctuary patients are the "little deaths"—of hope, of innocence, of love, and of joy. For some, the sources of grief constitute the loss of already established assumptions and beliefs about self, home, family and society. For others, the assaults to their integrity began when they were so young that they had no time to even develop a coherent assumptive world before their lives were shattered. Complicating the process of grieving for adult survivors is the fact that the losses that accompany child maltreatment are cloaked in silence, lost in the shrouds of history, and largely unrecognized. In general, their grief for these losses is unaccepted, rejected, denied and stigmatized. But these "little deaths" remain as unremoved splinters in the survivor's psyche for decades. Although new protective psychic tissue may form over these wounds and new experiences may allow the child to develop assumptions about the world that contradict the traumatic and abusive experiences, the psychic splinters remain, surfacing again in adulthood, often triggered by a new insult to the individual's well-being. Child neglect represents particular challenges for adult survivors because they must grieve for things they never had and thus never had the chance to lose.

This chapter will focus on these losses. Over the last fifteen years, we have specialized in the treatment of adult survivors of child abuse and neglect in our inpatient treatment programs and followed many of them as outpatients (Bloom, 1997, 2000; Bloom & Bills, 1998; 2000). We have learned about how difficult it is to form healthy attachments as an adult when your childhood attachments have been so scarring that the pain of the past continues in the present. Attachment theory and our growing understanding of the impact of trauma and traumatic grief provide ways to understand how trauma and loss in childhood affect adult relationships and impact the capacity to grieve. Our patients have taught us a great deal about loss and the difficulties they encounter in grieving for the omissions that accompany child neglect as well as the more flagrant commissions of physical, emotional, and sexual abuse. In this chapter I will detail many of those losses through the testimony of several people who agreed to be interviewed. Finally, we will look at the process of recovery. Our treatment model uses an acronym to describe the phases of recovery that trauma survivors must work through in the process of their recovery: S.A.G.E. The four letters stand for safety, affect management, grieving, and emancipation (Foderaro, in press; Foderaro and Ryan, in press). This chapter focuses on the G in S.A.G.E., and we will look at the losses—and the discoveries—that accompany the healing process.

Attachment and Grief

The losses that accompany childhood exposure to terror and violence can only be grasped within the context of attachment theory. One of John Bowlby's great contributions was to recognize that attachment behavior is a fundamental part of our evolutionary heritage and therefore has high survival value. Primates—including humans—need to attach from cradle to grave, and any disruption in normal attachment relationships, particularly those being established in early childhood, is likely to cause developmental problems (Bowlby, 1988). He recognized that "grief and mourning occur in infancy whenever the responses mediating attachment behavior are activated and the mother figure continues to be unavailable" (Bowlby, 1960, p. 9). He went on to discuss how "the experience of loss of mother in the early years is an antecedent of relevance in the development of personalities prone to depressive and other psychiatric illnesses and that these conditions are best understood as sequelae of pathological mourning" (Bowlby, 1960, p. 11). He identified four main variants of pathological responses by bereaved adults: (1) anxiety and depression, which he saw as the persistent and unconscious yearning to recover the lost person, originally adaptive because it produced strong motivation for reunion; (2) intense and persistent anger and reproach expressed toward others or the self and originally intended to achieve reunion with the lost relationship and discourage further separation; (3) absorption in caring for someone else who has also been bereaved, sometimes amounting to a compulsion; and (4) denial that the relationship is permanently lost (Bowlby, 1963).

Since Bowlby originally made these astute observations, other clinicians and researchers have been busily extending his work to show the relationship between disrupted attachment in childhood as a result of maltreatment and the development of adult pathology (de Zulueta, 1994). As far back as 1963, Khan discussed the idea of cumulative trauma and the impact of protective failures: "cumulative trauma is the result of the breaches in the mother's role as a protective shield over the whole course of the child's development, from infancy to adolescence" (Khan, 1963). He went on to discuss how this can leave a person vulnerable to breakdown later in life. There is a long-established connection between childhood loss and depression (Bowlby, 1980). Adam has recently reviewed the strong connection between suicidal behavior in adolescents and adults and disrupted attachment

(1994). In the last decades, other workers have concretized the relationship between insecure forms of attachment in childhood and the evolution of personality disorders (West & Keller, 1994). Fonagy and colleagues have helped illuminate the important relationship between disrupted attachment and borderline states (1998), while Liotti has written about the development of dissociative disorders within an attachment framework (1995, 1999). Others have looked at both highly conflicted families and violent couples from the point of view of disrupted childhood attachment relationships (Henry & Holmes, 1998; Roberts & Noller, 1998), while Main and Hesse (1990) and Solomon and George (1999) have provided abundant theoretical and evidence-based data showing how the disrupted childhood attachment relationships of parents can be carried over into the ways in which they parent their own children.

Complex Posttraumatic Stress Disorder

Of the patients we treat, most have been victims of severe physical, psychological, or sexual abuse or neglect. Some have experienced only one form of child maltreatment; many have experienced two or more. Childhood maltreatment is associated with a wide variety of physical, psychological, and social dysfunction in childhood and in adulthood, and there is now a significant body of literature reviewing various aspects of comorbidity (Ellason, Ross, Sainton, and Mayran, 1996; Grady, 1997; Koss, Koss, & Woodruff, 1991; Leserman et al., 1996; Salmon & Calderbank, 1996; van der Kolk, 1996). There are well-established connections between childhood exposure to overwhelming, traumatic events and chronic depressive disorders, somatization disorder, anxiety disorders, and various personality disorders, especially borderline personality disorder (Kessler, Sonnega, Broment, Hughes, & Nelson, 1995; Solomon & Davidson, 1997). However, many of the patients we see enter treatment carrying two, three, or even more psychiatric labels, many of the same diagnostic categories that have been implicated as the long-term results of disrupted attachment relationships. In many ways, the trauma-related disorders can be seen as disorders of disrupted attachment.

Children can be maltreated in a number of different ways, and it is common for maltreated children to have multiple victimization experiences. In a recent survey of a large HMO adult population performed by the Centers for Disease Control in Atlanta, more than half of respondents reported having had at least one type of childhood exposure to adverse experience, and one-fourth reported having had two or more. The seven categories of adverse childhood experiences included: psychological, physical, or sexual abuse; witnessing violence against the mother; or living with household members who were substance abusers, mentally ill or suicidal, or ever imprisoned.

The overlapping symptoms and complex clinical picture characteristic of adults who have experienced childhood maltreatment is more comprehensible if we formulate the problem as one of complex posttraumatic stress disorder (Herman, 1992; van der Kolk, Roth, Pelcovitz, & Mandel, 1994). Field trials for *DSM-IV* (American Psychiatric Association, 1994), demonstrated that there are significant differences between survivors of disasters who suffer from posttraumatic stress disorder and childhood survivors of maltreatment. These differences fall into seven major categories of dysfunction: alterations in regulating affective arousal, alterations in attention and consciousness, somatization, alterations in self-perception, alterations in perception of the perpetrator, alterations in relations to others, and alterations in systems of meaning. These symptom clusters have been demonstrated to differentiate sufferer of acute adult-onset trauma syndromes associated with disaster victims from adult victims of childhood interpersonal violence and abuse (Van der Kolk et al., 1994).

When viewed from the point of view of the grief literature, difficulties with managing affect and alterations in attention and consciousness may reflect two of the final adult personality outcomes of two of Bowby's sequelae of pathological mourning. The unrelenting yearning and searching for the lost love relationship and the defenses built up to protect against this yearning can be seen as an underpinning for many of the symptoms that lead people to seek treatment. The persistent anger and reproach originally intended to achieve reunion and discourage more separation are common problems for our patients in all of their relationships and strongly color the nature of the therapeutic alliance.

Alterations in self-perception, in perception of the perpetrator, and in relationships with others all can be understood in the context of an expectable developmental outcome in the face of disrupted early attachments. It is well established from studies of captive victims of all kinds—political prisoners, torture survivors, hostages, and both adult and child victims of family violence—that when people are placed in situations of inescapable danger for prolonged periods of time, they may develop very strange relationships with their captors and alter their perception of themselves. This phenomenon has become known as "trauma-bonding" (Herman, 1992; James, 1994; van der Kolk, 1989). Trauma-bonding is a relationship that is based on terror and the twisting and manipulation of normal attachment behavior in service of someone else's malevolent intent. People who are terrorized experience the perpetrator as being in total control: the source of pain but also the source of pain relief, the source of threat but also the source of hope. Victims come to internalize the experience of helplessness and the role of perpetrator and then later in life unconsciously re-create the pattern of these early and traumatizing relationships in new relationships. Successful grieving means letting go of these patterns as well as letting go of the former abusive relationships, even though these relationships are also associated with a deep sense of fear and foreboding at their loss.

Somatization may represent not just the effects of prolonged stress but also the long-term effects of suppressed grief on the body. In the study of childhood exposure to adverse experiences, there was a graded relationship between the number of categories of childhood exposure experienced and each of the adult health risk behaviors and diseases that were studied. People who had experienced four or more categories of childhood exposure, compared to those who had experienced none, had a four- to twelvefold increased risk for alcoholism, drug abuse, depression, and suicide attempt; a two- to fourfold increase in smoking, poor self-rated health, likelihood of having fifty or more sex partners, and risk of sexually transmitted disease; and a 1.4- to 1.6-fold increase in physical inactivity and severe obesity. The number of categories of adverse childhood exposures showed a graded relationship to the presence of certain adult diseases, including ischemic heart disease, cancer, chronic lung disease, skeletal fractures, and liver disease (Felitti et al., 1998). In another study looking at the connection in women between childhood adverse experiences and physical health, a history of childhood maltreatment was significantly associated with several adverse physical health outcomes, including perceived poor overall health, greater physical and emotional disability, increased number of distressing physical symptoms, and a greater number of health risk behaviors (Walker et al., 1999).

Disrupted systems of meaning can be understood as the logical outgrowth of growing up within intimate childhood contexts of mistrust, deceit, hypocrisy, and cruelty that are embedded within a larger social context that insists that children are to be valued, loved, cherished, and protected from harm. A child's exposure to deliberate malevolence at the hands of a primary caregiver powerfully confuses the ability of the child to correlate his or her own experience of reality with the realities of other people. The contradictions are shattering. Most importantly, perhaps, this bears on the issue of justice, a fundamental human striving that is rooted in our primate-derived sense of reciprocity and is the basis of all social relationships. If children are treated unjustly, they will seek justice for their hurt. If their family or their larger society denies them justice, then they will seek revenge against themselves, others, or both. When children discover that the adults who hurt them were never held accountable by society for the harm they inflicted, this causes disruption not only in the attachment relationship with the perpetrator but also with the self, other members of the family, and society at large. As Charny (1996) points out, "The avoidance of defining perpetration of evil as a disturbance in its own right reaches its bizarre extreme in the classic literature on child abuse—violence to the child. According to the prevailing definitions, the majority of parents who abuse children are not emotionally disturbed . . . it is utter nonsense to ignore the fact that anyone who seriously abuses his or her child is seriously disturbed" (p. 483).

Traumatic Grief

While attachment theorists have been carefully formulating theory and analyzing data from the perspective of developmental psychopathology (Cicchetti & Lynch, 1995), clinicians and researchers in the overlapping fields of traumatic stress studies and thanatology have been broadening our understanding of what happens to people who are traumatized and the ways in which traumatic bereavement differs from normal bereavement. Jacobs has described traumatic grief in relation to any death that is personally devastating and is characterized by traumatic separation. Traumatic grief has been shown to be associated with impaired role performance, functional impairment, subjective sleep disturbance, low self-esteem, depression, and anxiety, as well as a high risk of cancer, cardiac disorders, alcohol and tobacco consumption, and suicidal ideation (Jacobs, 1999). Other authors have looked at the various ways that traumatic bereavement and exposure to death and dying affect various populations and age groups (Figley, 1997; Figley, Bride, & Mazza, 1999), while still others have looked at the way entire communities grieve after mass tragic events (Zinner & Williams, 1999).

Rando (1993) has written extensively about the treatment of complicated mourning and has connected unresolved grief to many of the symptoms of chronic and complex posttraumatic stress disorder. She has also looked at the difficulties survivors encounter mourning someone who has victimized them, as is so often the case in survivors of childhood maltreatment. At least since Lindemann's seminal work (1944), the connection between the normal somatic manifestations of grief and symptoms of complicated mourning have been recognized (Engel, 1961; Rando, 1993).

Although the literature is by now rich and persuasive in conceptualizing the relationship between traumatic loss and disrupted attachment, relatively little has been detailed about the losses that do not involve actual death but do represent extraordinary loss for adults who were maltreated as children. These "little" losses occur in the context of a long-standing pattern characterized by the absence of sustaining and loving caregiver behavior. As children, our patients often had parents who were physically present, but the nature of their parenting was so abusive and/or neglectful that their losses are seen not as losses at all but as a way of life.

Nonetheless, recovery from loss requires the working through of a mourning process. Ochberg (1988) has talked about some of the necessary tasks required to complete the process of grief. Mourners must be able to express their emotions, understand the meaning of the lost person or object, and be able to surface and work through the ambivalence in the relationship, all of which will eventually free them up to attach trust and love to new significant others and find appropriate replacements for the lost relationships. These tasks are very difficult to complete for adult survivors of child abuse and neglect. Being raised in abusive homes characterized by disruptive attachment relationships almost guarantees that people will have difficulty in managing their emotions. The problems associated with disrupted meaning schemas will make it difficult for them to understand the meaning of the lost person, lost experience, lost self. Trauma-bonding may make it feel very unsafe to deal with the ambivalence in the earlier relationship, even if it occurred decades before. The consequent lack of resolution interferes with the capacity to establish new, safe, and loving relationships, and even to find appropriate people to love in order to replace the old abusive ones. Some people will stay aloof from relationships altogether so as not to become involved in more abuse. Others, having no other internalized standard, use the abusive relationships as their only norm. In this way the past becomes the present. As has long been pointed out in the field of grief studies, failure to complete the tasks of grieving can impair future development and adaptation (Engel, 1961). Lack of grief resolution can also impact on physical health. The study of childhood exposure to adverse experiences mentioned earlier (Felitti et al.,1998) may provide links between traumatic grief, traumatic stress, disrupted attachment, and childhood maltreatment.

Recovery from the Impact of Child Maltreatment

There is by now an extensive literature on the treatment of people who suffer from the complex syndromes related to a past history of child maltreatment. Since Pierre Janet first talked about the process of trauma resolution and the need to "liquidate" traumatic memory, there has been an understanding that trauma treatment progresses in stages or, perhaps more accurately, phases (van der Kolk, Brown, & van der Hart, 1989). Like the descriptions of bereavement, however, these phases are dynamic, interpenetrating and spiraling, rather than indicative of a clear stepwise progression.

We use the acronym S.A.G.E to describe the way we understand this dynamic movement. Our patients have helped us develop the concepts over the last fifteen years, and as a result the S.A.G.E. model has become a practical and useful way for our patients and their therapists to map out a road to recovery. *S* represents safety—the starting point for all efforts at healing. We understand that there are four levels of safety: physical safety or the ability to be safe from physical or sexual harm; psychological safety, or the ability to be safe with oneself; social safety, or the ability to be safe with others; and moral safety, or the ability to live and work within a personal and professional context whose guiding value is a respect for life (Bloom, 1997).

In practical terms, people generally enter treatment because they are not safe in any of a number of ways. They may be self-mutilating or have attempted or are threatening suicide. They may be abusing drugs or alcohol, may have an eating disorder, or are becoming increasingly nonfunctional because of escalating anxiety. They may be in dangerous relationships or placing themselves at unnecessary risk without understanding why or feeling able to control their behavior. Whatever the reason, the first step in recovery is to confront existing issues of safety, develop a plan for the restoration of safety, and implement that plan.

In the course of learning to manage safety by inhibiting dangerous or damaging behavior, however, it quickly becomes obvious to people that their unsafe behaviors have been serving a useful purpose. The behaviors have helped them exert control over emotions that are otherwise overwhelming, toxic, oppressive, and extremely painful. In order to be safe, they must learn how to manage emotions in health-promoting ways. This process is reflected in the *A* phase of S.A.G.E.: affect management. With enough social support, cognitive restructuring, skill development, inner fortitude, and perseverance, our patients allow themselves to trade in their self-destructive behaviors for healthier relationships. But the very act of taking such a relational risk with therapists, teachers, friends, and family opens the door to the next phase of S.A.G.E: grieving.

Unresolved, Stigmatized, Disenfranchised Loss

Adults who were maltreated as children carry around with them the impact of delayed, unresolved, "stigmatized" loss (Sprang & McNeil, 1995). According to the descriptions of stigmatized grief, the incidents giving rise to the loss happen suddenly, are associated with violence, result in others fearing contagion and blaming the victim, and result in victims believing that they should have done something to prevent the events or that they deserve what happened. Several of the characteristics of stigmatized grief describe the situation of abused children. In some cases, as in sexual abuse, the loss of a secure relationship with the parent can be quite sudden and unexpected. Child abuse is clearly associated with violence, and the victims are usually told that they have done something to deserve the violence. Their parents and society at large tend to blame them, and frequently they are told that if they had behaved differently, they could have prevented it. Social denial of the magnitude of the problem is still a prominent feature of our social environment.

Victims' grief is delayed because most abused children learn how to adapt to even astonishingly difficult circumstances in order to survive, but they do pay a price. A later crisis or loss in adult life may unmask an underlying vulnerability that has been lurking beneath the apparently normal surface of their lives for years. The losses they sustain are unresolved because for most survivors of childhood abuse, there is no clearly established and socially acceptable pathway for grief resolution if actual physical death has not been involved. Their losses cannot even be acknowledged as loss. Their grief is stigmatized because it is seen as a "blemish of individual character" (Goffman, 1963). Losses associated with childhood maltreatment that are only recognized or surfaced in adulthood are not considered legitimate reasons for grief by the larger society. Such individuals are not "legitimate" mourners.

According to Doka (1989), who has written about "disenfranchised" grief, there are three general types of people who suffere such grief: individuals whose relationships are socially unrecognized, illegitimate, or in other ways unsanctioned; persons whose loss does not fit the typical norms of appropriateness; and people whose ability to grieve is in question or who are not considered to be legitimate grievers. Victims of child maltreatment experience many losses that carry with them no social legitimacy. In the case of victims of sexual abuse, the losses they sustain are often not only unrecognized but denied by the perpetrator and by other family members. Victims of other forms of maltreatment are frequently labeled as "whiners" or "complainers" who manipulate others with their "victim mentality." As for normative appropriateness, the society at large barely is willing to deal with death as a legitimate cause for bereavement behavior. The social attitude toward most other losses is generally "get over it." And even among therapists and otherwise supportive others, there may be great resistance to empathizing with the grief victims feel at finally having to give up a relationship with someone who has been abusive, dangerous, and cruel or letting go of a behavior that has helped them cope and feel in control, even if that behavior appears "crazy." They are not legitimate grievers because the losses they experience are usually not considered appropriate causes for grief. After all, they survived, didn't they?

Bearing Witness to Childhood Loss

The seven categories associated with complex posttraumatic stress disorder are a useful way to classify the various losses our patients experience. In the following pages, several people were willing to share their experiences of loss secondary to childhood abuse and neglect. Each person is at a different point in her personal recovery, and each one has suffered unique experiences. All, however, were able to relate to the concept of loss and the questions I asked them in the interview. I have changed their names and identifying information and, after transcribing their conversations, received their permission to use the quotations I have included.

Samantha (S) is in her thirties and has been diagnosed with schizoaffective disorder. She has a history of self-mutilation, suicide attempts, multiple hospitalizations, and substance abuse and has been considered to be chronically mentally ill. Along with everything else, she episodically has a thought disorder and has difficulty separating reality from her paranoid ideation. She has been tried on many medications and is currently on antidepressants, antianxiety medication, and antipsychotic agents. She is living in a sheltered apartment, is no longer self-mutilating, and is determined to get well. Despite her long history of mental health problems, Samantha managed to complete college. She recognizes that she is currently grieving for the many losses she has sustained throughout her life as the result of her extremely abusive, chaotic, neglectful, and dangerous home life. She was sexually abused by her father and physically abused and neglected by both parents, both of whom were and still are active alcoholics.

Jodie (J) is also in her thirties. College-educated, she has a responsible position in business. Sexually abused by a relative beginning at a very young age, she lived with a number of symptoms until seeking treatment. She originally sought treatment because of posttraumatic symptoms secondary to her involvement in a violent relationship.

Helen (H) is thirty-seven years old, college-educated, and employed by a state government agency. She suffered physical abuse at the hands of her father, emotional abuse by her mother, and severe neglect from both parents. One of five children, her graduate-school-trained father refused to spend money on the family home or his children, so there was not even sufficient clothing or shoes or heat in the house when they were growing up. Neither Helen nor her siblings were given sufficient health care as children, and these tangible omissions were paralleled by a complete lack of affection, love, or empathic regard for the children. She originally sought treatment because her frequent negative encounters with authority figures and coworkers made it impossible for her to hold a job.

Rachel (R) is in her early forties and runs a successful hair salon with her husband. She was raised by a mother whom she describes as a hippie who ran with the avant-garde set in New York City in the '50s and '60s and left her children to fend for themselves emotionally, though she did provide for them financially.

Losses Secondary to Child Maltreatment

Alterations in Ability to Manage Emotions

Children require loving and empathic relationships in order to develop properly. The immature central nervous system needs caregivers who are willing to serve as protective shields against overwhelming arousal. The hallmark characteristic of all forms of child maltreatment is empathic failure (Weil, 1992). When exposure to abuse and neglect corrupts the family environment, children lose—or fail to develop—the ability to modulate their own level of emotional arousal, and as a result they are forced to use whatever coping skills they happen to hit on that calm them down. Often those coping skills are self-destructive—drugs, alcohol, aggression, self-abuse—but these behaviors, which are within the child or the adult's control, are preferable to the noxious experience of overwhelming distress. The inability to manage emotions in a relational, constructive way means that later the individual must grieve for how much more difficult life is and has been for him or her than for other people. It means that the individual loses a sense of being safe and secure in the world, if he or she ever had it in the first place. The prolonged effects of exposure to overwhelming stress means that it is very difficult to finish the grieving process that enables more successful relationships, because being able to grieve means being able to tolerate and work through very painful emotional experiences.

Loss of Ability to Manage Emotions Like Other People

Samantha has great difficulty in managing her emotions, especially now that she has given up self-abuse as a way of coping. Samantha provides us with an example of one way in which maltreated children, without supportive adults to help them adequately express themselves, may fail to develop the ability to associate feelings with words, also known as alexithymia (Krystal, 1988). As a result, she lives with what is now a state of pain, and finding verbal expression is difficult. People from more secure homes learn how to use other people as resources to help manage feelings when they are overwhelming, but children deprived of empathic care have great difficulty relying on others or even knowing how to get the help they need.

> S. My day-to-day living now is so painful because I never really felt anything and now I am. I had no words to attach to even asking for help. Even now I struggle with feeling and talking. . . .
>
> There was nothing else, nothing else but self-abuse. Anytime I felt anything I had to dissociate. I couldn't handle feelings at all.

Loss of a Sense of Safety

A basic sense of safety is what serves as the foundation for all developmental achievements. Children who grow up in violent homes are robbed of this basic necessity. For them, emotional, intellectual, and creative energy must be put in the service of protecting their minds and bodies from assaults at the hands of the people they are supposed to be able to trust. Samantha's home was so chaotic, violent, and deprived that the listener is more amazed at her capacity to go on, despite her limitations, than at the extent and magnitude of those limitations. Rebecca talks about the terrible and pervasive anxiety that accompanies a child without context, a child living with emotional neglect, while Helen focuses on the daily fear of living with the violence of physical and verbal abuse.

> S. All my life I had to worry about things like how early in the day I should wet my pants so I could go home and check on what was happening at home. It was pure chaos—addiction to drugs and alcohol, sexual and physical abuse. I had to be one step ahead all the time. . . .
>
> My sister's best friend was killed in the house too—she was twelve and I was ten. They were playing with guns and it went off accidentally. The girl and my sister were getting high, they got out the gun, I had the gun and my sister went to get the gun from me, and the girl was shot in the head. Then my father started shooting at all of the kids to teach them a lesson.

> R. I remember always feeling afraid. I was always afraid of going out to the playground for recess at school, but things were even worse if it rained. Then we would have to go to the cafeteria and I would be terrified. I would get so distressed that the teacher would send me home with my brother and I would miss more time from school and make my brother miss school as well.

> H. I was always afraid of my father because of his violence, his angry outbursts. My mother was verbally abusive but not violent, just haranguing. I was not safe in those regards. Did I fear for my life? Not really, but there was never a sense of safety or comfort.

Loss of Ability to Complete Mourning

The disruption in the developing ability to manage emotions makes enduring and working through loss extremely difficult. Our patients have great difficulties in tolerating the painful affects that accompany the resurfacing of unresolved grief. As a result of the process of therapy at Sanctuary, our inpatient program, Samantha has learned about the importance of grieving and is allowing herself to grieve as best as she can. She is even struggling to educate the staff of the transitional living facility where she lives about the importance of the grieving process. Jodie has come out on the other side of the mourning phase of her treatment, at least for now, and has come to recognize how much her failure to grieve has impacted on her developmental progress. Helen has not yet really even begun to grieve. Before she can allow herself to work through her losses, she must allow herself to feel the emotions associated with the losses in the first place. Helen's protective mechanism as a child was to detach herself from relationships and from her own emotional states, and now those states have become foreign to her.

> S. My doctor and Sanctuary encourage me to work through my grief, but even with them it feels too big to manage sometimes, especially in front of someone. With my doctor, I have to take care of how she is going to manage my feelings and I feel protective of her. With where I live now, a lot is going to be about me educating them. They seem to miss the whole grieving piece. And that makes it harder for me to deal with it, because I need them to understand. I am still struggling to put words to how I feel. I don't have words. One of the things I am working on is staying in the present, keeping the past and the present separate. I get pissed off, because why should I have to educate them when they are supposed to be helping me?

> J. I am not avoiding grieving any longer but it took a long time to get to it—about twenty-nine years.

> H. I don't like people seeing me sad or emotional in any way. It is embarrassing to have emotions in front of people. Particularly crying in front of someone. People tell me that I should have sadness about not having a relationship with my parents. I don't talk to them. But I don't feel it. They are probably right. This male therapist I was seeing kept telling me that I have a lot of anger towards my parents and one day I had an explosion of anger towards them. I guess you could be quite debilitated by it, if it is bad enough. But that is just conjecture. Like people don't let themselves get angry because they might do something violent. But that is all intellectual.

Alterations in Attention and Consciousness

Exposure to chronic states of physiological hyperarousal interferes with the capacity to learn, to voluntarily direct attention, and to maintain focus (Perry, 1994; Putnam & Trickett, 1993). Traumatized children have little ability to self-protect. Confronted with the massive physiological hyperarousal that accompanies exposure to violence, there is little they can do to fight back or to flee. But they can dissociate—fragment their experience in a way that protects them against the very real danger of physiological overload. But the price they pay for this protection is substantial—the loss of a sense of wholeness, of an integrated self that adults from functional families simply take for granted.

Loss of Wholeness

Jodie's experience gave me the title for this chapter. She offers her childhood experience of fragmentation up as a way of helping us understand what this "beveled mirror" effect looks like, feels like. And then she goes on to describe the separateness, the state of dissociation she felt that she now understands as grief.

> *J.* I had this thing when I was a child, this fantasy. My parents had a beveled mirror in their room and the regular mirror was in the center. I thought that everyone in the world must see me as in the beveled part of it, the part that was screwed up, with the eyes over here and the nose separate, in pieces, in shards, because that is how I felt— disconnected. I had this fantasy that my parents must be paying doctors all over the world to fix everyone's eyes so that they would see me as they would see a normal person because nobody knew really, what was going on inside of me. I was around seven or eight....
>
> Before I came to Sanctuary, I never really knew what these symptoms were about because the grief was like something separate from me. Now I am feeling it in my body as well. Now it is all inside of me and I can feel the grief bubbling instead of just being outside of me somewhere. I thought of this separate entity as a kind of blackness that was separate from me. It held so much power that it could control me and turn me against myself like wanting to kill myself or wanting to starve myself or just doing negative things to myself. I really thought about it as a separate thing. I knew it had something to do with my trauma—that the trauma was still controlling me. I could tell by the power and the impact it had on me that it had something to do with the past.

Alterations in Relationships

Abused children lose relationships. Some maltreated children have no one to relate to from the very beginning. But many parents are adequate in supplying an infant's basic needs but cannot handle the demands of a growing, active child. For such a child, the loss of the formerly nurturing parent can be experienced as a death for which there are no words. The loss of early attachment relationship is devastating in its impact upon the capacity to establish safe and trusting relationships as an adult. And it is not just individual relationships that are affected. It is within the family that we first learn about political, social, and economic arrangements between people. Dysfunction in family relationships will directly carry over into the school, the workplace, and the community-at-large. As a result, many survivors of systematic abuse do not feel a sense of place in their social system, and they do not know how to achieve such a place without paying a price similar to the one they have already paid in their families. History repeats itself in the life of the individual inside and outside the family, and then history repeats itself on the part of the whole group.

Loss of Attachment Relationships

Children can lose siblings, friends, pets, and other important relationships secondary to the abuse. Samantha's story about the puppy, below, is particularly poignant because in responding with understandable rage to her father's perfidy, she becomes complicit in his murderous behavior—yet another loss that she cannot begin to touch. The priest's failure to respond is another way that her capacity to trust other human beings is compromised, based on a realistic notion of what she could expect from other people. When Jodie's parents failed to protect her from the sexual proclivities of her mother's stepfather, even though he had previously molested her mother, she experiences a secondary empathic failure, one that is possibly even harder to resolve than the original abusive incident. For abused and neglect children, relationships with animals can take on an even greater significance than the usually deep attachment that secure children have with their pets. In Helen's case, the pets were as neglected as the children, and there was nothing she could do to help herself or them. Sometimes siblings can serve as buffers against the abuse of the parents, but in cases like Helen's, the children are turned against each other, competitively struggling for what little affection and care is available.

S. My older sister was removed from our home when she was ten by Child Protective Services. I was eight at the time. I was responsible for the younger children. My little sister that died was my baby doll. My father made me watch while he smothered her. I still have flashbacks about that. I was afraid about what was going to happen next. I got in the crib with her and tried to wake her up afterward, and then when my mother came home, my father blamed me, said I had killed her. Mother didn't believe him. They called it a crib death. . . .

S. I had gotten a puppy for Christmas and my father knew it meant so much to me, after my sister was killed. I could attach to the puppy. But he would destroy anything I liked. He took the puppy and me into the bathroom, put peanut butter between my legs and had the puppy lick it. I put rat poison in the honey my father used in his cereal and he gave some to the puppy. The puppy died, but my father didn't. He got sick, that's all. I had my father's baby when I was in eighth grade. I already had had one abortion. I went to the priest for help and told him who the father was. The priest told me to keep going to church and did nothing else about it.

J. I remember longing for protection from my mom, that she would act like a parent instead of a sibling that I was supposed to take care of. I had a longing for a dad that didn't rage and try to make us something we weren't and a longing for a grandfather who didn't use me for whatever he wanted.

H. I remember losing one particular teacher in third grade who was really good to me. This teacher recognized my plight. And I lost pet cats that died. They were sickly because my parents wouldn't pay for veterinary care and they would die off. They were very important to me. Also, I had a close relationship with my younger sister and when I was about nine or ten, my older sister convinced her I was the devil incarnate. I had five brothers and sisters but no one would play with me. My older sister had this practice of taking away my friends and one of them was my younger sister. It happened several times. I also lost two very close friends because of her. I have had devastating experiences when boyfriends broke up with me over the past fifteen years—a number of times. In the last ten years, three have broken up with me. The last one was that we couldn't agree on children—I didn't want any and he did.

Loss of the Capacity to Establish Safe and Trusting Relationships

Children who come from abusive and neglecting homes may have no models for relationship other than the ones they experience at the hands of their parents. Without such a model it is extremely difficult to establish trusting and safe relationships with others. We are conservative creatures and tend to repeat the past because we so easily adapt and form habits. If the definition of relationship that we behaviorally experience is one based on empathic failure, it will be difficult for us to establish any other kind of relationship, even as adults. Samantha's tentative moves to create a friendship in college are brave, and for a while effective, but even so, the course of normal endings or change takes on a significance for her that is overwhelming because of all the unresolved experiences of loss from the past. She has no pathway for knowing how to lose and begin again. Her extreme vulnerability to the disorganization of loss manifests as eruptions in clearly symptomatic behavior. Jodie, aware of the dangers of vulnerability, spends most of her life keeping herself away from confronting the demands of intimacy, although she is aware of her fear and clearly wants to overcome it. Helen stays away from intimacy as well, and what relationships she has now are with men. She overtly declares that she cannot trust women. Although both parents were abusive, her mother emotionally violated her with verbal abuse, manipulation, deception, and cruelty.

> S. It makes me so sad to remember trying to keep one step ahead of what was going to happen. The energy that took deprived me of ability to have any relationships myself. I now realize that is almost the biggest part of what I have to deal with now. At least now I can make a connection with someone, but I cannot transfer it to friendships. It has affected my ability to make attachments—once they are gone they are gone. My doctor is the first person that I can't say that about. So, never having the opportunity to have friends, to go through that process of finding out that you can work through conflict, that has been a big loss. . . .

> S. I was in college and I had made a friend who was older than me. I felt very attached to her and when she graduated I felt that she was leaving me. I was hospitalized shortly after that for the first time. I was drinking a lot at the time. The closer it got to the feelings about this woman, the more the drinking increased, along with blackouts, terrible flashbacks, reliving everything. I was sure my father was there, chasing me.

> J. I have been shut down emotionally and socially from people for my whole life. Also, whenever I reached out to people I felt like myself would be lost if I was rejected.

> H. No, I don't have a best friend. I did have one for fourteen years, between age eighteen and thirty-two, but she had a multiple personality disorder of sorts and once I got into therapy and she didn't, we stopped being able to identify with each other. I don't have a boyfriend or close relationships with my siblings. I have a couple of friends that I can call for some support and some intimate conversations. If you add them together, they are like having one best friend—all men.

Loss of Feeling Like a Meaningful Part of the Community, of Society

Feeling like a member of society is about feeling related. Victims of child abuse often experience themselves as "beyond the pale," stigmatized, outsiders, aliens. Neglected children may have particular holes in their comprehension of what is expected of them, how they are to behave. Peers commonly reject neglected children, and as a result, these children may miss out on a particularly important facet of the socialization experience. Helen talks about how as an adult, she has had to learn how to live in society, how to get along with others in order to even function in a job.

H. I am avoiding it [grieving] and I'm not there yet. I don't think I have much grief experience. The last nine years have been about learning how to live in society. I am learning how to do that after coming from a family that couldn't do that. How to relate to people I work with, how to have friends, how to accomplish something.

Alterations in Self-Perception and Perception of the Perpetrator(s)

We develop a sense of self-esteem in the context of our significant relationships. The baby learns to view himself or herself with the same regard that he or she sees mirrored in the mother's and father's eyes. Likewise, abused and neglected children come to believe the image of themselves that their parents create, an image that usually has very little to do with the reality of the children's abilities, skills, or dispositions. They are told they are bad, evil, or worthless, just like faithless Aunt Sadie or Uncle Bill. Repeat a lie frequently enough and people come to believe it. Children are particularly vulnerable to this kind of parental systematic brainwashing because of the large power imbalance that exists between parents and children.

As adults, people often maintain the same connection with their parenting figures they had as a child, and consequently they experience similar fears, powerlessness, and helplessness in the face of their parents or their internal image of their parents. We may experience that internal image as the voice of conscience and have taken it on board as our own without fully realizing that it is the internalized voice of an abusive parent. As a result, even within our own minds we continue to reenact the childhood trauma between ourselves and our parents. As outsiders, we may look at a six-foot-two young man intimidated and quivering before a frail old man half his size and fail to understand that the grown man is experiencing the same terrors as when his now frail father would beat him into submission every day after school. Our perceptions of ourselves do not just automatically change as we mature, nor do our perceptions of the people who have perpetrated violence against us. Without working through the grief and the anger connected to the relationship we can remain terrorized and humiliated by past figures in our lives, even though they may be out of sight or even dead. In the process we lose our sense of self-esteem, any role models that guarantee our success in the world, the capacity to figure out how to resolve problems without violence, and the ability to let go of the past and move on as a whole person, and along the way we miss out on many important educational and vocational opportunities that could have led our lives in very different directions.

Loss of Self-esteem

Helen talks about how her childhood impacted—and is still impacting on—her self-esteem. The physical and emotional impoverishment of her childhood, deliberately induced by her parents, profoundly affected her view of herself in a multitude of ways. She has been struggling for years, and with great perseverance, to reclaim her natural birthright, but she knows she still has years to go. In the conversation she reveals her continuing relationship with the perpetrators she no longer sees and how their influence, now deeply embedded in her psyche, continues to exert a powerful influence over the way she treats herself.

H. The way I was raised had a terribly devastating effect on my self-esteem. It is getting better because I have been in therapy for nine years. I still have years ahead to repair the damage. It is now to the point that I can at least hold a job. For the longest time I couldn't hold a job without being fired. People like me more now. I had abusive relationships for a long time. I deprived myself of basic things that most people have, even though I can afford them—like a decent place to live. I still live in a seedy place. I don't have a microwave or a computer or a VCR, even though I could. I don't take nice trips to places. My self-esteem was really bad ten years ago, but there is still significant headway to be made. I realize that in not allowing myself to have things I am repeating the pattern of my parents. Money does play a factor. Not having money growing up, I tend to put a lot away.

Loss of Successful Role Models

Human beings are great imitators. "Children will do as we do, not as we say" is an expression we have all grown up with. Having viable role models for normal human development is vitally necessary for every child. Unfortunately, this is one of the mechanisms for the intergenerational transmission of faulty attachment relationships. Abusive and neglectful parents provide lousy models for how people are supposed to behave—as parents, as adults, as citizens. Rebecca puts it most succinctly and perhaps cynically. Jodie talks about how difficult it has been for her to develop anything resembling a healthy relationship with a man. Helen's role models were astonishingly barren of any redeeming human qualities.

R. I was raised by wolves.

J. My mom is a very asexual, very inhibited person, and I also grieve about that because I had nobody to look up to for that type of a role model. It is hard trying to create a self or a person that you don't really know since there is no one to model yourself after. At least you can know enough to say, "I don't want to be like that," but if you don't have something there to work with, you can't really say that. I also had no positive male role model that is actually a good human being. I have had a hard time relating to men in general because of that. I haven't been able to see men—I have basically negated half of the population because I was so afraid of them. Or I shut them out because of knowing I was going to be rejected and not knowing how to be a woman because I never saw that either. I was always looking for that as a child.

H. My father is highly intelligent but he has some kind of a personality disorder. He was very cheap. He wouldn't buy clothing for his children, didn't want to pay to fix a furnace so we had to live without heat for years. He wouldn't take us for medical care. He had his master's degree in microbiology, was very smart, but did not have a single friend. I lived my whole life in complete, abject poverty. He did and still does insist on the house being in a state of disrepair to keep the taxes down and puts junk in the yard to keep the taxes down. It was too embarrassing to bring friends home. He was violent towards his kids, although he didn't drink. It was meted out based on how much a threat you were to him. My brother was intelligent and he got 80 percent of the violence—he would break chairs over his head. I was ambitious and so I got about 15 percent of the violence. He is not a nice person. Very opinionated and feels he can tell the world how to run their lives. My mother is a schizoid personality and cannot form relationships with anyone, even with her children. She is bright but incompetent in life. She is verbally abusive to her own family, but outside of the family she puts on an act of a loving mother, then she is nasty.

Loss of Ability to Resolve Problems or Conflicts in a Positive Way

How do we learn to resolve problems or conflicts? As children, we watch how the adults around us resolve problems, and if they are successful, we develop the confidence that we can do that too. If we don't expect the world to mistreat us, we often create self-fulfilling prophecies and don't get mistreated. Children raised in abusive families have very different experiences. They learn that the way adults resolve conflicts is through abuse, violence, or denial. The child who refuses to imitate the behavior of his or her violent family will be faced with an empty spot where good judgment and problem-solving skills should be. In Helen's case, this meant that she became overly reliant on the judgment of others, even though she had no guideposts for how to choose people to relate to who have good judgment and good conflict resolution skills. In situations of conflict, it is vitally important that people know what their boundaries are and know how to protect them without overreacting or underreacting. Helen has had to gradually develop such skills—it didn't come naturally.

> H. There are many ways I have had problems in my ability to resolve problems or conflicts. My mother was very big on telling us how stupid we were, so I grew up thinking I was stupid, so whenever I was in a disagreement with someone I would go with their way of doing things because I thought they were smarter than me, including men who wanted to date me. Other things too, like people advising me to get into dangerous or unsuitable situations—I would go along with them because I thought, "I am stupid!" Therefore they must know more than I do. Only in the last three or four years have I realized that I can use my own judgment. It is not because I am stupid, it is often because they are. And also, I would just do what other people wanted. I had a lack of boundaries, difficulty in setting my own boundaries. I was prone to have problems in work situations, trouble with authority figures. I would get petulant and resentful. Of course you don't like authority when the authority figures you know are so abusive. I would tell my boss off, and so then I often had to quit before I got fired. That was one of the first things I was able to change as a result of psychotherapy.

Loss of Capacity to Individuate, Separate, and Let Go of the Past

The compromised ability to handle emotions that accompanies childhood abuse leads to the inability to mourn. The inability to mourn means that it is very difficult to let go of the past. The past remains a living, haunting presence instead. Helen is beginning to understand that depriving herself of material goods when she does not have to do so is a form of reenactment, a way of not grieving for what has been lost in the past and will never be restored. She still reacts to people in the present as if her mother were talking to her and cannot fully differentiate her reactions in the present from the triggered memories of the hurtful past. It is as if her mother is still with her much of the time, even though she has not spoken to her parents in years. In this way, her mother could be dead but still influence her behavior in the present as if she were right by her side.

> H. I have a big problem with people who are histrionic or have any kind of affect or phony behavior. I have to put my hands over my ears and walk away. My mother used to put on an act of being a good mother and if I am in a store and someone waits on me who is overly nice, I walk away. My mother had an affected air in public and then when she would come home she would be terribly nasty. I can't say good morning because it is too phony. I sometimes see it on TV and I have to walk out of the room.

It is a sincerity factor, not an emotional factor. I can pick up lying too, but for years I never paid attention to it—I felt too stupid to know better. It has 100 percent to do with the other person's intention—that is the issue. It all goes back to my mother. I also live in the past by generally depriving myself—I haven't let go of that. There are a lot of things but it would take some time to think them out. For example, allowing myself to be successful at something. Often I will find myself sabotaging myself. I just feel uncomfortable, conflicted about being successful.

Loss of Educational or Vocational Opportunities

If adults repeatedly tell a child that he or she is stupid, worthless, ugly, or crazy, the brainwashing takes hold and it becomes difficult, if not impossible, for the child to face with confidence the challenges that life brings. But every human being needs an identity and for too many adults abused as children, their identity becomes that of a professional mental patient, as Samantha puts it, or a person too stupid to make good judgments, as Helen explains it. To relinquish such an identity and claim a new and better one, the survivor must be willing to tolerate the grief associated with all of the lost opportunities that will never be restored. Samantha has begun to wrestle with her own personal losses. Helen made some critical life decisions based on a desperate attempt to get from her parents what they were and are unable to give—love and acceptance. In doing so, she sacrificed many opportunities and has lost educational and vocational time that she can never get back.

> S. I am just now getting in touch with all the losses of my adult life. I have no clue about all of the opportunities I have missed, all those lost years. I have been stuck for fifteen years. I have been a professional mental patient. I was forbidden to go away to college by my father even though I had full scholarships to Bucknell and Duquesne. But I did go to community college.

> H. All my choices in life were formed by those experiences. I majored in something I didn't want to—chemistry—because I thought it could get my parents to like me. My father was a microbiologist and my mother was interested in environmental concerns. But I had no interest in chemistry, and I am an environmentalist but largely because I am a moral person. I would have majored in history and English. But I had to choose something that would get them to like me. That was not where my aptitude lay, so it took me seven years instead of four. Now I am basically a writer. If I had had any sense of self I wouldn't have done that. I would have gone away to college, but I thought we were too poor. I have led a very restricted life, went to a state college. Not that my parents paid for anything, I did. But I didn't see how I could go from abject poverty to going into debt for college. When you don't have money you don't feel you can pay it back.

Somatization

Descriptions of the mourning process have always been strongly colored by the somatic presentation of grief. But our patients are grieving events from the long-buried past, events that may not be considered "appropriate" causes for grief. Nonetheless, their descriptions of their own grieving processes reveal to us that when loss is worked through, the body does a great deal of the work along with the mind. The body remembers what the mind forgets, the body keeps the score (van der Kolk, 1994). In the case of chronic grief, this can mean the loss of health and well-being. In the particular case of sexual abuse, it can also mean the loss of a healthy and fulfilling sexuality.

Physical Sensations Associated with Grief

Samantha talks about her experience of grief as utterly paralyzing and powerfully physical. She also must contend with her conflicts about crying, so typical of the abused and neglect child who is not allowed to express normal and appropriate affect without shame and punishment. As in Jodie's case, it is quite typical for victims of child abuse to describe themselves as having died or as being dead, or a part of them as being dead. The grieving process is one of restoring life, an internal sort of resurrection. Jodie also can now talk about the transformative process of moving the grief, along with an associated feeling of badness and hopelessness, out of her psyche and into her body to be available to be worked through.

> S. I am in the midst of it now. I feel heavy. Almost like I can seem okay, just feeling really sad and then I become paralyzed and unable to move. The people at the apartment try to get me out of bed but I cannot move. It gets into my body so much because I cannot get it out. They are trying to figure out how much is real and how much is isolation. I am holding back the tears because if they come they won't stop. I can't let anybody see me that way. My body gets so involved and that has surprised me—I feel so overstimulated and overwhelmed. My muscles start to spasm, my body feels like it is on fire, I have no clue how to get through that. It feels like there should be openings in the ends of my fingers so it can come out. I also have a thought disorder so if I get overstimulated, I can confuse reality with the sensations. Crying can bring a sense of relief.

> J. The abuse started when I was two. When I was working with [her therapist] in a therapy session about another traumatic experience, I was holding my arm and he asked me why I was holding my arm and it was because I wanted to strike out at my grandfather, like my grandfather was in the room, but only in those ways, not in fantasy ways. Like a body memory. It was when my body was finally waking up for the first time and everything was being integrated and all these feelings were flooding in and I was still trying to find a balance between being completely overstimulated and being shut down and dead and that was one of the things that came up.
>
> Just recently I have been having experience with it physically, but in the past it was just an overwhelming sense of badness and hopelessness combined with that little inkling of wishing and hoping that things had been different.

Loss of Physical Health and Well-being

The state of chronic hyperarousal associated with posttraumatic stress disorder puts a terrible burden on the body, as is demonstrated by the stress-related comorbid conditions that accompany trauma-related syndromes. We also know something about the impact of acute grief on physical health and mortality. But we are only beginning to comprehend what the impact of chronic and unresolved grief may be on the health of the physical body, including the immune system. Jodie connects her previous eating disorder, stomach problems, and migraines to her sustained grief. Helen is convinced that her physical problems are related to chronic stress.

J. My body would always feel things, like I had an eating disorder and always had stomach problems and migraines. I never really knew what these symptoms were about because the grief was like something separate from me. Now I am feeling it in my body as well. Now it is all inside of me and I can feel the grief bubbling instead of just being outside of me somewhere. I felt physically disconnected and dead both spiritually and physically until I started to do the work at Sanctuary. Only in the last two years have I been able to integrate the emotions and the physical aspects of myself.

H. I have my theories about the connection between stress, anxiety, and autoimmune disorders. I had a lot of anxiety and for most of my life didn't even realize I was anxious. I think that had physical effects. I had muscle spasms in my back that have gone away since I started therapy. I had endometriosis, which I think was related to anxiety, though doctors would say that's not possible. I had to be operated on to take care of that—a cyst was removed ten years ago. I have had hormone treatments and birth control pills to treat the problem. However anxiety affects your body. For a while I was underweight, in my late teens, early twenties, because I was too anxious to eat.

Loss of Sexual Function

Sexual abuse is particularly damaging to one's capacity to engage in loving, enjoyable, and relational sexual behavior. Some sexually abused people avoid sexual relationships altogether, as in Jodie's case. Others engage in promiscuous sex without enjoying it or without being able to establish true intimacy. Helen, physically abused but not sexually abused, used sex as a form of exchange because she was bewildered about the nature of establishing healthy and reciprocal relationships. As she is struggling to achieve a better state of health, she has stopped the former behavior but has not yet learned how to achieve an intimate, loving sexual relationship.

J. I have not been able to have satisfying, successful physical relationships with either sex.

H. Before I got into therapy my relationships with men weren't productive but at least I knew how to relate on a dysfunctional level, so I could relate to them. In my twenties I had lots of relationships. Because I was so deprived of basic necessities, when someone would do something for me, I felt I owed them something, including sex.

Alterations in Systems of Meaning

Human beings are meaning-making animals. The structure and function of our minds compels us to make sense of our reality. In a very real way, we need to put everything we know and experience into some kind of logical, coherent, and integrated framework. Out of this framework, we develop a philosophy of life and derive the basic principles and assumptions that guide our decisions. It is exceedingly difficult for someone to make sense of the world when he or she have not been cherished and protected as a child, when the very people who were supposed to love the child were the people who abused, neglected, and abandoned him or her. This is particularly true in a society that routinely instructs us that children are to be cherished and protected. Victims of childhood abuse must grieve for the childhood that was stolen from them, that they are given to believe is their birthright. More subtle issues of neglect mean that survivors must grieve for what they did not have. Early in their lives, victims of childhood abuse and neglect are exposed to the commission of deeds on the part of their caregivers that are deliberate, harmful, and wrong. This early exposure to uncontrollable evil can have a grave impact on the child's moral development and make discovering moral clarity even more difficult. As a result of all of these experiences, many adults abused as children make conscious or semiconscious decisions not to "inflict" themselves on another vulnerable human being, and so they sacrifice their own desire to have children and, in doing so, their own future. The compounded result may be joylessness and difficulty in finding purpose or meaning in life.

Loss of Innocence, Loss of Childhood

The innocence and protection that cherished children receive serve as a protective buffer, a stable foundation, for whatever storms a person must survive later in life. While maltreated children are young, they may not even recognize that their childhood was missing something. Only later as they grow and compare themselves to others do they come to recognize the pain of all they missed.

> S. The most basic losses are easier to face. Like never being a kid, realizing all the jobs I had in my family related to protecting my parents and taking care of them and my siblings. Never being a kid—never having time to even think about me or how I felt.

> J. The loss that has most affected me has been the loss of innocence in childhood. And the grief in coming to terms with the childhood that I never had and the hopes and dreams that were destroyed along with it that every child is supposed to have and carry into adulthood and grow out of in a natural way when they get their hard knocks in life, but not when they are two.

The Loss of What Wasn't There but Should Have Been

The losses one feels as a result of childhood neglect pose a particularly difficult problem because, as Jodie puts it, it is "grieving for what you don't know." It is hard to make sense of losing something you never had, hard to feel you have a right to it, hard to get anyone else to understand the sadness of this. There are empty holes where meaning, purpose, and fulfillment should be. There are things you can't do, ways of relating that are absent and arduous to discover as an adult.

> J. Neglect is grieving for what you don't know. Some fantasy that what you don't know is supposed to be there. And then there is the fantasy of what you see in the movies or television of what other families show to the outside world, which of course isn't reality either. So you really don't have any idea, you just know something is missing, something that is not there that should have been, something is missing inside of you but you don't really know what it is.

> H. To lose something you have to have it first. I never had a family member die that I was close to. But some people would say I experienced a loss in having no parental affection, no material support from my parents, no medical support, or a decent place to live. The basic fundamentals of living were not provided.

Loss of Moral Clarity

A particularly challenging problem for many survivors is making some sense out of the role they were compelled to play—actively or passively—in the violation of others. Here, Samantha touches on the choices she was compelled to make between self and others. As we already know, Samantha was forced to witness and be the victim of the most serious criminal behavior on the part of her father, while neither her mother nor other bystanders did anything to stop him. And for those of us who listen to these stories, even more puzzling is this question: How does a child like Helen or Samantha, growing up in conditions of such depravity still develop concepts of ethics and morality?

S. He was sexually abusing me and he would threaten to hurt the other children if I didn't cooperate with him and let him do whatever he wanted.

H. I am actually a very moral person. But why is that? Because one of my brothers turned out to be very immoral but he has turned himself around. My parents were like law-abiding sociopaths. You dare not do anything against the law, even things that people commonly do. Like cheating on financial aid packages. They were bluntly honest when they didn't have to be. So, I am on the highly responsible moral end—that has been my approach in life.

Loss of Ability, Desire, or Willingness to Have Children

For most people, starting a family, being able to create a future, is perceived not as a gift but as a right. For abused children such a "right" can be instead funneled into the fervent desire not to reproduce, often for fear of reproducing the same trauma, grief, and rage that the children have themselves experienced. If a child's parents took no joy in parenting, it is difficult to even comprehend the possibility of joyous engagement with a child. Helen begins by speaking very rationally about her decision not to have children, having previously admitted that her last significant relationship ended because the man she was seeing wanted to have children and she did not. As she describes her relationship with his nephews, she lights up and talks about how special they were, but when she actually imagines children for herself, it's "not for me."

H. I know I don't want children. Or at least I don't think I do. It just does not appeal to me. I find nothing attractive about that scenario. I am not really sure why. I know one factor is that I dislike the loss of freedom involved. But the other reason is that it seems like a dreadful experience. I don't see kids as being appealing types of people. They seem to have negative attributes about them. I did meet a few kids in my life that I really liked, including my ex-boyfriend's nephews. They were really cute, but that does not sway my opinion. When I imagine my own, it's not for me.

Loss of Purpose, Meaning, Joy in Life, Will to Live

Samantha describes the utter emptiness of her life before she got into treatment and contrasts that later with how much better she feels. Helen describes her recognition that she is "stuck" between being dysfunctional and being functional, as she calls it, still not feeling much purpose or joy in her life. But it is Rebecca who is most revealing about her experiences of neglect and how she remains unable to find much purpose in living, to view her life as a precious gift.

S. There was nothing else, nothing else but self-abuse.

H. Basically, the reason I got into therapy was because I was having trouble making career decisions, though I had some insight based on watching TV that my family was dysfunctional. But then I realized how screwed up I was, I couldn't keep a job, my friends were crazy, I had no focus in my life. So what happened was, I was in therapy for a long time and it helped me learn to relate to society better, and I realized that I was out of focus and in disarray. And it helped me understand just how much in disarray. I am going from being dysfunctional but I'm not functional yet. I am in the middle, so I don't feel much purpose and joy—because I am stuck there.

R. As a result of the neglect I experienced as a child, I am unable to view life as a gift but instead I experience life as a burden that I didn't ask for.

Process of Recovery

Samantha, Jodie, and Helen are all very different people, with different problems, coming from very varied backgrounds. But all three are in the process of recovery. They, as well as others, have helped us begin to understand the nature of that process and some of the tasks that must be completed, particularly as these tasks relate to the grieving process.

Recognizing the Problem

People suffering from chronic, unresolved grief can present for treatment in many different ways. The most obvious and probably frequent manifestation is chronic depression that responds only partially or episodically to antidepressant medications. These patients are high utilizers of psychiatric and medical services, repeatedly seeking out some kind of direction or relief. Because of current changes in the health care system minimizing any form of therapy except medication, these patients are likely to receive inadequate or poor care. Chronic suicidality and a preoccupation with death may be indicators of the same problem. It is not uncommon for patients to make early progress in treatment and then "hit the wall" of grief without knowing that is what is happening. Progress in treatment slows, the patient appears to be continually circling around the same issues that go nowhere, and the therapist may become increasingly frustrated, bored, and angry. The resort to a change in medication or adding medications is a frequent response to this situation.

Chronic somatic complaints often accompanied by the overuse or abuse of prescription pain medications is common. When physical symptoms are a manifestation of unresolved grief, the pattern may be one of doctor hopping or drug seeking while the person and his or her health care providers seek a physical solution to a nonphysical problem. The result is bound to be an increasing level of frustration, chronicity, and compounded rage on the part of everyone involved.

Continuing to behaviorally reenact negative relationships despite insight and a commitment to treatment can also be a sign that the survivor is avoiding taking on the task of grieving. The yawning, dark chasm that grief represents may feel overwhelming, endless, or like a bottomless pit, particularly when those feelings are not identified as what they are—feelings of bereavement—and legitimized as part of the normal process of mourning. Here Jodie points out how important it was to have someone support but not interfere with her process, someone wise enough to know that not all human problems can be fixed with a pill.

J. In the process of my treatment, I was stuck for about three months. My doctor helped me so much. It looked like depression on the outside but on the inside I was doing all this processing and little bits and pieces would come out, of very distinct emotion and very compact emotion, but it looked on the outside as if I was depressed. Other people might have treated it with medicine to get me out of it but she knew I was going through the grieving stage, and I was. The internal processing that I was doing was leading me toward grieving and toward putting the pieces together. If I had been in a different program I don't know what would have happened because I felt very stuck. If the only treatment I had received was medication at the time, I could have been stuck there for years rather than months.

Experiencing the Grief

The hardest part of the grieving process may be allowing the process to begin. People whose attachments have been disrupted are so ill equipped to process loss and to have confidence that the pain will eventually go that they often spend decades doing everything they can think of to avoid confronting the pain of the past. Having toyed around the edges of grief for so many years, they may view it as something they can keep at bay and never have to resolve, not fully realizing just how much the past is robbing them of a vibrant present. So the first task is letting the experience happen, feeling the enormousness and uncontrolled nature of grief, and then, as Jodie has, coming to recognize that in struggling to control an act of nature, you are simply prolonging and being controlled by a process that would otherwise pass on.

> J. It was more like a welling up from inside of very, very strong feelings—sadness and despair. But now I know that it is inside me and that it cannot control me and I can control it or work with it. I still have body reactions. I still have stomach problems. But I pretty much can know where it comes from. Writing about it helps a lot.

Loss of Previous Coping Skills

Grieving for the past losses that accompany childhood abuse means giving up reliable coping skills. As long as the survivor is not safe with himself or herself, he or she cannot learn to manage affect, and without learning how to safely manage affect, it is impossible to safely work through the grief. But this does mean sacrificing habits that have helped manage overwhelming affect for decades—things such as drugs and alcohol, compulsive working, smoking, destructive eating behaviors, and, as in Samantha's case, self-mutilation. Coming out the other end of the tunnel, Jodie is able to recognize how comfortable it was to repeat the predictable past, how safe even if it was miserable.

> S. Today, there was a group session. A younger person had overdosed as a manipulation and a lot of the group focused on self-harm and suicidal behavior. I couldn't stay for it. I was so upset because three and a half years ago I was a self-abuser and I made a commitment to no self-harm and that option is not available to me anymore. I got so sad and felt so alone in the group. I was the only one who totally gave it up. It's another loss. It's so much easier to cut yourself, to scratch and stop the feeling. If that was available to me, then I wouldn't be in pain now. I am not sure you can grieve without giving up the self-harm. If you haven't, there is really danger. The more subtle danger is having compartmentalized everything in my life and then I get stuck in another repetitive pattern, especially with a thought disorder.

J. The unknown used to be very scary to me just because at least in my old patterns of reenactment I knew how I was going to react to things. I knew I was going to be left alone and that is just how it was going to be. So the only danger or fear I have now is what is going to happen next, but it is more exciting than scary to me. Right now at least.

Fearing Loss of Attachments

For many adults who were abused as children, the key to recovery is the restitution of the capacity to attach. But in allowing oneself to attach, there is also the fear of losing that precious attachment. Implicit in the process of therapy is that inevitable loss, because therapy cannot substitute for the creation of a long-lasting support system that you don't have to pay for. Samantha, having allowed herself to attach to her therapist, recognizes that the love is not unconditional. Her therapist has structured the relationship so that for Samantha to continue with it, she has to value herself at least as much as the therapist does. Balanced properly, the fear of losing attachments, of losing a potentially better future than the awful past, can be a powerful incentive for positive change.

S. It wasn't until I decided I was going to live—that's what has made the difference. The thing that changed things was video work—I had tried to hang myself and came into the hospital. I was doing video work about my mother—her voice was so dominant and internalized that I could not separate from it. My doctor came back from vacation and found me in the hospital after trying to hang myself and she was totally pissed off. I knew I had to get pretty serious pretty quick. So I worked really hard at the video stuff, really hard.

Losing Attachments

Recovery can mean losing attachments as well, and although the relationships may be highly pathological, they are all the person knows, and something is better than nothing. Jodie describes how working toward her own recovery necessitated getting out of the relationship she had. Helen describes, with some regret, how important it has been for her to be out of relationships altogether in order to avoid getting into more bad ones.

J. I had an unhealthy relationship when I first entered Sanctuary. I think I probably wasn't in the process of fully grieving yet but in the process of trying to get to some recovery path and still somehow grieve the childhood I didn't have. I moved through that relationship and that person did not react very well to my becoming healthier.

H. I stopped talking to my parents. That was the biggest change. I haven't talked to them in over eight years. I have had to avoid getting into relationships while I try to figure out how a functional relationship works. So in the past six and a half years I have only dated for a year. I am avoiding relationships until I feel I am not so impaired, until I can figure out what I want and need. I guess my relationships with men beore I got into therapy weren't productive but at least I knew how to relate on a dysfunctional level, so I could relate to them. Now I wish sometimes I could still because at least I could be relating to somebody.

Giving up the Fantasy of Restoration

Inside every adult who was abused as a child, there is a child hoping to be rescued, actively fantasizing about how different things will be someday. Continuing the symptomatic self-destructive behavior is a disguised way of holding on, of waiting for the rescue that never comes. Grieving for the losses of the past means giving up the fantasy that amends will be made, that the loveless parents will turn into loving ones, that innocence will be retrieved—the fantasy of restoration. Jodie describes that process of holding on, toying with the fantasy, and letting go, seeing in her sister an earlier version of herself. Samantha talks about the process of allowing herself to be overwhelmed by the grief as a fundamental part of being able to let go of the fantasy that her parents would ever be there for her; she also describes how critical her present therapeutic relationship was in helping her let go of that continuing engagement with them through her own self-harming behavior.

> J. I find myself wavering once in a while about still wanting it to be, or wishing it had been, different. But overall, no, I have let it go. I can see my sister going through the same process. She hasn't been in therapy yet and she is still at the point of saying, "Wouldn't it be nice to move back to [the Midwest] where my parents are and stay in a little house in the back?"—still looking to them for certain things that they are never going to be able to give.

> S. We were talked about discharge for Monday. On Friday I got hysterical crying—I could not stop. The nurses started to panic. But my doctor told them to leave me alone, that it was something I needed to do. I was wailing. I was realizing that no matter what I do, my parents are not going to come through. I remembered when I had been anorexic at [another hospital]. The social worker who was working with me called my parents to try to get them involved and I heard them on the speakerphone saying not to bother them until the situation was grave. Through this feeling of overwhelming loss I felt in the hospital, I finally gave up on my parents. I thought of my mom's mom, who had killed herself. The next day in the community, I felt like shit, I didn't want any help. My doctor challenged me and said that if I wanted to be like my parents, she didn't want any part of it, that as long as I keep hurting myself I am like my parents. That was the last time I did anything to hurt myself.

Working with the Nonverbal

It may not be possible to resolve grief, particularly long-standing, unresolved, traumatic grief, through the use of verbal abilities alone. From what we now understand about the way the brain processes overwhelming experience, we need art, enactment, story, and ritual to help us safely integrate the verbal and nonverbal aspects of our experience. As Samantha described earlier, the work she did using video therapy was vital to her progress, and here Jodie touches on the importance of her artwork in surfacing feelings and making the entire experience available for verbal integration.

> J. It starts with just feelings and emotions and I do a lot of artwork as well. The trauma happened before I was verbal. It started just with putting a lot on paper with colors and shapes and then I became able to write the words. But it started just as dictating what was happening in my life and looking at it as an outside observer, as if I were a

director or something. Finally I became integrated so I could talk as it was happening to me. But I still think in colors a lot. I think it will make me a better artist and a more integrated person.

The Vital Nature of Social Support

Social support throughout the grieving process is vital to the course of normal bereavement. Just as vital is the restoration of social support for the victims of grief that has been disenfranchised and stigmatized. Jodie talks about how vital it was for her to get validation of the work she was engaged in during the most deadened part of her grieving experience.

> J. The worst thing is not to got get validation that you are doing anything. I remember one day when my doctor showed me a graph that I was actually at the peak of doing the work and for someone like me that meant all the difference in the world. It was awful, feeling so down, to think that I was stuck for that long and not doing any work after all the work I had done. I felt like I was in the valley. There would be nothing worse than throwing more medicine at someone like that because you just feel like you aren't getting anywhere, like "Oh my God, I am back at the beginning and I am never going to get out of all this."

Making Meaning

We now understand how vital it is for trauma survivors to make meaning out of their experience (Janoff-Bulman, 1992). But making meaning out of an abusive childhood is a difficult task. Samantha survived with her integrity as a human being intact because she was intelligent, she had a vivid fantasy life in which people behaved differently, and she modeled herself after people she saw but did not know. Jodie is actively wrestling with her own sense of spirituality and her relationship with a higher power and with forgiveness.

> S. I can't make sense out of it. There were senseless acts of violence, abuse, neglect, but they also crossed the line into making bad things happen. They created violence when it didn't have to happen. I want to make sense out of it. I think a lot of people lose their will to survive. All the time this was going on I knew I was different from the other kids. I knew it wasn't happening to other people. I knew our family was different, that people could not understand me because I was different. I created a life in my head that was a fantasy. The only way I could get to sleep was a fantasy of other families in my head, other brothers and sisters from other people I saw but could never approach. I created all kinds of scenarios like that. I dreamed it could be different. I was always aware of people and what they did. I always knew what was going on around me. I never miss a trick, I guess it is what you call hypervigilance. I would watch what other people did and the decisions they made, people who were passionate about things in their lives, their work, other things and that is what keeps me going. I want to have that kind of passion about things. Being a part of something deeper than routine and ritual. I have some ideas about educating people about misconceptions, misperceptions about people who are victimized and people who are trying to help. So many doctors told me you will never get better, you have this or that disease. I have the opportunity to contribute something other people can't—art, writing. There are times I don't use it for healing but just for fun, just to express myself.

J. Somehow I have actually only recently come to terms with an idea of God or spirituality. For the first time this weekend I looked up at the stars and thanked God for my family and at least the best they thought they could do at the time. I was raised Catholic, but I am not Catholic now, mostly because of issues with the Catholic Church. I have looked at many different things trying to find an organized religion that I can relate to and haven't really found anything yet. So I was just kind of thanking the universe, or the idea of God, unformed as yet. I guess I was thanking my parents despite all of their flaws that they still have now. They have finally managed to come together as a unit, far away from us, and have managed to make a go of it somehow. My father has been broken, he has not been able to find a job for four or five years. He's got migraines every day, but though this is awful to say, he is much more easy to be around, I can relate to him as a person now. My mom is now the main breadwinner of the family, so things have completely switched and she is finding it in her power somehow, although of course, she won't talk about it. She is still the meek person but she is finding some kind of self-confidence. It is interesting to see. My sister is turning into an interesting young woman, very caring, and my brother is as well and I was just thanking God for that. . . .

It still doesn't make any sense to me. I still don't understand how anyone could do that to a child. I can understand how things can go through the generations and how my mom and dad had their own awful childhoods but at some point someone has to be accountable for it, somebody has to stop it. And I haven't really made sense of that yet.

Making Sense of the Intergenerational Nature of Abuse

Part of the struggle to make some meaning out of the abusive past is trying to understand how, if not why, this could have happened. The automatic question that arises in some point on the road to recovery is "What happened to my parents that they could have so mistreated me?" Jodie has learned that her abuser also had abused her mother, who suffered from childhood amnesia as well. Helen attributes much of her family pathology to her great-grandmother, an active participant in the Ku Klux Klan.

J. My abuser was my mom's stepfather who also did things to her that I am just finding out. She doesn't remember a lot of her childhood but she remembers when she first got engaged to my dad that there was a lot of alcohol in the family and her stepfather exposed himself to her when she was just getting engaged. Her mother found out and wanted to get her out of the house.

H. I was able to figure out something about why my parents behaved the way they did. My father was always putting me down for going to college, considered me selfish for going to college. He did that because he didn't want his children to succeed because they would see he was a failure. He gave the impression that failure was a badge of honor. If I got too successful I might figure out that he didn't really want it that way, that it was just a show he was putting on. My mother called me stupid because she was so incompetent. I met my father's mother and she was very abusive. My mother is a harder story but I know enough of the family history to know there was a lot of dysfunction. My great-grandmother was in the women's auxiliary of the Ku Klux Klan. I heard stories about her. She used to go to lynchings and kept mementos of them. When you have that in your history it is going to affect you. She was a terrible woman.

Moving On

As the grieving process progresses, the darkness begins to lift and survivors become involved in the process of moving on that is represented by the *E* in S.A.G.E.— emancipation. Here Samantha compares her own progress to the absence of any change in her siblings while recognizing that there is always going to be pain. She can talk about how hard it is and has been.

> *S.* I think I have an uncanny sense of perception about people and integrity about people. When I see it I am drawn to it. I lost a lot, but I really can't say what my life would have been like without it. All I know is that it is getting better, I look at my brothers and sisters but they are still addicted and not learning to feel and they are not where I am. As hard as it is, it is exciting self-discovery. . . .
>
> People don't get the grieving thing. There are always anniversaries, always reminders. No matter how far I get in my life I am always going to feel a heartache, a loss for the things I never even knew were available or couldn't get to because I was so sick. A lot of grieving for me is that I never thought it would be this hard, I never realized how much work is involved in taking responsibility for myself, how much I have to struggle just to let people know how I really am. I never expected anything to be this hard. That is the kind of thing I would like to give to people for a week, just to know how difficult it is. To keep moving forward and to have them get it.

Transforming the Pain

Ultimately, we hope that adult survivors of childhood abuse and neglect will be able to transform their pain into something of value to themselves and others, what Judy Herman has called a "survivor mission" (Herman, 1992). Helen talks about how she believes that good has already come from bad in that she is proud of some characteristics that she has developed that she attributes to her abusive past. Jodie shares her creative aspirations and how her wish is to be able to change the world for children as a result of working through her own painful experiences.

> *H.* I think there is always something to be said for every experience. I don't have a sense of entitlement that I know some people have and I am glad I don't and that comes from not having very much. I don't have the sense of materialism that other people have. I think that the insight you get from going through that experience and then evaluating the experience in therapy gives you insight about human nature I wouldn't otherwise have and gives me in the ability to apply it to other situations. I can deal with harsh situations better than the average person.
>
> *J.* I can feel that I am on the verge of turning my experiences into something positive. For the first time I feel like I am grieving as an integrated person and it feels like there might be positive energy coming out of that. I remember talking to my therapists in the beginning about anger and grief and asking them why I couldn't turn it all into something positive right away, why can't I just take a shortcut? But you have to go through the intermediate shit before you can do that. I can feel I am on the verge of finally doing that. I think in terms of my creativity. I think it has affected my creativity. And I think in terms of what I want to do and being able to change the world—that sounds too idealistic—but to affect children's lives in a positive way. I don't think I could have done it in the same way if I hadn't gone through it myself.

Conclusion

Grief is one of the natural outcomes of human attachment. Predictably, then, anything that interferes with the course of attachment produces the potential for loss and bereavement. The more trauma the person has experienced, the more likely it is that traumatic and complicated grieving will be involved. Individually and socially we are relatively comfortable with supporting the mourning process when someone has literally died. But the losses attendant upon child abuse and neglect are not usually about literal death, although actual death—particularly traumatic death—of an attachment figure can compound and complicate other losses. Instead, the losses that adults must recapitulate and work through in order to recover are long delayed, sometimes tangible, but at other times metaphorical, spiritual, or moral. In this chapter I have reviewed those losses utilizing the testimony of several adult survivors who volunteered to share their experiences. Finding a new life path always means shedding the old, and the recovery process involves loss as well if the survivor is to move past the fragmentation of childhood trauma and heal.

References

Adam, K. S. (1994). Suicidal behavior and attachment: A developmental model. In M. B. Sperling & W. H. Berman (Eds.), *Attachment in adults: Clinical and developmental perspectives*. (pp. 275–298). New York: The Guilford Press.

American Psychiatric Association. (1994). *Diagnostic and Statistical Manual of Mental Disorders* (4th ed.). Washington, DC: American Psychiatric Press.

Bloom, S. L. (1997). *Creating sanctuary: Toward the evolution of sane societies*. New York: Routledge.

Bloom, S. L. (1999) The complex web of causation: Motor vehicle accidents, comorbidity and PTSD. In E. J. Hickling and E. B. Blanchard (Eds)., *International handbook of road traffic accidents and psychological trauma: Theory, treatment and law*. Oxford: Elsevier.

Bloom, S. L. (2000). Creating sanctuary: Healing from systemic abuses of power. *Therapeutic Communities: The International Journal for Therapeutic and Supportive Organizations*.

Bloom, S. L. & Bills, L. J. (1998). From chaos to Sanctuary: Trauma-based treatment for women in a state hospital systems. In B. L. Levin, A. K. Blanch, and A. Jennings (Eds.), *Women's Health Services: A Public Health Perspective* (pp. 348–367). Thousand Oaks, CA: Sage Publications.

Bloom, S. L., & Bills, L. J. (2000). Trying out Sanctuary the hard way. *Therapeutic Communities: The International Journal for Therapeutic and Supportive Organizations*.

Bowlby, J. (1960). Grief and mourning in infancy and early childhood. *The Psychoanalytic Study of the Child, 15*, 9–52.

Bowlby, J. (1963). Pathological mourning and childhood mourning. *Journal of the American Psychoanalytic Association* 11: 500–541.

Bowlby, J. (1980). *Attachment and loss*. Volume III: *Loss, sadness and depression*. New York: Basic Books.

Bowlby, J. (1988). Developmental psychiatry comes of age. *American Journal of Psychiatry, 145*:1–10.

Charney, I. (1996). Evil in human personality: Disorders of doing harm to others in family relationships. In F. W. Kaslow (Ed.), *Handbook of relational diagnosis and dysfunctional family patterns*. New York: John Wiley & Sons.

Cicchetti, D., and M. Lynch. (1995). Failures in the expectable environment and their impact on individual development: The case of child maltreatment. In D. Cicchetti and D. J. Cohen (Eds.), *Developmental psychopathology.* Volume 2: *Risk, disorder, and adaptation*. New York: Wiley.

de Zulueta, F. (1993). *From pain to violence: The traumatic roots of destructiveness.* London: Whurr Publications.

Doka, K. J. (1989). *Disenfranchised grief: Recognizing hidden sorrow.* Lexington, MA: Lexington Books.

Ellason, J. W., C. A. Ross, K. Sainton, & L. W. Mayran. (1996). Axis I and II comorbidity and childhood trauma history in chemical dependency. *Bulletin of the Menninger Clinic, 60(1),* 39–51.

Engel, G. L. (1961). Is grief a disease? A challenge for medical research. *Psychosomatic Medicine, 23,* 18–22.

Felitti, V. J., Anda, R. F., Nordenberg, D., Williamson, D.F., Spitz, A. M., Edwards, V., Koss, M. P., & Marks, J. S. (1998). Relationship of childhood abuse and household dysfunction to many of the leading causes of death in adults: The Adverse Childhood Experiences (ACE) Study. American Journal of Preventive Medicine, 14(4):245–58

Figley, C. R. (Ed.). (1997). *Traumatology of grieving: Conceptual, theoretical and treatment foundations.* New York: Brunner/Mazel.

Figley, C. R., Bride, B. E., & Mazza, N. (1999). *Death and trauma: The traumatology of grieving.* New York: Brunner/Mazel.

Foderaro, J. F. (2001). Creating a nonviolent environment: Keeping Sanctuary safe. In S. L. Bloom (Ed.), *Violence: A public health menace and a public health approach.* London: Karnac Press.

Foderaro, J. F., & Ryan, R. A. (2000). S.A.G.E.: Mapping the course of recovery. *Therapeutic Communities: The International Journal for Therapeutic and Supportive Organizations.*

Fonagy, P., Steele, M., Steele, H., Leight, T., Kennedy, R., Mattoon, G., & Target, M. (1995). Attachment, the reflective self, and borderline states: The predictive specificity of the Adult Attachment Interview and pathological emotional development. In S. Goldberg, R. Muir, & J. Kerr (Eds.), *Attachment theory: Social, developmental, and clinical perspectives.* (pp. 233–278). Hillsdale, NJ: The Analytic Press.

Goffman, E. (1963). *Stigma: Notes on the management of spoiled identity.* New York: Simon & Schuster.

Grady, K. T. (1997). Posttraumatic stress disorder and comorbidity: Recognizing the many faces of PTSD. *Journal of Clinical Psychiatry, 58 (suppl. 9):* 12–15.

Henry, K., & Homes, J. G. (1998). Childhood revisited: The intimate relationships of individuals from divorced and conflict-ridden families. In J. A. Simpson & W. S. Rholes (Eds.), *Attachment theory and close relationships.* (pp. 280–316). New York: The Guilford Press.

Herman, J. L. (1992). *Trauma and recovery.* New York: Basic Books.

Jacobs, S. (1999) *Traumatic grief: Diagnosis, treatment and prevention.* New York: Brunner/Mazel.

James, B. (1994). *Handbook for treatment of attachment-trauma problems in children.* New York: Lexington Books.

Janoff-Bulman, R. (1992). *Shattered assumptions: Towards a new psychology of trauma.* New York: The Free Press.

Kessler, R., Sonnega, A., Broment, E., Hughes, M., & Nelson, C. B. (1995). Posttraumatic stress disorder in the National Comorbidity Survey. *Archives of General Psychiatry, 52,* 1048–1060.

Khan, M. M. R. (1963). The concept of cumulative trauma. *Psychoanalytic Study of the Child, 18,* 286–306.

Koss, M. P., Koss, P. G., Woodruff, W. J. (1991). Deleterious effects of criminal victimization on women's health and medical utilization. *Archives of Internal Medicine,* 151(2): 342–347.

Krystal, H. (1988). *Integration and self-healing: Affect, trauma, alexithymia.* Hillsdale, NJ: Analytic Press.

Leserman, J., Drossman, D. A., Li, Z., Toomey, T. C., Nachman, G., & Glogau, L. (1996). Sexual and physical abuse history in gastroenterology practice: how types of abuse impact health status. *Psychosomatic Medicine, 58(1),* 4–15.

Lindemann, E. (1944). Symptomatology and management of acute grief. *American Journal of Psychiatry, 101*: 141–148.

Liotti, G. (1995). Disorganized/disoriented attachment in the psychotherapy of the dissociative disorders. In S. Goldberg, R. Muir & J. Kerr (Eds.), *Attachment theory: Social, developmental, and clinical perspectives.* (pp. 343–365). Hillsdale, NJ: The Analytic Press.

Liotti, G. (1999). Disorganization of attachment as a model for understanding dissociative pathology. In J. Solomon & C. George (Eds.), *Attachment disorganization.* New York: The Guilford Press.

Main, M., & Hesse, E. (1990). Parents' unresolved traumatic experiences are related to infant disorganized attachment status: Is frightened and/or frightening parental behavior the linking mechanism? In M. T. Greenberg, D. Cicchetti, & E. M. Cummings (Eds.), *Attachment in the preschool years: Theory, research and intervention.* (pp. 161–182). Chicago: University of Chicago Press.

Ochberg, F. M. (1988). *Post-traumatic therapy and victims of violence.* New York: Brunner/Mazel.

Perry, B. D. 1994. Neurobiological sequelae of childhood trauma: PTSD in children. In M. M. Murburg (Ed.), *Catecholamine function in posttraumatic stress disorders: Emerging concepts.* (pp. 253–276). Washington, DC: American Psychiatric Press.

Putnam, F. W., & P. K. Trickett. (1993). Child sexual abuse: A model of chronic trauma. *Psychiatry, 56 (1),* 82–95.

Rando, T. A. (1993). *Treatment of complicated mourning.* Champaign, IL: Research Press.

Roberts, N., & Noller, P. (1998). The associations between adult attachment and couple violence: The roles of communication patterns and relationships satisfaction. In J. A. Simpson, & W. S. Rholes, (Eds.), *Attachment theory and close relationships.* (pp. 317–351). New York: The Guilford Press.

Salmon, P., & Calderbank, S. (1996). The relationship of childhood physical and sexual abuse to adult illness behavior. *Journal of Psychosomatic Research, 40(3),* 329–336.

Solomon, S., & Davidson, J. R. T. (1997). Trauma: Prevalence, impairment, service use, and cost. *Journal of Clinical Psychiatry, 58(suppl 9),* 5–11.

Sprang, G., & McNeil, J. (1995). *The many faces of bereavement: The nature and treatment of natural, traumatic and stigmatized grief.* New York: Brunner/Mazel.

van der Kolk, B. A. (1989). The compulsion to repeat trauma: Reenactment, revictimization and masochism. *Psychiatric Clinics of North America, 12,* 389–411.

van der Kolk, B. A. (1994). The body keeps the score: Memory and the evolving psychobiology of posttraumatic stress. *Harvard Review of Psychiatry, 1,* 253–265.

van der Kolk, B. A. (1996). The complexity of adaptation to trauma. In B. A. van der Kolk, A. C. McFarlane & L. Weisaeth, (Eds.), *Traumatic stress: The effects of overwhelming experience on mind, body and society.* (pp. 378–397). New York: Guilford.

van der Kolk, B. A., Brown, P., & van der Hart, O. (1989). Pierre Janet on posttraumatic stress. *Journal of Traumatic Stress, 2,* 365–378.

van der Kolk, B. A., Roth, S., Pelcovitz, D., & Mandel, F. S. (1994). Disorders of extreme stress: Results from the DSM-IV Field Trials for PTSD. Paper presented as 1994 Eli Lilly Lecture to the Royal College of Psychiatrists, London, February 2.

Walker, E. A., Gelfand, A., Katon, W. J., Koss, M. P., Von Korff, M., Bernstein, D., & Russo, J. (1999). Adult health status of women with histories of childhood abuse and neglect. American Journal of Medicine, *107(4),* 332–339.

Weil, J. L. (1992). *Early deprivation of empathic care.* Madison, WI: International Universities Press.

West, M., & Keller, S. (1994). Psychotherapy strategies for insecure attachment in personality disorders. In M. B. Sperling & W. H. Berman (Eds.), *Attachment in adults: Clinical and developmental perspectives.* (pp. 313–330). New York: The Guilford Press.

Zinner, E. S., & Williams, M. B. (1999). *When a community weeps: Case studies in group survivorship.* New York: Brunner/Mazel.

11.

The "Curse" of Too Good a Childhood

Therese A. Rando

The topic of this chapter is not an earth-shattering one. Not earth-shattering, that is, unless one happens to fit its parameters or work with an individual who does. It is a topic that has received relatively little clinical attention, despite pertaining to a good percentage of persons contending with trauma and major loss. The goal of the chapter is to illuminate a relatively lackluster phenomenon—one that most clinicians have encountered, but which far fewer have an explicit comprehension of and even fewer take into account in treatment. The topic is the deleterious impact on the assumptive world of a particularly positive premorbid history that was relatively devoid of adversity—known colloquially in this essay as "too good a childhood"—and how this plays out after trauma and major loss.

Many readers may wonder why attention is being paid to this issue. There are, after all, more substantially pathological or detrimental issues for an individual. Yet, to me, it is particularly distressing to witness a previously well-functioning, successful, in-control person painfully and confusedly struggle with the traumatization and profound disillusionment that can ensue when one of their prior strengths (their good psychological background) devolves into a risk factor, exposing them to additional hardship over and above that brought to them by the precipitating trauma or loss.

In over twenty-five years of practice, I have treated numerous individuals who have had specific difficulties coping with negative life events due to issues stemming directly from a relatively idyllic prior life marked by trustworthy attachments and positive experiences. There often appears to be a phenomenon of distress in these individuals consequent to the effects of an earlier life that was too pleasant and which was missing, for lack of a better term, a healthy dose of misfortune. The fundamental premise of this essay is that those who experience too good a childhood are relatively cursed when forced to contend with trauma and major loss later in life for two reasons, both of which are intrinsically related to the assumptive world.

Before going further, a note about language is in order. It is explicitly recognized here that the terms *cursed* and *too good a childhood* may have strong connotations for some readers. It is hoped that the reader will understand usage of these words in this chapter as defined herein, resisting adding additional nuances. By way of clarification *cursed* should not be taken to imply any retribution for any wrongdoing on the part of the individual, nor that anyone has imprecated for injury, harm, or evil to be visited upon the afflicted individual; the term is in no way to be associated with the divine or supernatural. The word is used solely to describe the phenomenom of an ordeal, problem, or tribulation befalling an individual specifically because of another experience (i.e., too good a childhood). It is this initiating experience that justifies the usage of the term *curse* by meeting the definition of serving as "a cause of great harm or misfortune" (*Merriam-Webster's Collegiate Dictionary*, tenth edition).

The term *too good a childhood,* as has been mentioned above, is used colloquially to refer to a premorbid history that has been marked by an abundance of positive, fortunate life experiences and/or a lack of negative, disadvantagous ones. Clearly, it must be granted that problems or issues can arise after childhood. Nevertheless, the term is retained here because of its usefulness in locating, identifying, and explaining the primacy and relative resistance to change of the core assumptions developed during this time of life.

Finally, the reader should be aware that, conceptually, major loss—although frequently mentioned in its own right—is considered in this chapter as a specific type of trauma and as a type of victimization. Hence, when trauma and victimization are specifically mentioned herein, they should be understood as generic experiences that incorporate major loss. (See Rando, 2000, for a detailed discussion of the critically important associations among trauma, loss, traumatic stress, grief, mourning, bereavement, and victimization.)

Assumptive World Vulnerabilities Due to an Overly Positive Premorbid History

There are two reasons why persons with too benign a prior history have difficulties when confronting trauma and major loss. First, such individuals tend to have developed assumptive worlds that are particularly shattered by those two experiences. Specific assumptions, expectations, and beliefs constituting the fundamental content of these assumptive worlds are especially vulnerable for being overly positive, unrealistic (if not totally naive), and overgeneralized (e.g., "All people are trustworthy"). While not every assumptive world element is unrealistically positive, the core ones are predominantly so. The issue here is not that they are positive per se, but that their particular degrees of positivity, realism, and overgeneralization are such that the individual essentially is set up for more than the typical amount of disillusionment and distress when these assumptions are violated.

The second reason that these persons have difficulties when contending with trauma and major loss is that they are likely to be unpracticed in defending and revising their assumptive worlds. These processes, of course, are mandated in human beings following significant occurrences of trauma and loss. Persons with little or no experience in defense and revision of the assumptive world are therefore relatively deficient in critically important process skills.

Thus, assumptive world content and process areas are predisposed to be compromised in the individual whose life experience was so positive as to generate unrealistic assumptive world elements, or whose experience did not include sufficient negative experiences to promote the capacity to contend with defense or revision of the assumptive world when necessitated. In the remainder of this chapter, these problems created by past life assets and deficits will be termed *assumptive world vulnerabilities*. (It must be noted that there exist a variety of causes for assumptive world vulnerabilities; the focus in this chapter is on just one of them.)

Extending from these concepts, I propose that there are two groups of individuals who sustain difficulties in these two areas. This translates into two ways in which one can have too good a childhood. This distinction between the two groups is made below and is mandated because of the following important caveat pertaining to our thinking on this topic.

Conventional clinical wisdom appears to suggest that a person cannot have too positive an upbringing. An insufficiency of favorable developmental experiences is routinely identified as a substantial risk factor for all manner of human suffering. As a corollary, individuals with a dearth of negative events in their background are presumed to be better able to deal with hardship later in life. The implicit reasoning appears to be that if childhood difficulties tend to lead to subsequent problems, then a minimal amount of such difficulties, or none, should leave the person relatively better off.

As will be discussed below, the empirical and clinical evidence suggest that this is not necessarily true. Yet it is important to note that there is one main problem with the thinking described above. It is an error that is unfortunately perpetuated by many clinicians. The absence of "bad events" does not necessarily signal the presence of "good things." For instance, just because one was not abused does not mean that one necessarily has had a good life. It may merely have been devoid of major problems, although it did not contain much of what would be considered healthy, good, or constructive. In other words, it was effectively neutral. The above mentioned distinction between two categories of individuals contending with too good a childhood develops from this point.

The first group of persons (Group I) with assumptive world vulnerabilities have prior histories characterized by both overwhelmingly and unrealistically positive experiences *and* a lack of adversity. As a result, Group I individuals have life experiences that (1) generate overly positive, unrealistic, overgeneralized assumptive world elements and (2) result in an absence of adversity that could provide knowledge about and practice in defending and revising the assumptive world. Consequently, they are relatively compromised in coping with trauma and major loss because of some of the specific content and nature of their assumptive worlds, as well as their inability to successfully meet challenges to them.

The second group of people (Group II) with assumptive world vulnerabilities have had a relative lack of adversity in their premorbid life. This comparative absence of misfortune in Group II individuals, as noted above, does not automatically mean that there was a corresponding presence of positive experience sufficient to generate unrealistically positive or overgeneralized assumptions. If there were, these individuals would fit into the first group. Instead, this second group is marked by the presence of difficulties in defending challenged assumptive worlds and in subsequently revising them as necessary. These stem from the lack of sufficient prior experiences to enable them to cope successfully with assumptive world violation. They definitely can maintain positive assumptions in their assumptive world; the assumptions just are not as excessively positive, unrealistic, or overgeneralized as those held by persons in Group I.

It should be noted that there is a third group of individuals who come from among those with too positive a background; however, they are not construed to have assumptive world vulnerabilities and are not considered "cursed" as discussed in this chapter. These Group III individuals are people whose life histories have provided them both with overly positive, unrealistic, overgeneralized assumptive world elements *and* successful experiences of meeting challenges to these elements. Since these challenges have been met successfully, there are now more realistically positive elements existing in their assumptive world. Its elements are not as glowing, naive, unrealistic, or inappropriately generalized as before, yet are still predominantly positive. Indeed, Group III individuals embody what has been delineated by Janoff-Bulman (1992) in her description of the new psychological world of the survivor of victimization:

> The inner worlds of victims who have "recovered" now reflect an acknowledgment of misfortune, an awareness of vulnerability. These survivors know that their prior assumptions were naive, that tragedy can strike and that no one is invulnerable. Their new assumptive worlds, however, are not completely negative. . . . Rather, these survivors recognize the possibility of tragedy but do not allow it to pervade their self- and worldviews. . . . [S]urvivors reestablish positive, yet less absolutely positive, core assumptions.
>
> They balance what they know can happen with more benign views of themselves and the world. They know they are not entirely safe and protected, yet they don't see the entire world as dangerous. Long after the rape, assault, serious accident, diagnosis of life-threatening disease, or disaster, the victim's assumptions remain somewhat more negative than that of their nonvictim counterparts. *The world is benevolent, but not absolutely; events that happen make sense, but not always; the self can be counted on to be decent and competent, but helplessness is at times a reality. Survivors are often guardedly optimistic, but the rosy absolutism of earlier days is gone.* (p. 174, emphasis added)

In summary, there are two groups of individuals incorporated under this chapter's rubric of too good a childhood: those in Group I, who have earlier histories that create overly positive, unrealistic, or overgeneralized assumptive world elements, and who also lack sufficient successful experience of defending and revising their assumptive worlds; and those in Group II, who lack such experience. The first group has two areas of assumptive world problems to contend with, content and process; the second group is restricted to process problems only. In the remainder of this chapter, the focus primarily is upon Group I people, although Group II folks are discussed as necessary for instructional purposes.

Putting this all together, what can be said so far about the topic of this chapter? Simply put, there seem to be definite costs or downsides to too good a childhood, although these are counterintuitive and certainly typically have been neglected in clinical practice. It seems that there can indeed be too much of a good thing. While it appears to me at the end of the day that it clearly is better for an individual to have to deal with sequelae of too good a childhood as opposed to dealing with the consequences of a bad childhood, the point to be made here is that such salubrious backgrounds are not necessarily positive, or even neutral, in all respects when it comes to handling trauma and major loss. Clinicians who fail to appreciate this reality not only do their patients or clients a disservice but actually can contribute to iatrogenic treatment effects.

Without a doubt, there are important questions that remain to be researched in the consideration of this issue. For instance, exactly what is a "healthy dose" of adversity? Might there be one or more core assumptions that are more vulnerable than others? Are there additional groups of persons with issues contributing to assumptive world vulnerability after positive upbringings other than those identified here? Are there other similarities and differences between Groups I and II? Precisely what, in the abstract, do persons need in order to be optimally prepared for contending with assumptive world issues subsequent to trauma and major loss? These and other questions need to be answered.

Following a selected review of literature about the assumptive world and identification of associated premises underlying this work, attention is turned to support for the notion of assumptive world vulnerability resulting from too good a childhood. The chapter continues with a discussion of clinical implications for therapists.

The Assumptive World:
Relevant Literature and Associated Concepts

This review of literature pertaining to the assumptive world and some of its associated concepts is not intended to be exhaustive in scope, but should provide a sense of the differing realms from which knowledge has come, as well as give some indication of important areas of concern to be considered in treatment with such individuals.

For purposes of this essay, literature about the assumptive world and associated concepts derives from four main source areas: psychology, particularly social, developmental, and cognitive psychology; studies of victimization and trauma; thanatology; and studies of transcendence of adversity.

Psychology

Psychology—particularly in the spheres of social, developmental, and cognitive psychology—initially was the realm from which sprang the fundamental concepts underpinning knowledge about the assumptive world. One of the early references most often cited is Kelly's (1955) work on personal constructs, in which emphasis is placed upon the importance of understanding people's own systems of meaning, which are organized around a set of core assumptions that govern their perceptions of life events and channel their behavior in relation to them. In essence, personal constructs are the formulations and the lenses through which people perceive, appraise, feel about, and respond to the world and the people and events therein.

Particularly relevant to this, among a number of other associated concepts, are Rotter's (1954) social learning theory construct of "expectancies," Berger and Luckmann's (1966) concepts of social construction of reality, Bowlby's (1973) notions of "working models of the world," Epstein's (1973) theories of reality, Marris's (1975) "structures of meaning," Paivio's (1986) work with mental structures and schemas, and Fiske and Taylor's (1991) analysis of schemas and their functioning. Constructivism, as put forth by Mahoney (1981, 1991) and Neimeyer and Mahoney (1995), among others, went further than these formulations and pointed out how individuals actively create and construe their personal realities, constructing their own representational model of the world, which in turn becomes a framework from which subsequent experience is ordered and assigned meaning. Rather than holding the representational model as a mere template through which experience is filtered, constructivism asserts that the model actively creates and constrains new experience, determining what is perceived as "reality" (Mahoney & Lyddon, 1988). Subsequently, this school of thought has underpinned other germane psychological theories, such as Epstein's (1985) cognitive-experiential self-theory.

Generic coping-related issues are particularly relevant to what occurs to, and happens because of, the assumptive world after trauma and major loss. In their classic work on stress and coping, Lazarus and Folkman (1984) make it clear that one of the two main personal factors influencing appraisal of stress and, in turn, coping with it, is the individual's beliefs. These include, among others, beliefs regarding personal control and efficacy (Bandura, 1977, 1986) and locus of control (Rotter, 1966), as well as existential beliefs. Related to this is Taylor and Brown's (1988) work on the adaptiveness of "positive illusions" in the maintenance of mental health via the provision of filters through which individuals can "distort" information in a positive direction and foster of positive emotions. Three types of positive illusions they identify include seeing oneself more positively than is true, believing that one has more control over events than is actually the case, being unrealistically optimistic about the future.

Victimization and Trauma

A second arena from which literature pertinent to the assumptive world springs is that formed by the study of victimization and trauma. As observed by Wortman (1983) in her review of the literature and delineation of implications for future research, most of the research on victimization has fallen within two general areas: basic assumptions about the world, and causal attributions and other cognitions. Regarding the former, Wortman notes that the literature indicates that (1) assumptions held by victims of undesirable life events may play a critical role in the coping process, (2) assumptions may influence reactions to life crises, (3) assumptions about the world may influence one's behaviors prior to victimization and thus can alter one's chances of being victimized, (4) assumptions can affect one's reactions to a victimization, and (5) experiences of being victimized can alter a person's basic assumptions.

Arguably the most notable work on the assumptive world within the area of victimization and trauma has been provided by Janoff-Bulman, who observes that the psychological disequilibrium ensuing from victimization and trauma stems from the shattering of three fundamental assumptions—that the world is benevolent, the world is meaningful, and the self is worthy (1985, 1992; Janoff-Bulman & Frieze, 1983). Extending this work and providing what is often perceived as the most comprehensive work in the field, McCann and Pearlman (1990) integrate three major psychological systems—the self, psychological needs, and cognitive schemas—to originate constructivist self-development theory and, with particular emphasis upon psychological needs and their corresponding cognitive schemas, utilize it successfully to integrate insights from object relations theory, self-psychology, and social cognition research to conceptualize trauma, explain its varying impacts upon victims, and generate treatment guidelines for adult trauma survivors.

Other well-recognized proponents for the critical role of assumptive world violation in victimization and trauma include Horowitz (1986), who perceives it as the central experience that precipitates the stress response syndrome; Ulman and Brothers (1988), who maintain that trauma "shatters the self" and that subsequent symptomatic expressions are manifestations of faulty restorative efforts at healing shattered "central organizing fantasies"; Epstein (1991), who reports that the disruption of an individual's schemas has a destabilizing effect on the entire personality, producing a state of disequilibrium characterized by symptoms of posttraumatic stress disorder (PTSD) and a mandate for the person to develop a modified theory of reality that can assimilate the trauma; Hyer (Hyer and Associates, 1994), whose focus of treatment is to change "happenings into meanings" and to enable "change of one's inner assumptive world or schema to the realities of the external world"; and Meichenbaum (1994), who adopts a constructive narrative perspective in the conceptualization and treatment of PTSD.

Thanatology

A third locus of information about the assumptive world is found in the field of thanatology. In fact, it is the thanatologist Parkes (1971) who is credited with coining the original term, one that he adapted from Cantril's (1950) "assumptive form world" so as to broaden the idea to include conceptual as well as perceptual elements. He asserts that major psychosocial transitions, including bereavement caused by the death of a loved one, necessarily demand changes in the mourner's assumptive world (1988). Rando (1993) expands upon this notion, making the relinquishing of invalidated attachments to the old assumptive world and the revision of that assumptive world two fundamental operations within the six processes of mourning she postulates as necessary to a healthy accommodation of the loss of a loved one. Within the assumptive world, Rando locates both global assumptions (those pertaining to the self, others, life, the world in general, or spiritual matters) and specific assumptions (those that had been predicated upon and associated with the deceased's continued, interactive presence in the world).

Other thanatologists informing this topic include Bowlby (1973), whose "working models of the world" already have been mentioned above. Also among this group would be Woodfield and Viney (1984–1985) and Viney (1991), who identify the stressful psychological sequelae of bereavement as deriving from the dislocation of personal constructs occasioned by the death of a loved one, with the ability to ultimately adapt one's personal constructs determining adjustment to bereavement. Nadeau (1998) integrates symbolic interaction and family systems theories to investigate meaning making within the family subsequent to the death of a family member, illustrating that meaning making occurs at all system levels; involves selected strategies and active processes to make sense of the death, with such meanings significantly affecting how family members mourn; and implicitly includes the "family paradigm" (Reiss, 1981), "family schema" (Patterson, 1988), or what would be termed there the family's assumptive world. Neimeyer (2001) thoroughly examines meaning reconstruction and the experience of loss, providing compelling evidence, anchored in a constructivist approach, that mourning entails affirming or reconstructing one's personal world of meaning—one's assumptive world—which has been challenged by loss. It is the central process in mourning, with adaptation involving restoration of coherence to the narrative of one's life.

Transcendence of Adversity

A final subject area having a direct bearing on the revision of the assumptive world following trauma and major loss is that devoted to transcendence of adversity. In their classic work on trauma and transformation, Tedeschi and Calhoun (1995) synthesize the literature and provide a model for growth in the aftermath of suffering. Such growth, they write, inherently demands modification of schemas; they "propose that growth *is* change in schemas" (p. 81). Similarly, works by Lauer and Lauer (1988), Segal (1986), Slaikeu and Lawhead (1987), and Weenolsen (1988) offer concerted proof of and instruction in coping with and growing through all types of personal crises, with each of them addressing aspects of reworking the assumptive world. Similarly, although with a more specific focus upon transcending loss through death, quite useful contributions have been provided by Jozefowski (1999) and Prend (1997).

Six personality characteristics have been associated with successful coping with negative life events (Tedeschi & Calhoun, 1995), and each constitutes an area replete with myriad implications for those with assumptive world vulnerabilites who are contending with trauma and major loss. These include: internal locus of control (Rotter, 1966); self-efficacy (Bandura, 1982); optimism (Scheier & Carver, 1985); hardiness (Kobasa, 1979); resilience (Rutter, 1987); and sense of coherence (Antonovsky, 1987).

Premises Assumed in Relation to the Assumptive World

Parkes' (1988) definition of the assumptive world is used to form the basis for all subsequent remarks. Parkes defines the assumptive world as

> an organized schema ... which contains everything that we assume to be true [about the world, the self, others] on the basis of our previous experience. It is this internal model of the world that we are constantly matching against incoming sensory data in order to orient ourselves, recognize what is happening, and plan our behavior accordingly. (p. 56)

Integrating other concepts, the assumptive world can be elaborated further to include all of the assumptions (including expectations and beliefs) that the individual sustains, with most of these becoming virtually automatic habits of cognition and behavior. In large part, the assumptive world determines the individual's needs, emotions, thoughts, and behaviors and gives rise to that person's hopes, conations, wishes, fantasies, and dreams. As additionally conceptualized here, the assumptive world is viewed as being fueled by the individual's experiences, memories, and needs and confirmed through that person's experiences, behavior and interaction patterns, and role relationships. It is critical in influencing appraisal and attribution processes and is fundamental in the anticipation, organization, and processing of experience.

In terms of trauma and bereavement, there are two categories of assumptive world elements (Rando, 1993). *Global assumptions* pertain to the self, others, life, the world in general, and spiritual matters. *Specific assumptions* pertain to precisely what has been or is being lost (e.g., a belief in one's invulnerability, a loved one); to its continued interactive presence in the world; and to the idiosyncratic expectations held for it, its meanings, and ties to it.

As utilized in this essay, the conceptualization of the assumptive world is further informed by constructivist self-development theory (CSDT) (McCann & Pearlman, 1990). What is particularly useful about this is the premise that schemas—or, as addressed here, assumptive world elements—are the cognitive manifestations of psychological needs that are affectively laden. As modified in 1997 (Traumatic Stress Institute/Center for Adult & Adolescent Psychotherapy, 1997), CSDT holds that schemas develop within five core need areas, which evolve in relation to the self and others and which motivate behavior. The five psychological needs are: safety, trust/dependence, control, intimacy, and esteem. Working with the premise that trauma disrupts one's central needs and alters, disrupts, or disconfirms one's beliefs, assumptions, and expectations in those central need areas, the CSDT explanation for individual differences after trauma is the degree to which emotionally significant schemas—those that reflect the particular individual's central needs prior to the victimization—are altered by the traumatizing experience.

In fact, the violation of core assumptions of the individual's world is held by most authors, including myself, as one of the most central experiences in trauma, if not the defining experience. As Janoff-Bulman (1992) concludes, the essence of trauma is the abrupt disintegration of one's inner world, in which overwhelming life experience splits open the interior world of the victim and shatters his or her most fundamental assumptions. As McCann and Pearlman (1990) define it, a traumatic experience is one that is sudden, unexpected, or nonnormative; that exceeds the individual's perceived ability to meet its demands; and that disrupts the person's frame of reference and other central psychological needs and related schemas. In both cases, as with so many other authoritative works in the field, violation of the assumptive world is held to be an intrinsic ingredient whenever trauma is found.

Another fundamental premise underpinning this chapter is that since there is, by definition, violation of the assumptive world to a greater or lesser degree in trauma and major loss, the individual's assumptive world necessarily functions as a critical factor in how experiences of trauma and loss are construed by that person. Wortman, Silver, and Kessler (1993) conclude that the impact of life events appears to be determined by whether they can be incorporated into an individual's philosophical perspective or view of the world, that is, the person's assumptive world. Neimeyer (1997) addresses the same issue when he observes that premorbid assumptions can either mitigate or exacerbate the impact of a loss, as when a particular loss either can be given meaning within the framework of one's existing constructions or can appear to actually undermine this very framework. Therefore, it is taken as axiomatic in this work that the individual's preexisting assumptive world is the matrix from which appraisals of trauma and loss are made, through which they are responded to, and in which modifications typically are necessitated in order to accommodate these two major negative life events.

Janoff-Bulman (1992) has argued persuasively that at the core of our assumptive worlds, among the global assumptions maintained, human beings hold abstract beliefs about themselves, the external world, and the relationship between the two.

She proposes three fundamental assumptions: the world is benevolent, the world (and life) is meaningful, and the self is worthy. She regards these as broad, abstract conceptions that are emotionally potent, having been the very first assumptions established in the individual's internal world; the logical outcome of these is a sense of personal invulnerability. With a colleague, she notes the illusory nature of these core assumptions, offering explanation for why disillusionment is such a basic part of human response to trauma and major loss:

> Our fundamental assumptions are not illusions in the sense that they are simply wishes
> ... lacking any substantial correspondence with reality. ... They are, nevertheless, false
> conceptions, because they go too far; our fundamental assumptions are illusions
> because they are overgeneralizations. Derived from our real interactions in the world,
> they are generally true, but not always. (Janoff-Bulman & Berg, 1998, p. 38)

Finally, while it is clear that trauma violates the assumptive world, it also must be appreciated that the violation of the assumptive world caused by trauma, in turn, can cause its own additional trauma. In no other situation is this as apparent as in the case of the Group I person.

In summary, the assumptive world is taken as the mechanism through which all human experience is filtered and processed. As pertains to trauma and loss, it contains both global and specific assumptions, the former of which develop in five psychological need areas. At the core of the global assumptions in the assumptive world lie three fundamental assumptions—essentially illusory overgeneralizations—regarding the benevolence and meaningfulness of the world and the worth of the self. Trauma and major loss violate essential elements of the assumptive world by shattering core and other assumptions and disrupting associated central needs. The long-term impacts of these negative life experiences are determined in large part by the preexisting assumptions maintained by the individual involved. While trauma violates the assumptive world, assumptive world violations, in turn, can create their own trauma.

Support for the Notion of Assumptive World Vulnerability Resulting from Too Good a Childhood

To the extent that an individual sustains assumptive world vulnerabilities of any kind, that person is subject to difficulties when encountering trauma and major loss given that these experiences mandate revision of the assumptive world. Persons who have these vulnerabilities secondary to the sequelae of too good a childhood are as much at risk as anybody, and then some. The purpose of this section is to examine some of the generic and specific issues that contribute to their assumptive-world-related problems when contending with trauma and major loss.

The Development, Resistance to Change, and Primacy of Core Assumptions

In her writings, Janoff-Bulman (1992; Janoff-Bulman & Berg, 1998) has clearly delineated how our fundamental assumptions originate in our earliest experiences with caregivers and how these provide the basis for preverbal representations of the world and the self (see also Bowlby, 1969, 1973, 1980).

> By responding to the child's cries, for example, a caregiver provides the earliest basis for perceiving a person-outcome contingency and a benevolent other; the seed is also planted for the infant to perceive the self as worthy of such care. In these early social interactions, then, the child begins to develop a representation of the world as benevolent and meaningful, and of the self as worthy. (Janoff-Bulman & Berg, 1998, p. 38)

These fundamental assumptions become the bedrock for the adult's assumptive world. They constitute the individual's most abstract, general schemas and reside at the very foundation of the cognitive-emotional system. Janoff-Bulman (1992) points out that human beings tend to process information in ways that serve to maintain old schemas rather than change them. This accounts for the conservatism of our conceptual system and explains our tendency to preserve already established beliefs. Established schemas (the term is used here interchangeably with *assumptions*) influence all subsequent interpretations of information, both new information and information from memory. They guide perception, memories, and inferences. The human being's motivation for cognitive conservatism is to provide the self with stability and coherence.

According to Janoff-Bulman, people need a "stable, unified conceptual system in order to impose order on a complex, confusing, chaotic world." This explains why so much social psychological research demonstrates that people are highly motivated to maintain cognitive consistency. In order that preexisting schemas remain intact, the person notices and attends to schema-relevant information more readily, processes it more rapidly and easily, behaves in schema-consistent ways to confirm preexisting beliefs, and discounts or isolates contradictory evidence. In this way, individuals can provide themselves with an intelligible, orderly, stable, secure, comfortable, and recognizable world.

This is the reason that our fundamental assumptions, formed so early in the development of our conceptual system, have undue influence upon us. Human beings generalize from their earliest interactions in the world, and these representations, in terms of assumptions, serve as guides and selective filters for subsequent experience. Janoff-Bulman concludes that fundamental assumptions or theories of reality are at the very core of our conceptual system. They are incredibly strong cognitively and affectively as, in their primacy, they shape our subsequent interactions and interpretations of the world and become reinforced as they do.

This explains the focus of this chapter on childhood. It is during this period when the earliest assumptions are developed and inlaid. Certainly others can be developed at later ages, but as noted above, all subsequent experience and meaning making is highly directed by the assumptions established in childhood. Too, as we mature, it becomes harder in general to change, thus explaining the relatively greater adaptability of youth. Unless taught otherwise by life, the human being will continue to believe, interpret, feel, and behave in accordance with the earliest and most central core assumptions.

Although the cognitive conservatism of the human being is responsible for the tendency to resist change, it would be untrue to say that change never occurs. When change does take place in cognitive structures, it most often occurs at the level of narrower rather than fundamental schemas, and it is gradual and incremental as opposed to sudden and swift (Janoff-Bulman, 1992). While narrower, more specific, superficial schemas change whenever any new learning occurs in the human being, the fundamental ones tend to stay intact. While it is possible for these core assumptions to transform gradually over time, they most often remain consistent, providing stability, continuity, and security.

It is during times of trauma—including major loss—that there is significant violation of fundamental assumptions, creating the demand for change in order that the experience can be accommodated. Despite this, the premorbid assumptive world, although shattered to varying extents depending upon the circumstances, remains a most powerful factor influencing the success of its own revision. Those persons whose assumptions are overly positive, unrealistic, and overgeneralized, or who lack sufficient experience in defending or revising their assumptive world, will be at a relatively greater disadvantage than those individuals who are more realistic in their assumptions and more practiced in dealing with challenges to their assumptive world.

In terms of the content of their assumptions, Group I individuals, as with all people, have core assumptions that tend to be quite old, very entrenched, and powerfully influential. They differ from others in that the nature and characteristics of their core assumptions are so unrealistic that they are predisposed to being overwhelmingly disillusioned, and even traumatized, when those assumptions are shattered and invalidated by a traumatic experience. To the extent that the content of their assumptive worlds is relatively out of sync with the vicissitudes of human existence, they labor under expectations and filter their experience through assumptions that do not stand them in good stead when striving to cope.

Issues Associated with the Lack of Experience in Defense and Revision of the Assumptive World

If an individual has not had the right kind or necessary depth of experience to contend with serious challenges to their fundamental assumptions, that person continues to maintain them as they initially were. As previously observed, the cognitive conservatism of the human being, particularly with respect to the core assumptions, results in few changes in the fundamental elements of the assumptive world unless occasioned by a significant enough life experience.

In those situations where there have been no previous substantial challenges to fundamental assumptions—as is the case for persons in Groups I and II—the individual is particularly at risk for problems when confronting trauma or major loss. This can occur despite the presence of resources in these people that traditionally have been identified to be associated with positive outcomes (e.g., high self-esteem, ego strength, affect tolerance, resilience). This is because despite the fact that such resources are important for healthy coping with trauma and loss, they do not obviate the problems caused by insufficient experience in defending and revising the assumptive world, although ultimately they can enable the individual to cope better with the problems that the lack of experience engenders.

Without a doubt, there are real difficulties for individuals facing major negative life events when they lack enough experience in successfully contending with challenges to their assumptive worlds. Such success would be operationalized as defending and/or revising the assumptive world in such a fashion that a stress experience can be accommodated. There remains no dissonance between the external reality and the individual's inner world. This does not mean that the person necessarily is happy, unmoved, or unscarred by what has occurred, only that that he or she has been able to incorporate it within the assumptive world by revising the content of that internal world (through adding, deleting, or changing specific elements) and/or by altering the appraisals and meanings assigned to the event. This is what has been referred to by Horowitz (1986) as "working through," that is, facing the reality of what has happened, processing the emotional and ideational aspects of the stress experience, and integrating it into the assumptive world with the rest of life.

An absence—or insufficient amount—of experience in successfully defending or revising the assumptive world essentially leaves the individual without knowledge and practice upon which to rely when confronted by trauma and major loss. In such instances, the person is missing important content and process pieces and is consitutionally more vulnerable because of not having been "inoculated" by earlier life stressors. They are missing the many positive impacts that rehearsal with minor assumptive world challenges could have upon future experience with major challenges.

Support for this in the literature is found in numerous areas. Lazarus and Folkman (1984), in examining adaptational outcomes of coping, observe that people who as children are protected from certain kinds of stress are likely to be all the more vulnerable to stress later because they fail to learn coping skills needed for day-to-day living. Holahan and Moos (1990) write that environmental events leading to resilience may not be pleasant happenings but rather stressors that are successfully engaged, resulting in additional strength. Rutter (1987) describes such events as inoculations against future difficulty.

Fisher and Fisher (1993) elaborate upon this further. They feel that witnessing family and friends go through difficulties, and observing strangers suffering in the media, can provide an individual with vicarious experiences that may inoculate against trauma to the extent that the experiences are perceived as potentially relevant to one's own life: They contend that "imbibing absurdity in small doses may hopefully build up a degree of immunity against it" (p. 193). Corroborating this, Tedeschi and Calhoun (1995) assert: "Some events can present doses of challenge great enough to highlight the randomness, injustice, meaninglessness, and absurdity of things, but small enough for us to learn to tolerate it" (p. 79). Plainly, previous experience in this realm has the potential to be therapeutic when it is of the kind that involves relevant or central issues to the person, it constructively teaches, and it is of a sufficient amount or type that the person is not overwhelmed or underengaged.

Finally, while the role of prior experience in assumptive world defense or revisions is an important one, it is not the experience itself that is the operative factor, but how it is contended with. Not unlike what is described in the thanatological literature on the influence of prior loss on bereavement outcome, it is not the objective number of prior losses sustained per se that is critical, although that is one factor. When they occurred, whom and what they involved, what they meant to the person, and whether they have been successfully accommodated—the last being the most important determinant—also determine if they constitute assets or liabilities for the mourner.

Literature Findings Pertaining to Problems Associated
with Too Good a Childhood

The clinical observation that individuals with overly positive premorbid histories and/or the lack of sufficient practice in assumptive world defense and revision have particular vulnerabilities when contending with trauma and major loss has been confirmed in the empirical and clinical literature. Support for this contention comes from several areas.

After analyzing the meaning of loss and adjustment to bereavement, Wortman, Silver, and Kessler (1993) conclude:

> Our analysis suggests a new way of thinking about vulnerability to major losses. In the past, vulnerability has been assumed to be a function of the coping resources that one possesses—one's self-esteem, socioeconomic status, belief in the ability to control one's environment, social support. Our analysis suggests that people who appear to have considerable coping resources—successful, control-oriented people who have a history of accomplishment and who have generally been rewarded for their efforts—may be particularly vulnerable to certain kinds of sudden, undesirable life events. Such people may be more devastated by a loss that challenges the view that efforts are generally rewarded than those who possess considerably less coping resources. (p. 365)

In other words, individuals who have considerable psychological coping resources and previous success in utilizing them can be more devastated after major losses than those who don't have such assets. These are primarily Group I individuals, who sustain unrealistically positive assumptive world elements and have not had sufficient experience to teach them how to cope with a violation of their assumptions. Group II individuals can also fall victim to such vulnerability after undesirable events because of their lack of experience with defense or revision of the assumptive world. However, to the extent that they did not also initially sustain unrealistically positive assumptions, their distress is likely to be relatively less than that of Group I people.

Research has identified a number of commonalities among the assumptions maintained by Group I people that come to be violated in trauma and major loss. To the extent that any Group I person sustains these assumptions, that individual is more "cursed" by the positive prior life experience that generated them. Individuals who have extreme beliefs in their own ability to control outcomes may find traumatic events significantly more difficult to cope with than persons with more moderate assumptions of personal control (Perloff, 1983; Swindle, Heller, & Lakey, 1988). People with extreme belief in their ability to control might unrealistically believe that they can influence existential aspects of problems (Fisher & Fisher, 1993). After conducting a preliminary study within the learned helplessness paradigm, Peterson and Seligman (1983) suggest that if people believe that they have control over the choice, planning, and changing of contingencies in a given situation, experiencing uncontrollable outcomes within that situation may be particularly debilitating.

Drawing on the research of Perloff (1983) and Scheppele and Bart (1983), Wortman (1983) concludes that there is clear evidence that people who assume that they are invulnerable to a crisis, or that others are trustworthy, will appraise situations differently than those who do not share these assumptions. Such a person might take longer to initiate coping strategies to deal with the crisis and might therefore cope less effectively with crises that demand immediate attention. Thus, assumptions can put people at risk when they are in a truly dangerous situation. As well, it appears that they can exacerbate the persons's reactions to the victimization.

Related to this, Scheppele and Bart (1983) found that when individuals were victimized despite the precautions they had taken, they may be especially likely to have their assumptions shattered and to experience deleterious aftereffects from the victimization. Also, they found that individuals were more likely to have extreme reactions to their victimization if it took place in circumstances where the individuals had believed themselves to be safe. In illustration, they report that women are less likely to change their views of the world if a rape takes place in a situation where they had some reason to believe they were in danger already. If the attack occurred in circumstances the woman had defined as safe, a much more extreme reaction is likely.

Perloff's (1983) investigation of perceptions of vulnerability to victimization is of particular interest for our central topic. She found that individuals who had not been victimized by negative life events tend to perceive themselves as "uniquely invulnerable," as less vulnerable to victimization than others. However, Perloff finds that victims who have the most difficulty coping with their misfortune appear to be precisely those individuals who initially had felt least vulnerable prior to being victimized.

> A second potentially maladaptive consequence of perceived unique invulnerability concerns people's ability to cope after they have actually been victimized. Several literatures suggest that people, in underestimating their own personal vulnerability to negative events, may have more difficulty adjusting to victimization should it occur. In general, unexpected, unforeseen, or unpredictable events are more difficult to cope with than expected, foreseen, or predictable ones.... An illusion of unique invulnerability may be related to what Janoff-Bulman and Brickman (1981) have called a "pathology of high expectations." Just as the pursuit of high expectations may have negative consequences when a task is insoluble, so too may illusions of unique invulnerability have debilitating consequences when people actually encounter misfortune. (1983, p. 49)

This echoes precisely Wortman's (1976) suggestion that

> people with exaggerated notions of personal control, or with considerable past experience at controlling the important events in their lives, may find uncontrollable outcomes all the more difficult to accept when they occur. (p. 45)

Perloff notes that other researchers support her findings as well. Disaster researcher Wolfenstein (1957) observed that there is likely to be more emotional disturbance following a disaster on the part of those who beforehand warded off all anxiety and denied the reality of the threat than on the part of those who were able to tolerate anxiety and to acknowledge that the disaster could happen. Similarly, Scheppele and Bart (1983), as previously mentioned, found that rape victims who cope worst may be those who initially felt safest, that is least vulnerable. Kübler-Ross (1969) suggested that among terminally ill patients, those who have lived active, controlling, high-pressure lives have more difficulty adjusting to the prospect of death than do simpler, more passive people. Janoff-Bulman and Marshall (1982) discovered that the elderly residents who coped least well with living in a nursing home were those who felt they had had a great deal of control over their lives prior to entering the home. And Taylor (1979) offered that persons who have been most accustomed to controlling and managing their environment in the past and have the strongest expectations of controlling and managing it in the future tend to have the most difficulty coping with hospitalization.

All of this research has a direct bearing upon the individual with too good a premorbid history who faces trauma and major loss and its resultant demands for assumptive world revision. Such individuals, by virtue of their prior experiences, tend to share traits, among others, of considerable personal coping resources, a history of previous personal success, high belief in personal control, and a sense of personal invulnerability. Surely no one would suggest that any of these four factors is psychologically detrimental in and of itself. In fact, these factors are among those often perceived as positive and therapeutic resources. Ironically, when it comes to coping with all types of victimization, the research suggests that those assets can become liabilities, at least for a period of time.

It should be recognized as well that just as trauma can lead to assumptive world violation, so too can assumptive world violation—secondary to trauma—cause its own traumatization of the person. Group I individuals, therefore, often receive a double dose of trauma—the first from the event itself, and the second from the violation of assumptions (and their inexperience in dealing with this) that stems from the trauma.

Clinical Implications

While, as we have discussed, the individual who has experienced what in other circumstances would be construed as an extremely good premorbid history is disadvantaged when it comes to dealing with assumptive world revision after trauma and major loss, the good news is that Group I persons (those with overly positive, unrealistic, and overgeneralized assumptions, along with an absence or insufficient amount of experience in defending or revising an assumptive world that has been significantly violated) usually have relatively good coping resources and other personal assets that act to minimize long-term distress despite intense initial reactions. Janoff-Bulman (1992) describes how for these individuals, impact and recovery are not parallel:

> Consider the adult trauma victim who experiences intense difficulties in the immediate aftermath (i.e., impact phase) of the victimization but who has the coping capacities to readily resolve the trauma and recover. In such cases there will be considerable short-term distress but good long-term adjustment. This best describes the survivor who had very positive assumptions prior to the victimization; he or she felt relatively invulnerable to misfortune and thereby has great difficulty in the immediate aftermath of an overwhelming life event. This is the quintessential mismatch of expectations and reality.
>
> It is those with the most positive preexisting assumptions whose core schemas are most deeply violated. Extreme negative events produce tremendous psychological

upheaval and anxiety, for their inner worlds are shattered. The intense impact of victimization, however, does not imply a similarly difficult recovery process. In fact, these survivors may have a relatively easy time rebuilding a stable, comfortable assumptive world, the essence of the recovery process. The same psychological makeup, history, and social environment that provided these optimistic people with their prior positive assumptions are also likely to have provided them with the psychological resources to cope successfully postvictimization. Thus, positive core assumptions may be a risk factor for initial psychological disruption, but they may also be associated with long-term recovery. (pp. 88–89, reference numbers removed)

I would add that the Group I person has several other issues that must be kept in mind. First, although Janoff-Bulman notes the better odds for recovery, it is by no means guaranteed. There are, unfortunately, Group I people who are so traumatized by the shattering of their assumptive world and the consequent demand for defense or revision that they get stuck in their incredulity and posttraumatic responses to the violation (which I artificially differentiate here from the posttraumatic responses stemming from the trauma or major loss event as a whole). The scenario witnessed can be akin to that seen after a sudden death where the survivor develops unanticipated mourning syndrome (Parkes & Weiss, 1983). In this situation, the lack of warning creates an impact so disruptive that uncomplicated recovery can no longer be expected. Along with other manifestations, the mourner is unable to grasp the full implications of the event and has difficulty accepting that it happened despite intellectual recognition of its occurrence. The mourner's adaptive capacities and coping abilities are seriously assaulted. Such individuals suffer extreme feelings of bewilderment, anxiety, self-reproach, depression, and despair that render them incapable of functioning normally in any area of their lives.

While not a huge percentage of Group I persons necessarily would respond in this fashion, varying degrees of it can be seen in those whose traumatization from assumptive world violation is sufficiently severe. The implication is that uncomplicated recovery cannot be automatically assured for each Group I person. This brings up the issue of additional distress caused by specific aspects of the Group I individual's background. For instance, along with contending with the unrealistically positive assumptive world elements and the lack of sufficient experience in defending or revising the assumptive world, there often can be an extra assumptive world element that gets created in the situation: "I *shouldn't have to change my world.*" This brings about further distress and often exacerbates any anger or bitterness that may be present.

A second issue pertains to the incredulity that this trauma or loss has happened. Such a feeling stems not only from the reaction to the event itself happening, but from the person's reaction to the violation of the specific assumption that had been predicated upon the belief that it wouldn't happen since it never had before. Finally, a third additional issue for Group I people comes from the particular problems that can develop when personal betrayal is a part of the experience. For many of these individuals, their major relationships have been marked by relative consistency, honesty, and trustworthiness. For this reason, they often have more extreme reactions than others when the traumatizing event entails personal betrayal. They are completely discombobulated by this, which adds greatly to their difficulties.

There is some literature that elaborates on the notion of differential impacts caused by diverse types of victimization. Janoff-Bulman (1992) writes that the meaning of the event for the survivor—which is determined by how the experience is interpreted in light of the victim's prior assumptions—determines which assumptions are most affected. She distinguishes between discrete and chronic events, individual and group victimization, and events caused by a perpetrator with malicious intent andacts of God (i.e., natural disasters). This last distinction is important in that her research suggests survivors of human-induced victimizations are most apt to hold negative assumptions about themselves and the benevolence of the world. The question of meaning is addressed in terms of the perpetrator and the self, with the greatest impact found in assumptions about self-worth and the perceived benevolence of the world. For such survivors, the two assumptions seem to move in concert, as if one mirrors the other; the world is viewed as more malevolent and the self is viewed more negatively. In contrast, victims of natural disasters develop an acute awareness and concern about randomness and chance in their lives. Many view themselves more negatively and appear to have lost confidence in their autonomy and strength, or see the world as more malevolent. The meaningfulness of the world is shattered.

Taking into consideration the information presented in this chapter, what would be useful agenda items for the clinician to adopt when treating a Group I person after trauma or major loss? The following suggestions are offered, with the expectation that they will be incorporated into traditional generic psychotherapeutic intervention in trauma (see, for example, Courtois, 1988, and McCann & Pearlman, 1990), major loss (see, for example, Rando, 1993, and Worden, 1991), and assumptive world revision (see, for example, Janoff-Bulman, 1992, and Thompson, 1998).

1. Do not assume that because of prior success, personal coping resources, and a positive premorbid history the individual will *not* have difficulties contending with necessitated assumptive world revision.
2. Thoroughly assess the individual's assumptive world—global and specific assumptions—and areas of psychological need that correspond to cognitive schemas.
3. Look not just at amount of prior experience and loss but at the types of it and whether and how it was successfully addressed.
4. Recognize that different victimizing experiences affect various fundamental assumptions. Appreciate that human-induced events are particularly problematic for the Group I person, particularly those associated with personal betrayal.
5. Recognize that the person's resilience may be affected by his or her assumptive world vulnerability; immediate impact—and, for some, longer-term impact—may not progress toward trauma accommodation, as would otherwise be predicted by the individual's personal psychological assets.
6. Understand that the trauma causes assumptive world violation and that that assumptive world violation, in turn, causes additional trauma. This means that the Group I person often needs recognition of and intervention into twin doses of trauma.
7. Explain to the affected individual the dynamics of the situation in order to render it more comprehensible and manageable, and to illustrate that despite intense initial reactions, successful coping and adaptation is not only possible but quite likely.

Conclusion

Individuals with too good a childhood meet trauma and major loss with inherent specific deficits because of overly positive, unrealistic, overgeneralized assumptions and/or insufficient experience in defending or revising their assumptive world. Clinicians must pay attention to the particular dilemmas facing such persons when contending with major negative life events, and need to design interventions to specifically target them. As well, clinicians have to avoid assuming that effective coping ability and resilience will be present in the early aftermath of a traumatic event merely because of the positive premorbid history of the person involved and the assets that it has provided to that individual. In fact, this person may be both more vulnerable to and devastated by major adversity precisely because of that previous history.

There is considerable suggestion that the psychological assets of the affected person ultimately can enable him or her successfully to accommodate the trauma or major loss and its mandated revision of the assumptive world. Nevertheless, this does not occur without much interim distress, destabilization, and additional traumatization. It is hoped that this chapter will sensitize the clinician to these intermediate experiences in order to enable therapeutic efficacy in assisting those individuals struggling with the "curses" described herein.

Note

This chapter is lovingly dedicated to the memory of Ms. D., who was her own person even though she wasn't one, which was much to her chagrin.

References

Antonovsky, A. (1987). *Unraveling the mystery of health: How people manage stress and stay well.* San Francisco: Jossey-Bass.

Bandura, A. (1977). Self-efficacy: Toward a unifying theory of behavioral change. *Psychological Review, 84*, 191–215.

Bandura, A. (1982). Self-efficacy mechanism in human agency. *American Psychologist, 37*, 122–147.

Bandura, A. (1986). *Social foundations of thought and action: A social cognitive theory.* Englewood Cliffs, NJ: Prentice-Hall.

Berger, P., & Luckmann, T. (1966). *The social construction of reality.* Garden City, NY: Doubleday.

Bowlby, J. (1969). *Attachment and loss,* Vol. 1: *Attachment.* New York: Basic Books.

Bowlby, J. (1973). *Attachment and loss,* Vol. 2: *Separation: Anxiety and anger.* New York: Basic Books.

Bowlby, J. (1980). *Attachment and loss,* Vol. 3: *Loss: Sadness and depression.* New York: Basic Books.

Cantril, H. (1950). *The "why" of man's experience.* New York: Macmillan.

Courtois, C. (1988). *Healing the incest wound: Adult survivors in therapy.* New York: Norton.

Epstein, S. (1973). The self-concept revisited, or a theory of a theory. *American Psychologist, 28*, 404–416.

Epstein, S. (1985). The implications of cognitive-experiential self-theory for research in social psychology and personality. *Journal for the Theory of Social Behaviour, 15*, 283–310.

Epstein, S. (1991). The self-concept, the traumatic neurosis, and the structure of personality. In D. Ozer, J. Healy Jr., & A. Stewart (Eds.), *Perspectives in personality* (Vol. 3, Part A, pp. 63–98). London: Jessica Kingsley.

Fisher, S., & Fisher, R. (1993). *The psychology of adaptation to absurdity.* Hillsdale, NJ: Lawrence Erlbaum.

Fiske, S., & Taylor, S. (1991). *Social cognition* (2nd ed.). New York: McGraw-Hill.

Holahan, C., & Moos, R. (1990). Life stressors, resistance factors, and improved psychological functioning: An extension of the stress resistance paradigm. *Journal of Personality and Social Psychology, 58,* 909–917.

Horowitz, M. (1986). *Stress reponse syndromes.* (2nd ed.). Northvale, NJ: Jason Aronson.

Hyer, L., and Associates (Eds.). (1994). *Trauma victim: Theoretical issues and practical suggestions.* Muncie, IN: Accelerated Development, Inc.

Janoff-Bulman, R. (1985). The aftermath of victimization. Rebuilding shattered assumptions. In C. Figley (Ed.), *Trauma and its wake: The study and treatment of post-traumatic stress disorder* (pp. 15–35). New York: Brunner/Mazel.

Janoff-Bulman, R. (1992). *Shattered assumptions: Towards a new psychology of trauma.* New York: The Free Press.

Janoff-Bulman, R., & Berg, M. (1998). Disillusionment and the creation of value: From traumatic losses to existential gains. In J. Harvey (Ed.), *Perspectives on loss: A sourcebook* (pp. 35–47). Philadelphia: Brunner/Mazel.

Janoff-Bulman, R., & Brickman, P. (1981). Expectations and what people learn from failure. In N. Feather (Ed.), *Expectations and actions.* Hillsdale, NJ: Erlbaum.

Janoff-Bulman, R., & Frieze, I. (1983). A theoretical perspective for understanding reactions to victimization. *Journal of Social Issues, 39*(2), 1–17.

Janoff-Bulman, R., & Marshall, G. (1982). Mortality, well-being, and control: A study of an aged population of institutionalized elderly. *Personality and Social Psychology Bulletin, 8,* 691–698.

Jozefowski, J. (1999). *The phoenix phenomenon: Rising from the ashes of grief.* Northvale, NJ: Jason Aronson.

Kelly, G. (1955). *The psychology of personal constructs.* New York: Norton.

Kobasa, S. (1979). Stressful life events, personality, and health: An inquiry into hardiness. *Journal of Personality and Social Psychology, 37,* 1–11.

Kübler-Ross, E. (1969). *On death and dying.* New York: Macmillan.

Lauer, R., & Lauer, J. (1988). *Watersheds: Mastering life's unpredictable crises.* Boston: Little, Brown and Company.

Lazarus, R., & Folkman, S. (1984). *Stress, appraisal, and coping.* New York: Springer.

Mahoney, M. (1981). Psychotherapy and human change process. In J. Harvey & M. Parks (Eds.), *Psychotherapy research and behavior change* (pp. 73–122). Washington, DC: American Psychological Association.

Mahoney, M. (1991). *Human change processes.* New York: Basic Books.

Mahoney, M., & Lyddon, W. (1988). Recent developments in cognitive approaches to counseling and psychotherapy. *The Counseling Psychologist, 16,* 190–234.

Marris, P. (1975). *Loss and change.* Garden City, NY: Anchor/Doubleday.

McCann, I., & Pearlman, L. (1990). *Psychological trauma and the adult survivor: Theory, therapy, and transformation.* New York: Brunner/Mazel.

Meichenbaum, D. (1994). *A clinical handbook/practical therapist manual for assessing and treating adults with post-traumatic stress disorder (PTSD).* Waterloo, Ontario, Canada: Institute Press.

Nadeau, J. (1998). *Families making sense of death.* Thousand Oaks, CA: Sage.

Neimeyer, R. (1997). Meaning reconstruction and the experience of chronic loss. In K. Doka with J. Davidson (Eds.), *Living with grief: When illness is prolonged* (pp. 159–176). Washington, DC: Hospice Foundation of America.

Neimeyer, R. (Ed.). (2001). *Meaning reconstruction and the experience of loss.* Washington, DC: American Psychological Association.

Neimeyer, R., & Mahoney, M. (Eds.) (1995). *Constructivism in psychotherapy.* Washington, DC: American Psychological Association.

Paivio, A. (1986). *Mental representations: A dual coding approach.* New York: Oxford University Press.

Parkes, C. (1971). Psycho-social transitions: A field for study. *Social Science and Medicine, 5,* 101–115.

Parkes, C. (1988). Bereavement as a psychosocial transition: Processes of adaptation to change. *Journal of Social Issues, 44 (3),* 53–65.

Parkes, C., & Weiss, R. (1983). *Recovery from bereavement.* New York: Basic Books.

Patterson, J. (1988). Families experiencing stress: The family adjustment and adaptation model, Applying the FAAR model to health-related issues for intervention and research. *Family Medicine, 6(2),* 202–237.

Perloff, L. (1983). Perceptions of vulnerability to victimization. *Journal of Social Issues, 39(2),* 41–61.

Peterson, C., & Seligman, M. (1983). Learned helplessness and victimization. *Journal of Social Issues, 39(2),* 103–116.

Prend, A. (1997). *Transcending loss: Understanding the lifelong impact of grief and how to make it meaningful.* New York: Berkley Books.

Rando, T. (1993). *Treatment of complicated mourning.* Champaign, IL: Research Press.

Rando, T. A. (2000). On the experience of traumatic stress in anticipatory and postdeath mourning. In T.A. Rando (Ed.), *Clinical dimensions of anticipatory mourning: Theory and practice in working with the dying, their loved ones, and their caregivers* (pp. 155–221). Champaign, IL: Research Press.

Reiss, D. (1981). *The family's construction of reality.* Cambridge, MA: Harvard University Press.

Rotter, J. (1954). *Social learning and clinical psychology.* Englewood Cliffs, NJ: Prentice-Hall.

Rotter, J. (1966). Generalized expectancies for internal versus external control of reinforcement. *Psychological Monographs, 80 (Whole No. 609),* 1–28.

Rutter, M. (1987). Psychosocial resilience and protective mechanisms. *American Journal of Orthopsychiatry, 57,* 316–331.

Scheier, M., & Carver, C. (1985). Optimism, coping, and health: Assessment and implications of generalized outcome expectancies. *Health Psychology, 4,* 219–247.

Scheppele, K., & Bart, P. (1983). Through women's eyes: Defining danger in the wake of sexual assault. *Journal of Social Issues, 39(2),* 63–81.

Segal, J. (1986). *Winning life's toughest battles: Roots of human resilience.* New York: Ballantine Books.

Slaikeu, K., & Lawhead, S. (1987). *Up from the ashes: How to survive and grow through personal crisis.* Grand Rapids, MI: Pyranee Books.

Swindle, R., Heller, K., & Lakey, B. (1988). A conceptual reorientation to the study of personality and stressful life events. In L. Cohen (Ed.), *Life events and psychological functioning: Theoretical and methodological issues.* Newbury Park, CA: Sage.

Taylor, S. (1979). Hospital patient behavior: Reactance, helplessness, or control? *Journal of Social Issues, 35,* 156–184.

Taylor, S., & Brown, J. (1988). Illusion and well-being: A social psychological perspective on mental health. *Psychological Bulletin, 103,* 193–210.

Tedeschi, R., & Calhoun, L. (1995). *Trauma & transformation: Growing in the aftermath of suffering.* Thousand Oaks, CA: Sage Publications.

Thompson, S. (1998). Blockades to finding meaning and control. In J. Harvey (Ed.), *Perspectives on loss: A sourcebook* (pp. 21–34). Philadelphia: Brunner/Mazel.

Traumatic Stress Institute/Center for Adult & Adolescent Psychotherapy (1997). Handout on constructivist self-development theory. South Windsor, CT: Author.

Ulman, R., & Brothers, D. (1988). *The shattered self: A psychoanalytic study of trauma.* Hillsdale, NJ: Analytic Press.

Viney, L. (1991). The personal construct theory of death and loss: Toward a more individually oriented grief therapy. *Death Studies, 15,* 139–155.

Weenolsen, P. (1988). *Transcendence of loss over the life span.* New York: Hemisphere.

Wolfenstein, M. (1957). *Disaster: A psychological essay.* Glencoe, IL: The Free Press.

Woodfield, R., & Viney, L. (1984–1985). A personal construct approach to the conjugally bereaved woman. *Omega, 15(1)*, 1–13.

Worden, J. (1991). *Grief counseling and grief therapy: A handbook for the mental health practitioner.* (2nd ed.). New York: Springer.

Wortman, C. (1976). Causal attributions and personal control. In J. Harvey, W. Ickes, & R. Kidd (Eds.), *New directions in attribution research* (Vol. 1). Hillsdale, NJ: Erlbaum.

Wortman, C. (1983). Coping with victimization: Conclusions and implications for future research. *Journal of Social Issues, 39(2)*, 195–221.

Wortman, C., & Brehm, J. (1975). Responses to uncontrollable outcomes: An integration of reactance theory and the learned helplessness model. In L. Berkowitz (Ed.), *Advances in experimental social psychology* (Vol. 8). (pp. 277–336). New York: Academic Press.

Wortman, C., Silver, R., & Kessler, R. (1993). The meaning of loss and adjustment to bereavement. In M. Stroebe, W. Stroebe, & R. Hansson (Eds.), *Handbook of bereavement: Theory, research, and intervention* (pp. 349–366). New York: Cambridge University Press.

12.

The Assumptive World of Children

Linda Goldman

Children entering this new millennium are faced with life issues that were unspeakable to us growing up as children. Death-related tragedies such as suicide, homicide, and AIDS, and nondeath-related traumas such as divorce and separation, foster care and abandonment, bullying and terrorism, and abuse and violence have left our children sitting alone in their homes, unfocused and unmotivated in their classrooms, and terrorized in their communities. They are overwhelmed with their feelings and distracted by their thoughts.

Survivorship of these traumas creates for any child a loss of their *assumptive world* of safety, protection, and predictability. The role of the media as a surrogate communal parent and extended family further creates this same traumatic loss of the *assumptive world for* many if not most of our children.

Children naturally assume their world will be filled with safety, kindness, and meaning as they attempt to answer the universal questions of "Who am I?" and "Why am I here?" All too often these qualities seem to disappear into a nightmarish universe of randomness, isolation, and unpredictability. This leaves many of today's young people immersed in a new assumption: "There is no future. There is no safety. There is no connectedness or meaning to my life." By joining together as a global grief team, caring adults can co-create an assumptive world that again allows children to presume that love, generosity, and value will be integral parts of their lives.

We are raising a segment of our youth that are numbed, disconnected from their hearts, their minds, and their consciousnesses. They choose all too easily other alternatives such as drugs and alcohol, crime, and violence as ways of coping with the loss of their assumptive world. In yesterday's world we may have protected ourselves from trauma by having fire drills in our schools. In today's world our kids protect themselves from danger in the schools by having gunfire drills.

Too many of today's schoolchildren are grieving children. So many of our boys and girls are born into a world of grief and loss issues that live inside their homes and lie in wait for them outside their doorsteps, on their streets, and in their schoolyards and classrooms. Increasingly, children are traumatized by prevailing social and societal loss issues in their families, their schools, their nation, and their world.

A major percentage of America's children face the loss of the protection of the adult world as homicide, violence, abuse, and terrorism infiltrate their inner and outer worlds. Issues involving shame and secretiveness, such as suicide and AIDS, create a grieving child who is locked into the pain of isolation and loneliness. The following is a statistical picture of today's youth and the all-too-prevalent loss issues that unfortunately are becoming the norm.

- By high school's end
    Around 50 percent of students experienced divorce
    About 20 percent experience the death of a parent
    One out of three girls will be in some way sexually abused
    One out of seven boys will be in some way sexually abused
- By age fourteen, children have witnessed eighteen thousand deaths on TV, usually violent
- About 3.3 million children in America witness domestic violence each year
- An estimated forty-one million children globally will be orphaned by one or both parents from the AIDS virus by the year 2010
- About 160,000 children in the United States stay home from school daily for fear of bullying
- One out of six children between the ages of ten and sixteen report they have seen someone or know someone who has been shot
- In 1992, 632 children under the age of five were murdered—two-thirds of these children were murdered by one or both parents
- Suicide has become the second leading cause of death for our young people today, with one young person completing suicide every ninety seconds.
- Ten percent of the teenagers polled in Washington, D.C., stated they had attempted suicide in the past year

Children need to grow their hearts in order to grow their consciousness. If they assume the world of love, support, and meaningfulness no longer exists, they may shut down their humanness and get lost in a new assumption of a terrifying, chaotic, random, unprotected universe, whereby the life they knew and the people they thought they were have dissolved into a scary, unpredictable environment with an uncertain future ... or no future at all.

Caring adults need to create safe havens in our homes, offices, schools, and communities. Kids need a space that allows them to regain an assumptive world of benevolence, meaning, and worth in order for them to grow socially, emotionally, intellectually, and spiritually to reach their fullest potential as human beings.

What Is a Child's Assumptive World?

Children make basic assumptions about their world around them. They assume it will be kind, protective, safe, consistent, and meaningful. They assume their caretakers will be there to provide love, protection, and meaning. They need predictability, structure, and reassurance that their life and world have meaning and value.

When a child experiences a death-related trauma his or her world becomes fragmented. Terror, rage, guilt, feelings of abandonment, self-hatred, and a sense of isolation are a few of the many thoughts and feelings that take the place of their perceived normalcy. When a loved one dies, life changes forever for a child. When a parent is murdered or dies of suicide, fear, betrayal, projected rage, and revenge can replace childhood sweetness. The loss of the assumptive world of fairness and sensibility means that the child is at risk of being abandoned to new assumptions about a futureless and unprotected new life.

Sudden or traumatic deaths, suicides or homicides creating shame and stigma, difficult relationships with a person who died, emotional or physical abandonment or neglect from a surviving caretaker or guardian, or multiple losses leave children bewildered and shaken. These complicated grief issues shatter the emotional and physical equilibrium and stability a child may have had. The terror, isolation, and loneliness experienced by too many of today's children leave them living in a world without a future, without protection, and without role models. Children normally and naturally assume the adult world will care for them, support them, and nurture them. When Dad is murdered, Mom dies of suicide, or a sister overdoses on drugs, a child's assumptive world is shattered. "How could this have happened to me?" Is their first question.

Children's Loss Issues

Loss of Trust: Fear and Betrayal

Alex was a fifth-grader whose dad died of suicide on Alex's tenth birthday, two weeks before a planned summer vacation with him. "How could he have done this to me?" was Alex's first question when he came in for grief therapy. The assumed world of Dad always being there and wanting to be with him had ended forever. His summer was spent alone, feeling angry, ashamed, and terrified. Afraid to face his peers for fear they would question him about his dad's death, Alex stopped seeing them. The fear of having to explain the way his dad died kept him from talking about his dad's death. Angry and bored, much of his summer was spent fighting with his mom and friends.

Alex was frozen in time, unable to progress through the natural grief process for his dad because he couldn't talk about his death. When school began that fall, he said he needed to make new friends and refused to call friends who didn't know of his dad's death. Remaining ashamed and silent, Alex experienced not only the loss of his dad and friends but the loss of a loving and accepting world. He now assumed his world would be a judgmental one, thinking less of him and his dad because of the way that his dad died.

Loss of Worth: Guilt and Magical Thinking

Alice was a ten-year-old whose magical thinking convinced her that she had killed her dad. When she confided these feelings to me, I asked her how she felt she had murdered her dad when she was only six years old at the time of his death. She quickly explained: "My dad picked me up the night he had his heart attack. If he hadn't done that, he wouldn't have died. It's my entire fault."

Her belief that she was a worthy person was destroyed by her dad's sudden death. Now she lived in an assumptive world of murder, and through a child's magical thinking she could be the only cause. Reality checks were used to reestablish freedom from overwhelming guilt. Discussing the medical facts about the cause of her dad's heart attack, such as being overweight, forgetting to take medication, and smoking cigarettes lifted doubt. Creating visits to her dad's doctor and the school nurse reinforced for Alice a world that released her from the prison of killing her parent.

Loss of Meaning: Projection

Jason was a ten-year-old fourth-grader. His dad was randomly murdered as he was driving his UPS truck. Jason struggled with terror that this could happen to him or his mom, thoughts he had never had before his dad's killing. Several months after the death he walked into my grief therapy office, sat down on the floor, looked up at me, and asked: "Linda, I only have one question. Why did God have to kill my father?"

His faith in God was replaced with the new assumption of God as murderer rather than benevolent protector. Only when he could ask this question out loud could we begin to explore his angry feelings, which may have been projected onto God about not saving his dad, and his unique spiritual beliefs. We could then begin reality checks about the facts of his dad's death. Interviewing the police, reading media accounts, and creating outlets to explore perceived understandings about the shooting allowed Jason to rebuild trust in his shaken world.

Loss of Faith: Abandonment

Janie's mom died when she was five. At six, her dad remarried and she and her older brother Tom moved into a different home with two stepsiblings. When she had unpacked her boxes of clothes and toys, Janie suddenly realized she couldn't find her favorite stuffed bear, Emily, which Mom had given her the Christmas before she died. She searched for weeks and weeks, asking everyone and looking everywhere. Her father even took her back to the old house to see if Emily was there. Every night she prayed and prayed to God to help her find that stuffed animal. After three months she stopped praying. Janie told me this story when she was ten. She explained: "The night I stopped praying and realized I would never find Emily was the night I realized there is no God."

Violence, Media, Murder:
Shattered Assumptions of a Benevolent, Meaningful World

Continuous Media Coverage: Loss of Trust

A nation of children and adults watched nightly for almost a week as a young mother, Susan Smith, pleaded for help to find her missing children. Families prayed with her for relief from her hellish vigil.

Adam was a first-grader who cried with Susan Smith and worried a lot. "Where were the children? What happened to them? Could it happen to me?" Adam awoke one day to a strange twist to this story: Susan Smith was the murderer. She put her kids in seat belts and let the car go into the water. The kids drowned. "How could this be?" he wondered "Moms don't kill kids." At dinner that night he asked his mom some important questions: "Mom, would you ever kill me?" and "What could those kids have done that was so bad their mom would have murdered them?"

An assumptive world of parental security and trust was shaken by the reoc-curring saga of murder and betrayal on the nightly news. Adam's mom began dispelling her child's magical thinking that children could ever be the cause of murder.

Visual and Auditory Impact: Trauma and Regression

Seven-year-old Mary heard on the news about the horrific car crash of Princess Diana. Mary's own mom had died in a car crash when she was five. Witnessing Princess Diana's demolished car on the TV retriggered terror of what happened to her mother and anxieties about herself and dad. As she watched the tragedy with her dad, she crawled onto his lap and began crying and sucking her thumb, regressing to earlier childhood habits. Sobbing through her tears, she asked: "Dad, could you ever get killed when you drive to work too?"

Safety in Mary's assumptive world was destroyed when her mom died, a natural shift of perception for grieving children. Filled with apprehensions, she was fear-ful that her dad would die in a car crash too. Mary told me how much she worried about dad not wearing his seatbelt. I suggested she write dad a letter telling him how she feels. Safety and protection were brought back to her assumptive world when her dad assured her he would wear his seat belt.

Retrigger Past Trauma: Visual and Auditory Memories

Tony's dad was killed in a sudden car crash too. Watching details of Diana's fatal car accident retriggered terrors that his mom would also be killed in an automo-bile accident. With his assumptive world shaken by media bombardment, past memories flooded in. He explained: "I can see the car crash, and I can hear the car screech again and again in my mind."

Over and over, he reread his memory book about his dad, reviewing his expla-nation about how his dad died and the picture he made of what happened. He became clingy and infantile and worried about leaving his mom's sight—common signs of a grieving child.

Tony's mom was planning a weekend trip with her new boyfriend, and Tony arrived for grief therapy angry and upset. He pleaded with his mom: "Please don't leave me. I'm too scared you'll die too. Stay home so I can see you are safe. Please don't go!"

Tony's mom and I listened. I then asked Tony what his mom could do in order for him to feel she would be safe (and his assumptive world protected) if she went on this trip. He urged her to take his uncles sport utility vehicle, which had airbags and antilock brakes, and we set up a schedule of times when his mom would call. This satisfied Tony, as he experienced control and choices, a feeling of being listened to, and assurance of a secure world.

Home, School, and Community Violence: Terror and Worry

A very poignant event that shocked and saddened our nation was the mass murder by high school students in Colorado of their fellow students. The assumption that schools are a safe place was shattered as a world of youth watched the massacre on TV. Not only the students at Columbine High but students throughout our country were shaken and traumatized by the scene, which they could too easily witness on TV.

Thirteen-year-old Jonathan called his mom at work, upset and scared. "I can't believe this is happening," he cried as he watched the terrifying event on the TV news. "I'm scared to go to school tomorrow and I don't want to go to high school. I'm afraid I'll get killed too!"

Eight-year-old Wanda watched the same news on TV and started to cry. "They are going to kill those kids the way they shot Floyd [her sixteen-year-old brother]." She ran over to her grandmother, sat in her lap, and began sucking her thumb and holding her grandmother tight.

These visual images instill terror in children and rekindle old wounds. Reassurance of a safe assumptive world was an important task for Wanda's mom. Creating reality checks and options, she reminded Wanda of the metal detectors, security guards, and policy of zero tolerance for weapons or violence at her elementary school. Her mom emphasized the neighborhood police protection and the community neighborhood watch, and suggested a buddy system before and after school and on the playground. Children are reassured when they feel the adult world has implemented concrete protection measures for safety in their world.

A World Forever Changed: Loss of the Familiar Assumptive World

At Home: Loss of the Routine, Day-to-Day World

Jennifer's mom died after a difficult bout with cancer. Jennifer was fourteen. Six months later she relayed a story in grief therapy about the depth of her loss. She was hungry and opened the refrigerator door to get out the noodles her mom always made for her after school. Realizing that there were no noodles—and no mom—she burst into tears.

Seven-year-old Peter had a similar experience. His mom had recently died in a sudden car crash, and his dad was trying very hard to keep the structure and routine of life the same as it has been before she died. Every Sunday morning she had made pancakes with her special pancake recipe. Peter's dad began making pancakes with this recipe. On the third Sunday of this ritual, Peter sadly explained to his dad, "Please don't make these pancakes. I don't like pancakes anymore."

In School: Loss of a Future

James, a ninth-grader, was sent to the principal's office for not doing his homework. He lived in a dangerous and violent neighborhood, and he had witnessed murders and had friends and family members who had been shot. When the principal asked James why he didn't do his homework, he responded in an abrupt, angry voice, "Why should I do my homework? I won't live until seventh grade. I think I'll plan my funeral instead."

The principal asked him to write about that for homework. The loss of James's assumptive world of a healthy tomorrow led his principal to create an assignment about a new assumptive world. James, in his assignment, used fantasy, imagination, and creativity in exploring what his own funeral could be. He experienced the excitement of creative writing perhaps for the first time; the assignment was one he could relate to. It was real and relevant to him. Therapeutically, getting to externalize what was really a long-held fear (of his own death and funeral) was very freeing. The principal used a sensitive moment to help, to heal, and to teach.

Henry's dad was murdered in a drive-by shooting. The trauma was excruciatingly painful for Henry, and he began having nightmares, wetting his bed, and experiencing frightening thoughts and feelings about being left alone. His schoolwork suffered, he began to become more restless and inattentive, and he became disruptive in class. He was showing the same behavioral symptoms used to diagnose attention deficit disorder: hyperactivity, impulsivity, distractibility, and inability to concentrate. They are also common for grieving children, but his school did not realize this, and they labeled him a slow learner and put him in a special-education class. Because of this, he assumed he was stupid and unproductive and lost all motivation and confidence.

In the Community: Loss of Identity and Self-worth

Mandy went to get her hair done for a special party. The woman who cut her hair asked if her mom was going to pick her up today. She relied, "No, she's home sick." Mandy didn't feel like explaining to a stranger that her mom had died of suicide last year. She felt so different and ashamed. Before her mom died, Many loved to share her world with everyone. In her new world, she felt isolated and alone . . . different and alien.

Re-creating a Safe Assumptive World: Recommendations and Conclusions

Know the Common Signs of Grieving Children

As a community grief team, all parents, educators, and health care professionals must familiarize themselves with the common thoughts, feelings, and behaviors of grieving boys and girls. By identifying these natural behaviors, we can normalize them and reduce fears and anxieties for parents and children. Becoming familiar with these signs can help us re-create a new assumptive world of consistency and understanding for a child's grief process.

The bereaved child may:

- Become the class clown
- Become withdrawn and unsociable
- Wet the bed or have nightmares
- Become restless when seated
- Speak out of turn
- Not complete schoolwork
- Have problems listening and staying on task
- Become overly talkative
- Become disorganized
- Exhibit reckless physical behavior
- Show poor concentration around external stimuli
- Show difficulty in following directions
- Complain of stomachaches or headaches

Sometimes bereaved children:

- Talk to their loved one in the present
- Imitate gestures of the person that died
- Idolize the person that died
- Create their very own spiritual belief system
- Worry excessively about their health and the health of the surviving parent or guardian
- Worry about death, theirs or a loved one
- Display regressive behaviors

Allow Children to Re-create a Safe, Protected, and Loving Assumptive World

Children can gain control of their world and feel they again have choices by symbolically re-creating a safe, assumptive world. Using drawings and stories, children can relay unacknowledged feelings, express memories, and create pictures of where they visualize their loved one to be. Ashley missed her mom on Mother's Day and decided to write her a letter. She created a dialogue with her mom, wondering what to get her for Mother's Day and drawing a picture of where she felt her mom was. After writing the letter, we decided to buy a big I Love You balloon and send it off symbolically to her mom for Mother's Day.

Grieving children often need to place their lost loved one somewhere, and lots of time children choose heaven. Ten-year-old Michelle wondered what heaven was like, and so she drew a picture and wrote the following story. This was a wonderful way for Michelle to re-create her loving and meaningful assumptive world with her mom.

What Is Heaven?

This is what heaven is to me. It's a beautiful place. Everyone is waiting for a new person, so they can be friends. They are also waiting for their family. They are still having fun. They get to meet all the people they always wanted to meet (like Elvis). There are lots of castles where only the great live, like my Mom. There's all the food you want and all the stuff to do. There's also dancing places, disco. My mom loved to dance. I think she's dancing in heaven.

Animals are always welcome. (My Mom loved animals.) Ask her how Trixie is? That's her dog that died. Tell her I love her.

Instill Safety, Connectedness, and Meaning in a Student's World

Alan, a fourth-grader, was disappointed that his teachers never mentioned the Columbine shootings. He wanted to talk about it. "These killings are the only thing on my mind," he explained. Matthew, a student in another school, was glad his school chose to discuss the shootings. The following are some of the questions his class was asked and children's reactions in discussion as they began to re-create a protected and meaningful assumptive world.

Do you feel safe at our school?
What do you wish we would do to make our school safer?
What do you think about Columbine?
Do you feel you understand what happened?
Is there anything you don't understand?
Would you like to do something to remember the students that died?

"This is so scary," said Mary. Suppose it happened to us!"

"The news is always blaming this on violent games and music. What about the parents, the school?" urged Joe.

"I think Columbine is a real eye-opener to everyone across the country to look out for each other and treat people with respect," offered Liam. "The kids that murdered were reclusive—bullied a lot."

Fear after a trauma can lead to new choices that vigilantly re-create safety. Children can be allowed to participate in ways to help restructure a meaningful assumptive world. When students were asked for suggestions about what they thought might help, they responded with: "Have gun detectors." "Have no-bully policies." "Stay home from school."

Educators can use these teachable moments of national trauma as a spontaneous mini-lesson, explaining school policy on violence and bullying and what procedures are necessary if children hear a threat. This lays the framework to begin to reduce fear after a trauma and reinstate a secure and meaningful assumptive world.

Students may feel at a time of national trauma that they are suddenly powerless and there is nothing they can do. One school encouraged their students to actively participate in the commemoration of the students who died in Colorado. This created a connectedness to the tragedy and began to give meaning to their world again. Fourteen-year-old Liam made a poster to represent his school's feelings of grief. Every child in the entire school signed the poster and it was sent to Columbine High. Liam's assumptive world had expanded to become a part of his country.

Conclusion

Grieving children naturally feel different, scared, angry, and unprotected. The enormous reservoir of unexpressed grief feelings so many of these children have are being consciously or unconsciously projected onto the outside world in the forms of bullying, abuse, violence, and homicide, or they are being projected onto the children themselves in the forms of victimization, feelings of helplessness self-hatred, suicide ideation, and death by suicide.

Losses from death-related and nondeath-related trauma could create for all too many children the additional loss of the assumptive world of kindness, meaning, and self-worth. Einstein suggested that perhaps the most basic of all questions might be, "Is the universe a friendly place?" Its answer is the foundation for one's basic set of assumptions about life. We can re-create a universe of friendship for our grieving children. We can instill benevolence, protection, self-esteem, and meaning in our children by offering security, connectedness, and caring hearts.

Parents, educators, professionals, and caring adults need to recognize the problem and assure our children that the assumptive world they held so dear before their trauma can exist again and that meaning can return in their lives. Kindness, protection, and a loving sense of self can be reestablished in their assumptive world by recognizing the signs of traumatized grieving children; allowing understanding and expression of feelings, thoughts, and behaviors that are natural for grieving children; and creating a the space of consistency, openness, and patience to allow these children to safely experience their grief process.

References

Goldman, L. (1996a). *Bart speaks out: Breaking the silence on suicide.* Los Angeles: WPS.

Goldman, L. (1996b). *Breaking the silence: A guide to help children with complicated grief—suicide, homicide, AIDS, violence, and abuse.* Washington, DC: Taylor & Francis.

Goldman, L. (1996c). We can help children grieve: A child-oriented model for memorializing. *Young Children: The National Association for the Education of Young Children, 51(6),* 69–73.

Goldman, L. (1996d). The meltdown process in children's complicated grief. *The Forum Newsletter: Association for Death Education and Counseling, 22(3),* 10–12.

Goldman, L. (1997). Children grieve too: Lessons in how to support children through a normal, healthy grief process. *Children and Families: The Magazine of the National Head Start Association, 16(2),* 22–31.

Goldman, L. (1998). Helping the grieving child in the school. *Healing, 3(1),* 15–24.

Goldman, L. (2000a). *Life and loss: A guide to help grieving children.* (2nd ed.) Washington, DC: Taylor & Francis.

Goldman, L. (2000b). *The grieving child in the school: Opportunities to help and enhance learning.* Washington, DC: Phi Delta Kappa.

Goldman, L. (2000c). Suicide: How can we talk to the children? *The Forum Newsletter: Association for Death Education and Counseling, 26(3),* 6–9.

part 4.

Traumatic Loss
and What Cannot Be Said

13.

Safety and the Assumptive World

A Theory of Traumatic Loss

Jeffrey Kauffman

Traumatic loss differs from nontraumatic loss in the psychological impact of the experience. The difference lies not in the nature of the event but in the nature of the experience, though types of events in which the self is particularly violated are specifically traumatizing. The difference between traumatic and nontraumatic grief, as either an absolute difference or a difference in degree, is in the experience of violation that shatters or fragments the self, that violently breaks the self into pieces. These pieces are dissociated fragments of self. The greater the degree of fragmentation, the greater the degree of psychological traumatization.

Traumatic grief is characterized by fragmentation of the self, *and* by efforts to hold together what is already broken. This dynamic constructs an underlying psychological economy of traumatic grief. The psychological phenomenon consists of the impact (being violated, which fragments the self) *and the self's resistance or cohesion.* The struggle with fragmentation that ensues in the wake of traumatic loss ripples from the point of impact on, without losing energy, and destines the self's experience of itself to the urgency of repair. This urgency echoes throughout the individual as screams that feel as if they are never heard, and yet they may be invisible to the therapist's. The therapist may disavow, dissociate, overlook, get caught in affective surges and undertows of, and keep secret from himself or herself what may be as subtle as a draft or overtly destructive as a hurricane: *the presence of the other fragmenting and resisting fragmentation.* Keeping safe and secure the boundaries threatened by fragmentation *and* attentively registering the danger as clinical information helps contain the violence of fragmentation.

Loss of the assumptive world occurs in both traumatic and nontraumatic loss. We see this in the difference between Janoff-Bulman's use of the term (Janoff-Bulman, 1992) and Rando's use (Rando, 1993). Janoff-Bulman's concept is about the loss of basic *valuations:* beliefs or convictions in the benevolence of the world, in the worth of the self, in meanings. Rando's use of the term is especially attentive to the psychosocial assumptive world: the loss of assumptions about belonging and fitting into the social world, and the loss of diverse expectations about one's self and one's life. Loss of the assumptive world in both Janoff-Bulman's and Rando's uses of the term, is present in traumatic loss like vertical and horizontal axes, but the loss of the dimension of normative valuation more specifically characterizes traumatic loss.

The assumptive world, as the concept is developed by Janoff-Bulman and Rando, both following Parkes, is a *cognitive representation* of, on one hand, valuations that organize the self, and, on the other, the value of a sense of connection and belonging. These underlying valuations constitute and cohere the self—its relation to itself, its being attached to itself. The psychological damage in the traumatic loss of the assumptive world is the self's breaking up. The foundation of assumptive world cognitions is the implicit value of cohesion.

The concept of an assumption refers to the beliefs that ground and the norms that protect—that is, that these valuations are *merely taken for granted*. Taking for granted is an act in which taking means both *giving* (to oneself) and *receiving*. The assumptive world is psychologically received from an archaic constitutive (but nonthetic) omnipotence of the self, which *gives* the assumptive world as a dwelling place—though this giver is often taken to be not self, and the affirmation of that assumption to be a grounding in humility. Nonetheless, this difference within self between giver and receiver cradles the capacity for assumption.

Assumption is the *power* of making real, constituting, constructing, or bringing forth, as in *bringing forth the human world*. The *power* of assuming is received from primitive omnipotence; the self receives the assumptive world, yet the giver is the self's very own root omnipotence. Assuming is an act of communication between giver and receiver. In the wake of traumatic loss the gift of the ability to assume is damaged; the receiver is busted, the giver is out, the connection between them is disrupted.

The assumptive world order is the set of illusions that shelter the human soul. We recognize assumptions that are normative in the sense of creative and protective, and need to *account* for assumptions that are destructive, ugly, shameful, dangerous, and bad. This accounting may be pivotal in mourning traumatic loss, for it often appears that these self-valuations are the most affectively significant clinical material in processing the traumatic loss of the assumptive world.

Traumatic loss *overwhelms* and floods the self with negative assumptions, assumptions deviant from the protective norm of the good. The utter, nameless horror at the heart of traumatic experience, which both defies and calls out for naming and containment, is represented in the loss of assumptive world values and safety by the specific assumptions that are lost. *Traumatization is an exposure of the self in which the self fragments, loses its protective illusions and value, and hides in unnamable shame.* In the loss of assumptive world protections, the self disintegrates *in shame*. Safety is the condition that permits the self to come out of hiding and to speak. Safety fosters integration.

Loss of the assumptive world coincides with terrible shame, helplessness, loss of control, panic, primitive affect disturbances, greatly heightened dissociative activity, and intensely self-destructive reliving of the traumatic loss. These trauma features all signify loss of safety.

The terror that shatters the assumptive world is a violent deprivation of safety. Exposure to violent death or other violence breaches the boundary of the self, inflicting *a sense of profound and enduring peril*. Psychologically, the loss of the assumptive world is the inward elaboration of this violence in terms of value and meaning and self-experience. In traumatic grief the sense of unsafety, as distrust and extreme guardedness, anticipates violence that has already happened but has not been sufficiently taken in and secured, violence that is *continuous* as the inner reality of self-experience and that keeps *repeating* in day-to-day experience of the self in the world. We are inclined to hedge, to refuse to acknowledge or reckon with irreversible loss of safety, to dissociate the traumatic loss of security. While transcendence and resilience emerge as adaptive prospects, whose heroic significance is the revaluation of a protective assumptive world, the primary clinical matter is concern with the shattered self.

The difference between traumatic and nontraumatic loss of the assumptive world is the difference between panic and anxiety. In traumatic loss there is persistent helplessness panic and annihilation panic, and in nontraumatic loss there is helplessness anxiety and annihilation anxiety more or less persistently. In panic, the boundary of the self is breached and ruptured. In panic resulting from a loss of safety, silent or voiced, the vulnerable core of the self, out of which the self in all its values and meanings is spun, experiences itself to be at risk of annihilation. What is *lost* in the traumatic loss of the assumptive world? The answer to this question is all. All is lost. Traumatic loss of safety is loss of all. "All is lost" expresses an awareness of annihilation *plus* a sense that the all is of the greatest worth. "All is lost" means that hope is lost, that there is no future. Assumptive world convictions maintain belief in the future, maintain an open horizon to the future. No safe future imaginable means that no future is imaginable. In traumatic loss this dilemma is prone to be intense and overwhelming.

Basic Woundedness

This account of the loss of the assumptive world involves both three basic dimensions (self-worth, meaning, and safety) and a framing of the basic woundedness.

Janoff-Bulman, whose work leads the way in approaching the concept of the assumptive world, says the basic dimensions of the assumptive world are meaning, self-worth and benevolence; safety is not conceptualized as a component in this schema. Benevolence, however, is a part of safety. "The world is good" implies moral value and means, at least or at bottom, not dangerous (safe). But even the moral judgment that the world is good or not good usually expresses a sense about the safety of the world, that is, good for me. The illusion of the benevolence of the world is an expression of the sense of safety of the self. A sense of safety is *projected* in the belief that the world is good. When we listen clinically to assertions about the benevolence of the world, we may hear assertions about sense of safety. Safety is *the* clinical issue. Janoff-Bulman argues strongly that safety is central; leaving the concept out of her influential theoretical construct of the assumptive world (the assumptive world as convictions about self-worth, meaning, and the benevolence of the world) has, among its many advantages, the shortcoming that the theoretical construct no longer directs research and clinical attention to the central concern (another shortcoming is, perhaps, that it overvalues the significance of a belief that the world is good). The nature of mortality, sacred and hidden—and, likewise, the guts of animal fear—urges upon self a primary concern with safety. And, in the mortal urgency of traumatic loss, the primary concern for safety, for protection against (traumatizing) violation, is, at the time of traumatic loss and continuing afterward, urgent and radical.

Clinically framing *basic woundedness*, the core of the inner self in traumatic loss, focuses clinical attention on the affects and psychodynamics associated with the loss of the assumptive world. Traumatic woundedness, reverberating in the deepest vulnerabilities of the self, is *reflected and represented* in the loss of the assumptive world. Basic woundedness in traumatic loss has to do with a loss of power, such as loss of the power to assume a safe world. The psychodynamics of loss of the assumptive world, of loss of the power to assume safety, has to do with the power of infantile omnipotence to provide sufficient protection. Assumptive world beliefs and convictions ground or orient human experience in normative valuations, the underlying affects and psychodynamics of which derive from infantile omnipotence.

When protective cognitions are shattered by helplessness panic, illusions of invulnerability become more primitive, inflated, tenuous, and fragmented. The greater the danger of helplessness, the greater the urgency of omnipotent protection. The assumption of invulnerability opposes the danger of out-of-control powerlessness, the abyss between the two deepening as helplessness panic unfolds. The normal developmental and lifelong ongoing process of integrating helplessness into a capacity to be vulnerable, to mourn loss, and for the self to grow is disrupted by traumatic loss, and a regression to more primitive tensions between helplessness and omnipotence is prompted.

The most primitive, global, powerful psychological resource is infantile omnipotence. Loss of safety, in the most radical form, is a loss of the protective cover constituted by normal infantile omnipotence, the psychological root out of which meaning and self-worth develop. Psychologically, catastrophic loss is an endangerment of the most basic safety provided to the self by its own infantile omnipotence. Yet this same infantile omnipotence, on its own terms, disavows, or simply has no accountability for, its violence.

The Self in Traumatic Loss

McCann and Pearlman (1990) review some basic and important concepts of self. The theory about the safety of the self recounted here is closely related to the theories that they reference, and I should like to start out by taking their discussion of the self for granted and zeroing in on a few aspects of a theory of the self that come to light, especially with regard to the loss of safety and the loss of the assumptive world.

The self is understood to be *that which fragments* in traumatic loss. This fragmentation is the focus of our practical and theoretical concern and prompts clinical and theoretical interest in the self in traumatic loss. The implosive disintegrative force of traumatic loss focuses our attention on the self as *that which is disintegrating*. A nucleus of identity, of the self's experience of itself, is damaged. The fragmented self, riddled with dissociated identities, has, at its core, experienced violation and been overwhelmed by annihilation panic. When we recognize that the assumptive world is shattered, we implicitly recognize that the self that *constitutes* the assumptive world is shattered; that self *as* power or ability to assume a normative safe world is seriously compromised.

Janoff-Bulman points out that assumptions are illusions. Psychodynamically, these illusions are projections, acts of the self projecting itself, *creating* illusions in

duality of the word says, cover/exposure. An underlying violation, vulnerability, *possibility*—the possibility of exposure and the necessity of cover—point to the very nature, the form, of the human soul: cover/exposure. The boundary, or, we may say, the skin, cover/exposure is the soul's container. On this boundary, that is, shame, the self sentiently experiences itself (to be). Darwin said that shame (blushing), being the expression of self-consciousness, is the uniquely human expressive emotion. "Uniquely human" means it is the mark distinguishing humankind from other species. It inaugurates the vertical dimension of human existence. Shame both determines and safeguards the sacred, or as Bruno Snell wrote, "shame originates as the reaction which excites the holy in man" (Schneider, 1977, p. 110). Traumatic violation is unholy. It profoundly shames. The horrifics of defilement, sacrificial self-loathing, or traumatic exposure to violence obliterate sacred cover. The dangerous presence of the unholy may contaminate clinical space through its effect on the therapist, so far as it is too shameful or too horrifying to be in its presence. The holiness or sanctuary of the clinical setting is providing safety for the presence of the unholy.

While shame *is* self-relating and installs subjective order, in the same action it regulates social order, that is, relation to other, to each other who is every bit other. Shame enforces the normative functioning of assumptive world convictions as constructs maintaining the social order and subjective order in the same stroke. However, shame also differentiates the self from others, as a private, separate realm. Safety provided by assumptive world beliefs is *being under cover of a norm*. The assumptive world is a language of shame enforced through protective (though not necessarily effectively so) norms.

References

Husserl, E. (1962). *Ideas*, tr. W. R. Boyce Gibson, NY: Collier Books.

Janoff-Bulman, R. (1992). *Shattered assumptions: Towards a new psychology of trauma*. New York: The Free Press.

Kauffman, J. (2001). "Shame" In G. Howarth and O. Leaman (Eds.), *Encyclopedia of death and dying* (pp. 407–409). London: Routledge.

Kauffman, J. (In press.) "The psychology of disenfranchised grief." In Ken Doka (Ed.), *Disenfranchised grief: New directions, challenges and strategies for practice*. Research Press.

Levinas, E. (1973). *The theory of intuition in husserl's phenomenology*, tr. Andre Orianne. Evanston: Northwestern University Press.

McCann, L. A., & Perleman, I. L. (1990). *Psychological trauma and the adult survivor*. New York: Brunner/Mazel.

Mohanty, J. N. (1972). *The concept of intentionality*. St. Louis: Warren H. Green.

Rando, T. (1993). *Treatment of complicated mourning*. Chicago: Research Press.

Rank, O. (1971). *The double: A psychoanalytic study*, tr. Harry Tucker Jr. Chapel Hill: University of North Carolina Press.

Schneider, C. D. (1977). *Shame, exposure and privacy*. Boston: Beacon Press.

Straus, E. (1966). "Shame as a historiological problem." In *Phenomenological psychology* (ch. 11). New York: Basic Books.

14.

What Cannot Be Remembered or Forgotten

Henry Krystal

If we could, each survivor would need to write something like Wiesel's *Night*. It would do justice to what needs to be said. But Wiesel struggled with this testimony over a number of years Originally he wrote the story in 700 pages, and it ended closer to 110 pages. He wrote it in Yiddish, later in French, and was finally able to publish it with the help of Françoise Mauriac in 1960. He has been writing this story in many ways ever since. Sometimes I think of him as the chief mourner for the Holocaust. This idea takes us right to the heart of the matter, namely, that testimony is an act of mourning made necessary by impacted mourning. There are many limitations to how much a person can successfully deal with through mourning. Some derive from one's individual characteristics and attributes. Common knowledge leads us to acknowledge that the loss of a child leaves a parent changed and grieving for the rest of his or her life. Which bereavement can be completed depends on the quantity of the loss, the circumstances of the loss, and the object of the loss. The people who have lost everything really have no chance of completing mourning successfully. We are dealing with impacted grief.

While many people think of testimony as an important act of future historic significance, from the point of view of the individual it is unfortunate to have to become a witness, especially an angry witness. The need to witness represents a failure to reintegrate one's life, to fill the void. It is a testimony to uncompleted bereavement. The need to go over some element of the past may become an all-consuming task. No amount of retelling relieves the inner compulsion. There seems to be not enough time, not enough listening to do justice to the compulsion. If the story cannot be fully captured in thought, memory, and speech, then enactment may be necessary. Uncompleted mourning may be expressed in a penitential life as illustrated in *The pawnbroker* by Wallant (1962).

Greenspan (1998) has recorded an interview in which the subject, while describing his business, realized that there needed to be some explanation why his business was remaining in the inner city despite the danger and the distress to him involved. As he was telling the story it was not "adding up" for him anymore. He reflected: "The city, it reminds me of the ghetto. Everything is boarded up and ruined. You know what I mean? Maybe ... maybe I am punishing myself.... I don't know." The pressure to witness goes becomes part of some self-reevaluation in the context of the consequences of the traumatic events in one's life pattern.

Laub (1991, p. 80) made the point that it was part of the uniqueness of the Holocaust experience that "during its historical occurrence *the event produced no witnesses*. Not only did the Nazis try to exterminate the physical witnesses of their crime; but the inherently incomprehensible *and* deceptive psychological structure of the event precludes it own witnessing by its very victims." In addition, it was inconceivable that any historical insider could remove herself from the contaminating power of the event so as to remain a fully lucid, unaffected witness, that is, sufficiently detached from the inside so as to stay entirely on the *outside* of the traumatizing roles, and the consequent identities, of either victim or executioner (p. 81).

For the above-stated reasons, words convey messages neither intended nor recognized by the witness. They become a vehicle through which the struggle continues. Not telling the story serves as a perpetuation of the tyranny. Survivors who do not tell their story sometimes become victims of distorted memory, that is of the forcibly imposed "external evil" that causes an endless struggle within oneself, and with a delusion, that is, that the Jews deserved it. The distortion of memory is that if one could not stop the atrocities, rescue, and comfort the victims, one is responsible for their pain. No victim observer could remain untainted, that is, maintain integrity, wholeness, and separateness (Laub, 1991).

The emerging of the Holocaust prevented the maintenance of an intact self-feeling that alone could keep itself uncompromised by the very act of being a witness to these horrible events. Perpetrators, in their attempt to rationalize the unprecedented scope of destructiveness, literally imposed upon the victim a delusional ideology whose grandiose coercive pressure totally excluded and eliminated the possibility of an inviolate, unencumbered, and thus sane point of reference in the witness (Laub, 1991, p. 81). The story of testimony and memory involves an active process. Memory happens in the course of retelling. But memory is determined by a number of events; mental elements are involved. Among the factors are the nature of the original perception, the degree and mode of registration, the nature of the retention, and finally, the capacity for recall and the form in which the recall takes place. Ultimately the recollection will be additionally shaped by the anticipation of the impact of the story on the audience and the audience's reaction to the teller of the tale.

Returning to the first mental act in the chain: what could be the nature of perception in the traumatic state? The recognition that the danger is unavoidable, unmodifiable, means that one has to submit to it. When that happens, the emotions change from fear, which is activating and energizing, to an affect related to the submission, which we call the catatonoid reaction (Krystal, 1978). This development initiates the traumatic state. In this state there is a progressive blocking of mental and emotional functions. From the beginning there is a blocking of the nature of perception, narrowing it to the mere matter of survival. There is a narrowing of attention to a sphere dictated by the overwhelming situation or object (just as is observable in a hypnotic trance). Progressively there is a blocking of registration of pain and painful affects. The emotions go into a "blank," unmodulated state that can be later recognized in trances and fugues. In other words, the intrapsychic splitting so well known in posttraumatic states is established at the point of overwhelming self-containment and effectiveness in dealing with one's life and psychic reality. That is why the surrender to a danger one cannot deal with self-reliantly represents the *"erlebte Situation"* (Freud's 1929 term for the psychic reality of an experience) of the beginning of the traumatic state.

Next, there is a blocking of cognitive functions such as judgment, recall, problem solving, discrimination, and eventually a blocking of vitality. In the robot state in which survival was possible in the situations into which the Nazis forced their victims, the field of possible perception was limited to immediate survival. It was the extreme of an altered state of consciousness. That is, one could not represent it to himself the self organization and self. Zalman Loewenthal, while in the Sonder-Commando, and before he was killed in the Birkenau crematorium uprising, wrote notes that he buried in the ashes around the crematorium, some of which were found. They were published in a book entitled *The scrolls of Auschwitz* (Mark, 1985). One fragment reads: "We ran while being chased with raised clubs by SS guards until we were totally confused. None of us knew what we were doing, who was doing it, and what was happening. We completely lost our senses. We were like dead men, like robots, that when they rushed us, we did not know where to run and what was to be done. No one looked at anyone else. I know for a fact that none of us was alive at the time. None of us thought or exercised judgment" (p. 219), and "thus in time they succeed in blunting all emotions, all thoughts of any action" (p. 222). Another typically laconic note: "There were times in this camp in 1941–1942 that every man, every single person that lived more than two weeks was living at the expense of other victims or stealing from them.... I want to say that [they] will certainly not reach the truth that no one has the strength to imagine. As no one can imagine the events, he will not believe [knowing] that we have been left alive by the power [i.e., the Nazis]" (p. 239).

In traumatic states, memories do not register in the normal way, and the traces are unreliable. Contrary to early psychoanalytic opinions that unconscious and repressed mental elements are not subject to change, but are preserved unaltered, my own research indicates that unconscious mental contents are subject to constant revision (Krystal 1988). The recall of the events experienced in a conflictual, painful, and particularly traumatic situation is spotty and highly distorted. Many memories are recovered in a conspicuously improbable way with evident displacements, amalgams of dreams and fears. Some of them are screen memories substituting for the original registration of the traumatic state, serving to protect one from the possibility of retraumatization.

The most consistent findings in posttraumatic states are disturbances of memory: amnesias and hyperamnesias that are part of the flashbacks, endless reexperiencing, and intrusive symptoms and thoughts. A major lifesaving operation is the creation of traumatic screens, false memories functioning as a protection against the unthinkable. Another disturbance follows from the other inevitable consequence of the trauma: the splitting of one's self-representation. There are many split patterns, the most conspicuous of which results from a fixation on the past. One has to live in the present but is never able to stop living in the past as well. Another major dissonance is between believing and not believing what happened and how could it have happened. Finally, there is a splitting within oneself along the polarization between victim and oppressor representation. These two parasitic self-representations must be kept rigidly apart at almost all cost. In some cases they cannot be brought together without causing a severe disturbance to the object (Shaw, 1967).

Langer, studying the Holocaust survivors' testimonies, described his interpretation in a book entitled *The ruins of memory* (1991). He discussed the nature of survivor testimonies as representing (1) unheroic memory, (2) tainted memory, and (3) humiliated memory. There were other ways of trying to conceptualize what factors in the traumatic state interfere with all the mental functions and the consequent state, such as death immersion, psychic closing off, and more. There is no clue here to the memory of the event because the victims who have not survived are in many ways the most important characters in the narratives. But there is no personal voice represented. The object representations can only be evoked, spoken about. We wrestle with the rerun of a permanently unfinished tale, full of incomplete intervals, faced by the spectacle of faltering witness often reduced to a distressed silence by the overriding solicitations of these memories. The recall is also disturbed by the fact that in the traumatic state the registration is on a sensorimotor level, that is, preverbal, and therefore no language is available for the presentation of the memory. The recollections are presented in an understated way. There is a staccato way in which the memories are presented, without emotions, rigid, and unmodifiable. This is recognizable by the aprosodic state of the presentation. The melody is gone out of the speech. Even though statements appear lucid, their heuristic value is like a memory of a *nightmare*. Memory is unreliable.

One instance: a survivor was able to recall and retell the death march from Auschwitz westward to the next camp; he was able to describe the circumstances of the terrible night, the frost, and the killing of everyone who couldn't keep on marching. Recently, through a set of circumstances, he started examining himself to see what he really recalled. It turned out that he remembered only certain unconnected vignettes, isolated fragments of the event. One of them was waiting to be marched out from Birkenau. Another was on the march, beginning to hear and then realizing that people were being killed by the side of the road. Another was that he was marching close to two friends and one of his friends became weak and wanted to just sit down and not go any farther, which meant that he would be killed. Our reporter and his other friend held him up and marched with the man. He does not remember for how long it went on or how it ended. In his next image he finds himself at dawn marching alone. No columns, no other prisoners. He marches alone on a empty road and encounters an old (Volkssturm) German soldier who is leaning against a fence and carrying his rifle. The soldier seems to be in as bad a shape as the teller of the story, but no dialogue is remembered. He does not know how it happened, but the two of them were marching through the city, in which he visualizes a busy intersection with traffic regulated by military police. Somehow he finds himself in the camp where the prisoners are "stored." Sometime later (possibly the next evening) he is being loaded on a cattle car, and with him are the two men with whom he had been marching on the first night; they stay together in a defensive position.

The spottiness of his recollections was discovered recently and somewhat accidentally. This man told about his death march many times without ever scrutinizing his tale critically. The "official," pithy version was all he and his audience cared to deal with.

Traumatic memories are not repressed in the ordinary sense of the word. Something worse happens to them. They are repudiated. Freud used the word *verwerfung* instead the verb *verdrängung*, meaning "to repress." Their return to consciousness may produce a life-threatening situation and/or a sanity-threatening situation. Some traumatic perceptions are not compatible with the survival of the self and are never registered consciously or in a form that is recoverable by any normal means; and these are the memories that cannot be remembered or forgotten.

Another deep-seated problem is that of *shame*. The unrecognized, not consciously registered problem of latent shame drives some people to overcompensate through presenting an emphasis on competence, effectiveness, invulnerability. But the compulsive nature of this behavior is betrayed by the lack of choice and control, the drivenness, and the need to constantly maintain this victorious attitude in order to prevent the emergence of shame. It is not just because the past involved enforced passivity, submission, and surrender, but because the emotional regression to certain infantile forms of relatedness causes an evocation of the infantile and childhood trauma encapsulated within their memories of the major trauma. There are many other issues involved in the consequences of the loss of safety, the confrontation with death (resulting in an injury to one's natural narcissistic state), and the irreparable damage to one's own omnipotence (Krystal, 1997).

When we reflect on the nature of the presentations we have just reviewed, what could be the reaction of the listener? What could be the impact on the listener? There is a common history of host populations' reaction to immigrants who came bearing this tale. For the most part, it was not possible for people to hear the story. In turn, they discouraged the survivors from talking about it. It took actually about twenty years after liberation before a hearing could be obtained and before survivors could hear and listen to themselves. We had gone through a preparatory period in which a movement was started by Dr. Eva Fogelman in Boston. She started to work with children of survivors and the issue of how their parents talked to them and what they were able to hear. She related the story of this work in a movie called *Breaking the silence* (1984). But it was hard. Think of *The diary of Anne Frank*. Her rescuer, Miep Gies, who found the diary, put it in a desk drawer and never looked at it until Otto Frank returned. Her explanation given later in the book she wrote (1987) was that if she read it and then was arrested and interrogated, she might have to reveal the names of other rescuers. That does not hold water because in fact she knew them all the time. Otto Frank had a much harder time dealing with Anne's diary. He could never bring himself to see the movie or the play based on it. Actually the play was based on an expurgated, purified copy of the diary. The screenplay was prepared by two comedy writers from Hollywood, and together they eliminated Anne's sexuality, anger, and Jewishness (Ozick 1997). Danieli (1984) studied the reaction of therapists who worked with survivors. She reported that therapists struggled with anger, horror, fear, privileged voyeurism, shame, emotional coping with mass murder, identification, bystander guilt, perception of survivors as heroes, mourning, sadness, and anxiety. Judith Herman who wrote a book (1992) based on her work with survivors of rape, summed up her observations as follows: "After every atrocity one can expect the same predictable apologies. It never happened. The victim lies. The victim exaggerates. The victim brought it on herself. Anyway, it is time to forget and move on." In another place she said, "The bystander succumbs to the temptation to look the other way. This is the experience even when the victim is an idealized and valued member of the society. Soldiers in every war, even those who have been regarded as heroes, complain bitterly that no one wants to know the real truth about the war." After Vietnam this reaction was very strong and very important. In therapy, teaching, and psychoanalysis, the audience has to live through a crisis, because the listener becomes a co-owner of the traumatic event and has to construct the trauma in his or her own mind. In the detailed story of interviewers in Israel, Mazur, Gampel, and Horwitz (1997) found that the interviewers' recall and relating of the material was fragmented. Interviewers reported having been afraid to hurt survivors. In their words, there was a tremendous impact of the survivors relating their traumatic experiences on the interviewers' life, professional stance, family relations, and sociopolitical attitude. Bolkowsky (1987) reported, "The questions always seemed impertinent, gratuitous, insensitive. The answers always seemed incomplete, like shadows that are simultaneously real and unreal. Nothing is certain, no words adequate. Every statement seems equivocal and leaves the impression that it is simultaneously true and untrue. . . . Survivors and listeners know that there lurks an infinite and unfathomable number of meanings that are inexplicable and ungraspable."

Note

Paper read to a meeting sponsored by the Michigan Psychoanalytic Institute and Society, C.H.A.I.M., and the Michigan Jewish Federation, May 10, 1998, West Bloomfield, MI.

References

Bolkowsky, S. (1987). Interviewing victims who survived. *Annals of Scholarship, 4*, 33–51.

Danieli, Y. (1984). Psychotherapist's participation in the conspiracy of silence about the Holocaust. *Psychoanalytic Psychology, 1(1),* 23–42.

Fogelman, E. (1984). *Breaking the silence: The generation after the Holocaust* [documentary film].

Freud, S. (1926). *Inhibition, symptom and anxiety.* In *The standard edition of the works of Sigmund Freud* (pp. 77–175). London: Hogarth Press.

Gies, M., with A. L. Gold. (1985). *Anne Frank remembered.* New York: Simon and Schuster.

Greenspan, H. (1998) *On listening to Holocaust survivors recounting and life history.* Westport, CT: Praeger.

Herman, J. (1992). *Trauma and recovery.* New York: Basic Books.

Krystal, H. (1978). Trauma and affects. In A. Solnit, et al. (Eds.), *Psychoanalytic Study of the Child* (Vol. 33, pp. 81–116). New Haven: Yale University Press.

Krystal, H. (1988). On some roots of creativity. *Psychiatric Clinics of North America, 2(3),* 475–491.

Krystal, H. (1997). The trauma of confronting one's vulnerability and death. In C. Ellman & J. Reppen (Eds.), *Omnipotent fantasies and the vulnerable self* (pp. 149–185). New York: Jason Aronson.

Langer (1991). *The ruins of memory.*

Laub, D. (1991). Truth and testimony: The process and struggle. *American Imago, 48,* 15–41.

Mark, B. (1985) *The scrolls of Auschwitz.*

Mazur, A., Gampel, Y., & Horwitz, G. (1997). Interviewer's reactions to Holocaust Survivor's Testimony. *Echoes of the Holcaust, 5,* 31–54.

Ozick, C. (1997, October 6) "Who owns Anne Frank?" *New Yorker,* 76–87.

Shaw, R. (1967). *The Man in the Glass Booth.* London: Chatto and Winders.

Wallant, E. D. (1962). *The pawnbroker.* New York: McFadden.

Wiesel, E. (1960). *Night.* New York: Farrar, Straus & Giroux.

15.

Parting Words

Trauma, Silence, and Survival

Cathy Caruth

Freud begins his groundbreaking work *Beyond the pleasure principle* with his astonished encounter with the veterans of World War I, whose dreams of the battlefield repeatedly bring them back to the horrifying scenes of the death that they have witnessed. As with the victims of accident neuroses, these dreams seem to bring the soldiers back to a moment of fright or surprise that constituted their original encounter with death:

> Now dreams occurring in traumatic neuroses have the characteristic of repeatedly
> bringing the patient back into the situation of his accident, a situation from which he
> wakes up in another fright. This astonishes people far too little. (Freud, 1961)

The repetition of battlefield horrors in the dreams astonishes Freud, because dreams, in psychoanalytic theory, had always served the function of fulfilling wishes: of allowing the unconscious, conflictual desires of childhood to find expression through the symbolic world of the dream. In the dreams of the returning veterans, however, the encounter with death and horror cannot be assimilated to the fulfilment of desire, rather than turning death into a symbol or vehicle of psychic meaning, these traumatic dreams seem to turn the psyche itself into the vehicle for expressing the terrifying literality of a history it does not completely own. But the peculiarity of this returning, literal history also strikes Freud because it brings back not only the reality of death but the fright or unpreparedness for it: the dreams not only show the scenes of battle but wake the dreamer up in another fright. Freud's surprised encounter with the repetitive dreams of the war—the beginning of the theory of trauma, and of history, that has become so central to our contemporary thinking about history and memory—thus raises urgent and unavoidable questions: *What does it mean for the reality of war to appear in the fiction of the dream? What does it mean for life to bear witness to death? And what is the surprise that is encountered in this witness?*

Immediately after discussing the disturbing dreams of the war, however, Freud proposes to "leave the dark and dismal subject of the traumatic neurosis" and to pass on to the "normal" activity of child's play. Freud embarks here upon a story of his encounter with another repetitive behavior, the "puzzling activity" of a "good little boy" of one and a half, just beginning to speak. Freud says he observed the strange game of this child who repeatedly threw a wooden spool on a string into his crib, uttering the sound "o-o-o-o," then retrieved it, uttering "a-a-a-a." With the help of the mother, Freud first interprets these sounds as meaning *fort*, "gone," and *da*, "here," and ultimately suggests that the child is reenacting the departure and return of his mother, which he had just recently been forced to confront. The repetitive game, as a story, thus seems to represent the inner symbolic world of the child: as a story of departure and return, the game seems not only symbolically to fulfill a wish by telling the story of the mother's departure as the story of her return, but also to substitute, for the pain of loss, the very pleasure of creation itself.[1] But Freud himself unexpectedly proceeds to challenge his own first interpretation:

> Our interest is directed to another point. The child cannot possibly have felt his mother's departure as something agreeable or even indifferent . . . It may perhaps be said in reply that her departure had to be enacted as a necessary preliminary to her joyful return, and that it was in the latter that lay the true purpose of the game. But against this must be counted the observed fact that the first act, that of departure, was staged as a game in itself and far more frequently than the episode in its entirety, with its pleasurable ending. (Freud, 1961, pp. 15–16)

The creative activity of the child's game, Freud recognizes with surprise, does not ultimately involve a symbolic representation of the mother's pleasurable return but repeats, in a kind of stammer that interrupts its story, the painful memory of her departure. Like the soldiers' dreams, the game thus reenacts the very memory of a painful reality. What is most surprising in the child's game, however, is that this reenactment of reality in the game places repetition at the very heart of childhood, and links the repetition to a creative act of invention. In the introduction of the child's game Freud's original question—How does life bear witness to death?—is linked to another question: What kind of witness is a creative act?

I will propose in what follows that Freud's insight into trauma in *Beyond the pleasure principle*, its new understanding of personal and of collective history in the face of war, lies precisely in the striking and enigmatic leap that juxtaposes the nightmares of war to the child's game. This juxtaposition is not ordinarily taken into account in the critical reception of Freud's text—the study of trauma in contemporary fields tends to focus on a theory of history and memory derived ultimately from the example of the nightmare and the theory that grows out of it, and the writing on the child's game is not part of the tradition of trauma theory—but it is crucial, I will suggest, for understanding the insight of Freud.[2] My own understanding of this insight did not emerge, however, simply through a reading of Freud's text but began, in fact, in my encounter with a real child in Atlanta, a child whose best friend was murdered in the street and who is interviewed by the friend's mother. By reading together the language of the nightmare and the language of the child in Freud's text—two very distinct kinds of language whose intertwining strands are at the heart of Freud's theory—and in then understanding how Freud's text and the language of the real child shed light upon each other, we can begin to understand Freud's enigmatic move in the theory of trauma from the drive for death to the drive for life, from the reformulating of life around the witness to death, to the possibility of witnessing and making history in creative acts of life.

Death and Awakening

Freud's analysis of repetition compulsion in the origins of consciousness attempts to explain the significance and surprise of the traumatic encounter with death in terms of a new relation between consciousness and life.[3] Consciousness first arose, Freud speculates, as an attempt to protect the life of the organism from the imposing stimuli of a hostile world, by bringing to its attention the nature and direction of external stimuli. The protective function of consciousness as taking in bits of the world, however, was less important, Freud suggests, than its more profound function of keeping the world out, a function it accomplished by placing stimuli in an ordered experience of time. What causes trauma, then, is an encounter that is not directly perceived as a threat to the life of the organism but that occurs, rather, as a break in the mind's experience of time:

> We may, I think, tentatively venture to regard the common traumatic neurosis as a consequence of an extensive breach being made in the protective shield against stimuli. . . . We still attribute importance to the element of fright. It is caused by lack of any preparedness for anxiety. (Freud, 1961, p. 31)

The breach in the mind—the psyche's awareness of the threat to life—is caused not by a direct threat or injury but by fright, the lack of preparedness to take in a stimulus that comes too quickly. It is not the direct perception of danger, that is, that constitutes the threat for the psyche, but the fact that the danger is recognized as such one moment too late. It is this lack of direct experience that thus becomes the basis of the repetition of the traumatic nightmare:

> These dreams are endeavoring to master the stimulus retrospectively, by developing the anxiety whose omission was the cause of the traumatic neurosis. (Freud, 1961, p. 32)

The return of the traumatic experience is not the direct witnessing of a threat to life but rather the attempt to overcome the fact that it was not direct, to master what was never fully grasped in the first place. And since consciousness cannot bear witness to death, the life of the survivor becomes the repetition of the reality that consciousness cannot grasp. In the traumatic encounter with death, life itself attempts to serve as the witness that consciousness cannot provide.

The repetition exemplified by the nightmare, indeed, concerns not only the repetition of the image in the dream (as I have analyzed in Caruth, 1996), but the repetition of waking from it:

> Dreams occurring in traumatic neuroses have the characteristic of repeatedly bringing the patient back into the situation of his accident, a situation from which he wakes up in another fright. (Freud, 1961, p. 13)

If *fright* is the term by which Freud defines the traumatic effect of not having been prepared in time, then the trauma of the nightmare consists not simply in the experience within the dream but in the experience of waking from it. It is the surprise of waking that repeats the unexpectedness of the trauma. And as such, the trauma is not only the repetition of the missed encounter with death but the missed encounter with one's own survival. It is the incomprehensible act of surviving—of waking into life—that repeats and bears witness to what remains ungrasped within the encounter with death. The repetition of trauma, therefore, is not only an attempt or an imperative to know what cannot be grasped that is repeated unconsciously in the survivor's life: it is also an imperative to live that still remains not fully understood. And it is this incomprehensible imperative to live that Freud ultimately places at the very origin of life when he suggests that life itself began as the drive to death:

> The attributes of life were at some time awoken in inanimate matter by the action of a force of whose nature we can form no conception. . . . The tension which then arose in what had hitherto been an inanimate substance endeavored to cancel itself out. In this way the first drive came into being: the drive to return to the inanimate state. (Freud, 1961, p. 38, translation modified)

Life itself originates, Freud here suggests, as an awakening from "death" for which there was no preparation. Life itself, that is, is an imperative to awaken that precedes any understanding or consciousness and any possible desire or wish.[4] The witness of survival itself—the awakening that constitutes life—lies not only in the incomprehensible repetition of the past, that is, but in the incomprehensibility of a future that is not yet owned. Freud's central question raised by the war nightmare—What does it mean for life bear witness to death?—thus ultimately leads to another, more urgent and enigmatic question: In what way is the experience of trauma also the experience of an imperative to live? What is the nature of a life that continues beyond trauma?

The Child's Game

It might appear that with this analysis Freud had replaced the notion of the child, and its central place in psychoanalytic theory, with the theory of trauma. The child's repetition of its mother's departure could be explained as the unknowing reliving of its mother's (anticipated) death, and the child's life as the unconscious reliving of what is not yet grasped within the mother's departure. From the perspective of Freud's rethinking of life around its traumatic significance, the child's game thus peculiarly reenacts the incomprehensible moment of the mother's act of leaving and reshapes the very life of the child as the unconscious witness to the death he has survived. Repeating the *fort* that is not his own but his mother's act of leaving, the child's own life story—his departure into life—becomes inextricable from his mother's silent departure into death. In this incomprehensible departure, the child's life—like the origin of the drive—thus silently enacts a larger history he does not completely own.[5]

Freud's analysis indeed suggests that the encounter with traumatic repetition requires a rethinking of psychoanalysis itself, which had previously focused its model of the mind on the notion of childhood as the site of the pleasure principle. By modeling the mind on the encounter with war trauma, Freud thus appears to shift the center of psychoanalytic thinking from the individual struggle with internal Oedipal conflicts of childhood to the external, collective activities of history, and to make of childhood itself a reflection of a more obscure painful encounter. Thus Robert Jay Lifton writes that the reversal of adult and child trauma as a model for the human mind was at the center of *Beyond the pleasure principle*, and produced the "image-model of the human being as a perpetual survivor" (Lifton, 1979). The questions raised by war trauma concerning the nature of life thus require a new model for psychoanalytic thinking and, in particular, for the relation between psychoanalysis and history.

Beginning Again

Yet the game of the child playing *fort* and *da*, there and here, with his spool, seems to become not less enigmatic but more so when it is understood in relation to traumatic repetition. If the child's reenactment of his mother's departure repeats, ultimately, her loss and her death, the game still remains an act of creation that, unlike the dream of the war veterans, does not simply compulsively repeat a history it doesn't own but creates, in its repetition, something new.[6] This very movement from the example of traumatic repetition in the war nightmare to the example of the child will, moreoever, reappear surprisingly in Freud's text, and will reappear precisely at the moment that Freud has explained the notion of trauma in the very origins of life. For shortly after introducing the origin of life as an awakening out of death, Freud pauses abruptly and starts again:

> But let us pause for a moment and reflect. It cannot be so. The sexual instincts, to which the theory of the neuroses gives a quite special place, appear under a very different aspect. . . . The whole path of development to natural death is not trodden by all the elementary entities which compose the complicated body of one of the higher organisms. Some of them, the germ cells, probably retain the original structure of living matter and, after a certain time . . . separate themselves from the organism as a whole. Under favourable conditions, they begin to develop—that is, to repeat the performance [*das Spiel wiederholen*] to which they owe their existence; and in the end once again one portion of their substance pursues its development to a finish, while another portion harks back once again as a fresh residual germ to the beginning of the process of development. . . . They are the true life drives. (Freud, 1961, p. 39–40, translation modified)

The origin of life as the death drive—as the beginning of the repetition compulsion, and as an awakening—is itself repeated, Freud audaciously suggests, and is repeated, moroeover, precisely in the form of a game (*Spiel*). After disappearing for most of his text since his original introduction of the child—and disappearing in particular from the theory of trauma, which is entirely governed by the language of consciousness and awakening[7]—the language of the game reappears, and reappears to describe a different form of repetition: a repeating of the origin of life in another kind of beginning.[8] This repetition brings back, moreover, for the very first time the explicit language of the child's game, the language Freud uses at the moment he recognizes the game as a game of departure:

> But against this must be counted the observed fact that the first act, that of departure, was staged as a game in itself and far more frequently than the episode in its entirety, with its pleasurable ending [*dass der erste Akt, das Fortgehen, für sich allein als Spiel inszeniert wurde, und zwar ungleich häufiger als das zum lustvollen Ende fortgeführte Ganze*]. (Freud, 1961, p. 16)

This game and the event of departure that it reenacts is now repeated as the very action of the life drive:

> Under favourable conditions, they begin to develop—that is, to repeat the perfor-
> mance to which they owe their existence; and in the end once again one portion of
> their substance pursues its development to a finish [*Unter günstige Bedingungen gebracht,
> beginnen sie sich zu entwickeln, dass heisst das Spiel, dem sie ihre Entstehung verdanken, zu
> wiederholen, und dies endet damit, dass wieder ein Anteil ihrer Substanz die Entwicklung bis
> um Ende fortführt*]. (Freud, 1961, p. 40)

Freud thus reintroduces the language of departure not as the origin of the death drive, but as the way it repeats itself, differently, as the drive for life.[9] The departure into life is not simply the awakening that repeats an original death, but an act of parting that distinguishes, precisely, between death and life.[10] The repetition of this game, then, as an origin is the beginning of life as a surprising repetition that both bears witness to and breaks from the death drive, that bears witness and repeats precisely by breaking away. It is a language of departure, that is, that does not repeat the unconscious origin of life as death but creates a history by precisely departing toward survival.

This creative act takes place, moreover, not only in the child's game, but in Freud's own text as well, through the very transformation undergone by the language of trauma: from the departure—the *fort*—that appears to be the repetition of the mother's anticipated death in the child's game, to the *fortführen* of the drive that is the pressure toward life.[11] This transformation also differentiates or parts the traumatized subject, the soldiers of war repeating death, from the individual testimony of Freud's own text, the creative act of language that becomes not only the story of departures but also the language of play, a language that would, in fact, become a new language for psychoanalysis in the future. In the life drive, then, life itself, and the language of creativity, begin as an act that bears witness to the past even by turning from it; that bears witness to death by bearing witness to the possibility of origination in life. Here history is reclaimed and generated not in reliving unconsciously the death of the past but by an act that bears witness by parting from it. The language of the life drive does not simply point backward, that is, but bears witness to the past by pointing to the future. The return of the child's language in *Beyond the pleasure principle* thus transforms the original questions of trauma—What does it mean for life to bear witness to death? What is the nature of a life that continues beyond trauma?—into an ultimately more fundamental and elusive concern: what is the language of the life drive?

Mementos

The significance of this question arose, for me, not from within Freud's theoretical text nor in the history of World War I but in my own encounter with a child in Atlanta, within the contemporary history of urban violence in America. I encountered this child shortly after leaving New Haven and arriving in Atlanta, when I became familiar with a group established in Atlanta to help traumatized children who had witnessed violence, a group called Kids Alive and Loved. This group was established by a woman named Bernadette Leite, whose oldest son,

Khalil, was shot in the back one night when he was out with friends, shortly before graduating from high school. The impulse for the group came specifically, as she tells us, not only from witnessing the symptoms of anger and the violent reenactment of trauma in the kids' responses to the death at the funeral and afterward, but when the mother of the dead boy, Bernadette, overheard the peculiar language of children:

> After his death I noticed that his friends were coming over every afternoon and hanging out in his room. And I began to listen, and I heard them speaking to him. They would come over every afternoon and hang out in his room and speak to him. And I realized that they needed someone to talk to. (Bernadette Leite, personal communication.)[12]

Hearing the language of the children addressed only to her dead son, Bernadette recognized the unresolved trauma of many of his friends in their inability to speak about their feelings to the living. She thus decided to found a group to allow the children to talk about their feelings to each other concerning the violence they had experienced, in weekly Wednesday night meetings and through videotaped interviews she has made for the Kids Alive and Loved Oral History Archive. Giving the group the name Kids Alive and Loved, whose initials—KAL—reproduce the initials of her child, Khalil Aseem Leite, Bernadette hoped to make the group a way not only of helping the living children to get over their trauma by talking about Khalil (as well as other murders they had experienced), but also of providing a kind of living memorial to her dead son through the living children's words and lives.

The complexity of this process was most movingly portrayed for me, however, through the words of a single child, in the recorded interview of Bernadette with Gregory, Khalil's best friend. Gregory was seventeen at the time of his friend's death. He had received a call from Khalil that morning to go out that evening, but argued about being called so early, and then was not at home when he was called again.[13] Gregory speaks, throughout the interview, in a language that tries to convey the difficulty of grasping Khalil's death: when asked to say something about Khalil's life he answers, "He lived for everything. He died for nothing." This inability to grasp the meaning of his friend's death resonates in his own difficulty in extricating a description of Khalil's life from his own survival of Khalil's death:

B: What do you want people to know about his life?
G: He had a good heart.

B: What does [the experience of Khalil's death] feel like?
G: It's like when somebody is actually pulling your heart out, or just repeatedly stabbing it.

The dead Khalil's life and Greg's survival of it are tied around a heart that they share and that has now been removed. Greg's heart, it would appear, being removed and stabbed, tells the story of Khalil's death. In the exchange between Bernadette and Greg, we see Bernadette's attempt to help Greg memorialize Khalil in a kind of language of memory, and we witness Greg's own transformation of her language of memory into a parting that allows for both a memorialization of his friend and a recognition of his own life.

Parting Words

This possibility opens up, strikingly, in a moment of surprise, in a remarkable moment of his interview with her, just at the place, moreover, when the interview turns to the topic of memorialization. Bernadette has been asking about Gregory's feelings concerning Khalil's death, and the interview has become very sombre and at times filled with sorrow. Then Greg makes the interview take a sudden turn:

> B: Do you have any mementos of Khalil?
> G: Let's see . . .
> B: Do you have personal belongings of his?
> G (suddenly smiling): He has something of mine!
> B (laughing): I know he has something of yours . . . a couple of things!
> G: He had . . . That's what also made me feel good, because he was buried in my shirt that I loved, and my watch. At first that shirt bothered me because I loved that shirt—
> B: And I didn't know at the time . . . Mark picked it out and I only found out later. It's too bad—I wanted to get him a Tommy Hilfiger shirt he'd seen downtown but I didn't have time to get it and get to the funeral parlor. It's too bad—but then maybe he wouldn't have been buried in your favorite shirt.
> G: That's okay, because it was my favorite shirt and my favorite friend.

Greg's first response to Bernadette's question—"Do you have any personal belongings of his?"—comes as a surprise because it reverses the order by which the living Greg would memorialize his dead friend and suggests that it is the dead friend that is keeping mementos of him: "He has something of mine!" Greg says. This is also, in its irony and humor, a kind of maintenance of the playful relationship that Greg had with the living Khalil: the implicit joke that Khalil got away with his favorite shirt seems to re-create the very humorous relationship they had when Khalil was alive. Greg thus, in effect, says "Gone!" to his shirt and, in so doing, establishes a relationship with Khalil that recognizes, even within the fiction of personification, the ineradicable difference between his life and Khalil's death.

Bernadette's response, likewise, turns both to the dead and to the living at once, although in a somewhat different fashion. On one hand she tells, very movingly, of a mother who wants to get one last gift for her dead son, to buy him the shirt that he had seen and wanted. But the telling of this story is simultaneously, and equally movingly, a kind of playful mothering of the living boy in front of her, because she empathizes with the fact that it is too bad that he could not have had his favorite shirt back. To Gregory's "*fort*" or "gone" Bernadette thus says, in effect, "*da*" or "*here*" and, in this way, makes her act of mothering the living boy a continuation of her mothering of the dead one, and makes of Greg the living memory of the dead Khalil.

It is thus particularly striking that Greg's final words, which are the true climax of the exchange for me, once again give up the shirt to Khalil: "That's okay because it was my favorite shirt and my favorite friend." If his first response brought Khalil to life as a youthful friend—and reanimated Greg too as he was before he had the horrible knowledge of Kahlil's death—this final response, in giving the gift to Khalil, gives up that former innocence and re-creates Greg through his ability to give to and thus memorialize his dead friend. By once again saying "gone," Greg indeed departs from his former self and turns the memento—and the language of the memento—into an act, not of a symbolic return or wish for possession but of an ability to give to the dead something that can never, now, be returned.[14]

This double act is repeated a few minutes later in the next exchange, an exchange that now, significantly, concerns a game:

> B: So it made you feel good that your favorite friend was buried in your favorite shirt and your watch.
> G (smiling again): And he has my—it's not really a hat, it's a cap. It's a little like a stocking cap, that colorful thing on his wall. Yeah, him and me and Maurice would play this game, "left hand," where you call out what's in the person's left hand and you get to keep it. And he called that and he got it.
> B: I should give that back to you, you could take it with you as a memento.
> G: Uhuh, I would feel better if it would stay in his household. Because it's a memento of him but it's a memento of me too.

The game with his friend, Greg tells us, had been a game of naming and possessing; by calling out the other's clothing it could become yours, just as the friendship was perhaps a kind of reciprocal possession of each boy by the other. But when Bernadette offers, once again, to give the possession back—"I should give it back to you, you could take it with you as a memento"—Greg once again repeats his *fort*: "I would feel better if it would stay in his household. Because it's a memento of him but it's a memento of me too." Naming the cap as a memento of both Khalil and himself, not only does Greg give up the part of himself that existed before Khalil's death, he also ties his life with Khalil's death: the cap is not only a memento of him for me, he says, but of me for him. This bond, however, does not confuse the living child with the dead one, nor does it symbolize the dead one in the living one, but precisely separates Greg, whose younger self is buried in the coffin, from the dead child who will not grow past this moment. Indeed, this refusal of Bernadette's offer to give the cap back is also (as my own mother pointed out to me), a way of saying "I will not be your dead child." In giving up the language of memorialization offered by Bernadette, however, he creatively transforms the language of the memento and achieves another language and another memorialization: a memorialization that takes place precisely through his separation and his own act of creation. It is in this reclaiming of the meaning of the memento, even while giving it up, that Greg's *fort*, I would suggest, does not simply reenact his friend's departure or attempt to return to his life, but bears witness, creatively, in the very act of parting from his dead friend.

This language, I would suggest, is the language of the life drive. It is this drive for life that is at work in Greg's description of how the death of his friend is also motivating him to achieve goals in his life, achievements that will also incorporate Khalil's name:

> B: How has his death changed your life?
> G: I am more determined to make it in the music business somehow and I know it will be because of him. We used to talk about it all the time. He did rap....

[W]e were to go to Clark Atlanta, him for business management and me for communication, music, and combine our talents. But now he can't do that.... But that's okay, because when I do it I'll bring all the people jobs, Mike, Maurice ... When we get that studio [Khalil's] name is going to be the name of it. And I have to have a son and his name will be in there.

In this language we can see the drive for life, a language of parting that itself moves the speaker forward to a life that is not simply possessed, but given, in some sense, and received, as a gift from the dead. In the memento, as Greg teaches us, the two children take leave from each other: as Greg gives Khalil back to death, Khalil, in a sense, gives Greg back to life. This is a creative act, an act that bears witness to the dead precisely in the process of turning away. It is indeed a new language of departure, parting words that bind the living child to the dead one even as he takes leave from him, bind him to his dead friend even in the very act of letting go.[15]

Freud's Game

In Greg's words, we see the insight of Freud's text as it touches on and resonates with our contemporary crises and with the actual struggles of children in contemporary culture. But Greg's words also shed light on the way in which the language of the child itself reemerges at the very heart of Freud's own theoretical writing.[16] For Freud's elaborate staging of the game of the fort/da can be understood not only as a description of the puzzling game of the child staging the departure and return of the mother, but as Freud's own oscillation in his understanding of the child's game. This oscillation takes the form, moreover, of the alternation between a *fort* and a *da*:

> I eventually realized that it was a game and that the only use he made of any of his toys was to play "gone" with them. (Freud, 1961, p. 15)

> This, then, was the complete game—disappearance and return. As a rule one witnessed only its first act, which was repeated untiringly as a game in itself, though there is no doubt that the greater pleasure was attached to the second act. (Freud, 1961, p. 15)

> It may perhaps be said ... that [the mother's] departure had to be enacted as a necessary preliminary to her joyful return, and that it was in the latter that lay the true purpose of the game. But against this must be counted the observed fact that the first act, that of departure, was staged as a game in itself and far more frequently than the episode in its entirety, with its pleasurable ending. (Freud, 1961, pp. 15–16)

As Freud's interpretation passes from the *fort* to the narrative of *fort* and *da*, and back again to the *fort*, Freud shows himself as struggling in the face of a child whose language, in its shifting meaning for Freud, first brings him nearer and then distances him in Freud's understanding.[17] What is striking in Freud's example, that is, is not simply the child's struggle and reenactment of the distance of its mother, but Freud's struggle with and reenactment of the distance of the child. Freud's text, it would appear, repeats the story of the child he has encountered, and does so, moreover, in the very act of distancing. Paradoxically, then, it will be in his repetition of the child's distance, in his own distancing of the child at the moment of his failed comprehension of the game, that Freud's own text will connect with, and transmit, the story the child cannot quite tell. Freud's text, that is, itself repeats the child's traumatized *fort*—the stammered word that marks the very loss of the child's own story—but does so as the very creation of its own new language, a language that does not return to the pleasurable compensations of the narrative but speaks, precisely, from beyond the story. It is not necessarily on the level of the child's own game, that is, but on the level of Freud's repetition of it that the creative act of the game, the new conceptual language of the life drive, will take place.[18]

We could, moreover, understand the entire theory of trauma in *Beyond the pleasure principle* not as simply an explanation of trauma from the distance of theoretical speculation, but as the very passage of the story of the child in a theoretical act of transformation.[19] For what is the story of the mind's attempt to master the event retrospectively if not the story of a failed return: the attempt, and failure, of the mind to return to the moment of the event? The theory of repetition compulsion as the unexpected encounter with an event that the mind misses and then repeatedly attempts to grasp is the story of a failure of the mind to return to an experience it has never quite grasped, the repetition of an originary departure from the moment that constitutes the very experience of trauma. And this story appears again as the beginning of life in the death drive, as life's attempt to return to inanimate matter that ultimately fails and departs into a human history.[20] Freud's own theory, then, does not simply describe the death drive and its enigmatic move to the drive for life, but enacts this drive for life as the very language of the child that encounters, and attempts to grasp, the catastrophes of a traumatic history.

A Final Parting

The most striking appearance of Freud's own speaking as the child will occur, however, not within the theoretical language of the text, but in a footnote that refers, in fact, to the entrance of a real death into the life of the child as well as into his own life: "When this child was five and three-quarters, his mother died. Now that she was really 'gone' ('o-o-o'), the child showed no signs of grief."

In noting the real death of the child's mother, Freud first explicitly links the child to himself, since the child's mother was also, in reality, Freud's daughter Sophie, who died toward the end of the writing of *Beyond the pleasure principle*. But whereas the (already traumatized) child shows no signs of grief, Freud himself begins to repeat not simply the language of the *fort*, but the inarticulate sounds of the "o-o-o-o" that constituted the very origin of the game (and the only moment in which the living mother had appeared in the example, when she agreed with Freud as to the meaning of the "o-o-o-o" as indicating the word *fort*). By reintroducing the lost "o-o-o-o" of the original child's game in his words, and in this footnote that announces his daughter's (*the mother's*) real death, Freud implicitly connects the origin of the child's game with the very significance of his own theoretical text, a significance that now, in its very inarticulate stammer, serves as a kind of memory of and parting from Freud's own dead child.[21] The language of the theory, much like the child's stammering language, articulates the very notions of the trauma and of the death drive as a creative act of parting: a parting from the real child, and a parting from the psychoanalytic child—or from the mere psychoanalysis of childhood—toward an analysis of the collective catastrophes of death encountered in war, and toward the pressing cultural imperative for a new kind of survival.[22]

I would propose that it is through the child's words—through this literary, not fully articulated language of theory—that Freud's text speaks, moreoever, most powerfully, in its full historical relevance, to us. For it is through the child's own stammer—the stammer of Freud as he faces the encounter with World War I, the reduction of the theoretical mind to the stammering struggle of the child—that Freud will first tell us about the necessity of witnessing the effects of death in the century of trauma. But it is also through the creative transformation of this stammer into a new language of psychoanalysis—not only the language of departure, which will be his language of history *in Moses and monotheism*, but the very future language of psychoanalysis itself, in the rethinking of psychoanalysis, for example, around the individual's capacity for play—that the possibilities of Freud's not yet articulated insight are handed over to us.[23] I would suggest that it is only in listening to this second and literarily creative element in Freud's own writing that the theory of trauma, now so prevalent in numerous disciplines, can extend itself beyond the theory of repetition and catastrophe, beyond the insight of the death drive, into the insight enigmatically passed on in the new notion of the drive to life. As such, the theory of trauma does not limit itself to a theoretical formulation of the centrality of death in culture, but constitutes—in Freud's, and our own, historical experience of modernity—an act of parting that itself creates and passes on a different history of survival.

Notes

This article will also be published in *Cultural Values*, special issue on testimony, ed. Jackie Stacey, fall 2000, and in *Between the Psyche and the Polis: Refiguring History in Literature and Theory*, Michael Rossington and Anne Whitehead (eds.) (Aldershot, UK: Ashgate Press, 2001.)

This work is dedicated to Elaine G. Caruth, Ph.D., my mother. She was a psychoanalyst who worked for many years with children and adolescents and later with adults. She had discussed an earlier version of this text with me a number of times before her death in March 1998.

1. Freud describes the game as the child's "first great cultural achievement" and suggests that the child rewarded himself for not expressing his distress by creating a game instead. Thus the game not only represents the mother's wished-for return but, by substituting itself for the mother, the game itself becomes a kind of symbolic return.

2. The game has been read, for instance, as a game of mourning. Within the literary critical tradition, see, for example, Santner (1990). The received understanding of the game is that it represents a form of mastery and is thus not, strictly speaking, purely traumatic repetition—unless traumatic repetition is understood as already itself a form of mastering. Freud does suggest at one point in his analysis that the game may express a principle of mastery "beyond the pleasure principle" but the peculiarity of such repetition is rarely explored within traditional analyses. Exceptions to this line of thought can be found in Derrida (1987). Jacques Lacan (1978) analyzes the game in the context of a reading of traumatic repetition. See also Gasché, (1997). On the crucial structure of the game in relation to the speculative structure of *Beyond the pleasure principle*, see Weber (1982, 1991).

3. For a related analysis of this aspect of Freud's text with a slightly different emphasis, see Caruth (1996, ch. 3, "Traumatic Awakenings.")

4. Life is thereby separated from the desire to live; survival is no longer linked to the wish to live but to another imperative that appears to have ethical force (thus the survivor mission to tell) as well as a relation to knowing or witnessing (as an "awakening").

5. Thus the theory of individual trauma in *Beyond the pleasure principle* will lead to the theory of historical (and collective) trauma in *Moses and monotheism*. I have analyzed this in terms of the story of departure in Caruth (1996, chs. 1 and 3). The notion of an attempt to return that becomes a departure is a pattern that originates in *Beyond the pleasure principle* in the description of individual trauma and ultimately the foundation of life; in *Moses and monotheism*, Jewish history is itself structured by a trauma that turns Moses' attempt to return the Hebrews to Canaan into an endless departure into a Jewish history of survival.

6. Freud emphasizes the creative element of the game by remarking that it is the "first self-invented game" of the child (*das erste selbst-erschaffene Spiel*), an emphasis we see again in his letter to Wilhelm Zweig concerning his insight behind *Moses and monotheism* that "Moses created the Jews," which uses a related although slightly different verb form (*hat . . . geschaffen*). Freud's use of the word *create* in *Beyond the pleasure principle*, which I am echoing in my own use of the word *creative*, thus has a specific, foundational meaning and is also, in both *Beyond the pleasure principle* and *Moses and monotheism*, ultimately linked to a traumatic history. The creative element in the *fort/da* game appears, moreoever, to be associated specifically with the origins of language; Freud notes that the game begins when the child is just beginning to make articulate sounds. Jacques Lacan thus suggests that this game represents the origin of symbolic language as such in the differentiation of the phonemes *o* and *a* (see Lacan, 1977). The game is not, that is, about symbolizing the literal but about moving from silence to speech. The foundational nature of the game—or of the scene as Freud presents it—points toward its link to the foundational moment that traumatic repetition repeats, which is the ultimate concern of *Beyond the pleasure principle*.

7. One line of theoretical (or in Freud's terms, "speculative") elaboration of the notion of trauma in *Beyond the pleasure principle* begins in chapter II with the example of the nightmares of battle—which are compared to the nightmares of an accident that wake the patient up from his sleep—continues with the explanation of trauma in chapter IV, which speculates on the origins of consciousness and proposes that trauma is a break in the stimulus barrier that consciousness provides for the living organism, and culminates in chapter V, in which Freud suggests that life itself was an awakening from inanimate matter for which there was no preparation. This line of speculation appears to have an independent logic and does not completely align itself with the language of play that accompanies it in an apparently separate line of argument. The *Spiel* appears first in the example of the child, is repeated in chapter III in regard to the reenactment behavior in transference, and thenceforth is mentioned only in regard to children's play and theater, until the introduction of the notion of the life drive. (Interestingly, the discussion of analysis in chapter III suggests that the entire theory of the Oedipal origins of unconscious conflict in childhood needs to be rethought after the encounter with trauma; at this point in his argument, then, Freud appears to be incorporating the earlier theory of neurosis into a larger speculation concerning traumatic neurosis.)

It is notable that the distinction between the terminology of the nightmare (a terminology of seeing and awakening) and the terminology of the game (a language of play and speech) also appears in contemporary discussions of the problem of traumatic imagery as opposed to the resolution of trauma in (symbolic) language. See, for example, van der Kolk (1996).

8. The movement from the death drive to the life drive seems, in fact, to carry out a possibility contained in Freud's double denomination of trauma in chapter II, as both

fright (*Schreck*) and surprise (*Überraschung*): "dass das Haputgewicht der Verursachung auf das Moment der Überraschung, auf den Schrech, zu fallen schien," "Schreck aber benannt den Zustand, in den man gerät, wenn man in Gefahr kommt, ohne auf se borbereitet zu sein, betont das Moment der Überraschung."

9. Interestingly, it is not until the introduction of the life drive that the *fort* makes its appearance again literally in the language of Freud's text. Here we might see a possibility of bringing together Jean Laplanche insight into the shared single energy of the life drive and death drive and Harold Bloom's insistence that Freud is a dualist. See Laplanche (1970) and Bloom (1982).

10. The repetition of the origin as the new beginning of the life drive thus distinguishes itself from the confusion between death and life enacted in the death drive. One thinks of the repeated confrontation with death in life in traumatic repetition associated with the sense of being a living dead by survivors (cf. Lifton, 1967) or the writing in Charlette Delbo's trilogy) or of the literary example of the woman in Duras' and Resnais' *Hiroshima mon amour*, having missed the moment of her lover's death, exclaiming, "I could not find the least difference between his dead body and mine." So too, in that piece, the slap that breaks the traumatic repetition in her encounter with the Japanese man can be understood as a new beginning that distinguishes death from life, not as understanding but as act. One might say that the event of trauma is repeated, in the moment of parting in the life drive, as the act of survival, an act that, in a sense, fulfills the imperative to live that begins life, but fulfills it differently (the imperative and its fulfilment are not continuous). This act, though, is not just any act; since it repeats the "awakening" of the life drive, it is inextricable from questions of witnessing or knowing that govern traumatic repetition (which is life and is also awakening) and thus can be understood as a different form of witnessing. To this extent, the question of creativity—as a creativity arising in the context of trauma—is bound up with the question of truth. Rather than providing an affective response to trauma, the life drive can be understood as providing another means of bearing witness. In other words, the life drive (unlike, say the pleasure principle) cannot be understood within the economy of pleasure (which is also the economy of symbolization, as we see in the *fort/da* game) but must engage the epistemological problems of truth and knowing introduced by the trauma.

11. It should be noted that the passage from chapter II is already fairly complex and appears to be somewhat playful in its own use of *fort* and *da*, in naming the never-achieved pleasurable end of the game (the hoped-for *da*) as "das zum lustvollen Ende fortgeführte Ganze"—i.e., in naming the longed-for *da* by means of a *fort*. The question of departure could also be thought as a meditation on the nature of the return (Derrida suggests something of the sort [1987]); here it would be interesting to examine the shift from the *da* of the child—seen as the marker of the pleasure principle—to the *zurück* of the drives beyond the pleasure principle.

The new meaning of *fortführen*, moreover, brings out a remarkable reversal that occurs in the movement from chapter II and chapter IV (where trauma is an exception to ordinary experience, an encounter with death that disturbs consciousness) to chapter V (where the traumatic delay defines the very origin of life itself, and ultimately, in its repetition in the life drive, the possibility of a new beginning). For whereas consciousness was understood, originally, to protect life against death (chapter IV), we can see (from chapter V) that, since trauma ultimately reenacts an origin that marked the beginning of life, consciousness ultimately serves to protect the organism not from death but from life—or more accurately, from the surprise of new beginnings.

12. Bernadette Leite has spoken of this (and reiterated the importance of speaking) in the *Atlanta Journal-Constitution* (7/24/99, 8/15/99, among other dates) and is honored in the November 1999 edition of *Redbook*. She has worked for the last several years in association with the Minority Health Institute at the Rollins School of Public Health at Emory University.

13. As Greg says, "He called early, like ten or eleven ... But again, that was the night I went to my cousin's home, he called again, but I wasn't there."

14. The tone of Greg's language here might be understood as being achieved through a giving up of a certain kind of pathos, although even in its humor it attains a different pathos, perhaps the pathos of giving up pathos. I would like to thank Elizabeth Rottenberg for her insights into questions of humor and tone in the exchange between Greg and Bernadette Leite.

15. It is interesting to note that the question of departure and parting arises at the end of the interview between Bernadette Leite and Greg: "B: Any parting words? G: Departing words? B: Parting words. ... Words to say to others" (KAL Oral History Archive).

16. Thus the future of Freud's text could be understood as a "beyond" in the strict sense, both inside and outside of Freud's text in the language of a child both inside (in the game) and outside (in the experience of the real child), already there but not yet there, just as, perhaps, the life drive is beyond the death drive.

17. On the self-reflexive dimension of the scene, see, for example Derrida (1987); on the self-reflexivity of *Beyond the pleasure principle* see Bloom (1982), where he suggests that Freud's citation of Tasso in chapter III is "an allegory of Freud's own passage into the Sublime," and Meisel (1984). Freud's argument, as we have outlined, thus first appears to replace the notion of childhood Oedipal conflict with a kind of trauma modeled on the adult (war trauma), but on the self-reflexive level of Freud's writing reintroduces the child's centrality or priority not as a concept but as a kind of language. Likewise, the notion of beginning wrapped up in the death as the awakening at the origin of life becomes associated with a kind of origination in language.

18. Thus Freud's own creative act could be said to arise (as in the interview of Greg and Bernadette) out of an encounter: his encounter with the child. The shift from death drive to life drive, which remains fairly enigmatic in its original speculative introduction in chapter V—Freud just stops with the description of the death drive and starts again with the life drive—could be said to take place on the level of the encounter rather than as something that could simply be an object of speculation or knowledge within the theory. In other words, if one were to ask, pragmatically or clinically, what would make possible the move from death drive to life drive in an individual—what makes possible, for example, the language of the life drive for Greg—the answer would have to be found, in this particular text by Freud, on the level of the encounter, that is, as taking place in the context of an encounter.

19. Not the distance of theoretical knowing, then, but the distance of the child's game.

20. On the fort at the origin see Weber (1982); Caruth (1996, ch. 3).

21. As Freud insists in his own letters, *Beyond the pleasure principle* was mostly written before the death of Sophie and thus does not (in the strictest sense) refer directly to her death; by introducing her death in a footnote, however, Freud allows the resonances to take place and also sets up another parallel with the child, for whom the mother died after the game just as Sophie died after the writing of Freud's text. On the death of Sophie see, for example, Derrida (1987), Bronfen (1993). Anne Whitehead (in an unpublished lecture) also remarks on the important contribution of Luce Irigaray to the unread position of the mother in the *fort/da* game in Irigaray (1987).

22. The interweaving of language and history, once again, emerges in Freud's peculiar association of the death drive with something "unobtrusive" and, in later texts, "dumb," and the life drive with noise or "clamour." This distinction occurs first in *Beyond the pleasure principle* and is reiterated in *The ego and the id* and *Civilization and its discontents*. Reading the death drive in terms of its historical shape in *Beyond the pleasure principle* and *Moses and monotheism*, we could say that what the language of the life drive bears witness to is precisely the silence of history (or, in the child's game, the silence of the mother's departure).

23. To the extent that the life drive moves us away from the direct line of argument that leads from *Beyond the pleasure principle* to *Moses and monotheism*, or from individual to

collective history, the imperative for survival could be understood here as taking place within acts (or within a language of the life drive) that is neither simply individual nor simply collective in the sense of those terms that preceded the death drive/life drive analysis. In a sense, the introduction of the life drive in my argument is also the reintroduction of the notion of individual acts on the other side of the collective analysis of historical catastrophe implied in the death drive argument that leads to *Moses and monotheism*. Here, the "individual" act (or the language of the life drive) might itself carry with it the force of a larger history.

On psychoanalysis and play see Winnicott (1971). Here we might recall the importance of the word *create* for Freud discussed above in fn. 10, and its passage into Winnicott in the notion of living creatively. It is also interesting to note that this later thinker of play was also interested, in this context, in the notion of surprise.

Bibliography

Bloom, H. (1982). Freud's concept of defense and the poetic will. In *Agon: Towards a theory of revisionism*. New York: Oxford University Press.

Bronfen, E. (1993). Eine Frau verschwindet: Sophie Freud und Jenseits des Lustprinzips. *Psyche*, 47, 6.

Caruth, C. (1996). Traumatic awakenings. In *Unclaimed experience: Trauma, narrative and history*. Baltimore: The Johns Hopkins University Press.

Derrida, J. (1987). To speculate—on Freud. In *The post card: From Socrates to Freud and beyond*, tr. A. Bass. Chicago: University of Chicago Press.

Freud, Sigmund (1961). *Beyond the pleasure principle*. In *The standard edition of the complete psychological works of Sigmund Freud*. Translated from the German under the general editorship of J. Strachey in collaboration with A. Freud, assisted by A. Strachey and J. Tyson (vol. 18.). London: Hogarth (German quotations are taken from S. Freud, *Studienausgabe*, Band III [Frankfurt am Main: Fischer Verlag, 1969–1979].

Gasché, R. (1997). The witch metapsychology. In Todd Dufresne, (Ed.), *Returns of the French Freud: Freud, Lacan, and beyond*. New York: Routledge.

Irigaray, L. (1987). Belief itself. In *Sexes and genealogies*, tr. G. C. Gill. New York: Columbia University Press.

Lacan, J. (1978). *The four fundamental concepts of psycho-analysis*. tr. A. Sheridan, ed. J.-A. Miller. New York: Norton.

Laplanche, J. (1970). Why the death drive? In *Life and death in psychoanalysis*. Baltimore: The Johns Hopkins University Press.

Lifton, R. J. (1983). Survivor experience and traumatic syndrome. In *The broken connection: Death and the continuity of life*. New York: Basic Books.

Santner, L. (1990). *Stranded objects: Mourning, memory, and film in postwar Germany*. New York: Cornell University Press.

van der Kolk, B. A. (1996). Trauma and memory. In B. A. van der Kolk, A. C. McFarlane, and L. Weisaeth (Eds.), *Traumatic stress: The effects of overwhelming experience on mind, body, and society*. New York: The Guilford Press.

Weber, S. (1982). *The legend of Freud*. Minneapolis: University of Minnesota Press.

Weber, S. (1991). *Return to Freud: Jacques Lacan's dislocation of psychoanalysis*, tr. M. Levine. Cambridge: Cambridge University Press.

Winnicott, D. W. (1971). *Playing and reality*. London: Tavistock Publications.

Postscript

Colin Murray Parkes

This book provides us with authoritative and detailed support for a new and valuable theory of traumatic stress. Every credit is due to Ronnie Janoff-Bulman for showing how the distress caused by psychological trauma can be explained by the unexpected and urgent need to revise our basic assumptions at a time when we have little or nothing to put in their place (Janoff-Bulman, 1996). The current editor and authors have developed and applied that model to a wide range of traumatic life events, linking it to other theoretical models and making important recommendations for the prevention and therapy of psychiatric disorder. In doing so they have generated a new set of assumptions about assumptions.

The concept of the assumptive world and a theory about the ways by which it can be changed arose out of a comparative study of the reactions to two very different life events: the loss by death of a loved person and the loss by amputation of a limb (Parkes, 1971, 1972). In that study it was found that amputees used much the same language to describe the loss of their limb as widows and widowers did to describe the loss of a spouse. Twelve of the amputees had suffered both types of trauma and had found much in common between the two experiences.

Both similarities and differences seemed to be important. Amputees did not miss their limb in quite the same way as widows miss their husbands, although they might miss the friends and workmates they had lost as a result of their disability. This unique aspect of the reaction to loss of a loved person, pining, is best seen, in traditional attachment theory, as a type of separation anxiety, the deep-seated need to search for those from whom we have become separated (Parkes, 1969).

On the other hand, both amputees and widows described feelings of emptiness and mutilation; both experienced a sense of dislocation and chaos, often accompanied by anger and resentment, which seemed to reflect their awareness of a major discrepancy between the world that preceded the loss and the world that now existed. It was these aspects that required a different explanation.

A widow, age twenty-five, put it this way two months after bereavement:

> It seems that when we got married we were one, and I was much richer and stronger than what I am now. So *I feel, in a way, crippled.* I have to learn to live this way... I feel not as strong as I was, *like somebody that just lost their arm or their leg or something.* I just have to live without it....

I was quite touched the other day, I was in the savings bank, and I saw this girl who had lost a hand and an arm—not quite half an arm—and she was able to sign her own name on a cheque and take the money out. I feel she must have had quite a bit of adjustment to do. That is going to happen to me. In a way its the same because I just have to learn it (Glick, Weiss, & Parkes 1974, italics added).

Of course, the assumptive world contains much more than assumptions about the way to sign checks, and it is useful to consider how it comes into being if we are to understand clearly why it is that some assumptions are more basic and more difficult to change than others.

One of the main differences between humans and nonhuman species is our resilience, our ability to survive in a variety of ecological niches. The equipment that enables us to survive is, of course, our cognitive capacity, our ability to develop a repertoire of behavior patterns to keep us safe in the particular environments to which we become accustomed.

From the moment of our birth we are building up a set of assumptions about the world, on the basis of which we recognize the world that we meet and plan our behavior accordingly. Because that world is based on a real world, it stands us in good stead. Most of the time we can count on the accuracy of our assumptive world, which includes not only assumptions about the world outside us but also assumptions about the consequences of our own actions and those of others to whom we are attached.

This last consideration is of particular importance during the first few years of life when human beings, to a greater extent than other species, are totally dependent for their survival on the protection of others, particularly their parents.

The assumptive world is not a static world; we are constantly adding to and refining it in the light of new information. In fact, one of the pleasures of life is to visit new places and do new things that will test our skills and enable us to expand our horizons. There are, however, as we have seen repeatedly in this book, certain life events that bring us face-to-face with the fact that our existing assumptive world can no longer keep us safe. What follows is a painful and protracted struggle to find a new set of assumptions to replace those that are now obsolete. I have termed these struggles "psychosocial transitions."

The life events that cause the most difficult psychosocial transitions are those that violate core assumptions concerning (1) self-trust, the assumption that, most of the time, I can cope with the world I meet; (2) other-trust, the assumption that, when necessary, I can count on others to keep me safe; and (3) world trust, the assumption that the world is a reasonably safe place.

These core assumptions can be further subdivided and the consequences of their loss predicted:[1]

1. Self-trust depends on
   a. Faith in my ability to perceive dangers ("I know where I stand")—the need to alter this assumption (e.g. as a result of illness or accident affecting the organs or skills on which we have relied to perceive the world) produces incomprehension, disorientation, and anxiety
   b. Faith in my ability to handle those dangers that arise ("I can cope")—loss of this faith (e.g., resulting from loss of motor skills or confidence in coping ability) leads to feelings of particular helplessness

    c. Faith in my body image ("I am an intact, whole person")—loss of this (e.g., by amputation of a part of the body) leads to phantom phenomena and a distressing sense of mutilation

2. Other-trust depends on
    a. The assumption that others will be available to protect me when needed ("You can rely on other people")—invalidation of this assumption (e.g., by desertion or death) leads to disillusionment, anger, and grief
    b. The assumption that I am capable of evoking the care of others and rewarding them for their support ("People love me")—invalidation (e.g., by humiliation or rejection) results in shame and self-abasement
    c. The assumption that I am powerful, dominant, or respected enough to be able to coerce or control others into supporting me ("People do what I tell them to")—invalidation (e.g., by rebellion or defeat) leads to bitterness and rage

3. World trust depends on
    a. Faith in the lasting absence of danger ("The world is a safe place")—loss of this faith (e.g., as a result of persecution or disaster) leads to anxiety and perpetual vigilance
    b. Faith in protective powers, God, laws, police, governments, and so on ("God's in his heaven, all's well with the world")—loss of this faith (e.g., following murder or manslaughter) leads to anger toward the supposed cause and distrust of the power and/or goodwill of authorities

Traumatic life events can undermine any or all of these assumptions of security. Sadly, traumatic events affecting other-trust and world trust can also make people distrustful of possible sources of help just when they most need them.

In my view the function of the assumptive world is not to protect us from reality but to enable us to cope with reality. Why, then, are some of the assumptions of our clients so out of touch with reality? To answer this question we need to look again at the nature of the assumptive world and the way in which it arises.

By their very nature, internal models of the world cannot be entirely accurate. When we perceive a person we do not take that person into our brain, we extract from the multitude of sensations that reach us from the person certain perceptual clues that, when we meet them again, are sufficient to enable us to recognize and relate to the person. Occasionally we make mistakes—we misidentify someone who resembles another person, or we misjudge them. But this does not invalidate the general assumption that perception is based on reality.

A person who has gone blind will continue to look toward the source of a sudden noise. This behavior, though out of keeping with current reality, is so easy to understand that we think nothing of it. It may be in keeping with a world that no longer exists, but it is clearly a part of the basic assumption that if you look toward a danger you will see its cause, and this basic assumption cannot easily or safely be given up.

In order to survive, a child must learn what is dangerous. Young children naturally look to their parents to teach them what is safe. If the parents see danger where none exists, we should expect their children to do the same. Again, the children's assumptions may be incorrect, but they are based on their attempts to perceive and predict reality.

By identifying with our parents we learn not only what is safe but also how to cope with the dangers that arise. Some children learn, at an early age, that their parents cannot tolerate closeness. They soon develop the assumption that closeness is dangerous and learn to keep a safe distance from those to whom they are attached.[2] In the course of time they will meet other people who are not intolerant of closeness, but as long as they keep at a safe distance they have no way of finding out that the assumption of danger is unjustified. In other words, an assumption that was true at one time *and which would have been experienced as essential to survival* cannot easily be abandoned simply because a therapist or other person says that it is an illusion. Nor should we see the illusion as a denial of reality.

In later life most people do indeed modify many of the assumptions learned in childhood. We become more independent and no longer see our parents as our main source of security. If we are honest, however, we will recognize that old habits of thought are not entirely lost; at times we turn to our mother or father for comfort in much the same way as we did as children, and we seldom resent the fact that they continue to treat us as if we had never grown up.

Our expectations of others continue to be colored by the memory of our parents even when we consciously attempt to correct obvious misperceptions. This is most likely to occur at times of stress, when our accustomed ways of coping fail to keep us safe. Thus a mother who was treated as a wicked girl by her mother may be determined not to make the same mistake with her own child. At times of stress, however, she may be horrified to find herself regressing, thinking and behaving toward her child in much the same way as her mother behaved toward her.

Denial of reality is often seen as a means of warding off overwhelming anxiety. An alternative view would be to say that since it takes time, sometimes a long time, to change basic assumptions, and since high levels of anxiety disrupt the concentration and assimilation that are essential to this activity, it makes sense to give priority to managing our own anxiety, even at the cost of avoiding painful issues. Looked at in this way, denial is better seen as postponement. Sometimes a particularly painful psychosocial transition may be postponed forever.

Cognition and emotion are often treated as opposed and cognitive therapies criticized on the assumption that they ignore emotional issues. In my view this fails to recognize the interdependence of the two. Emotions arise as a consequence of cognitions and, in their turn, influence the cognitions and the processes by which they are modified. Modification of one is likely to affect the other.

In helping people faced with the need to change their assumptive world, it is wise to take account of both emotions and cognitions. For the reasons given above very little cognitive change can be expected when people are experiencing disruptive levels of distress. Bowlby's notion of the therapist's role in providing a secure base from which the client can feel secure enough to tackle the problems that are making for insecurity (1988) is quite crucial.

Much has also been written about the importance of empathy in therapy, and it is true that empathic understanding of the client's assumptive world is an aid to therapy. This said, we need to be sensitively aware of the extent to which clients' assumptions may have been distorted by their particular experience. For instance, clients who see themselves as weak and helpless may induce us, empathically, to see them in the same light. But this makes it difficult for us to correct their misperception and to treat them with the respect they most need.

While counselors and therapists are right to expect that transformation of the assumptive world will usually lead to the inception of a more mature and realistic view of the world, this is not always the case. A desperate search for meaning can sometimes cause people to adopt and cling to paranoid, self-deprecating, or idealized assumptions, which may create fresh problems. Family members or others with similar assumptions may aggravate the danger. Thus the experience of violence may lead to ill-directed retaliation against supposed abusers or to self-destructive attempts to make retribution. The wish to maintain a continuing bond with a lost person may lead to extreme idealization of the dead and denigration of the living, as when a dead child is treated by its mother as more important than other children who have survived. Our role as therapists may require us to present to our clients—and, where possible and appropriate, their families—the possibility that there are alternative views of the world that they may choose to adopt.

In trying to help people in transition, we tread a narrow line between passive, nondirective tolerance of our client's misperceptions and intrusive confrontation. Support groups are often highly valued by those who take part in them, and they certainly help to overcome the sense of isolation and loneliness felt by people in transition. But if they are leaderless or poorly led, they can lead to collusive scapegoating, idealization of the role of mourner, and the perpetuation of distorted assumptions about the world (Goffman, 1963).

Our training, experience, objectivity, and insight should make us less likely than our clients to hold distorted assumptions and may enable us to recognize theirs. They come to us in the hope that we will place our knowledge at their disposal, and we let them down if we deny or withhold that knowledge. But we also need to remember that it takes time and a great deal of courage to change assumptive worlds. If we say too much too soon or deprive our clients of the opportunity to develop and use their own creative potential in order to find new paths in life, we will rightly be accused of therapeutic imperialism.

This book places at our disposal a wealth of assumptions that we can use in the service of others. It is up to us not to misuse them.

Notes

1. For a more detailed examination of these types of loss see Parkes and Markus (1998).
2. Note that the child does not become detached from this person, keeping a safe distance does not mean detachment. As Ainsworth, Blehar, Waters, and Wall have shown, insecure attachments are, if anything, more not less powerful than secure ones (1978).

References

Ainsworth, M. D. S., Blehar, M. C., Waters, E. & Wall, S. (1978) *Patterns of attachment: A psychological study of the strange situation.* Hillsdale, NJ: Erlbaum.

Bowlby, J. (1988) *A secure base: Clinical applications of attachment theory.* London: Routledge.

Glick, I., Parkes, C. M., & Weiss, R. S. (1974). *The first year of bereavement.* New York: Wiley.

Goffman, E. (1963). *Stigma: Notes on the management of spoiled identities.* Englewood Cliffs, NJ: Prentice Hall.

Janoff-Bulman, R. (1992). *Shattered assumptions: Towards a new pychology of trauma.* New York: The Free Press.

Parkes, C. M. (1969). Separation anxiety: An aspect of the search for a lost object. In M. H. Lader (Ed.), *Studies of anxiety.* London: British Journal of Psychiatry, Special Publications.

Parkes, C. M. (1971). Psychosocial transitions: A field for study. *Social Science and Medicine, 5,* 101–115.

Parkes, C. M. (1972) Components of the reaction loss of a limb, spouse or home. *Journal of Psychosomatic Research, 16,* 343–349.

Index

An environmentally friendly book printed and bound in England by www.printondemand-worldwide.com

PEFC Certified

This product is
from sustainably
managed forests
and controlled
sources

www.pefc.org

PEFC/16-33-415

MIX
Paper from
responsible sources
FSC® C004959

FSC
www.fsc.org

This book is made entirely of chain-of-custody materials

#0092 - - C0 - 229/152/14 - CB